This book examines the life and accomplishments of Christopher Columbus in the broad context of European and world history. It begins with the fragmented world of the fifteenth century, in which Europeans, Africans, and Asians did not know much about one another and did not even know that the peoples of the Western Hemisphere existed. It ends with the enormous consequences of Columbus's voyages, which started the irreversible process that linked the world together. In between, it explores the life and times of Columbus, who searched for a western sea route to Asia, but found something far more important.

The Worlds of Christopher Columbus

Departure of Columbus from the Port of Palos, painting by Joaquín Sorolla
y Bastida, 1910–11. Courtesy of The Mariners' Museum, Newport
News, Virginia.

THE WORLDS OF
CHRISTOPHER COLUMBUS

William D. Phillips, Jr., and *Carla Rahn Phillips*

CAMBRIDGE
UNIVERSITY PRESS

Published by the Press Syndicate of the University of Cambridge
The Pitt Building, Trumpington Street, Cambridge CB2 1RP
40 West 20th Street, New York, NY 10011-4211, USA
10 Stamford Road, Oakleigh, Melbourne 3166, Australia

First published 1992
Reprinted 1992 (twice)
First paperback edition 1992
Reprinted 1993, 1994, 1996

Printed in the United States of America

Library of Congress Cataloging-in-Publication Data
Phillips, William D.
The worlds of Christopher Columbus / William D. Phillips, Jr. and
Carla Rahn Phillips.
p. cm.
Includes bibliographical references and index.
ISBN 0-521-35097-2
1. Columbus, Christopher. 2. Explorers – American – Biography.
3. Explorers – Spain – Biography. 4. America – Discovery and
exploration – Spanish. I. Phillips, Carla Rahn, 1943-
II. Title.
E111.P67 1991
970.01'5–dc20
[13]   91-18790

A catalogue record for this book is available from the British Library.

ISBN 0-521-35097-2 hardback
ISBN 0-521-44652-X paperback

Partial funding for the publication of this boook has been provided by
The Program for Culltural Cooperation Between Spain's Ministry of
Culture and United States Universities.

For Helen Nader

Contents

Acknowledgments

In preparing this book we accumulated many debts that we acknowledge with gratitude. The National Endowment for the Humanities awarded William Phillips a fellowship for the academic year 1988–9, so that he could devote full time to Columbus. In addition, we both received grants-in-aid of research from the Graduate School at the University of Minnesota, which allowed us to hire several able graduate students for short-term projects: Thomas Perry-Houts, Allyson Poska, P. J. Kulisheck, and Timothy Coates.

An early draft of the manuscript benefited greatly from thoughtful and expert critiques by Peggy Liss and by two anonymous readers for Cambridge University Press. Their questions and suggestions helped us shape the final version, but any errors or omissions remain, of course, our own. John Parker and Carol Urness of the James Ford Bell Library at the University of Minnesota have been generous with their advice and help at various stages, particularly in providing illustrations from the rich collection of rare books in their care. We also thank John R. Jenson of the Special Collections Library, who prepared the index in record time, with his customary care and skill. The unflappable demeanor and unstinting support of Frank Smith, our editor at Cambridge, made our job a real pleasure.

Finally, our warmest thanks go to Helen Nader of Indiana University. Nearly ten years ago, she began to urge scholars to look toward the five-hundredth anniversary of Columbus's first transatlantic voyage as an unparalleled opportunity. Through conferences, symposia, academic associations, articles, and personal contacts, she called on scholars to present the best evidence about Columbus and his worlds to a broad reading public. This book is our contribution to that call. Recognizing that without Helen Nader's inspiration and support we would never have written it, we dedicate this book to her.

William D. Phillips, Jr.   Carla Rahn Phillips

Minneapolis
April 1991

A Note on Names

The spelling of personal names and place-names presents extraordinary complications in a book written for English-speaking readers but that nonetheless spans the world and centuries of its history. Logic demands spelling that is both consistent and comprehensible. Common sense recognizes that consistency must sometimes yield to comprehension. Foregoing rigid consistency, we have adopted a general set of principles governing the form of names of persons and places, using common sense and comprehensibility as our primary guides.

For major place-names, we have used the spelling most familiar to English-speaking readers, when English versions exist and when their pronunciation approximates the syllabic stress of the original language. Thus, we use Lisbon instead of Lisboa; Seville instead of Sevilla; Genoa instead of Genova; Castile instead of Castilla. For less familiar place-names, we have included the accent marks of the original language, where their absence could lead to mispronunciation. Examples include Alcáçovas, Cádiz, Córdoba, and León.

For most personal names, we have used the spelling and accent marks of the country of origin. For example, we use João in Portugal, Juan in Castile, and Giovanni in Italy, for names that could all be rendered as John in English. This helps to differentiate between similar names in diverse countries. Given the scope of the book, however, this approach could not be followed consistently. The names of the most prominent European explorers mentioned are almost always known to the English-speaking world in their English forms: for example, John Cabot for the Italian Jacobo Caboto, or Ferdinand Magellan for the Portuguese Fernão Magalhães. And for travelers whose tales are known only in translation to the English-speaking world, only the English version of their names seems to make sense: for example, William of Rubruck and John of Piano Carpini. In many cases, we include the original form of a name at its first mention and thereafter use the English spelling.

The most difficult set of problems concerns the names of members of Christopher Columbus's family. Although the family originated in Genoa, Columbus and several of his relatives moved to Portugal and later to Spain and its overseas colonies. Columbus and various members of his family became naturalized Spaniards. At each stage in their migrations, they adapted the form of their names to local spellings; we have tried to reflect their changing lives by changing the spellings of their names. Thus we refer to Christopher's brothers by the Italian version of their names, Bartolomeo and Giacomo Colombo, in the early period of their lives. Once they became naturalized in Spain, we shift to the Spanish version of their names, Bartolomé and Diego Colón. Christopher Columbus's legitimate son was born in Portugal and baptized Diogo Colombo. In his life in Spain, he was always known as Diego Colón. Columbus's natural son Hernando was born in Spain and was never identified with any other nation. We have therefore referred to him as Hernando Colón throughout his life.

Christopher Columbus himself presents the greatest challenge. Born in Genoa and called Cristoforo Colombo, he was later known as Cristóvão Colombo while he lived in Portugal. After his migration to Spain, he attained status and recognition as Cristóbal Colón. Late in life he adopted as his signature a Greco-Latin neologism based on his first name: *Xpo ferens,* or *Christo ferens,* the Christ-bearer. Virtually all authors who have written about Columbus have translated his name into the language used in their text. Writers in English call him Christopher Columbus, based on a translation of the Latin Christophorus Columbus. Because Christopher Columbus is a name universally recognized in the English-speaking world, we have used the English version of his name for every stage of his life – violating our naming principles but at least in his case opting for consistency.

1

The Worlds of Christopher Columbus

IN THE WORLD of the late twentieth century, events on one continent routinely influence developments on the others, for good or for ill. In the broad expanse of historical time, however, these extensive connections developed quite recently, starting in the fifteenth and sixteenth centuries. In one sense, the process began with Christopher Columbus's four voyages, the first transatlantic excursions to have far-reaching and long-lasting consequences. In another sense, however, Columbus's voyages were less a beginning than the continuation of a centuries-old human process of exploration and migration.

When Columbus was born, Europe, Africa, and Asia were each part of the Old World of the Eastern Hemisphere, but they were also separate worlds culturally, religiously, and politically. Over the long span of human history, sea and land routes intermittently connected these worlds, making their peoples at least aware of one another's existence. The world of the Western Hemisphere, on the other hand, stood completely apart and isolated from the Old World, as it had been for thousands of years.

Columbus's voyages shattered that isolation once and for all, in what is arguably the most fateful encounter between disparate human groups that history has ever known. Columbus's voyages, nonetheless, were part of a broader pattern. In just over thirty years, mariners from the Iberian peninsula tied the world together in unprecedented ways. Dozens of voyages figured in this rush to explore, but the most famous were Bartolomeu Dias's rounding of Africa's southern cape in 1488, Columbus's first voyage to the Caribbean in 1492, Vasco da Gama's arrival in India in 1498, and the first circumnavigation of the earth in 1519–22 by Fernão Magalhães (called in English Ferdinand Magellan), a Portuguese sailing for Spain, and Juan Sebastián del Cano, his Spanish Basque second-in-command. Magellan's voyage demonstrated the vast distance that separated Europe and Asia, even as conquest, trade, and settlement were already establishing long-lasting ties between Europe and the Western Hemisphere. The period is so short that it would have been possible for sailors on Dias's or Columbus's voyage to have sailed with Magellan as well. It seems unbelievable that such a momentous change could have occurred in just thirty years, especially considering the thousands of years that advanced civilizations had existed on earth. Yet

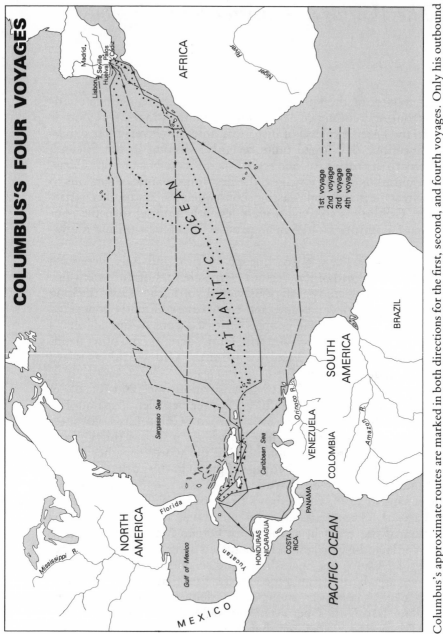

Columbus's approximate routes are marked in both directions for the first, second, and fourth voyages. Only his outbound route is marked for the third voyage, because he returned to Spain under arrest, rather than in command of the voyage. (Map prepared by the Cartography Laboratory, Department of Geography, University of Minnesota.)

those thirty years of rapid exploration marked the culmination of centuries of effort by Europeans, especially Italians and Iberians.

Columbus did not set out to discover the lands of the Western Hemisphere at all, even though his unplanned discovery of America is often defined as his most important accomplishment. Instead, Columbus's exploits marked the convergence of two long-term trends in Europe: the search for direct contact with Asia and the gradual mapping of the Atlantic Ocean. Columbus's originality lay in combining these two trends by seeking a western route from Europe to Asia across the ocean. His desire to succeed so consumed him that he never publicly acknowledged what many others suspected before his death: Columbus did not reach Asia at all. Instead, he happened upon a vast and populated area unknown to Europeans. He discovered – or made known – a New World, and within thirty years all of the great urban civilizations on the face of the earth became aware of one another for the first time in human history.

Educated Europeans in Columbus's time marveled at the *"news of such great and unexpected things"* that his voyages revealed, even if they could not be sure just what had been revealed, or where.[1] The next generation had a much clearer notion of the shape of the earth and could glory in Europe's expanding horizons. As the Spanish scholar Juan Luis Vives wrote in 1531, *"the whole globe is opened up to the human race."*[2] The Italian Lazzaro Buonamico wrote in 1539, *"Do not believe that there exists anything more honourable to our or the preceding age than the invention of the printing press and the discovery of the new world; two things which I always thought could be compared, not only to Antiquity, but to immortality."*[3] At the end of the sixteenth century, the Milanese physician Girolamo Cardano reflected on the high points of his life, noting that *"the first and most unusual is that I was born in this century in which the whole world became known; whereas the ancients were familiar with but a little more than a third part of it."*[4] Columbus received his fair share of glory for Europe's good fortune. In 1535, Gonzalo Fernández de Oviedo praised him as *"the first discoverer and finder of these Indies . . . a brave and wise sailor, and a courageous captain,"* but a man *"still more worthy of fame and glory for having brought the Catholic faith to these parts. . . ."*[5]

COLUMBUS AS HERO

Columbus assumed heroic proportions in the record of world history, partly because of his accomplishments and partly because of the magnitude of the processes he unleashed. The stunning success of his 1492 voyage won fame as soon as he returned to Europe, and its global implications became apparent by the end of the sixteenth century. Only a heroic individual could be credited with changing the dimensions of the world that Europeans knew in 1492. However, like the heroes of antiquity to whom he was often compared, Columbus was far from perfect as a human being. The sixteenth-century writers who glorified his memory rarely mentioned his flaws, and perhaps were unaware of them. Nonetheless, they expected heroes to display human weaknesses. All the heroes of antiquity and even the ancient pagan gods had flaws. In many classical legends savored by European intellectuals in Columbus's time, the negative aspects of the hero's character could be as instructive as his virtues. Nonetheless, perhaps even then there was less tolerance for failings in real historical heroes than in the legendary heroes of antiquity. And the modern world often seems to have no patience at all with flawed heroes, for reasons that lie more in the realm of psychology than history.

Conflicting notions about heroes and their uses in historical interpretation have clouded many attempts to explain and evaluate the life of Columbus and his place in history. Nowhere has that conflict been more apparent than in the United States. Columbus is one of the most familiar figures in history to Americans – the first European since the Vikings to reach the Western Hemisphere. Americans remember the date 1492 as easily as they remember the date 1776 and rightly assume that Columbus's first voyage was important to the foundation of their country. From the very beginning of the United States as an independent nation, Americans took Columbus, a Genoese merchant mariner sailing for Spain, as one of their national heroes. When the United States expanded westward in the nineteenth century, his reputation rose. Scores of cities, counties, and institutions from east to west were named after Columbus, or his poetic counterpart Columbia, all attesting to the special role that Columbus had assumed in the self-definition of the United States.

Nineteenth-century Americans identified Columbus with the spirit of the frontier, with the heroism of people leaving the security of settled homes to search for a new life. They applauded his invention of bold new ideas and viewed his life as a challenge to outmoded tradition and repressive authority. Americans saw Columbus as a misunderstood genius, far ahead of the scholars of his time. They credited him with scientific learning, a Renaissance man beating against the walls of medieval superstition. They celebrated his life as the triumph of a heroic individual standing alone and unafraid against society's ingrained prejudice. In short, Americans appropriated Columbus as a symbol of everything they admired in themselves as a nation. And in the early twentieth century, Americans of Italian and

Hispanic heritage spearheaded a drive to name a national holiday after Columbus, taking pride in their connection to the famous explorer.

COLUMBUS AS HUMAN BEING

Many aspects of the unblemished portrait of Columbus came directly from his own writings and from those of his closest supporters. Even in the nineteenth century, this one-sided portrayal was contradicted by hard evidence from other sources. Far from being an accomplished scholar or a misunderstood genius, Columbus held wildly inaccurate views of the world. From a limited reading of academic geographers and religious sources, he came to picture an earth reduced in size by one-third, with Japan located at the longitude of the Bahamas. The Columbus that nineteenth-century Americans portrayed as suffering at the hands of hidebound clerics in fact used biblical passages as significant geographical evidence. Deeply influenced by millenarian visionaries, his professed goal was to hasten the conversion of the world to Christianity. As early as his first voyage, he suggested that all profits from his enterprise should be used for the Christian reconquest of Jerusalem from the Muslims. Yet Columbus also had his mind on practical matters. He was an experienced businessman and an inveterate deal-maker, able to attract funding from both public and private sources to support his voyages. And, far from being an individual standing alone against a hostile world, Columbus seems to have been quite sociable, taking comfort from having family and friends close by when he was on land and never sailing from Europe with fewer than ninety others to accompany him. The historic Columbus was much more complex, and certainly much more human, than simple heroic legends portrayed him.

A significant part of that complexity was well understood by scholars even in the early nineteenth century, and persistent research throughout that century unearthed a wealth of additional documentation in Italy and Spain. Nonetheless, the simplified heroic version of Columbus's life and times remained entrenched, especially in the United States. Hundreds of school textbooks based their portrayals of Columbus on the vastly popular biography published by Washington Irving in 1828. Although Irving had access to the best European scholarship on Columbus when he wrote, his main goal was to retell a familiar story in an appealing fashion, not to reinterpret or detract from a man who had become a popular icon in the United States.[6] For the rest of the nineteenth century, variations on Irving's heroic portrait of Columbus continued to hold sway in the United States.

The fourth centenary of Columbus's 1492 voyage became the occasion for the United States to celebrate its new power as a vigorous, expanding nation, and the World's Columbian Exposition, held in Chicago in 1893, provided a grandiose finale to the festivities. The European commemoration of the fourth centenary included a much more lasting contribution: several published collections of documents dealing with Columbus's life and times, and a flurry of competent scholarship incorporating the information that the documents provided.[7] Scholars in 1892 knew nearly as much about Columbus as we know in 1992, with the exception of a few significant additions unearthed since then. Several Americans contributed to the outpouring of scholarly publications at the end of the nineteenth century, among them Henry Harrisse, John Boyd Thacher, and Justin Winsor.[8]

In Winsor, the heroic version of Columbus's life found its first great American debunker. Other authors had tried to chip away at the solid monument that Irving had erected, but their works had been so tarnished by religious or ethnic prejudice that they were easily dismissed by Columbus's admirers. Winsor could not be dismissed so easily. His careful examination of Columbus's character and accomplishments was based on the documentary record and presented in a spirit of unbiased scholarship. He portrayed Columbus as a daring mariner with great powers of persuasion and extraordinary dedication to his goals. Winsor also revealed Columbus as an inept administrator, so sure of his own rectitude that he openly disobeyed royal instructions and brought many of his troubles on himself. Among his other failings, Columbus unashamedly waged war against the native inhabitants of the Caribbean and enslaved hundreds of them, hoping to profit from a transatlantic slave trade. He angered the Spanish crown by waging war and taking slaves in direct contravention of a royal order, although under appropriate circumstances warfare against the Indians or their enslavement could have been justified by European law and precedent. Nonetheless, the depiction of Columbus as the first slave trader in the New World hardly enhanced his reputation. With Winsor's work, and the accumulated scholarship surrounding the fourth centenary, a more balanced portrayal of Columbus claimed a place beside the heroic portrayal that continued to dominate American historiography.

The irony is that a balanced portrayal of Columbus's character and accomplishments has rarely been presented in the textbooks that have informed generations of schoolchildren.[9] Authors of American textbooks in the nineteenth century were more concerned with presenting Columbus as a role model than with examining his life accurately. In the early twentieth century, much the same attitude prevailed, but Columbus and the early days of European exploration tended to get shorter shrift as events such as the First World War demanded space in history textbooks. A more critical attitude toward traditional heroes became prominent from the 1930s on, coupled with a trend away from seeing exemplary individuals as the moving forces in history. Writers could feel justified in ignoring individuals altogether and discussing larger forces such as population movements and economic and social trends. The social activism of the 1960s gave rise to an emphasis on certain groups in American society that had been largely ignored in earlier textbooks, especially people of color. Although each of these historical trends stimulated new research and new approaches, they did little to correct the old-fashioned heroic notion of Columbus or to keep alive the nuanced version of his life known in the late nineteenth century. In short, the United States seems to have lost, rather than gained, knowledge about Columbus since 1892. Most people reach adulthood with only the most rudimentary knowledge about him, half-remembered from a few lessons in elementary school.

Many popular misconceptions therefore continue to hold sway in the United States. Some of them are trivial, such as the Columbus Day advertisements that show him peering at the horizon through a telescope, an instrument invented a century after he died. Other misconceptions are more serious, such as the persistent belief that Columbus was the only man of his day to believe in a spherical earth. Taken together, however, these misconceptions reveal a profound lack of knowledge about Columbus and his historical context. Even worse, the general impression seems to be that Columbus is a mysterious figure about whom little is known and much needs to be conjectured. Even serious historians have often filled the gaps in their evidence about Columbus with suppositions about his life and times, as if heroic stories were somehow exempt from the ordinary rules of historical explanation. When serious historians fail to mention that their suppositions have no firm proof, they encourage a wild array of speculation from other authors ignorant of the historical record and the rules of inference.

Scholars have not done a good job of explaining their knowledge about Columbus to a broader public raised on the simplistic notion of Columbus the unblemished hero.[10] Or perhaps there has simply been too much resistance to any attempt to show Columbus as a fully rounded human being, with vices as well as virtues. Not surprisingly, from time to time popular authors and journalists discover the negative aspects of Columbus's life and set out to challenge traditional myths about him.

Some recent debunkers of Columbus approach the evidence with a sense of triumphant outrage, angered by their assumption that the full story has been hidden from them. They respond like the child in all of us after discovering that trusted adults have withheld part of the truth. Their sense of betrayal is genuine and justified. Unfortunately, their approach often serves a particular political agenda rather than an informed search for truth. For example, an environmentalist might portray Columbus primarily as the first European desecrater of the American environment, assuming that it was pristine before Europeans arrived. Supporters of American Indian causes might pillory Columbus as a genocidal maniac, blaming him by extension for five centuries of perceived injustices. Such furor is counterproductive, not because it tears down the distorted heroic myth of Columbus but because it merely erects other distortions in its place. The attention currently given to supposedly new negative evidence about Columbus's failings raises the possibility that the traditional – and false – heroic myth of Columbus will give way to a revisionist – and equally false – myth of Columbus as villain. If that were to happen, the true figure of Columbus would still be obscured, but this time behind flashy new curtains woven from various strands of current political activism. Such an outcome would be of dubious merit as a lasting legacy of the Columbian Quincentenary.

EVIDENCE AND SUPPOSITION

The difference between persuasive rhetoric and persuasive scholarly argument is the scholar's reliance on hard evidence, and the interpretation and presentation of that evidence in a balanced way. To understand the context and meaning of the Columbian voyage of 1492, we need to discard the misconceptions that have surrounded the historical figure of Columbus. This book is an effort to examine the best evidence available about Columbus and his worlds and to present it as fully, and clearly, as possible. Central to that effort is identifying the evidence and evaluating its validity.

After 1492, when Columbus was a celebrity, his career became fairly well documented, and we can track his movements and actions with some assurance. Before 1492, the situation is far less clear. Part of the problem arises from gaps and the ambiguities in his life history. The early documentary record of his life is obscure and incomplete, to such a degree that amateur historians, often quite ignorant of the fifteenth century, have produced a series of scenarios for his birth and early years. Most are contradictory, and although some are more plausible than others, many of them lack even the most rudimentary attention to standards of proof for a historian who knows the period and the documentation.

Even with less than a complete record, however, scholars can state with assurance that Columbus was born in the republic of Genoa in northern Italy, although perhaps not in the city itself, and that his family made a living in the wool business as weavers and merchants. For the periods in his young adulthood that Columbus spent in Portugal and Spain before 1492, historians rely on a somewhat fuller historical record. The two main early biographies of Columbus have been taken as literal truth by hundreds of writers, in large part because they were written by individuals closely connected to Columbus or his writings. One biography is attributed to Hernando Colón (1488–1539), the admiral's second son, who was born out of wedlock after Columbus went to Spain. The other is by Bartolomé de Las Casas (1474–1566), a Dominican monk who knew Columbus and his son and had access to the family papers.

Both biographies have serious shortcomings as evidence. Hernando became a rich and learned man and collected what may have been the largest private library in Europe. The only available version of the biography attributed to him is not the one Hernando wrote in Castilian Spanish but an Italian translation, first published in 1571.[11] In the early sections, the biography reveals a lack of knowledge about Columbus's background and early life, as well as a concerted effort to glorify his lineage and, by extension, Hernando's lineage as well. Based on many questionable statements in sections on Columbus's early life, the Spanish historian Antonio Rumeu de Armas concluded that Hernando never intended to write a full-blown biography but only an account of Columbus's voyages and a brief description of how he had developed his geographical ideas. Rumeu de Armas claimed that the first fifteen chapters, which tell Columbus's story before 1492, were not written by Hernando at all but inserted by someone else after Hernando's death. The altered manuscript in Castilian became the basis of the Italian translation that appeared in 1571. Rumeu de Armas therefore rejects almost everything in the biography covering events before 1492.[12] Few historians have followed him to that radical conclusion, but we will treat quite skeptically any information from those early chapters that cannot be corroborated by other evidence.

Bartolomé de Las Casas used Columbus's own writings and family papers, as well as Hernando's writings, to prepare the biography of Columbus that forms an early part of his massive *Historia de las Indias,* but he added his own particular twists of interpretation.[13] His summary of the log of Columbus's first voyage reveals a landsman's lack of familiarity with nautical terminology and procedures. Even worse, the well-educated Las Casas seems to have assumed far too much about Columbus's education and intellectual pursuits. In writing about Columbus's geographical notions, for example, Las Casas often cited a dozen or so classical sources that Columbus *could* have used in developing his ideas. Just because the work of a classical author was available, however, is no proof whatsoever that Columbus actually consulted that work. Ample evidence suggests that Columbus was a highly intelligent man, but he was much less the scholar and intellectual than Hernando Colón and Las Casas claimed. Moreover, Columbus had a strong sense of his own worth, rarely admitting any personal failings and tending to blame any and all misfortunes on the actions of others. By relying so heavily on Columbus's writings, both Hernando and Las Casas introduced a bias into their own works that modern historians cannot trust.

Because of the shortcomings in these early biographies, we must rely on other documents to fill out the details of Columbus's life and test the assertions of his biographers. Royal chroniclers in both Portugal and Spain have left some official accounts, but these deal with the relations between Columbus and the monarchs, not with how he arranged his personal life or related to his friends and associates. The best sources for that sort of information are the records of public notaries, whose archives are just beginning to be exploited in detail. Consuelo Varela and Juan Gil have provided some fascinating glimpses of Columbus's business dealings from the notarial archives in Seville, and similar documents may exist elsewhere.[14] The most frustrating gap in the record of Columbus's life concerns his years in Lisbon, where almost no records from the period exist. Fortunately, several men who accompanied Columbus on his second, third, and fourth voyages wrote about their experiences; their versions of events allow us to test the reliability of Columbus, his son Hernando, and Las Casas.

Some of the most valuable information about Columbus comes from legal records of the long series of lawsuits between his family and the Spanish crown.[15] Sworn testimony by friends, acquaintances, neutral observers, and foes of Columbus provides a variety of perspectives on the events of his life and times. Archives in Italy house other valuable documents, most of which were discovered in the late nineteenth century and published as part of the commemoration of the fourth centenary. These documents provide details about Columbus's family background and activities as a merchant that historians consider highly reliable.

Even using all of the available documents, the record of Columbus's life is not nearly as complete as a modern historian would like. His entire early life and much of his life as a young adult are virtually undocumented. Far too many writers have given in to the temptation to make the scattered shards of Columbus's early life into a complete mosaic, compensating for the missing 90 percent of the pieces with "might have beens" and "must have beens." In the absence of evidence, any number of explanations is possible – some are even plausible – but none is provable. In discussing Columbus's early years in Genoa, Portugal, and Spain, we will try to indicate clearly what is known for sure, what appears to be reasonable on the basis of reliable documents, and what is purely conjectural. After 1492, when the record of Columbus's life becomes much more complete, we will be able to follow nearly every twist and turn of his career and assess his accomplishments and failures with greater assurance. Although we make no claim to have found much that is new or startling in the documents, we hope to present a balanced view of Columbus's life and times, firmly based on the historical record and firmly placed in proper context.

COLUMBUS IN CONTEXT

To understand Columbus, we must understand fifteenth-century Europe, in particular what Europeans knew about the rest of the world and why they were so fascinated with Asia. European efforts to travel overland to the Far East had been going on since the twelfth century. As far as we know, the first European expedition to sail around Africa to Asia started in 1291 – exactly two centuries before Columbus – and its leaders were also Genoese. Italian and Iberian sailors probed the Atlantic sporadically thereafter, discovering islands and charting the mainland shores. Through trade and settlement, they also found ways to profit from their discoveries.

Columbus was not the only European to think about reaching Asia by sailing west, or even the first. If he had not found support for his voyage, some other mariner would have made the attempt. The logic of hundreds of years of sailing experience pointed in that direction. In the late fifteenth century, Basque whalers ventured farther and farther into the Atlantic as they hunted their prey. The king of Portugal sponsored at least one voyage toward the west before 1492, and in the same decade in which Columbus reached the Caribbean the king of England sponsored several voyages westward at more northerly latitudes, following earlier probes by English merchants.

Both Columbus and his contemporaries saw his first voyage as part of a long process extending European trade over increasing large areas. In that sense, Columbus's voyage differed only in direction from earlier voyages in the eastern Atlantic and along the western coast of Africa. Many Christians, including Columbus himself, also saw the voyage as an extension of the militant Christianity that had launched the Crusades against Islam in the eleventh century. Columbus thought the greatest accomplishment of his first voyage was that he had reached the outlying fringes of Asia, where he expected to find, as well as fabulous wealth, populations receptive to the Christian message. Until his death he publicly asserted that he had reached Asia, even though his private letters on the fourth voyage suggest that he knew the land he had found was not the part of Asia known to European travel books.

Why the dream of Asia loomed so large in his imagination can only be understood in the broadest possible context. Before focusing on the life of Columbus, we will spend the next three chapters defining the stable but isolated worlds of the late fifteenth century and examining when, why, and how Europeans began the process that linked those worlds irreversibly together.

2

Old Worlds in Isolation

E DUCATED EUROPEANS in Columbus's day knew a good deal about
their place in the world, even if some of their ideas bore little
resemblance to the geographical reality known to the late twentieth
century. In medieval maps the earth was depicted as a circle, on a flat
piece of parchment, vellum, or paper. Although the geographical
details varied, these maps all reflected the idea that only a portion of
the earth, well above the equator, was habitable. Below the equator
was thought to lie the Torrid Zone, too hot for human habitation.
Christians assume that the earth was created by God the Father and
that human history centered on the life and death of his son Jesus.
Accordingly, Christian mapmakers depicted Jerusalem – the holy
city of Judaism, Christianity, and Islam – at the center of the inhabited world. The known continents were arrayed around Jerusalem,
with Europe and Africa together shown as about the same size as
Asia alone.

Such depictions of the world are now called "T-O maps," a short-
hand description of their layout and presentation. The Mediterranean
Sea formed the base of the *T*, with Jerusalem at its top; the arms of
the *T* were the Don River and the Nile River. Reinforcing the blending of religion and geography, many of these maps located the Garden of Eden, described in the Bible as the terrestrial paradise, in the
eastern part of Asia. An all-encompassing and uncharted ocean, the
O of the map, surrounded the land mass of Eurasia.[1] The T-O maps
have frequently been used as evidence for medieval ignorance of the
true shape of the earth. A compelling counterargument is that the
T-O maps depicted spiritual rather than physical truths; they were
drawn schematically, in the full knowledge that the scheme did not
represent the physical world. In much the same way that maps of
modern subway systems bear little resemblance to the exact shape of
the tracks beneath the urban landscape, they were symbolic represen-
tations of an intellectual reality.[2]

In physical reality, Europe is a small, western peninsula of the vast
Eurasian continent. Educated Europeans in the fifteenth century knew
this, however incomplete their precise knowledge was of the world
as a whole. The Islamic world of North Africa and the Middle East
provided Europeans with access to the products of Africa and Eurasia, and European geographical knowledge tended to follow from
the trade goods that Europeans imported. For example, once they

This simple version of a T-O map, first published in the seventh century, set the form for countless others. (From Saint Isidorus, bishop of Seville, *Etymologiae* [Augsburg: Gunther Zainer, 1472], p. 111. Photograph courtesy of the James Ford Bell Library, University of Minnesota.)

began to import Asian products regularly, in the twelfth century, Europeans became fairly well informed about Asia. They were much less well informed about Africa, for several reasons: the limited trade in products from sub-Saharan Africa; European assumptions about the inhospitable nature of the Torrid Zone; and Muslim zeal to keep Christians out of direct trade to Africa. And, of course, the existence of two continents in the western ocean between Europe and Asia lay completely outside the knowledge of even the best-educated Europeans in the fifteenth century.

THE WESTERN HEMISPHERE

As far as we know now, the Americas were first populated by Asians, between fifteen and thirty thousand years ago, when a land bridge across the Bering Strait joined Asia to North America. These dates, like most others in prehistory, are subject to revision as new archaeological evidence is discovered. About 10,000 B.C. the land bridge disappeared, and thereafter the land masses of Eurasia and the Americas – together with their peoples, plants, and animals – developed in isolation from one another.[3] The prehistoric migrants to America settled in almost all the regions suited for human habitation, forming societies and economies that took good advantage of their natural surroundings, whether plains, highlands, deserts, forests, jungles, or islands. Over the millennia they developed a wide variety of societies, from nomadic hunter-gatherer groups to sedentary, agricultural civilizations.

Over most of the lands from the Arctic Circle to the southern tip of South America, the human population seems to have been widely dispersed in small nomadic or agricultural tribes. Centers of great civilization developed in only three areas, which supported dense populations with highly stratified and economically productive societies. Maya civilization developed in the Yucatan Peninsula and adjacent areas of Central America, flourishing from about 400 B.C. to A.D. 1000. Thereafter the Maya civilization declined, perhaps because their centralized empire had outstripped the productive capacity of the land. The Mayas are best remembered for their sophisticated astronomical calculations and their harsh gods, who demanded blood sacrifices from kings and commoners alike.

Shortly after the decline of the Mayas, the Mexicas or Aztecs created a large empire in the Valley of Mexico by conquering surrounding tribes and collecting tribute from them. The Aztecs organized a vast network of exchange between their tributaries and their capital at Tenochtitlán, demanding goods, services, and human captives for sacrifice to their gods. The subject tribes who accepted Aztec rule with good grace shared in the benefits of the empire; those who resisted met a harsh fate. The Aztec empire was flourishing in 1500, just before the arrival of the Europeans, but maintaining control over a diverse collection of unwilling subjects had put enormous strain on Aztec power.

A similar situation obtained in the Andean highlands of South America, where the Incas had created an empire through conquest and maintained it through bureaucratic management. Well organized, and skilled at providing for a large population in an inhospitable environment, Inca civilization was also near the peak of its power when the Europeans arrived, although straining like that of the Aztecs under the burdens of empire. These great civilizations in the Western Hemisphere knew the rules of the game of politics, diplomacy, and warfare and used them effectively to hold power over less developed peoples. The Europeans who invaded their world after 1500 knew a variant of the same game, however, and also possessed a technology much more advanced than anything that had developed in the Americas.[4]

Five hundred years before Columbus's first voyage, the Vikings of Scandinavia had touched the shores of North America, but their voyages had had little effect on the peoples living there or on the consciousness of Europeans. Certainly any collective knowledge of the Viking voyages had vanished in the five centuries between Leif Ericson and Christopher Columbus. Still, the great ocean to the west of Europe lured adventurous European mariners, intrigued by legends of islands in the "ocean sea," as the Atlantic was then called. In the two centuries before Columbus's voyage in 1492, Europeans found and settled several groups of islands near the European and African coasts, which we will discuss in the next chapter. Rumors of still-undiscovered islands inspired Columbus as he formulated his plans, and they inspired other voyagers as well. Nonetheless, islands occupied secondary importance in the dreams of Columbus and his contemporaries. Their longing for distant places focused on Asia.

ASIA AS A FARAWAY DREAM

Europeans gained their knowledge of Asia through contacts that began in ancient times. While the Roman Empire held sway in Europe and the Middle East, its trading networks radiated from Rome westward to the British Isles and eastward to the Indian subcontinent. Once the overarching authority of Roman rule disintegrated, those networks unraveled.[5] Asia receded from European reality, while persisting in European imagination as the source of luxury and wealth and the site of Christianity's terrestrial paradise. From the end of the Roman Empire until the First Crusade – that is, from the fifth to the late eleventh century – western Europe was poor, backward, and underdeveloped, both by the standards of the old Roman Empire and by comparison to its successor empires in Byzantium and the Islamic world. In the early Middle Ages, western Europeans had to defend themselves from a series of outside attacks. Beginning in the eighth century, the Muslims, following their explosive conquests in the Middle East and North Africa, conquered most of the Iberian Peninsula and raided the kingdom of the Franks, north of the Pyrenees. In the ninth century, Viking raiders harried western Europe and established their own kingdoms in France, England, and Italy. In the ninth and tenth centuries, the Magyars attacked central Europe from the east. The Catholic church was one of the few consistent forces acting for Christian unity during that tumultuous period.

By the tenth century the tide of invasion had ebbed, as the invaders were either incorporated (in the case of the Vikings), defeated (in the case of the Magyars), or held at bay (in the case of the Muslims).

Thereafter, in the absence of major external threats and with monarchs working with the church to limit internal warfare, Europe began to prosper. A rising population, stimulated by innovations in agriculture and stock breeding, led to the expansion of land under cultivation. The increased food supply supported not only a continuing rise in population but also the growth of towns, cities, and commercial activity.

In Spain, Christian leaders in the north directed a series of campaigns against the Muslim lands of the south. By the mid-1080s they had reached the center of the peninsula, conquering Toledo in 1085 and Valencia (though only temporarily) a few years later. During the same time, inspired by the Spanish Reconquest, legal scholars at the papal court in Rome developed the idea of the "just war." According to their formulations, war could be justified – despite the oft-professed pacifism of Christianity – on any of several grounds. The most important for the struggle against Islam was that war was justified to regain lands that once had been in Christian hands. This doctrine applied clearly in the Spanish case, and it could easily be applied to Syria and Palestine, which had been ruled by Christian emperors from 393, when Christianity was legalized in the Roman Empire, until the seventh century, when the Muslims conquered the area.[6]

CHRISTIAN CRUSADERS REDISCOVER ASIA

In the early 1090s, the Byzantine emperor Alexius Comnenus requested the help of Pope Urban II in enlisting a contingent of knights from western Europe to help protect Constantinople from the Muslim Seljuk Turks in Asia Minor. The pope agreed to help and preached a sermon in the southern French city of Clermont, in 1095, that went far beyond the emperor's request, calling for western knights to march to Jerusalem and free Christianity's most holy city from Muslim control. He described Palestine as a land of milk and honey and promised that those who died while fighting the Saracens (another European name for the Muslims) would enter into heaven. The rapid response must have exceeded his fondest dreams. In a few months, Urban witnessed the formation of four major armies of experienced knights, along with several mobs of inexperienced commoners. They set off for the Middle East to reclaim the birthplace of Christianity, and within five years Jerusalem was in their hands. This nearly spontaneous eruption of Christian militancy has come to be known as the First Crusade, which would be followed by three other major ones and several minor ones in the course of two centuries.

The Crusades owed their origin to a complex set of conditions in several cultural regions around the Mediterranean.[7] It is not sufficient to account for them solely on the basis of the papal appeal in 1095. We must go back several decades and examine Near Eastern events, in order to understand the electrifying effect of Pope Urban II's call to arms.

In the middle of the eleventh century, a group of nomads from Central Asia, the Seljuk Turks, seized influence over the caliphate of Baghdad, the nominal center and directing force of Islam. First invited in as mercenaries, the Seljuks made themselves the most powerful group at the center of the Islamic world, able to dictate to the caliph. Thereafter, a group of Seljuks began to move into Anatolia, an important area of food production for the Christian Byzantine Empire. Beyond the economic losses that they suffered, the Byzantine rulers clearly recognized the strategic threat posed by the Turks to their Anatolian possessions. In that context, the Byzantine emperor Alexius Comnenus called on the pope for a contingent of western European knights to aid his own troops in driving the Turks from Anatolia. It was a limited request, and the emperor probably hoped for a limited response. He did not expect, or want, a full-scale western European crusade against the Turks.

Because Pope Urban II never recorded his reasons for summoning the First Crusade, much less for initiating an expedition to Jerusalem, historians have speculated about a number of possibilities. Most of them have little to do with the situation in Anatolia, but many relate to broad religious concerns in the eastern Mediterranean. The one strong connection that linked aid to the Byzantines with military action beyond Anatolia lay in the pilgrimages often made by western Christians to Jerusalem. These pious expeditions were quite popular, and the Seljuk advance threatened the routes used by pilgrims. Such a threat would surely have concerned the pope, as head of western Christendom. Perhaps the pope did not distinguish carefully among the several Muslim groups in the Middle East, equating the Seljuks in Anatolia with other Muslims in Jerusalem and considering it improper and unfortunate for Muslims to control the most holy places of Christianity. Perhaps the pope wanted to use the crusaders to help heal the division between Roman and Byzantine Christianity, a split that had existed for centuries but was formalized only in 1054. If so, he miscalculated the effect that rampaging western armies would have in Byzantium; their destructive presence probably widened, rather than narrowed, the breach between western and eastern Christians.

The pope may also have been influenced by internal changes in Europe. For some time, the papal administration had cooperated with secular authorities in an attempt to reduce domestic warfare in western Europe, establishing the so-called Truce of God and the Peace of

God to limit periods of war and to shield noncombatants from the destructive effect of pointless squabbles among the elite. What better way to save Europe from unwanted and destructive combat than to direct the energies of the knights, whose whole lives were devoted to war, toward acceptable goals outside their homelands? For the knights, and for the nobles who led them, the compensations that lay in a religious crusade were more than adequate. They could gain spiritual rewards for participation; they benefited from a papal moratorium on their debts while they campaigned; and they could hope to gain land for themselves in the conquered territories. The last incentive was especially important as Europe coped with an impressive rise in population, which made land for seignorial holdings increasingly difficult to find.

MERCHANTS IN THE CRUSADER KINGDOMS

Other Europeans beside the pope and the nobles had reason to look eastward in the late Middle Ages. The merchants and seamen of Italy's commercial cities – principally Venice, Genoa, and Pisa – saw great opportunity for trade if they could gain commercial privileges in the eastern Mediterranean. Four centuries before Columbus, northern Italians were already famous for seeking out new sources of profit from trade. Commercial needs presumably had little to do with the pope's call to arms in 1095, but there is no question that commerce was one of the main beneficiaries of the Crusades. By 1100, the crusading armies had established a line of enclaves along the shores of the eastern Mediterranean. The history of the Crusades usually emphasizes the crusader states such as the kingdom of Jerusalem, but equally important were the areas secured by Italian merchants. In return for their support in conquering numerous towns, including Acre, Tripoli, and Beirut, Italians received both urban property and land in the surrounding countryside. They engaged in agriculture, producing marketable commodities such as sugar and cotton; above all, they engaged in trade. Even before the Crusades, merchants from Amalfi, Venice, and Pisa had traded in Tyre for silks and sugar. In the division of spoils following the crusaders' victories, Venice gained control of Tyre. In 1240, the Venetian agent in Tyre reported on twenty-four Venetian-owned estates in the city's vicinity, including vegetable gardens, vineyards, orchards, and sugarcane fields, all producing for the market.[8]

The activities of western European merchants in the Middle East had a great impact on the growth of the European economy in the later Middle Ages. Italian merchants used their commercial bases in the crusader states to expand their trading contacts throughout the eastern Mediterranean. They extended their trading networks north into the Black Sea and south into Egypt, crossing religious frontiers in the process. One of the most profitable sectors of Italian commerce in the Middle East was the provision of eastern European slaves to Egypt, a trade that continued for two centuries after the last Crusade.

THE GROWING TASTE FOR EXOTIC IMPORTS

Europeans learned a great deal from their exposure to the sophisticated ambience of Middle Eastern civilization. After the Crusades, rich Europeans (both noble and bourgeois) embraced a more elaborate style of life, enjoying more luxurious clothing, a more varied diet, and fancier houses. The Italians in the eastern Mediterranean catered to their demands, providing spices, luxurious textiles, slaves, and sugar to markets in western Europe and enriching themselves and their home cities in the process.[9]

To take just one product as an example: sugarcane had been grown by the Muslims in the Middle East and the Mediterranean for centuries, but in Europe sugar was a rare luxury, prized as a medicine and aphrodisiac and sold in miniscule quantities at high prices. The Muslims introduced sugar to Sicily and parts of Spain centuries before the Crusades, and Venice imported Egyptian sugar in the late tenth century. Nevertheless, sugar and sugarcane plantations were new to the Frankish crusaders and attracted the attention of northern chroniclers.[10] Their reports helped to stimulate demand for sugar in western Europe.

The crusader states lasted for nearly two centuries before the Muslims regained control over the territory. Although by the late thirteenth century their existence had become precarious, the crusader states continued to produce sugar for their own use and for export. When the Muslims drove the last western Europeans from the Middle Eastern mainland, in 1291, Christian refugees took the knowledge of sugar production with them. In the islands of the Mediterranean and the eastern Atlantic and on the mainland of states in the western Mediterranean, they introduced large sugar plantations producing for export. The commerce in sugar between Muslim and Christian lands also continued, with ports in Syria and Egypt continuing to provide European merchants with sugar, as well as spices and other goods.[11] Sugar would be introduced to the Atlantic islands by Spanish and Portuguese settlers, and to the Americas by Columbus, who took sugarcane plants to the Caribbean island of Española on his second voyage. In other words, Columbus would provide the link between sugar production in the Old World and the New, as he would provide other crucial links in the development of global trade.

Even though the Crusades failed to establish lasting control of the Christian holy places, they gave western Europeans firsthand knowledge of the Middle East and a hint of the vastness of Asia that lay beyond. The end of the Crusades by no means ended Europe's connection to the Middle East and through it to the farthest reaches of Asia. Many of the luxurious and exotic products prized by the European elite continued to arrive from Asia via the Middle East, but political and economic conditions over the vast land mass of Asia determined whether trade was profitable, or even possible. For many years during the eleventh and twelfth centuries, competing empires in Asia habitually disrupted trade. During the thirteenth and fourteenth centuries, however, the long overland routes from the Black Sea to China opened again, in the aftermath – ironically – of a terrifying series of conquests.

RISE OF THE MONGOL EMPIRE

The conquerors and latter-day peacemakers of Asia were the Mongols, a tribe of nomadic warriors from the edge of the Gobi Desert. In the early thirteenth century, a young nobleman called Timujin gained control of the Mongols and a number of related tribes, totaling nearly one million people in all. Taking as his new name Genghis Khan, "ruler of the universe," he led them on a career of conquest and pillage that spanned all of Asia. The Mongols were superb horsemen who had mastered the techniques of mounted warfare. They traveled light – even with women and children in tow – normally living off the land and, if need be, subsisting on mare's milk and the blood of their horses. Their armament included powerful bows, light armor, and fine steel weapons, and they had also learned siege tactics and the use of explosives from the Chinese. The Mongols killed defeated enemies mercilessly, using espionage to learn about their foes and encouraging the spread of stories about their own ruthlessness. These characteristics, hardly designed to endear the Mongols to their contemporaries or to history, proved to be powerful advantages in their career of conquest.

The Mongols invaded northern China, took Beijing by 1215, and entered Russia and Persia in 1223. By the death of Genghis Khan in 1227, Mongol power stretched across Asia to the eastern fringes of Europe; one contingent of Mongols traveled nearly to Vienna. Tales of the Mongols reached as far as England, where Matthew Paris, a monk of St. Alban's near London, mentioned them in the entry for 1240 in his chronicle.

> overrunning the country, covering the face of the earth like locusts, they ravaged the eastern countries with lamentable destruction, spreading fire and slaughter wherever they went. Roving through Saracen territories, they razed cities to the ground, burnt woods, pulled down castles, tore up the vine trees, destroyed gardens, and massacred the citizens and husbandmen; if by chance they did spare any who begged their lives, they compelled them, as slaves of the lowest condition, to fight in front of them against their own kindred. And if they only pretended to fight, or perhaps warned their countrymen to fly, the Tartars following in their rear, slew them; and if they fought bravely and conquered, they gained no thanks by way of recompense, and thus these savages ill-treated their captives as though they were horses. The men are inhuman and of the nature of beasts, rather to be called monsters than men, thirsting after and drinking blood, and tearing and devouring the flesh of dogs and human beings; they clothe themselves in the skins of bulls, and are armed with iron lances; they are short in stature and thickset, compact in their bodies, and of great strength; invincible in battle, indefatigable in labour; they wear no armour on the back part of their bodies, but are protected by it in front; they drink the blood which flows from their flocks, and consider it a delicacy; they have large and powerful horses, which eat leaves and even the trees themselves, and which, owing to the shortness of their legs, they mount by three steps instead of stirrups. They have no human laws, know no mercy, and are more cruel than lions or bears. . . .[12]

Kublai Khan, grandson of Genghis, conquered all of China by 1276, but the Mongols had already begun to encounter resistance they could not overcome. In 1260, the Mamluks of Egypt defeated them in Palestine. They failed to take Burma and Vietnam, mainly because of their unfamiliarity with jungle warfare. They were unable to conquer Java with a naval expeditionary force and tried unsuccessfully to invade Japan in 1274 and again in 1281.[13] The Mongol Empire broke up in the fourteenth century, but for a period during the thirteenth and fourteenth centuries the *Pax Mongolica* (Mongol peace) reigned throughout Asia, guaranteeing the safety of travelers along the overland routes that spanned the Mongol Empire. The *Pax Mongolica* allowed contact between Europe and Asia at a level that had been impossible before, including a series of visits to Asia by remarkable European missionaries and merchants, who returned to tell their stories to Europeans fascinated by tales of faraway lands and untold riches.

PLAGUE, WARFARE, AND THE DISRUPTION OF TRADE

Long-distance trade with Asia suffered a stunning blow after 1347, however, when bubonic plague arrived, by way of the Asian caravan routes, at the shores of the Black Sea. From there it spread like wild-fire throughout Europe, where it was known as the Black Death, killing between one-quarter and one-third of the population of Europe in a few years. The Black Death also devastated the population of the Middle East and paralyzed long-distance commerce for a generation or more.

Political disruption added to the chaos. In China, the Mongols were pushed out of power in 1368 and replaced by a new dynasty, the Mings, who reversed the Mongol practice of welcoming outsiders and reestablished a traditional pattern of indifference to foreigners, their goods, and their ideas. In the Middle East a dissident Mongol tributary named Timur the Lame (whom Europeans called Tamerlane) carried out a series of brutal conquests from Persia to India during the late fourteenth century. At the same time the Ottoman Turks carved out an empire in Anatolia and the eastern Mediterranean. The combination of plague and political disruption, starting in the mid-fourteenth century, ended the golden age of trade and contact between Europe and Asia that had been protected by the Mongols.

While it lasted, the *Pax Mongolica* had brought more Asian goods, and Asia itself, within the reach of Europeans. Mediterranean merchants explored the possibilities for direct trade with the markets of Asia. Missionaries explored the possibilities of converting the huge Asian populations to Christianity. Popes and princes became aware that beyond the Islamic world lived other peoples who might be willing to form alliances against the Muslims of the Middle East. The more Europeans learned about the world east of Jerusalem, the more they searched for ways to travel there.

NORTH AFRICA AND THE WORLD OF ISLAM

In the late Middle Ages, Europeans were quite familiar with parts of the Islamic world, particularly North Africa and the kingdom of Granada in southern Spain. Despite centuries of European wars and the Crusades against the Muslims, and despite frequent attacks by Muslim pirates at sea, Christians of the western Mediterranean regularly traded in the ports of North Africa. The gold of West Africa enriched Muslim rulers in the black African empires, as well as en-

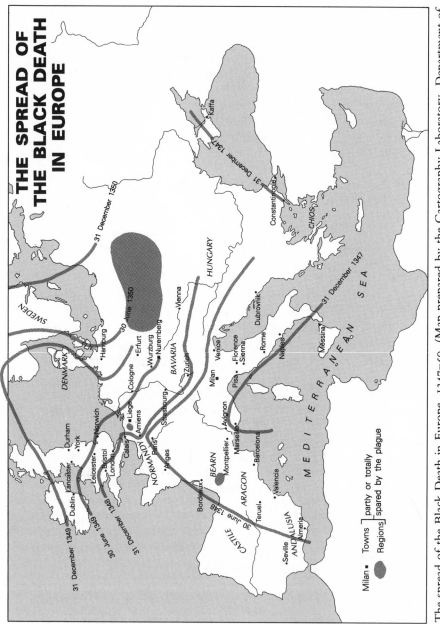

The spread of the Black Death in Europe, 1347–50. (Map prepared by the Cartography Laboratory, Department of Geography, University of Minnesota. Adapted from Philip Ziegler, *The Black Death*.)

riching trading cities south of the Sahara. Mansa Musa, the Muslim ruler of Mali, had wealth beyond the dreams of European monarchs. In 1324, while on a pilgrimage to Mecca, he and his entourage reportedly spent so much gold in Cairo on female slaves and luxurious garments that their purchases upset the local market in precious metals. Mansa Musa was prominently depicted on fourteenth- and fifteenth-century European maps of Africa as the quintessential symbol of Africa's golden treasures. In the ports of the southern Mediterranean, European merchants obtained African gold that had been brought across the Sahara Desert by Muslim caravans. But in Africa, as in the Middle East, a Muslim barrier stood between European merchants and the wealth they hoped to gain from direct trade. Europeans in Columbus's time were eager to challenge or at least evade that barrier, which had been an obstacle since the seventh century.

EUROPE AT THE CROSSROADS: THE ECONOMY

Historians disagree about how Europe arrived at the crossroads that would lead to European exploration and eventual domination of much of the rest of the world, but they generally seek explanations in the complex history and mental outlook of Europeans as a whole, and of Iberians in particular. In dealing with peoples they encountered around the globe, Europeans and their governments relied on traditions and skills developed over time, adapting them to a daunting array of new situations. By examining the European world before 1492, we can gain insights into the reasons for its successful career of exploration and exploitation of the world beyond Europe.

The standard of living of the average European in Columbus's time would be unacceptable to the developed world of the twentieth century. People who live in wealthy countries today benefit from advances in food production and medical care that developed slowly and incrementally for centuries before achieving dramatic success, beginning in the eighteenth century. Today's Europeans would be outraged if one in four children died before their first birthday or if half died before reaching the age of twenty, yet those were the realities that Europeans faced in the fifteenth century. With sufficient harvests, however, ordinary people could provide food for their families, and that was the key to continued population growth. Those who survived first waves of the Black Death in the mid-fourteenth century, and their descendants, enjoyed a higher standard of living than their ancestors a century before, because fewer people were competing for land and other resources. Eventually, enhanced economic opportunities enabled Europeans to marry sooner, have more children, and provide for them. Despite recurring plagues and other setbacks, the population of Europe was growing again by the late fifteenth century. By 1500, the population had risen far above its level in 1400, even if it was still far below the peak reached before the Black Death.[14] In the late fifteenth century, the European economy was expanding as well, and rising populations were nowhere close to exhausting the capacity of the land to feed them. That is not to say, however, that everyone was well provided for, as we shall see.

Some cities remained vital centers of manufacturing, trade, government, religion, and culture even during the depression that followed the Black Death. Those cities were poised for further growth once the depression had lifted. The seeming paradox of islands of urban prosperity in a sea of depression has perplexed many historians. They find it difficult to understand how manufacturing and commercial centers in Italy and the Netherlands, for example, could flourish during a Europeanwide depression. The explanation is deceptively simple but becomes more complex on closer examination. Simply, their wealth was built on the manufacture and sale of items that still found a market in the depressed economy, for the most part luxury goods. The complexity arises in understanding how that market took form.

Historians who study the European economy in this period often focus on the consequences of the Black Death. As large numbers of people succumbed to recurring waves of that devastating disease, the survivors as a whole had more money to spend – a phenomenon that has been called the "inheritance effect." At the very least, there was more land for the remaining population, and farmers could concentrate their efforts on the best land available, which would tend to yield more than poor land. Once people had supplied their basic needs for bread and other dietary staples, they acquired a taste for more meat and for fruits, nuts, and other items they could not have afforded when the population was large and bread prices high.

Groups in European society that were rich in earlier times became even richer with the inheritance effect. They not only wanted new foods but also new and better fabrics, jewels, medicines, and exotic items that often had to be imported. The market for fine woolen cloth and other luxurious textiles also expanded, even though the total market for manufactured goods probably shrank. A shortage of labor after the Black Death tended to push wages up in industries that were still profitable during the depression. Over time, entrepreneurs developed new products and technological innovations to cut their total production costs and circumvent the rising cost of labor. Agriculture and manufacturing became more efficient, as the use of

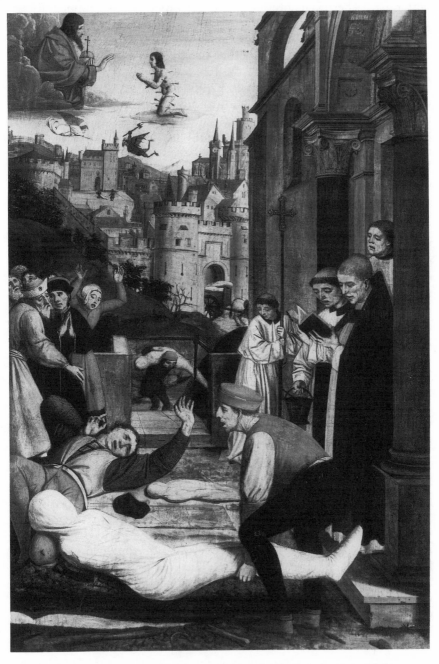

St. Sebastian Interceding for the Plague-stricken (1497–9), by Josse Liefer-inxe. (Walters Art Gallery, Baltimore.)

better land, better techniques, and improved tools allowed fewer workers to attain a higher output.

This combination of circumstances seems to have supported the outburst of economic growth that occurred in several parts of Europe during the depression of the late fourteenth and early fifteenth centuries. The city-states of Italy provide the most obvious example of economic growth. People with money spent it lavishly on clothing, jewels, buildings, furnishings, and decoration. They also spent large sums on the support of artists and intellectuals, who characterized the brilliant civilization of the Italian Renaissance. Elsewhere in Europe, other islands of economic health thrived amid the general depression.

International trade played an important role in supplying the luxuries demanded by the European elite, both during the depression and thereafter. In the Mediterranean, trade gave rise to sophisticated bookkeeping and credit instruments, as well as maritime insurance and international commercial law. These developments provided the structure for financing voyages and for organizing and regulating trade that would later be used for overseas exploration. Itinerant merchants carried their commercial techniques with them, helping to disseminate advanced methods all over Europe. Communities of foreign merchants played an important role in the commercial life of many important European cities in the late fifteenth century. Lisbon, for example, already harbored a community of Italians, many of them merchants, when Columbus arrived in Portugal in the 1470s. Some families had been there for a century or more. Italian communities were also well established in Seville, Cádiz, Córdoba, Cartagena, and elsewhere in Castile.

These foreign-merchant enclaves are sometimes described as outposts of their home countries, and there is no question that they provided a ready-made community for newly arrived compatriots far from home. Columbus married a woman with Italian-Portuguese ancestry soon after arriving in Portugal. Nonetheless, it seems that merchants of all nations in a foreign land had a good deal in common. Often abandoned by their governments, they learned to fend for themselves in order to prosper. The role that local and foreign-merchant communities in Iberia played in backing voyages of exploration has long been acknowledged. New research into business contracts and related documents is allowing us to broaden our understanding of those roles and the importance of expanding commerce in promoting European political expansion.[15]

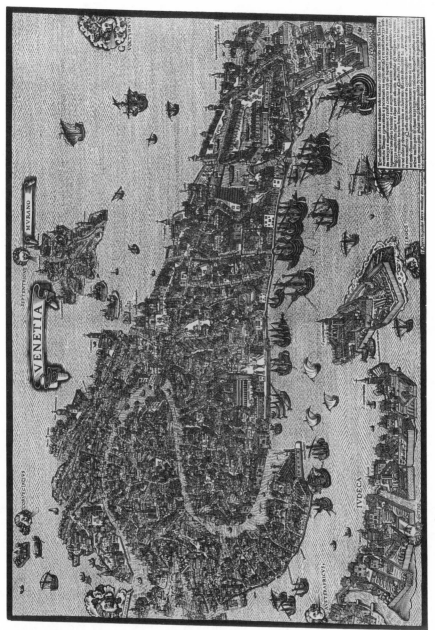

Venice, in the late fifteenth century, was one of the richest city-states of the Italian Renaissance, controlling an extensive hinterland as well as the city proper, with its islands and lagoons. Engraving by Vavassore. (Museo Correr, Venice.)

EUROPE AT THE CROSSROADS: SOCIETY

European society in the fifteenth century organized itself in a hierarchical pyramid. A very small, privileged elite, probably comprising no more than 10 percent of the total population, stood at the top of the pyramid, controlling much of the landed and movable wealth, as well as local and national government. Some members of the elite sprang from families that had earned their position through military service to a patron or lord. Others had grown wealthy through trade and then had abandoned trade for the more prestigious status of landowner, earning their income by renting land to tenant farmers. Still others were members of the elite by virtue of holding important positions within the religious hierarchy of the Roman Catholic Church, the only Christian church in western Europe in the fifteenth century. In one way or another, the elite had power over the vast majority of the population, which included everyone from the poorest beggar to merchants outside the ranks of the elite.

It is difficult to define levels of economic well-being precisely in fifteenth-century Europe, but general impressions provide grim reminders of the vast disparity between rich and poor. The truly destitute probably accounted for about 10 percent of the total population. In years of bad harvests, the proportion of people needing charity simply to survive might rise to 20 percent. The ranks of the destitute would rise and fall with the state of the working poor – those who managed to survive most of the time through farming or other labor but occasionally fell into destitution through illness, injury, a bad harvest, or some other catastrophe. The working poor probably included at least 50 percent of the population. Farmers with some land of their own (and perhaps a few animals), artisans, and shopkeepers enjoyed a slightly better lot in life, for they might have some small savings to tide them over in hard times. This group probably included no more than 15 to 20 percent of the population. Except for the elite, those who had sufficient food and other necessities all or most of the time would have been a small proportion of the total population. Members of the clergy came from virtually every part of the social hierarchy and ran the gamut of wealth and status from the highest church official to the lowest parish priest. By virtue of their membership in the clergy, however, they rarely faced starvation.

The social hierarchy was supposed to be unchanging, with everyone expected to remain at the same level into which he or she was born. Reality was rather different. Within the church, for example, bright and talented individuals might rise to the top ranks of the hierarchy, despite humble birth. Although men were the primary beneficiaries of social mobility through ecclesiastical careers, women of exemplary piety and administrative skills could also rise to distinction within female religious orders. A similar upward mobility was possible for men through a military career. European wars in the fourteenth and fifteenth centuries provided the opportunity for many men to acquire noble status, or at least to acquire wealth from the spoils of war. Service to the monarchy in one way or another was also a popular avenue to wealth and status for many men. As we shall see, Columbus himself, the son of a weaver and merchant of Genoa, could aspire to noble status as a result of his service to the Spanish king and queen. His career was by no means unique. Conversely, a family high in status – designated as noble because of illustrious deeds in the past – might lose its wealth and be forced to live quite humbly, while retaining the legal status of nobility. In short, there was much more social mobility in Europe than we might expect based on definitions of legal status alone, but the relative percentages of rich and poor persisted. As the population grew and the economy quickened its pace, the opportunities for social mobility, both upward and downward, tended to increase, and traditional definitions of wealth and status began to erode.[16]

EUROPEAN GOVERNMENTS AND THEIR ISLAMIC ENEMIES

Europe contained a wide variety of governmental types in the late fifteenth century, ranging from free cities and city-states to counties, duchies, principalities, and large territorial monarchies. Although European political units differed from one another in many ways, they shared certain characteristics. For instance, each was governed by a body of law, both written and customary, that placed limits on the actions of individuals and their leaders and regulated their behavior for the general good of society. In southern Europe, the traditions of written law were especially strong, stemming from the ancient law codes of the Romans but revised over the centuries. The law codes in effect in the late fifteenth century dealt with virtually every aspect of human existence: marriage and inheritance, civil and criminal wrongs, the definition and legal implications of social hierarchy, morals and manners, religion, relations between the states and the people, trade and commerce, and a host of other topics. Judges and lawyers were a crucial part of official hierarchies all over Europe, interpreting the law as a living reflection of their changing societies.

National monarchies far outstripped smaller units such as city-states in resources. In the late fifteenth century, their kings and queens enjoyed power and territories far beyond the dreams of their medieval predecessors. They had a permanent and substantial tax base for the support of internal administration and foreign policy. Moreover, they could use their authority to encourage activities such as exploration that benefited both the state and its subjects. It is no accident that Columbus and his brother sought support from Spain, France, Portugal, and England, perceived to be the wealthiest national monarchies of their time. Although Columbus himself was Genoese, the city-states of northern Italy did not command the resources of the new monarchies, nor, because of their Mediterranean orientation, were they as likely to be officially interested in Atlantic exploration. Genoese merchants who wished to enter the transoceanic Asian trade realized they would have to work through intermediaries or attach themselves to national monarchies in western Europe.[17]

We should, however, be careful not to assume too much about the power of the national monarchies. Their kings and queens had established centralized authority at the expense of powerful subjects within their realms, often through open warfare. In the fifteenth century, the matter of who should rule was by no means settled. For centuries thereafter European monarchs faced serious challenges to their authority from within, as well as having to deal with foreign rivals outside their realms. Besides, the amount of money available to the rulers of the national monarchies was seldom sufficient to cover the costs of their ambitious foreign policies. Rulers were forced to rely for support on the same powerful subjects that they were trying to control. The trick was to inspire their loyalty to the throne and at the same time to make it worth their while to cooperate with the crown. In this endeavor, the presence of a foreign enemy could prove useful, and enemies lay close at hand, in the Islamic world.

The eastern Mediterranean and almost all of North Africa lay firmly in the hands of the Muslims, beyond the control of Christian leaders in Europe. After the end of the Crusades, Christians and Muslims had entered a period of wary stalemate. Southern European merchants regularly traded in the Muslim ports, and military confrontation seldom escalated beyond piracy at sea and occasional skirmishes on land. That situation began to change in the fifteenth century, because of the expansion of a militant new force within Islam – the Ottoman Turks – who challenged the traditional Muslim rulers in the eastern Mediterranean and began a concerted campaign to extend the lands under Muslim control.[18]

The Ottomans directed their main thrust in the fifteenth century against the Christian Byzantine Empire, which ruled extensive lands in southeastern Europe from its capital at Constantinople. After gradually encircling the city with conquests in the Balkans, the Ottomans took Constantinople in 1453, marking a bitter defeat for Christian Europe. For the Genoese and the Venetians, the expansion of the Ottomans meant the loss of their colonial outposts in the Black Sea and the Aegean. For Christian Europe as a whole, the loss of Constantinople meant that the Ottomans held a dagger at the heart of Christian civilization. By the late fifteenth century, the essential hostility between Islam and Christianity was an acknowledged fact, although Italians still traded in Muslim port cities and Christian pilgrimages to Jerusalem continued. The dream of the warriors and crusaders of earlier times to recapture the holy places of Christianity from Muslim control continued as well, with renewed fervor. That dream served as a powerful inspiration for many of the explorers and mariners of southern Europe, whatever national differences divided them.

RELIGION IN FIFTEENTH-CENTURY EUROPE

Western Europe was better unified religiously than it was politically in the fifteenth century, with the pope in Rome acknowledged as the head of western Christendom, and Christianity by far the dominant religion. Charismatic preachers played an important role in shaping religious attitudes, because their sermons could reach an audience that was still overwhelmingly illiterate.[19] The church served as a focus and guide for the religious zeal of the fifteenth century and as a patron of art and culture during the Renaissance. The church also served as a powerful preserver of civil peace and the existing social hierarchy. The ritual of penance and forgiveness, the lavish public processions in honor of Christian unity, and the ecclesiastical hierarchy itself all reinforced the ideal of law and order under a just God.

Tensions existed within western Christianity, however. Medieval heresies, which had attempted to redefine the relations of believers to God and to the church, had been ruthlessly suppressed, without answering the questions they raised. The late-medieval papacy had been split in two between 1378 and 1417, presenting the confused laity with two rival claimants to the line of papal succession. At one point three individuals claimed the papal office, making a sham of Christian unity against Islam. Even after the split was healed, this Great Schism cast a shadow over the church. Even more damaging was the active involvement of successive popes in European politics and the scandalous personal lives of several of them. Taken together, these features of the fifteenth-century papacy seriously damaged its reputation in northern Europe.

In southern Europe, on the other hand, Christian orthodoxy and the struggle against the Muslims kept the church in a strong position. Some Christian pilgrims to the Holy Land might become disillusioned by the trade in bogus religious relics, but they rarely doubted that Christianity was superior to Islam. In the Christian kingdoms of Spain, for example, internal reform of the church and skillful diplomacy by successive monarchs bound church and state together, despite the dubious spiritual leadership of the Renaissance papacy. In Spain and elsewhere, clerics served the government as bureaucrats, and even as leaders of military campaigns, in addition to their function as religious advisers. Kings and queens also had a good deal of influence over the appointment of religious officials and took an active role in the governance and reform of the Catholic church in their lands. In short, there was no clear line between church and state in the fifteenth century, or between religious concerns and secular concerns. The blending of the sacred and the secular in Columbus's writings found a friendly reception at the royal court of Spain because they reflected a common fervor in southern Europe to use political power to spread the Christian message.

EUROPE'S INTELLECTUAL LIFE

The intellectual horizons of Europe broadened greatly in late medieval Europe, if only among the literate elite. The rediscovery of ancient works of literature, ethics, law, geography, science, medicine, and astronomy spurred the elite to learn more about distant cultures and languages. Even militant Christian clerics anxious to convert their Islamic enemies recognized that they themselves had to master the Arabic language and learn more about Islam before they could hope to persuade faithful Muslims to abandon their traditional religion. The result of the quickening of European scholarship was the richly textured intellectual life of the Renaissance, spreading from the courts of the Italian city-states and the papal court at Avignon (and later Rome) to nearly every corner of Europe.[20]

Wealthy rulers vied with one another to have the most distinguished scholars at their courts, for political as well as cultural reasons. Most of the rulers of the Italian city-states, as well as the kings and queens of the newly united monarchies, had won their positions through warfare and guile, rather than dynastic succession. Their patronage of learning and culture helped to legalize their rule and to silence would-be critics.

The dual concerns of Christian zeal and intellectual curiosity led to the movement called "humanism," which sponsored translations of works originally written in Greek, Arabic, Hebrew, and Aramaic into Latin, the scholarly language of Christian Europe. The expanded market for books related to one development that would have profound repercussions, far beyond the charmed circle of the elite. That development was the invention of movable type, sometime around 1450, which revolutionized the printing industry. We associate the name of Johannes Gutenberg with the invention, although little is known about him. In the half-century after Gutenberg's first Bible appeared in about 1455, printing by the new method spread all over Europe. The use of movable type enabled much faster production of books than was possible with hand copying and was much more efficient than wood-block printing. The books published in the first fifty years after the invention of movable type marked the infancy of the printing industry; that is why they are called *incunabula,* from the Latin for "cradle." These early works printed by the new method reached an astonishing number for the time: perhaps 20 million copies·arrived on the European market before the end of the fifteenth century. Once itinerant typecasters such as Gutenberg himself had carried the process to their courts, government and religious leaders immediately saw that printing could enhance the power and efficiency of their rule.

The new method allowed the classic works of ancient and modern learning to find a wider audience than ever before. Speculation and scholarly argument could be informed by citations of ancient authorities of classical Christian, Jewish, and Islamic civilization. Learned scholars and laymen alike could study a wide range of opinion on topics such as geometry, geography, and cosmography (the study of the shape of the known universe). The books in which Columbus found support for his ideas were readily available in Lisbon and Seville, as well as in the other major cities of Europe. Outside learned circles, by the late fifteenth century devotional works and the Bible began to find their way into quite humble homes. The net result was that knowledge, which had been the province of the wealthy and leisured elite, began the slow process of democratization, a process that is still unfolding. Perhaps the wider availability of learning stimulated the curiosity of Europeans to explore their world further. More likely, the printing press merely responded to a restless mentality that had already developed in the complex matrix of European culture.[21]

Asia and its legendary wealth had been a faraway dream to Europeans for much of the Middle Ages. From the time of the Crusades, Europeans rediscovered the reality of Asian wealth, and the European elite acquired a taste for the exotic Asian products arriving by land and sea. Even when direct European contact with Asia became virtually impossible, after the collapse of the Mongol Empire, travel books kept the vision of a populous and wealthy Asia alive, if out of date, in the European imagination. Based on his reading, Columbus still expected to find the Mongols ruling China in 1492, although the Ming emperors had replaced the Mongol khans about a century and a half earlier. The militant Ottoman empire had controlled all approaches to Asia by land from the early fifteenth century on, as well as access to the seaports of the Indian Ocean. The Ottomans formed a barrier between European merchants and the sources of Asian spices, silks, and other coveted goods. Unless a solution was found, the supply of these goods for Europe would forever be at the mercy of the Muslims. Europeans of the fifteenth century would come to see the circumnavigation of Africa as their best hope for reaching Asia and challenging the Muslims from behind.

Europeans were ideally positioned to explore the farthest confines of the Old World − both in pursuit of wealth and in service to a militant Christianity.[22] Of all the peoples on earth, they seem to have possessed the strongest combination of motives for overseas exploration, and the maritime technology necessary to carry it out. Neither the Muslim powers, nor the land-based empires of India, nor the Chinese and their neighbors in Asia, nor the empires of the Western Hemisphere had that same explosive mixture of motives for establishing long-distance links across cultural frontiers and the means to establish the routes and keep them open. Western Europeans, especially Iberians and Italians, had both the will to pursue those motives and the tools to ensure their success.

3

The Quest for Trade and Christians

THE EUROPEAN VOYAGES OF EXPLORATION and discovery that characterized the fifteenth and sixteenth centuries had numerous antecedents deep in the human past. In prehistoric times, migrating peoples from Asia had crossed the land bridge across the Bering Strait to the lands of the Western Hemisphere. Their great trek formed an important chapter in the ongoing saga of human migration, but it did not create lasting links among the continents of the eastern and western hemispheres. Thousands of years later, according to legend, in the sixth century after the birth of Christ, a monk named Brendan and his followers set out from Ireland in a sewn-leather boat, seeking a remote place to worship God and contemplate the infinite. They may well have reached land in the Western Hemisphere, and Brendan was posthumously sainted. Despite the breathtaking audacity of their quest, Brendan's voyage might as well not have happened, however, given its lack of consequence for the rest of the world.

Around the year 1000, Viking explorers began island hopping westward across the North Atlantic from Scandinavia, first to the Shetland and Orkney islands, then to Iceland and Greenland, and finally to what would later be called North America. But even the exploits of Leif Ericson had little effect, and only the Icelandic sagas kept their memory alive in his northern homeland. Columbus's voyages had their origins in centuries of tentative contacts that connected Europe to the rest of the Old World and inspired Europeans to seek a route to Asia.

In discussing the motives for European expansion, it is easy to assume that Europeans in general shared the desire to explore. In fact, most Europeans in the fifteenth century were too busy simply making a living to worry about anything else; the goals of mariners, merchants, and princes were far from their experience. Any discussion of European motivations for exploration should reflect the fact that a very small segment of society was responsible for initiating the vast changes grouped under the heading of European expansion. Even those who were inspired by the potential rewards of exploration were inspired in different ways and sought different rewards. Nonetheless, most of the identifiable motivations fell into two main categories – economic and religious – related directly or indirectly to the centuries-old rivalry between Christianity and Islam. Christopher Columbus responded to the same wide range of motivations that

St. Brendan's isle, with sea monster. (From Caspar Plautius, *Nova typis transacta navigatio* [N.p., 1621]. Photo courtesy of the James Ford Bell Library, University of Minnesota.)

influenced his contemporaries. What set him apart was the integrated whole that he created from ·those motivations and the vision and drive with which he pursued his goals.

TO CONVERT THE WORLD

One prime motive for European expansion, reiterated by nearly all of the early explorers, was a desire to spread Christianity. To the current cynical age, religious motivation is difficult to understand; it is much easier to assume that missionary zeal merely served to justify a lust for gold and glory. Yet Christian religiosity had extraordinary power in Europe in medieval and early modern times, touching virtually every aspect of human life. Europe had spawned generation after generation of charismatic preachers, who inspired and exhorted Christians to lead a good life and fear the consequences of sin. Columbus lived in a time of great religious ferment, when itinerant evangelists and reforming churchmen rallied the faithful to seek spiritual purification and renewal. In 1494, a fiery Dominican preacher named Savonarola gained control of the city government of Florence and whipped its residents into a penitential frenzy through his oratory. Only a few decades after Columbus died, Martin Luther and other great religious figures of the sixteenth century would lead their followers away from the Roman Catholic Church in search of a reformed spirituality.[1]

In this atmosphere, one of the oldest impulses in Christianity – the desire to send missionaries to nonbelievers – came to play an important role in European expansion. The conversion of non-Christians had been a necessary component of Christianity from the beginning; missionaries had played a crucial role in making the Roman Empire Christian by the end of the fourth century and in converting the remaining pagans of northern and western Europe by the eleventh century. The Crusades at the end of the eleventh century began with a focus on the conquest of Jerusalem, the historic and psychological center of Christianity. Christian crusaders in the Middle East concentrated on retaining control of Jerusalem and other crusader states and ruling over conquered Muslims. Nevertheless, during the two centuries that the crusader states lasted, some preachers began to approach the Muslims with an eye toward converting them. In 1216 Jacques of Vitry, bishop of Acre, became one of the first Christians to preach to the Muslims. His efforts were followed by missions to the Muslims in Spain and North Africa. Western European contacts with Asia during the *Pax Mongolica* also opened the possibility of finding new converts, as we shall see.

The beginning of new efforts at converting non-Europeans in the thirteenth century coincided with the foundation of two orders of friars, the Dominicans and the Franciscans. Both sought converts to Christianity from the moment they were founded, even though their primary attention was focused on the laity of Europe. In the first rule he wrote for the fledgling Franciscan order, Francis of Assisi (1181–1226) proposed a global mission to "all peoples, races, tribes, and tongues, all nations and all men of all countries, who are and who shall be."[2] The pope approved a milder statement of purpose, which, if not as encompassing as the earlier wording, still called for missionary work among Muslims and other infidels. Francis himself contrived to preach to the sultan of Egypt, and many of his followers in subsequent centuries fulfilled their founder's dream of missionary efforts beyond Europe.

Dominicans and Franciscans both stressed the need for missionaries to prepare themselves by learning languages. As early as the 1230s, Dominicans in the crusader states were learning Arabic. In the next decade, Raymond of Peñafort led a Dominican effort to establish schools for training missionaries in newly reconquered areas of Spain and in European enclaves in Tunis and other North African cities. In Majorca, Raymond Llull (ca. 1232–1316) established a school for missionaries to the Islamic world. After the Muslims reconquered

Acre, he wrote several tracts advocating a resumption of the Crusades and suggested strategies and tactics. Llull urged the formation
of a crusading army, accompanied by preachers well trained in the-
ology and Arabic. During the crusade they would preach to prisoners of war, and once Jerusalem was reconquered they would work
to bring the defeated Muslims within the Christian fold.

Llull's association of crusade with mission was by no means new,
and it would long persist. Missionary activities and proposed crusades, from the late Middle Ages on, were closely tied to apocalyptic, millenarian, and eschatological speculations and prophecies. One
group of mystical speculators, mainly associated with the Spiritual
Franciscans and influenced to some degree by the writings of Joachim
of Fiore (d. 1202), believed that certain conditions had to be fulfilled
to prepare for the Second Coming of Jesus Christ and its inevitable
sequels, the Last Judgment and the end of the world. First, a new
age would dawn, although this might not be readily apparent at once.
Joachim had prophesied that the third and final age of the world –
the age of the Holy Spirit – would begin in 1260, inaugurated by the
founder of a religious order. Spiritual Franciscans adopted some of
Joachim's ideas and developed others of their own. They believed
that in Joachim's new age all peoples of the world would be exposed
to the Christian message by dedicated missionaries and some, at least,
would convert to Christianity. They debated the precise meaning of
the revelations, but they generally agreed that at least some people
in all nations had to become Christian in order to fulfill biblical
prophecy. The Book of Revelation (7:9–10) foretold that at the Last
Judgment *"a great multitude, which no man could number, of all nations,
and kindreds, and people, and tongues, stood before the throne, and before
the Lamb, clothed with white robes, and palms in their hands; And cried
with a loud voice, saying, Salvation to our God which sitteth upon the
throne, and unto the Lamb."* Before the prophesy could come to pass,
the whole world had to hear the Christian message. Officials of the
Franciscan order tried to discourage belief in the apocalyptic vision
of Joachim, which had been branded in part as heretical, but it became deeply rooted in the Franciscan view of the world.[3] In the mid-
fourteenth century, the Catalan Franciscan Johannis de Rupescissa
predicted a quick conversion of the Jews and the Tatars and a rapid
extermination of the Muslims.

While missionary work proceeded, another essential event had to
occur: Jerusalem must be restored to Christian control. From 1187,
when Saladin's Muslim forces retook Jerusalem, crusaders tried to
no avail to recover the city. After 1291, when the Crusades ended
with the fall of Acre, western Europeans called for renewed crusades
to restore Jerusalem to Christian hands.[4] Even though no crusades

were launched, the impulse to reconquer Jerusalem remained a powerful Christian mandate. In the atmosphere of heightened spirituality in fifteenth-century Europe, it is not surprising that Columbus asked that the crown's share of the profits from his ventures be dedicated to a new crusade to reconquer Jerusalem.

The perennial strength of proselytizing zeal appeared clearly in the early years of European exploration, although not every voyage or every explorer shared that zeal. Both the Portuguese and the Spanish tried to spread Christianity in the empires they established. Spaniards in the Americas were more successful than were the Portuguese in Africa and India, however. The Portuguese in Africa remained guests on the margins of powerful states and had to be careful not to offend the religion of local rulers. Except where local rulers had their own reasons to adopt Christianity – as in the Kongo – the Portuguese initiated few religious missions. Their situation was even more tenuous in India and the Far East. In Brazil, on the other hand, where they established dominance over the local inhabitants, the Portuguese engaged in sustained missionary activity. In the Spanish Empire in the Americas, Christianization formed one of the continuing aims of colonization, particularly after the conquest of the Aztecs in Mexico and the Incas in Peru. Indeed, Spaniards generally believed that they had a duty to convert the Indians they had conquered, and Christianization aided their goal of assimilating native peoples into colonial society.

TO CONQUER THE WORLD OF ISLAM

Another religious aim for European expansion arose from the rivalry between Christianity and Islam. The centuries-long struggle between these rival civilizations had left a legacy of hostility that would continue into the sixteenth century and beyond. Muslims, particularly the Ottoman Turks, posed a major threat to Christian rulers in the late fifteenth century. The possibility that explorers could provide information about Muslim power induced several reigning monarchs to support early expeditions. The Portuguese dreamed of carrying a Christian holy war to the heart of Islam. The Castilians shared that dream, but first they had to complete their own reconquest of Muslim Granada.

A curious legend about a Christian emperor named Prester John encouraged the hope that a Christian holy war could succeed. The earliest report of this mythical figure appeared in 1145, shortly after the Turks took back the city of Edessa from the crusaders. A Frankish bishop of Gabala, near Antioch, returned to Europe and told the

Prester John, on the cover of *Preste Joam das Indias* by Francisco Alvares (Coimbra, 1540). (Photo courtesy of the James Ford Bell Library, University of Minnesota.)

pope that Prester (or Presbyter) John, a Christian ruler descended from the Magi, might be relied on to help the hard-pressed crusaders. Supposedly this ruler had fought his way through the Middle East, defeating the Medes and the Persians on the way, and had been prevented from linking up with the crusaders at Jerusalem only by his inability to cross the Tigris River. The bishop's report found its way into the chronicle of Otto of Friesing and thereby attained wide circulation.

Further news and rumors spread about this powerful Christian ruler who might be a valuable ally against the Muslims. In the 1160s a letter purportedly from Prester John himself reached the Byzantine emperor Manuel Comnenus and thereafter circulated in Europe. In response, Pope Alexander III appointed his physician Master Philip as the first papal envoy to Prester John. Philip carried the pope's response to Prester John's letter as he embarked on his journey, but he seems not to have got beyond Jerusalem. Later envoys, missionaries, and merchants from western Europe were also motivated in part by the search for Prester John; their search discovered valuable information about western Asia, although Prester John himself remained elusive.[5]

Portuguese voyages down the Atlantic coast of Africa carried instructions to collect news or even rumors about Prester John's kingdom, and its presumed location shifted several times. Concurrent with seaborne expeditions, in the late fifteenth century King João II of Portugal sent an overland expedition to the Middle East to seek Prester John. The Portuguese eventually did reach Ethiopia, a kingdom in East Africa whose people had been Christian since the fourth century, converted by the Copts of Egypt. But their leader, though called an emperor, hardly measured up to the legendary Prester John. He ruled over his own people and several tributaries, but his culture lacked the technological and material resources needed to launch any sort of crusade against Islam. Given the scope of these efforts, there is little doubt that the politicoreligious goal of attacking the Muslims with help from allies beyond the Middle East held an important place among European motives for exploration.[6] Both religious and economic motives for exploration came together in the European fascination with Asia, especially during the *Pax Mongolica* of the late thirteenth and early fourteenth centuries.

THE MONGOLS AS POTENTIAL ALLIES OF CHRISTENDOM

Given the horrific image of the Mongols in European chronicles, they would seem unlikely allies for western Christendom. Yet several popes saw good reason to seek contact with their empire. However bloodcurdling the stories about them, the Mongols were a distant threat. They might prove useful against a much closer threat – the Muslims – an especially appealing idea in the mid-thirteenth century, when the crusader states were falling to Islamic forces. As knowledge of the Mongols filtered through to the West, Pope Innocent IV (1243–1254) came to look upon them as potential allies. He was especially concerned because the fall of Jerusalem to the Muslims in 1244 demanded a bold response on the part of Christianity. Consequently, the pope assembled a diplomatic mission to send to the court of the Mongol khan, led by two Franciscan friars, John of Piano Carpini and Lawrence of Portugal, and later joined by a Polish Franciscan named Benedict. Their main assignments were to ask the khan to recognize the pope's religious supremacy and to suggest the possibility of a military alliance against the Muslims.

Piano Carpini had worked as a Franciscan missionary in northern and eastern Europe and knew part of the route well. He led his companions by land from Kiev to the Mongol court near Karakorum, where they witnessed the coronation of Guyuk Khan. Far from recognizing papal supremacy, however, the khan called on Piano Carpini to lead the kings of the west to the khan's court to render him homage. Nothing came, either, of papal plans for a military alliance with the Mongols, but Europeans at least gained more knowledge about Asia from the expedition, and hope remained that the Mongols could one day be brought into an alliance. Piano Carpini returned with a written account which he developed into his *Historia Mongolorum,* including the first description of China by a European. His account was also copied into a history of the world by Vincent of Beauvais, court historian of King Louis IX of France, and was used as well by the Franciscan Salimbene of Parma. Louis IX was so heartened by the prospect of aid against the Muslims that he sent his own emissary, Andrew of Longjumeau, to visit the Mongol court in 1248. The Franciscans William of Rubruck and Bartholomew of Cremona led another diplomatic mission in 1253–5. Their accounts are among the few that have survived, but we know that other Christian missionaries from western Europe also reached China during the *Pax Mongolica.*

PAX MONGOLICA AND THE SEARCH FOR ASIAN MARKETS

In direct contacts with China, Italian merchants were at least as active as missionaries, willing to try new ventures in their search for economic gain. In 1260, the Venetian merchants Nicolò and Maffeo Polo departed from the Crimean Peninsula on the Black Sea, where Italian (especially Genoese) merchants had been established for some time. They traveled through Mongol lands on a trading expedition, following the caravan routes through Central Asia and ultimately reaching China. They returned to Venice in 1269, reporting that the Great

Marco Polo sails from Venice, from "The Books of the Grand Khan."
(Ms. Bodley 264, fol. 218r, Bodleian Library, Oxford.)

Khan Kublai wanted to learn more about European society. When they left again for China a few years later, they took Nicolò's son, Marco, with them. Marco Polo lived for eighteen years in China, serving as a bureaucrat in the court of Kublai Khan. While Polo resided at the Mongol court, the Franciscan John of Monte Corvino arrived in Beijing (known as Khambalik under the Mongols). The friar spent some thirty years in China and became the first archbishop of Beijing, presiding over a large archdiocese (but very few Christians).

Marco Polo traveled throughout China and visited India as well before returning to Europe. His return journey brought him back by sea from India, which gave him a glimpse of the vast Indian Ocean trade that linked India with the ports of the Red Sea and the Persian Gulf. The Muslim merchants and mariners who dominated that trade had created an immense commercial network encompassing the East African coast, Egypt, Arabia, Mesopotamia, Persia, and India, with extensions to China by way of the Strait of Malacca. Regular trade over so vast an area depended upon the predictable annual shifts of the monsoon winds, blowing from the northeast from October to March and from the southwest from April to September. By planning their trips in the direction of the monsoons, traders in the Indian Ocean could have fairly easy sailing most of the year, except from June to August, when the winds were strongest.[7]

After Marco Polo returned to Venice in 1292, he fell victim to the seemingly endless wars among the Italian city-states. Captured by the Genoese, he spent 1298–9 as a prisoner of war, an unfortunate occurrence for him but an extraordinarily fortunate one for history. In jail he met another prisoner, Rustichello of Pisa, who was a writer. Presumably to while away the idle hours, Polo told him about his travels in China and the East. Rustichello wrote it all down, embellishing in places and not completely understanding all of it but nonetheless preserving a tale that might otherwise have been lost forever. Merchants such as Maffeo, Nicolò, and Marco Polo had other things to do than write their life stories.[8]

Many of the details in Marco's description of life in China – such as the Chinese cooking and heating with small black stones (coal) – seemed unbelievable to Venetians, and he was derided by many as "Marco Millions" for what they thought were his exaggerations or outright lies. Nonetheless, The Travels of Marco Polo became one of the best-known tales in western Europe, especially after the invention of movable type made cheap printed books available in the late fifteenth century. Even two centuries after Polo had returned to Italy, his wondrous stories of life in the Mongol court and the fabulous riches of Asia continued to bedazzle Europeans. Historians know that Columbus owned a copy and read it carefully, because his copy, with numerous comments in the margins, still exists. In fact, Columbus probably gleaned much of what he knew about Asia from reading Marco Polo.

By the early fourteenth century, the Italian merchant community knew a good deal about the products of Asia and the routes leading to their points of origin, thanks to a century or more of trade through ports in the eastern Mediterranean and on the Black Sea. In 1340, Francesco Balducci Pegolotti wrote La practica della mercatura, a commercial guide listing the goods to be found at markets around the Mediterranean, especially the high-priced spices that had made the fortunes of many Italian city-states. Pegolotti, a trusted employee of the Bardi trading company of Florence, had served in Cyprus and Antwerp and had for a time headed the Bardi branch office in London. From his commercial connections he had learned much about the routes to Asia, for which he listed itineraries and offered practical advice regarding mounts and pack animals, provisions, and safety precautions.[9]

Both Pegolotti's manual of commerce and the account of Polo's travels told how to buy spices from the East. Ironically, their stimulation of interest in Asian trade came at an inauspicious time. Just seven years after Pegolotti's book appeared, the Black Death arrived at the shores of the Black Sea. The disruption caused by the epidemics and economic depression that followed called a temporary halt to Europe's quest for religious and economic glory in Asia. Once the plague had become more or less domesticated in Europe and the economy had begun to revive, the quest could begin again.

ECONOMIC MOTIVATIONS

Among the potential economic motivations for European exploration and colonization in the fifteenth century, we must immediately discard one: the idea that Europeans sought new lands because of the pressure of excess population. In the late sixteenth century and also in the nineteenth and early twentieth centuries, many Europeans emigrated to escape the misery that accompanied a rapidly rising population. On the eve of expansion, however, Europe was only just recovering from the depression that had followed the Black Death. Although the population was clearly on the rise again by 1450, Europe was far from overpopulated. There were still lands to fill, jobs to hold, and opportunities for many to prosper in the quickening economic life of the fifteenth century. If ambitious European princes and some of their subjects had economic motives to explore new lands, it was not because Europe lacked opportunity but because they saw even greater opportunity elsewhere.

Economic motivations for exploration in Columbus's time stemmed from the strengthened European economy after about 1450, especially the expansion of trade. That expansion had two distinct but related goals, both of which would influence Columbus: the search for new trade goods and routes, especially in Asia; and the search for gold and other opportunities for profit in Africa.

THE QUEST FOR ASIAN TRADE GOODS IN THE MEDITERRANEAN AND BEYOND

Herbs and the few spices native to Europe had been staples of European cookery since ancient times, but the more durable, pungent spices of Asia added new interest to the diet of the elite and satisfied

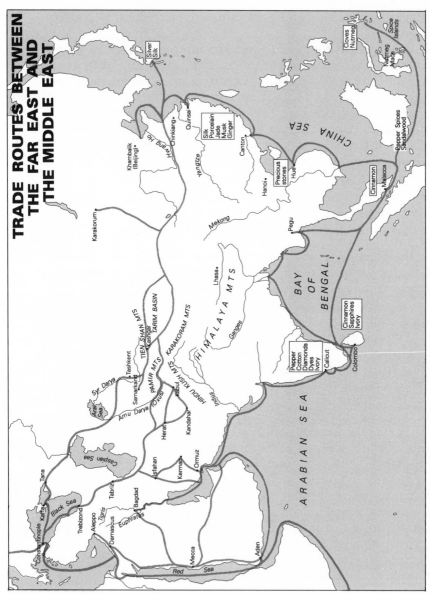

Trade routes between the Far East and the Middle East, showing the sources of pepper, ginger, cinnamon, and other commodities. (Map prepared by the Cartography Laboratory, Department of Geography, University of Minnesota.)

their desire for conspicuous consumption. Spices could also aid in the preservation of foods for long storage. Most of the spices entering European markets were grown in India and the islands of Southeast Asia. By sea, spices and other goods traveled from Asia and India along a variety of routes, passing from one group of local merchants to another at the limits of their respective spheres of influence. Many of the merchants were Muslims, whose widespread religion allowed them to bridge the gulf between different cultures. Once in the Arabian Sea, goods might travel via Ormuz and the Persian Gulf to Baghdad and the Levant, or via Aden and the Red Sea to Alexandria, within the Venetian trading orbit. Beirut and Alexandria specialized in medicines and in pepper, ginger, cinnamon, nutmeg, other spices, and aromatics. Several hundred such items were mentioned in price lists of the early fourteenth century, some of them brought from as far away as China and Southeast Asia, others from much closer. During the *Pax Mongolica,* the overland "silk road," or caravan route, for silks and spices passed from Khambalik (Beijing) and Quinsai through Turkestan to Tana on the Sea of Azov. The southern route traveled by Marco Polo used the Kashgar Pass to Kokand, Samarkand, Asterabad, and Tabriz, to Trebizond on the Black Sea. Trebizond was known for silks from Persia and the area around the Caspian Sea. These and various other routes, exotic as they undoubtedly seemed, were known by name to educated southern Europeans in the early fourteenth century, when Pegolotti wrote his famous commercial guide.[10]

The Black Sea and the Sea of Azov were also the end points for overland trade from Russia, the Ukraine, and the areas around the Danube basin. Italians (especially Genoese) in the region dealt in furs, pelts and hides, wax, honey, amber, slaves, and metals, imported from Russia, the Ukraine, and central Europe. In addition, dyes, saffron, boxwood, fir, and local cloth mingled with more humble products such as grain, fish, and wool from the local hinterland.

Many merchants had only the vaguest idea of the ultimate origins of the items they bought and sold. Despite the fame of Marco Polo and others who had traveled beyond the Mediterranean, few European merchants knew Asia firsthand, and Pegolotti's descriptions of Asian routes and markets had little relevance for them. Instead, they bought Asian exports at entrepôts on the borders between the Christian and Islamic worlds.

The political and demographic disasters of the late fourteenth century interrupted the overland trade routes that fed into the eastern Mediterranean. Fortunately, the mechanisms of long-distance trade proved strong enough not only to survive the depression but to enable certain merchants and the trade in some commodities to flourish.[11] During the depression, spices remained important in the markets of Egypt and Syria, where Venetian merchants held sway. Both Venice and Genoa were forced to rely on Muslim intermediaries for spices, however, which increased their cost and the difficulty of doing business. In addition to spices, the Egyptian market also reexported gold from the Sudan and balsam, importing wood, grain, salt, metal, local cotton, and cloth in exchange. Industrial products such as soda ash, used in soap and glass manufacture, also held a prominent place in Venetian purchases. Venetian merchants fared well during the fourteenth and early fifteenth centuries, and the late fifteenth century saw the golden age of their trade with the Levant. In part Venetian success depended on the active support of their government in negotiating the terms of trade with local rulers.

Genoese merchants faced a more difficult challenge. Around the Black Sea they continued purchasing local products, including Caspian silks, although the silk trade from central Asia had all but ceased during the depression that followed the Black Death. Often unaided by their government, they had to contend with increasing Ottoman pressure in the Black Sea region. When the Ottomans captured Constantinople in 1453, many Genoese foresaw the end of their eastern trade. Some of them had already relocated their business and themselves elsewhere, especially in the western Mediterranean and the Iberian Peninsula. Florentine merchants were also attracted to Iberia, especially Castile. By about 1450, the Castilian economy had begun an impressive rise, fueled by growth in population and agriculture and by trade with West Africa and the Netherlands.

MEDITERRANEAN TRADE COMES INTO ITS OWN

Overall, the adjustments to commerce during the depression of the fourteenth and early fifteenth centuries changed the character of trade in the Mediterranean. From exchanges based largely on a small number of high-priced goods, often transported by land, the trade became more broadly based and largely seaborne. As population began to recover in the mid-fifteenth century, western Europe demanded more foodstuffs and industrial raw materials. Such items could be transported cheaply and efficiently by sea, and the Genoese led the way in organizing their exchange. Although they seemed at a disadvantage by comparison with the Venetians in the eastern Mediterranean, Genoese merchants prospered in the western Mediterranean, sharing in Iberian expansion.

Among other strategies, Genoese merchants lessened their risks by attempting to control production of the products they traded. They obtained contracts for salt production in eastern Spain and the island of Ibiza, coral in Tunis, mercury in Spain, and iron ore on the island of Elba. Even more important was alum, crucial to many industrial and artisanal processes, including dyeing, painting, and tanning. The Genoese held a monopoly over the rich alum mines at Phocea in Asia Minor, on contract from the sultan. Shortly after the Ottomans captured Constantinople, a new source of supply was discovered at Tolfa in the Papal States, in 1462, which Genoese merchants also contracted to exploit. Considering the stranglehold the Ottomans would have had on European industry without these new sources, it is no wonder that the Tolfa discovery was considered a miracle in Christian Europe. Alum was also discovered in Spain, Italy, and the Tyrol, and there were additional sources in North Africa.[12]

The trading empire of Catalonia in the eastern Iberian kingdom of Aragón also profited from the increasingly diversified trade of the western Mediterranean during the fifteenth century. When the king of Aragón claimed Naples (already a favored port of call) as his rightful inheritance in 1443, that city became an important part of Catalonia's trading empire, which reached its peak in the late fourteenth and early fifteenth centuries.[13]

FIRST FORAYS INTO THE ATLANTIC

During the late fifteenth century, the nexus of European trade as a whole began to shift from the Mediterranean to the Atlantic. Merchants from the Mediterranean had been trading beyond the Strait of Gibraltar for several centuries, and Italians, Catalans, Castilians, and Basques were established in many port cities on the Atlantic coast of Europe. As the business climate in the eastern Mediterranean deteriorated during the fifteenth century, Mediterranean merchants intensified their efforts in the Atlantic, where, for a time, African gold supplanted the spices and other luxuries of the East as a prime motivation for trade.

Atlantic trade took centuries to develop. The first recorded medieval attempt to reach Asia by way of the Atlantic occurred in 1291, with a Genoese expedition led by two brothers, Ugolino and Guido (or Vadino) Vivaldi. That same year Muslims recaptured the town of Acre in the Levant, the last crusader stronghold in the Middle East. The loss of Acre provided a pointed reminder that Asian trade by the traditional medieval routes could no longer count on safe havens in the eastern Mediterranean. The Vivaldis planned to avoid the troubled Middle East altogether by sailing around Africa with their two ships, the *Allegraza* and the *Sant'Antonio*. They first called at

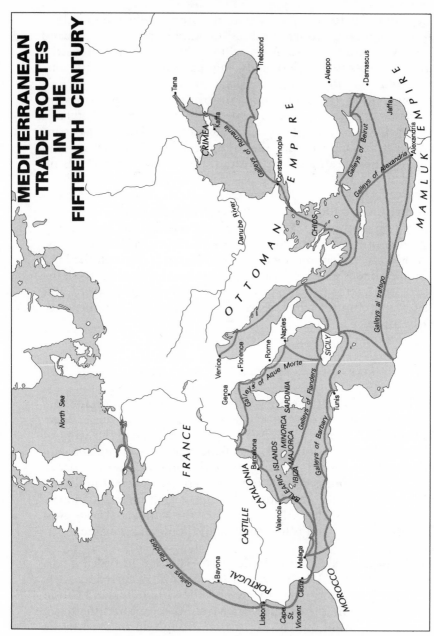

Mediterranean trade routes. (Map prepared by the Cartography Laboratory, Department of Geography, University of Minnesota. Adapted from Frederic C. Lane, *Venice, A Maritime Republic*.)

Majorca and then headed for the Strait of Gibraltar to begin a projected ten-year voyage *"which no one had ever attempted,"* traveling *"through the Ocean Sea to the regions of India, carrying goods profitable from there."* They reportedly reached as far as the African coast opposite the Canary Islands. Thereafter they vanished from European knowledge but not from the European imagination. Supposedly Sor Leone Vivaldi, Ugolino's son, went to seek his father in 1325 and found some trace of him in Africa near the Canaries. After that the stories became more fantastic, as the Vivaldi expedition passed from history into legend. One version of the legend had the Vivaldis landing on the African coast and later being taken to the court of Prester John. Another told of a white man found on the African coast a century and a half later who said he was descended from members of the Vivaldi expedition.[14] The Vivaldis stand out among the early voyagers into the Atlantic for the great ambition and daring of their plan. They were followed by a series of venturers who had other, less ambitious, motives, ones more easily fulfilled. Instead of seeking the Indies and other fabled parts of the Far East, they sought trade with nearby Africa and the islands in the ocean sea.

THE RICHES OF AFRICA

Gold provided a powerful lure for Europeans, not just in the fifteenth century but throughout recorded history. Since the time of the late Roman Empire, western Europe had tried to increase its meager internal supply of gold, the source and standard of wealth. Marco Polo had described in awed detail the vast quantity of gold in China and Japan. His images of golden-roofed temples and gold-covered palace walls dazzled his European readers and added to the mystique of wealth that colored their dreams of Asia. Optimists kept hoping that alchemy would find a way to transform baser elements into gold; realists settled for trade to obtain it. The Muslim world was better provided with gold than was Europe, largely because it tapped into sources south of the Sahara Desert. By the late Middle Ages, the most important gold supplies were in West Africa, in three major areas: Bambuk, Buré, and Akan. In the exotic ports of the southern Mediterranean, European merchants were able to acquire gold through Muslim intermediaries but often on unfavorable terms.[15] One of the main motivations to explore West Africa was to locate the sources of African gold and thereby circumvent the Muslim monopoly of trade across the Sahara.

Portugal was well placed geographically to undertake African exploration and possessed considerable maritime and commercial experience as well, including a tradition of ocean fishing and of trade with northwestern Europe. The Portuguese crown had close relations with the merchant community, supporting trade, granting licenses for commerce, sponsoring maritime insurance, and negotiating for capital with Italian merchants and bankers resident in Lisbon. The Portuguese also faced economic pressures that piqued their interest in African gold. Like the rest of Europe, Portugal in the early fifteenth century was just emerging from the effect of the Black Death a half-century before, and Portuguese nobles had developed the same taste for imported luxuries that characterized members of the elite elsewhere. The income of the Portuguese nobility was based largely on landownership and the rents they collected from farmers, but they had rented out much of their land at fixed rates, for long terms. As their demand for goods outstripped their income, they found themselves in need of more cash. The king and the merchants needed more money as well, particularly gold, to meet their obligations and expand trade to supply a rising demand. No wonder, then, that African gold became one of the lures drawing the Portuguese down the African coast.[16]

Africa had other attractions as well. To ease Portugal's chronic shortage of grain, merchants regularly bought wheat in North Africa, particularly Morocco, to supplement production at home. They found that the grain could also be sold in areas farther south along the African coast, where the desert limited suitable farmland. Similarly, Portuguese mariners found that African coastal waters were ideal venues to extend their fishing grounds. Mariners from southwestern Castile made the same discovery and skirmished with the Portuguese over the right to fish in African waters. The fishing industry was vital both to coastal Portugal and to coastal Andalusia in Castile, providing for home consumption as well as exports.

The Portuguese conquered Ceuta – just across the strait from Gibraltar – in 1415, establishing a base in the Mediterranean and a trading position in Morocco. In addition to grain and fish, Morocco also produced textiles, and Ceuta was one of the coastal destinations of the caravans that brought gold and slaves from the interior. Ceuta was not as profitable as the Portuguese had hoped, because after the conquest the Muslims diverted much of the town's Saharan trade to other ports. Nevertheless, with Ceuta the Portuguese had established a foothold in Africa, from which they could continue to explore and trade farther to the south.

Exploration provided a number of opportunities for profit, which the Portuguese learned to exploit as they went along. Throughout the fifteenth century, they slowly advanced southward. Between 1434, when the first Portuguese expedition passed Cape Bojador, and 1475, when they reached Benin, Portuguese sailors explored thousands of miles of the African coast. At suitable locations they established trading posts (*feitorias*) where they traded with local rulers. The post (and later fort) at São Jorge da Mina was one of the most important of these strategic locations. Along with other profit-making ventures, the Portuguese entered into the slave trade, which expanded significantly over a period of several decades. At first – roughly between 1434 and 1443 – the Portuguese raided the Saharan coast for slaves, but they soon realized that purchasing slaves was more acceptable to African rulers and also made better economic sense. They brought goods from Europe and Morocco that could be exchanged for slaves farther south. The European goods included horses, saddles, and stirrups; cloth, caps, and hats; saffron, wine, wheat, and salt; and lead, iron, steel, copper, and brass. In return they secured gold, especially at Mina; slaves; and a variety of exotic African items to be sold in Europe: animal skins, gum arabic, civet, cotton, malagueta pepper, cobalt, parrots, and camels. Some of the slaves went to Europe, but before the sixteenth century most went to the new European colonies in the Atlantic islands.[17]

Castilian explorers and merchants challenged the Portuguese for the African trade and profited greatly from it. The fifteenth-century fairs of northern Castile were fueled by African gold, attracting merchants and goods from all over Europe. And the port cities of Spain were ideally situated to serve as the nexus for trade between Africa and both Mediterranean and Atlantic Europe. The trade goods exchanged in Spanish ports might arrive legally, or they might arrive clandestinely, to avoid taxes and restrictions imposed by various governments.[18] Either way, they helped to drive the booming economy of fifteenth-century Castile.

CONQUEST AND EXPLOITATION IN THE CANARIES

The Canary Islands, known to classical antiquity as the Fortunate Isles, began to interest Italians and Iberians in the course of the fourteenth century. A Majorcan map of 1339 included the Canary Islands – and included as well the imaginary capital city of Prester John on the African mainland. Sometime before then a Genoese nobleman, Lancellotto Malocello, had sailed to the Canaries, giving his name ever after to the island of Lanzarote. The first European captains who visited the Canaries in the fourteenth and fifteenth centuries found the islands inhabited, unlike the other Atlantic islands, and in 1341 the king of Portugal sent an expedition to conquer the islanders. One of the two ships and crews he sent was Florentine, the other Genoese, and the expeditionary force included Portuguese and Castilians as well – a representative sampling of the pioneers of European expansion into the Atlantic. According to Giovanni Boccaccio, who recorded the venture, they carried everything necessary for a proper siege of cities, including horses, but what effect such equipment might have had in the Canaries is open to doubt; Boccaccio left us ignorant of the expedition's outcome.

Another major but curious effort to conquer and colonize the Canaries began in the 1340s, when the pope invested a Castilian nobleman with the lofty title of Prince of Fortune and gave him lordship over a collection of Atlantic and Mediterranean islands. The pope was Clement VI, who presided over the papal court in Avignon and maintained a pro-French foreign policy. The Castilian nobleman he invested was don Luis de la Cerda, also called don Luis de España, a great-grandson of Alfonso X of Castile and Louis IX of France. Don Luis had been born in France during a period when his father was exiled from Spain, and he retained ties with both countries throughout his life. As a young man he visited Spain briefly, early in the fourteenth century. While there he married doña Leonor de Guzmán, thereby gaining lordship of the towns of Deza, Enciso, and Puerto de Santa María, a town that would later figure prominently in the history of Castilian expansion and in the life of Columbus.

Returning to France, don Luis took part in the major campaigns of the Hundred Years' War and attained the office of admiral of France. In 1344, he was in Avignon as one of the ambassadors to the papal court on behalf of King Philippe IV of France. While there, don Luis petitioned the pope for lordship of a collection of eleven islands, and Clement VI (1342–1352) agreed, no doubt hoping to please the French king. In return don Luis swore vassalage to the pope for his new possessions. One of the islands (Goleta) lay in the Mediterranean, and the rest lay in the Atlantic. Don Luis named them specifically in his petition: Canaria, Ningaria, Pluviana, Capraria, Iunonia, Embronea, Athlantia, Esperidum, Cernent, Gorgones, and Goleta – names taken directly from the *Natural History* of Pliny the Elder, written in the first century after Christ. Because no more recent knowledge of the islands than the ancient names was mentioned, the papal grant was more ephemeral than it seemed on paper; later explorers gave new names to the islands they found. Don Luis was to raise the capital for the expedition on his own. Although the pope wrote the rulers of several countries urging them to provide financial support, he offered none himself. Presumably he knew perfectly well how speculative the venture was.

The papal grant of the Canaries evidently pleased no one but don Luis (and perhaps the king of France). Diplomatic response from other quarters was rapid, and less than enthusiastic. The English ambassador to the papal court, whose ignorance of geography was matched by his inability to clarify the terms of the grant, wrote a worried letter to his king, suggesting that the British Isles might be included. The kings of Portugal and Castile knew quite well where the Canaries were and were not disposed to see them granted to don Luis de la Cerda. Neither monarch directly challenged the pope's authority to make the grant, but each enunciated his own prior right. Portugal asserted its possession by dint of proximity to the islands and claimed that Portuguese explorers had previously discovered them. Castile asserted that the Visigoths of Spain had seized the islands from infidels centuries before; as heirs of the Visigoths, Castilians laid an ancient claim to the islands. Undeterred, don Luis set about raising an expedition in France and secured the aid of the king of Aragón. Although he died before launching his campaign, the possibility exists that one of his lieutenants may have taken one ship to Lanzarote. Don Luis's will, leaving his claim to his eldest son, was executed in 1348 – an ominous year. By then Europe was in the grip of the Black Death, which suspended plans for any large-scale attempts at conquest.

The Canaries were not forgotten, however. A series of smaller expeditions, some with only one vessel, probed the area both before and after don Luis de la Cerda's grant. The king of Aragón, Pedro IV, sent out several expeditions of his own from Majorca in the 1340s and thereafter, including both missionaries and settlers. Attempts to convert the Canary Islanders to Christianity had evidently been going on for some time. Clement VI had granted two Majorcans named Joan Doria and Jaume Segarra the authority to mount a mission to the Canaries. They were to be aided by twelve Canary Islanders who had been brought, perhaps as captives, to the court of the king of Aragón and taught the Catalan language. By the 1390s, sailors from Andalusia visited the islands fairly regularly, but only in 1402 was the expedition launched that began the definitive conquest of the Canaries by Castile.[19]

In the mode of its conquest, colonization, and economic organization, the experience of the Canaries set many precedents that would later be repeated in the Americas. At first, Enrique III of Castile simply granted lordship over the Canaries, in 1402, to the Norman noble Jean de Bethencourt, who, with Gadifer de la Salle from Poitou, began the conquest of the Canaries in 1402–4. The forces they assembled conquered the islands of Lanzarote, Fuerteventura, and part of Hierro. Maciot (or Mathieu) de Bethencourt inherited his uncle's claim to the Canaries, and in 1418 he turned title over to the count of Niebla, Enrique de Guzmán. In 1420, Juan II of Castile made a grant to Alfonso Casaus (or Las Casas) to conquer the uncontrolled islands, and he was able to complete the conquest of Hierro and to take over Gomera. Later, sales and marriage agreements brought the islands under the control of Inés de Las Casas and her husband Diego de Herrera in 1452, who governed the islands until 1477.

In that year Queen Isabel of Castile and her husband King Fernando of Aragón reclaimed jurisdiction over the three largest and still unconquered islands of the Canaries: Gran Canaria, La Palma, and Tenerife, leaving the Herrera family in possession of the four smaller islands. The royal decision reflected both an effort to assert stronger control over all lands in their jurisdiction and a recognition of the strategic importance of the Canaries in their struggle with Portugal. The monarchs made agreements with individual captains to conquer the three largest islands in the name of the crown. Gran Canaria's conquest began in 1478 with the bishop of Lanzarote, Juan de Frías, and a captain named Juan Rejón, who relied on ecclesiastical financing for the attempt. Disputes between Rejón and royal officials stalled the conquest until 1480, when Fernando and Isabel sent out Pedro de Vera as royal governor, with wide powers and a large army. After ousting Rejón, Vera subdued the inhabitants of Gran Canaria by April 1483.

A captain with previous experience in the conquest of Gran Canaria, Alonso Fernández de Lugo, made a pact with the crown, in June of 1492, to conquer the islands of La Palma and Tenerife. With backing from Genoese merchants resident in Andalusia, Fernández took a small army to La Palma in 1493 and subdued it. He had a harder time conquering Tenerife, even though he raised a larger army and followed the standard practice of securing allies among the Christianized islanders to use against the pagans. The conquest still took him nearly three years. At one point the local inhabitants (Guanches) ambushed his troops, defeating them and forcing the survivors to abandon the islands temporarily. In May of 1496, the surrender of the last local kings marked the end of the conquest of the Canaries, nearly four years after Columbus sailed from Gomera on his first transatlantic voyage.

Modern scientific studies have suggested that the Guanches were related to the Berbers of northwestern Africa, and their culture has been classified as Neolithic because they did not know how to work metal. Primarily herders, they had developed an agricultural economy only on the island of Gran Canaria and were organized politically into bands. The Castilians made treaties with some of the bands and conquered others. In the initial phases of conquest, the conquerors needed quick profits to repay creditors who had financed the expeditions. The capture and sale of slaves offered an obvious and easy way to repay those loans. Many enslaved Guanches were taken to be sold in Spain or in the Madeira Islands settled by the Portuguese; other slaves remained in the Canaries to work for European settlers, most frequently in household service. According to medieval law, it was legal to enslave members of bands that had resisted the Spanish incursion – those who, in other words, were captured during a "just war." It was not legal to enslave members of bands that had submitted voluntarily. However, bands allied with the Europeans that later rebelled or refused to carry out the terms of their treaties could be enslaved as "captives of a second war" (*de segunda guerra*).[20] Conquerors and colonists often circumvented the law, however, anxious for the profit to be made in the slave trade and from the use of slave labor on sugar plantations.

European settlers introduced sugarcane quite early in the Canary Islands, although production would not reach its peak, with twenty-nine mills in operation, until early in the sixteenth century. With time and increased European immigration, the Canaries were remade into true colonies, with similar patterns of economic, social, and political development – all dominated by a large group of European settlers. The Canaries acted as a way station between Europe and the Americas for Spanish sugar production. Cuttings for the propagation of sugarcane, and sugar-processing techniques, would be taken from the Canaries to the newly discovered Caribbean Islands early in the colonizing process.[21]

Just as the Canaries served as a link between Europe and the Americas in the history of sugar production, the relations between European and native peoples in the Canaries foreshadowed experiences in the Americas. In the Canaries slaves were used both as laborers and as commodities for sale elsewhere, but the Guanche population was relatively small to begin with, and its numbers were diminished by epidemic disease after the European incursion. Moreover, members of many bands could not be enslaved, at least legally, and those enslaved frequently attained manumission. Consequently, the natives of the Canaries did not account for a substantial or long-lasting addition to the international slave trade. The Canarian slave trade to Europe ceased altogether in the early sixteenth century, as the islanders increasingly assimilated European culture and intermarried with the colonists.

In short, local natives never filled the need for labor in the colonial economy of the Canaries, and other sources had to be found to develop the islands fully. The labor shortage was solved in several ways. Some wealthy settlers brought their own slaves with them from the Iberian peninsula. In addition, Portuguese slave traders brought in black slaves from the western coast of Africa, and Castilians raided the African coast for North Africans, Berbers, and others to enslave. Many of the Africans, especially the North Africans, were soon freed, and there was even a voluntary emigration of Muslims and converted Muslims (Moriscos) from Spain and North Africa to the Canaries. Following the first Spanish contact with the Americas, a few Caribbean natives were sold in the Canaries, but the Spanish crown quickly outlawed the slave trade in Indians. As free Castilian and Portuguese settlers increasingly emigrated to the Canaries, the need for coerced labor declined. The initial search for fast profits through the slave trade, followed by the establishment of more lasting bases for the colonial economy, shaped the relationship between Europeans and local inhabitants in both the Canaries and the Americas.

PORTUGAL'S ATLANTIC ISLANDS AND THE SUGAR BOOM IN THE MADEIRAS

Like the Canaries, the Madeira Islands were the focus of rivalry among several groups of European explorers between their discovery in the thirteenth or early fourteenth century and their definitive settlement by the Portuguese in the early fifteenth century. Given the wind patterns in the eastern Atlantic (which we will discuss in the next chapter), it was only a matter of time before some group of European seafarers discovered the Madeiras, and Iberian mariners were ideally situated to be the first.

In the late fourteenth and early fifteenth centuries, Portuguese and Castilian ships visited the Madeira Islands for easily obtainable products such as wood and the red dye called "dragon's blood," the resin of the so-called dragon tree. Pirates used the islands as occasional bases as well. The Portuguese crown was not very interested in the Madeiras until 1417, when their Castilian rivals visited the islands with a large force. Faced with potentially serious Castilian competition, João I of Portugal sent an expedition of about one hundred people, mostly from southern Portugal, to the principal islands of the Madeiras – Madeira and Porto Santo – to establish permanent settlements. The leaders of the expedition were two Portuguese, João Gonçalves Zarco and Tristão Vaz Teixeira, and an Italian naturalized in Portugal named Bartolomeu Perestrelo. Many years later Perestrelo's daughter would marry another Italian immigrant to Portugal – Christopher Columbus. All three men were members of the lower nobility in Portugal, as were some fourteen other men in the expedition. We can assume that they had been induced to settle the islands by promises of lands to exploit and rule. Zarco and Teixeira divided the island of Madeira, and Perestrelo received Porto Santo. In 1433

Portugal's new King Duarte made his brother Prince Henrique (known to history as Henry the Navigator) lord of the Madeiras for life. Prince Henrique later confirmed the grants made to Zarco, Teixeira, and Perestrelo, creating administrative divisions called "captaincies" that he bestowed on each of them as a hereditary right.[22]

The Madeiras were uninhabited and fertile, but the land required careful and extensive preparation before sugar or other crops could be successfully grown there. Forests were cleared by burning, and irrigation canals and terraces were built to balance the effect of irregular and insufficient rainfall. By about 1450, the Madeiras began to generate profits from grain production, and the Portuguese built a water-powered flour mill on Madeira in 1452. Thereafter, sugar production and other agricultural pursuits expanded to support a much larger population. The Venetian Cadamosto reported some eight hundred people living on the island of Madeira in 1455, and the Portuguese Azurara, writing in the same decade, gave a similar estimate. By the early sixteenth century, the population stood at between fifteen and eighteen thousand, including some two thousand slaves.

From the mid-fifteenth century on, the Portuguese took slaves to work in the Madeiras: Moroccans and Berbers, black Africans, and native islanders from the Canaries. There was a limit to the number of slaves that could be profitably employed, however, because the Madeiran sugar plantations were relatively small in comparison with the later Caribbean and Brazilian plantations. Besides, the growth of population in Portugal in the sixteenth century induced many free Portuguese laborers to migrate to Madeira, depressing the market for slaves. The use of slave labor soon began to decline, and there were even proposals to expel the Canary Islanders to reduce the labor supply. In short, during the fifteenth century the development of Madeira, like that of the Canaries, proceeded along lines that would later characterize American colonial development, with a reliance on slave labor for commercial plantations. In the sixteenth century, however, Madeira came to rely much more heavily on free labor, phasing out a system of slave labor that did not suit the situation.

Much farther south, the island of São Tomé, which later became a crucial entrepôt for the transatlantic slave trade, also experienced a sugar boom in the sixteenth century and in many ways served as a prototype for sugar production in the islands of the Caribbean. The Portuguese established sugar production on other Atlantic islands as well, but none rivaled the early profits drawn from the Madeiras and São Tomé. Sugar enjoyed little success in the Azores because of the unsuitable climate; grain and dyestuffs were always more important there. And Portuguese development of the Cape Verde Islands concentrated on grain and fruit, as well as cattle raising.

THE CREATION OF COLONIAL WORLDS IN AFRICA AND
THE ATLANTIC ISLANDS

In the fifteenth century, Iberians and their Italian associates developed two modes of exploitation in newly colonized areas. In one mode, the Portuguese set up *feitorias* (trading posts) along the African coast – sometimes fortified, sometimes not – that enabled them to tap into existing trade networks. In Africa, Europeans had to contend with major obstacles to any grandiose plans for Christian proselytizing or for control of local resources. Many African kingdoms and other states were willing to trade, but they would not allow Europeans to dominate them and had the strength to resist attempts at conquest in the fifteenth century. The Portuguese soon abandoned any thought of territorial conquest and instead negotiated with each local ruler for trading privileges. Endemic disease also prevented European colonial incursions into the African mainland. Tropical Africa hosted a variety of endemic diseases to which local populations had developed tolerance or even immunity. Europeans had never been exposed to them, however, and succumbed in great numbers. Together, the strength of African states and the insalubrious environment prevented Europeans from establishing a large territorial base in West Africa. The Portuguese found ample compensation in trade, however, and were content to act as merchants in their coastal enclaves.

The other mode of European exploitation, which developed in the Atlantic islands, was very different, even though the island groups were discovered and settled by Iberians simultaneously with their African exploration. Except for the Cape Verdes, the Atlantic islands were mild enough in climate and similar enough to Europe to allow Europeans to settle there easily. In all the Atlantic islands, European settlers developed a new mode of colonial control and exploitation, initiated by a forceful European incursion, then followed by the establishment of profit-making ventures in agriculture and mining, using coerced, non-European labor. This mode of exploitation would not work in regions such as mainland Africa and India, but it would be repeated profitably, and with devastating effect, across the Atlantic.

Exploitation of the Atlantic islands by Portuguese and Castilian settlers was a logical extension of the search for commercial profits that had engaged southern Europeans for centuries. That search formed one of the two major motivations that drove Europeans to try novel ventures and explore new lands. The other motive was religion, the militant Christianity that had inspired both the Reconquest of Iberia from the Muslims and the Crusades that took the battle to the heartland of Islam. Together, religious and economic motivations had shaped European experience for centuries, particularly in southern Europe. They would come together, in the late fifteenth century, to inspire Columbus's great leap of imagination. But as compelling as these motivations were, they would have had no practical consequence without the appropriate means for acting upon them. If motivations were to be turned into realities, Europeans needed a wide range of technology and technical skills, including suitable ships and the knowledge of how and where to sail them.

4

Tools of Expansion

B Y THE LATE FIFTEENTH CENTURY, Europeans had ships large and strong enough to make long deepwater voyages, but such voyages were neither easy nor without risk. An adequate ship alone hardly guaranteed success. The sea lanes of the age of discovery are liberally strewn with the wrecks of vessels that never reached their destinations. Columbus would lose his flagship, the *Santa María,* on his first voyage through the carelessness of a young sailor who let it run aground. Nevertheless, without reliable vessels the oceans of the world would have remained an impassable barrier to European dreams of exploration.

Europeans were not the only mariners capable of long-distance voyages. The Chinese enjoyed a maritime technology that was easily the equal of Europe's, but they chose not to exploit it. This is abundantly clear from the history of the massive fleets of Chinese ships sent out in the early fifteenth century. Between 1405 and 1435, the admiral Cheng Ho commanded several Chinese fleets involving hundreds of ships and thousands of people. They sailed throughout the lands rimming the Indian Ocean, even venturing as far afield as East Africa. But the Ming emperors discontinued the expeditions, and China officially withdrew within her own ample borders. The Chinese neither knew – nor, presumably, would they have cared – that European rulers at the same time were choosing to look outward rather than inward.

The vessels that proved most useful for European voyages of exploration were the product of a long evolution in ship design and construction, changing gradually as detailed improvements and innovations were made, especially during the fifteenth century, by the experienced shipwrights of Spain and Portugal. In the Middle Ages, Europeans constructed vessels of two basic types, one propelled primarily by oars and the other propelled primarily by sails.[1] Depending on circumstances, both types of vessel were suited for the landlocked and tideless Mediterranean and for the rougher waters of Europe's Atlantic coastline. The oared vessel, generally very long in proportion to its breadth, was represented in southern Europe by the Mediterranean galley and in northern Europe by the Viking longship. Both usually carried a single square sail, but the main power

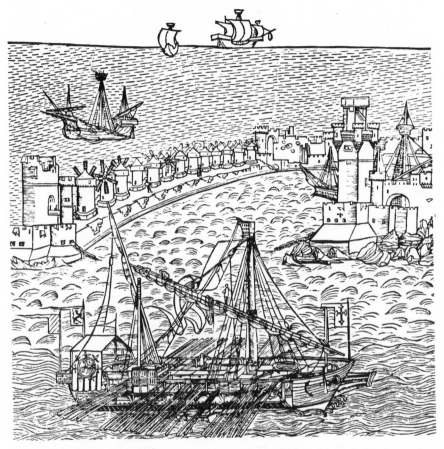

A great galley shown approaching Rhodes in the late fifteenth century, laden with chests of trade goods. (From Bernhard von Breydenbach, *Peregrinatio in Terram Sanctam* [Mainz: E. Reuwick, 1486]. Photo courtesy of the James Ford Bell Library, University of Minnesota.)

came from the oarsmen. A typical galley was about five to seven times as long as it was wide, and, when outfitted for warfare, might carry several hundred men. The ship had to be long, low, and narrow to be rowed effectively and was ill suited for long voyages because of the limited space in which to carry provisions for the crew. Cargo capacity was also limited. Only a highly lucrative cargo, such as spices or luxurious cloth, could offset the cost of the large crew and its provisions. On the other hand, because the ship provided its own propulsion, it could follow a much tighter schedule than a vessel dependent on the wind. Although the city-states of Venice and Florence frequently sent commercial galleys as far as England, in the fourteenth and fifteenth centuries, it is clear that the galley and the longship were better suited for warfare than for trade.

The sailing ship, or "round ship," depended mainly on the wind for its propulsion and was therefore much cheaper to run on long commercial voyages than the galley. As its nickname implies, it was much shorter in relation to its breadth than the galley or longship. A typical round ship had proportions often described as "one-two-three," which meant that for every unit of breadth, or beam, there were two units of keel and three units of length, measured on the first deck. In both northern and southern Europe, the ship was steered by large oars fixed at the stern; northern ships generally had one and southern ships two.

Although the proportions of round ships from northern or southern Europe were similar in the late Middle Ages, methods of hull construction were not. In northern Europe the hull was fashioned from the outside in. Shipwrights soaked and steamed planks to make them flexible, then bent them to shape. The planks were overlapped slightly, like clapboard siding on a house, and fastened together with nails clinched on the inside. After the hull was shaped, bracing timbers were added to the inside of the hull for additional strength. These "clinker" hulls were strong, durable, and fairly watertight, but they were also heavy and used a great deal of wood. In southern Europe, by contrast, standard hull building in the late Middle Ages proceeded from the inside out. First a skeleton of ribs was fashioned and erected on the keel, setting the shape of the hull. Then planks were steamed and attached to these ribs, edge to edge, not overlapped. Caulking and a waterproof coating such as tar and grease were added to the seams between the planks, in an effort to make them watertight. The southern hulls were strong enough for most purposes, relatively light compared to the clinker hulls of the north, and required much less wood. What the southern (or "carvel") hulls sacrificed in strength and watertightness, they gained in speed and agility, as well as in the economical use of raw materials.

In the late Middle Ages, the round ship of northern Europe was usually propelled by a single square sail. In the Mediterranean, the round ship was more likely to have two or three sails, called a "lateen" sail, each shaped like an obtuse triangle. Depending on the prevailing wind, each type of sail had advantages. The square sail performed best when the wind was blowing from behind, but it performed badly or not at all when sailing against the wind. The lateen sail was more effective with contrary winds and was particularly useful in sailing close to a coastline. The long yard on the lateen sail was difficult to adjust, however, and did not take full advantage of a following wind.

Seal of the city of Dover, England, 1305. The ship is a typical northern European design, double-ended, with a single, square sail, a clinker-built hull, and a steering oar. (Replica, owned by W. D. Phillips and C. R. Phillips.)

Because of their various limitations, both the long, oared ship and the square-sailed, round ship were unsuitable for long voyages to unknown regions. In European waters, the crew of a round ship could wait out contrary winds and sail when favorable winds arose. In unknown waters, however, the right wind might never arise, and the crew might be stranded forever on an alien shore. An oared ship, independent of the wind if need be, could return along any course chosen, if only its crew had sufficient provisions. In unknown lands, that was nearly impossible to ensure. The Viking longship voyages to Greenland and Iceland were extraordinary accomplishments, but the Norsemen benefited from the relatively short stretches of open sea they had to cross. Five hundred years later, the Portuguese of the fifteenth century would have been foolhardy to attempt exploration of the African coast in galleys. In much of northwestern Africa, the Sahara Desert meets the sea. In the fifteenth century, the coastal area supported only a small, mainly nomadic, population. Without convenient provisioning stations, a galley's crew could easily have starved.

Eventually, European mariners found a solution to the technical problems of oceangoing and coastal navigation by blending characteristics of the ship types from northern and southern Europe, once

Southern European round ship with carvel planking, constructed over a skeleton. (From Bernhard von Breydenbach, *Peregrinatio in Terram Sanctam* [Mainz: E. Reuwick, 1486]. Photo courtesy of the James Ford Bell Library, University of Minnesota.)

trade had opened up between those two areas. During the centuries of intermittent warfare between Christians and Muslims in the Middle Ages, long-distance voyages between northern and southern Europe were rare as well as dangerous. The volume of trade did not warrant taking the risk. During the thirteenth century, the political situation stabilized somewhat, and trade flourished. Once the Strait of Gibraltar was secured by the Christian kings of the Iberian Peninsula, commercial voyages could increase in number and regularity. Ships from the full length of Europe's Atlantic and Mediterranean coastlines came into regular contact with one another, and mariners were able to observe one another's vessels. In a classic example of technological transfer, shipwrights borrowed the best features from the northern and the southern styles of sailing ship. The changes that occurred deserve to be called a "revolution" in ship design, and they produced several types of vessels superbly suited to the needs of long-distance commerce and oceanic exploration.

Changes occurred gradually to both hulls and sails. A hinged rudder affixed to the stern, invented in the late twelfth century to replace steering oars, was one of the earliest features adopted by both northern and southern ships. The rudder's origins remain unclear, and its adoption was neither rapid nor universal. Nonetheless, over a century and a half the sternpost rudder became standard equipment on large ships in both northern and southern Europe, although steering oars remained the choice for many smaller vessels and remain so today. In hull construction, even though northern Europe still had vast forests, unlike the south, the southern style of edge-joined planking became widely recognized as a better design for large ships and was gradually adopted by northern shipwrights. In sail plan, the square sail of the north replaced the lateen sails of the Mediterranean as the main source of propulsion. By the mid-fourteenth century, both northern and southern ships often had a second, smaller, square sail, although it could be a lateen sail on southern ships. Paintings, town seals, and other illustrations from the late fourteenth century often show these ships, which were called "cogs" in English, *coques* in French, and *cocas* in Spanish. They tended to be double-ended and had high, permanent structures called "castles" both fore and aft, to help the sailors work the rigging lines and also to serve as fighting platforms in battle.

By the early fifteenth century, many ships had begun to use a third mast, called the "mizzen," at the rear of the ship, rigged with a lateen sail and balancing the large, square mainsail and the square foresail. Thereafter, the standard sail plan for oceangoing vessels would be some combination of square and lateen sails, especially the classic "full rig" consisting of a square mainsail, a square foresail, and a

Lateen caravel with two sails; large carrack with three sails. Facsimile of the portolan chart of Piri Reis, 1513. (Photo courtesy of the James Ford Bell Library, University of Minnesota.)

lateen mizzen sail. By using both square and lateen sails on the same vessel, mariners could take advantage of a wide range of wind conditions and avoid the limitations posed by using one type of sail exclusively.

In many ways Iberia was the nexus for this revolution in ship design. In addition to designing and building cogs that were sold all over Europe, Iberians developed the ship type called by variants of the name "caravel." The prototypes of these ships evidently had existed in the waters between southern Iberia and northern Africa from at least the thirteenth century. The vessel was small, agile, and much narrower than the typical Mediterranean round ship – perhaps four times as long as it was wide. It was also planked by the typical southern method of edge-to-edge construction over a skeleton of ribs. The identification of the caravel with the "carvel" method of planking in documents of the period was close enough to suggest that one took its name from the other, although scholars still argue about the identity of the borrower and the lender. Fishermen and other mariners who used caravels along the Atlantic coast of Portugal and the Cantabrian coast of Spain probably strengthened the hull to withstand the open ocean, perhaps using small whaling vessels as their model.

As the Portuguese explored the coastline of Africa, they used small caravels with a two-masted lateen rig for many tasks, especially after they rounded Cape Bojador. The lateen caravel could beat its way home while keeping within reassuring sight of the coast. Out in the open ocean, however, the small lateen caravel did not sail as well as a full-rigged ship. It is likely that shipwrights in southwestern Spain adapted the full rig to the hull of the caravel to make the ship handle better, resulting in the ship type they called the *carabela redonda,* or "round caravel," referring to the use of square sails that "rounded" with a following wind. The Portuguese also experimented with the caravel's hull and sail plan, developing a range of vessels with the same name but having little in common with one another except a slim hull and lateen sails. Caravels were also adopted and adapted in northern Europe at the same time, and some of those changes undoubtedly found their way back to Iberia. By the late fifteenth century, various small caravel types were well known along the Atlantic coasts of Europe and Africa.[2]

These new ships, which made oceangoing exploration possible, were all relatively small in the fifteenth century. The caravel averaged about 50 to 70 tons burden – just large enough, as it turned out, to carry a crew and its provisions across the Atlantic. Its larger counterpart – the merchant vessel with a full rig – was called a "carrack" in English, *nao* in Spanish, and variations of those names by other Europeans. The *nao* averaged about 90 to 200 tons, much smaller than the transatlantic ships of later centuries. With the hybrid ships of Europe's design revolution at their disposal, Spanish and Portuguese mariners had the means to travel virtually anywhere they wanted. Finding their way around the oceans of the world presented another set of challenges, which European technology in the fifteenth century only partially met.

NAVIGATIONAL INSTRUMENTS AND TECHNIQUES

Important advances in instruments of navigation, and skill in their use, came during the Middle Ages.[3] The most important navigational aid that European vessels carried was the magnetic compass, adopted from the Muslims by the twelfth century. The early compass was a rather primitive tool, consisting simply of a magnetized needle or pointer affixed to a compass card that indicated directional

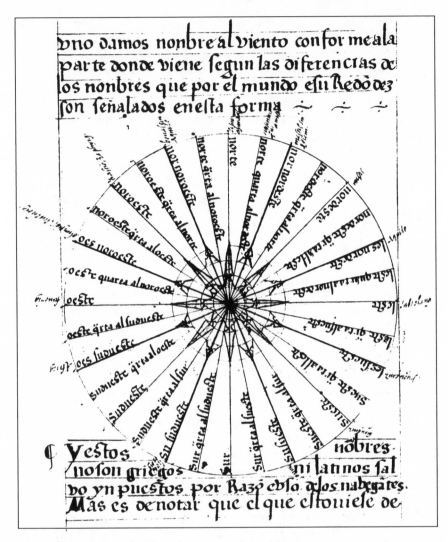

Compass card showing the names of the thirty-two compass points. (From Pedro de Medina, *Libro de cosmographía* [1538]. Bodleian Library, Oxford.)

points around a circle. The whole apparatus was mounted on a pivot to allow it to adjust its level against the rolling of the ship and was then placed in a box to protect it from sea spray and weather. From time to time the pilot had to remagnetize the directional needle with a lodestone that he carried as a crucial part of his equipment. By consulting the compass, the pilot could track his vessel's movement toward its destination.

For local voyages in the Mediterranean and in known regions of the Atlantic coast, fifteenth-century mariners could rely on charts called "portolans," prototypes of modern marine charts.[4] Produced for centuries by skilled mapmakers in the Mediterranean, they showed in detail the coastline, ports, and salient geographical features of the area. More important, they included compass directions for sailing from each port to any other point on the map. Most portolans devoted little attention to the inland areas beyond the ports. Their orientation was clearly toward the sea. As useful – and beautiful – as these portolan charts were, they were useful only in known waters. Beyond their borders, the world was literally and figuratively a blank. To aid in expanding the available store of knowledge about geography, early explorers reported to their governments the location and geographical features of any new places they visited, complete with compass directions. This ensured that all subsequent voyages would be easier. When political power or the ownership of new lands was at stake, however, governments had little interest in sharing navigational secrets with other nations. Precise sailing directions to new lands came to be defined as state secrets, jealously guarded against rival nations.

Sailing into unknown seas, an experienced mariner had to rely primarily on his senses and his powers of observation and calculation. The few pieces of equipment he carried with him seem pathetically inadequate for the task he faced. Once out of sight of familiar coasts, the best way to determine how far north or south his ship had traveled was to estimate its position in relation to known objects in the heavens.[5] In the Northern Hemisphere, the mariner's guiding light was the polestar, easily recognizable on a clear night. To observe the heavens, mariners of the fifteenth century used either an astrolabe, adapted from an instrument used by astronomers on land, or a quadrant. In its simplest form, an astrolabe was a flat, circular piece of brass, hollow in the center except for a strip across the diameter, to which was attached a movable pointer called an "alidade." To use the astrolabe, a mariner would hang the instrument from a ship's timber and hold it as steady as possible. (A good astrolabe could weigh as much as 10 pounds, because its weight helped to keep it steady against the rolling of the ship.) He would then peer through two viewing holes on the alidade, adjusting it until the viewing holes aligned with the star. As the pointer moved, it slid along a scale marked on the circular edge of the astrolabe. Once the star was sighted properly, its angle to the horizon could be read from that scale. From the observed angle the mariner could ascertain the latitude, or north–south position, of his ship, either by calculating the change from his earlier sightings or by consulting published tables calculated from the observations of other mariners. The larger the angle to the polestar, the farther north his ship had traveled; the smaller the angle, the farther south. The procedure was similar with a quadrant, for this instrument was merely a quarter-circle, with a simplified version of the astrolabe's scale. After the instrument was hung up to steady it, the quadrant itself was tilted until its two viewing holes aligned with a star. The star's altitude could then be read, at the point where a plumb line crossed a scale marked on the quadrant's lower arc. Typically, the scale would be marked not only by degrees of altitude but also by the names of known places where those altitudes had already been measured.

Making accurate observations on the heaving deck of a ship at sea depended on good luck at least as much as on experience and skill. It is hardly surprising that even the most experienced mariners could become hopelessly lost at times. Nonetheless, the use of fairly sophisticated measuring devices marked a major change in navigation. Earlier European sailors had relied on gross estimates of the altitude of the polestar; that was sufficiently accurate in the known waters of the Mediterranean and the Atlantic coast of Europe. Exploring the unknown waters off the African coast led the Portuguese to develop more reliable methods – hence the use of the astrolabe and the quadrant to scan the heavens. Various scholars have claimed that precise celestial measurements were used first in the Mediterranean, then later in the Atlantic by the Portuguese, but the weight of evidence seems to favor Portuguese innovation.

As Portuguese mariners ventured farther south down the African coast, the polestar sank ever lower on the horizon, creating a real dilemma. After about 1480, the Portuguese began to use the angle of the sun from the horizon at its noontime meridian as a way to verify their calculations based on observations of the polestar. Soon tables of the sun's declination at various places and seasons were available to oceangoing sailors. That only partially solved the problems of navigation in the Southern Hemisphere, once the polestar was lost entirely to view. If the sun was not visible at noon, mariners would lose a day's calculation of their course. Even if it was visible, they would have no nighttime observation to compare with their daytime calculation. Portuguese voyagers of the late fifteenth century felt this problem acutely and solved it by about 1500, when they identified the constellation called the Southern Cross, the Southern Hemisphere's equivalent of the polestar. With careful observation and the development of a new set of tables, the Southern Hemisphere could be incorporated into the expanding world known to Iberian mariners.

Careful observation of the sun, the polestar, and the Southern Cross effectively solved the problem of determining latitude. Columbus carried up-to-date tables of solar declination on his first voyage in 1492, and he had obviously learned from Portuguese innovations in celestial navigation relating to latitude. Despite present-day popular assumptions, however, Columbus did not have a telescope to aid in his observations; that would not be invented until more than a century after his 1492 voyage.

More difficult than the determination of latitude was the calculation of a ship's speed and its longitude, or position east to west. Columbus and other Europeans, as well as mariners in the Indian Ocean at the same time, sailed east or west by following the latitudes of known places. For example, on his third voyage Columbus sailed across the Atlantic at the latitude of Sierra Leone in Africa, knowing that this would put him where he wished to be. Only with great difficulty, however, could he estimate where his ship was on any given day of its westward course. Such estimates depended on experienced observations and on calculations of time and the ship's speed and direction. Time was measured at sea in the fifteenth century by a sand-clock or hourglass. Each running of the sand usually took half an hour, and the accuracy of the clock depended on the reliability of the person assigned to turn it over when the sand ran out. The ship's speed was measured by observing the hull as it passed through the water, and its direction was measured by noting each change in compass heading and its duration. By combining all these measurements and observations, an experienced mariner could calculate how far, how fast, and in what direction his ship had traveled each day. The method as a whole is usually described as "dead reckoning." A skilled dead reckoner such as Columbus might rely more on his intuition than on the evidence of his instruments, a method not necessarily less accurate than trusting the instruments entirely. The mariner's tools of the fifteenth century, and the conditions under which they were used, did not inspire confidence, even then. Nonetheless, without those tools, and without ships capable of withstanding the pounding of the open sea, the rapid exploration of the globe by Europeans could not have taken place.

THE TOOLS OF WAR

As another part of their technological legacy, Europeans had centuries of experience in warfare and its specialized technology. Guns –

both cannons and small-caliber long-guns called "harquebuses" –
were common in Europe in the fifteenth century. The knowledge of
gunpowder had passed from China, where it was invented, through
the Muslim world to the West, and by the late fifteenth century Europeans had the most advanced gunnery in the world. Strange as it
may seem, however, guns did not play a crucial role in European
successes at the beginning of their exploration and conquests around
the globe. Ship-mounted cannon were not important factors in European expansion until the Portuguese reached the Indian Ocean and
until other Europeans conducted pirate raids against Spanish shipping and settlements in the sixteenth century. The hand-carried harquebuses were crude, hard to load, and not particularly effective.
Their noise and novelty could terrorize those who faced them for the
first time, but even in battle other weapons were far more effective
– hardened steel blades, horses, and war dogs.[6] In the process of
European expansion as a whole, weaponry was much less important
than other aspects of European development, especially business
techniques and bureaucratic state organization. Influencing all else
was the collective mentality of Europe during the period of exploration.

THE INTELLECTUAL REVOLUTION IN ASTRONOMY AND GEOGRAPHY

The quickening pace of European commercial life in the fifteenth
century focused renewed attention on Asia, the fabled source of luxury and wealth. With the great overland routes to Asia inaccessible,
European speculation about the best route to Asia naturally turned
toward the sea. The new orientation relied heavily on knowledge
about the heavens and the earth that scholars had been accumulating
for centuries.

The astronomical knowledge of Europe, and of the Islamic world
as well, relied on the model proposed by Claudius Ptolemaeus, known
as Ptolemy, a classical astronomer and geographer. Ptolemy, who
had lived in Egypt in the second century A.D., had been trained in
Hellenistic science. His book on astronomy, usually known by the
title of its Arabic translation, *Almagest,* had been translated into Latin
in the twelfth century. In Ptolemy's universe the sun, the moon, the
planets, the stars, and the heavens revolved around the earth on perfectly formed spheres of transparent crystal, their purity and form
expressing the perfection of their divine creator. If we imagine viewing them in order, from the sphere closest to the earth to the one
most distant from it, Ptolemy's spheres held the moon; Mercury;

Venus; the sun; Mars; Jupiter; Saturn; the firmament, or starry heaven; the prime mover, or crystalline heaven; and finally the empyrean, the habitation of God.

Ptolemy's earth-centered, or "geocentric," theory was wrong, of course, but it retained its importance throughout the Middle Ages in both the Christian and Islamic worlds. Medieval astronomers were not careless observers. Even though they lacked the telescope and had to depend on observations made with the naked eye, they were able to determine that the planets do not describe perfectly circular paths in their apparent journey about the earth. Medieval astronomers accounted for these discrepancies between Ptolemy's theories and their own observations by suggesting that each planet described tiny circles, or "epicycles," on the surface of its larger sphere. As foolish as this may seem to anyone with a modern education, the notion of epicycles allowed medieval astronomers to explain the observed heavens within a consistent general framework. Other notions of medieval astronomers were correct even by modern standards. They knew, for example, that the moon has no light of its own and glows with reflected light from the sun. They also knew that eclipses of the moon occur when the earth casts a shadow on it and that eclipses of the sun occur when the moon blocks the sun's light from reaching the earth.

The first challenge to Ptolemy's model came just a half-century after the first voyage of Columbus through the work of Nicholas Copernicus, a Polish astronomer who published his theory in 1543, basing it on decades of observing the heavens. Copernicus postulated that the sun, not the earth, is the center of the universe, a new conception that challenged ancient and medieval wisdom about the heavens quite as much as the voyages of Columbus and his successors challenged the accepted view of the earth. Over a century and a half passed before the sun-centered, or "heliocentric," model was accepted by scholars, and even longer before ordinary people knew about it. Because modern European languages took shape during the period when the geocentric model held sway, we still speak of the sun "rising" and "setting," as if it were circling a stationary earth – the same visual illusion that fooled medieval astronomers.[7] Columbus's knowledge of astronomy undoubtedly developed during his years as a mariner, and it fit quite comfortably within the Ptolemaic universe accepted in his time.

The principal scholarly texts about geography did not offer European mariners much practical assistance. Over the centuries, however, scholars had developed enough information to suggest that ocean routes to Asia were possible. Academic geographers did not always agree with one another, or with ancient authorities, but their specu-

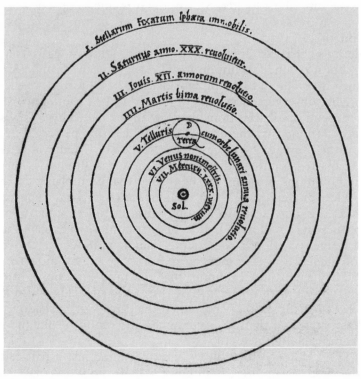

The heliocentric universe. (From Nicholas Copernicus, *De revolutioni-bus orbium coelestium,* Book 6, first published 1543; facsimile ed., Turin, 1943. Photo courtesy of Special Collections, University of Minnesota.)

lations stimulated discussion and controversy.[8] By the late fifteenth century Columbus, along with other merchants, popes, and princes, could pick and choose among the available theories, selecting the interpretations that they found the most persuasive or congenial.

In 1264, Roger Bacon had published his *Opus majus,* which summarized ancient geographical knowledge and integrated contributions from Muslim geographers in the Middle Ages. Bacon accepted the view common in his time: the habitable portion of the world was composed of three parts (Asia, Africa, and Europe), and the rest of the globe was covered by oceans. In a crucial break with tradition, however, Bacon rejected the common notion that seas and lands near the equator were too hot for human beings to survive. Instead, he believed that Asia and Africa extended down below the equator and might be inhabited. Once scholars began to doubt the existence of a Torrid Zone, the prospect of southerly voyages lost its fearsome quality.

Bacon's work was only one of many speculating about the shape and character of the world and questioning the wisdom of ancient and medieval authors. The *Geographia* of Ptolemy, greatest of the ancients, was translated into Latin in the early fifteenth century, providing a convenient framework for depicting the terrestrial globe in graphic form. Among his other contributions, Ptolemy divided the earth into 360 degrees of latitude and longitude, which became the basis for subsequent Western maps. He did, however, make two fundamental errors. First, his estimate for the size of the earth was about one-fifth too small. Second, he described Africa and Asia as being joined at their tips. This configuration would have made the rich trading network of the Indian Ocean inaccessible to ships sailing from Europe. Fortunately, there were other opinions to choose from. Enea Silvio Piccolomini (later Pope Pius II) published a work in the early fifteenth century summarizing much of Ptolemy's *Geographia* but rejecting the idea that the Indian Ocean was an enclosed sea. When Columbus was assembling academic support for his grand scheme in the late fifteenth century, he undoubtedly read Piccolomini's work and probably found it appealing.

Pierre d'Ailly, an early fifteenth-century cardinal, published a geographical work called *Imago mundi* that was to have a great influence upon many European scholars, merchants, and mariners, among them Columbus. The cardinal relied heavily on geographical treatises by classical and Muslim scholars, and to increase the accuracy of his work he disregarded the accounts of mere travelers such as Marco Polo. Nonetheless, he made several basic errors, exaggerating the size of Asia and underestimating the extent of oceans on the face of the earth. He was thus able to conclude that a voyage westward from Europe to Asia was eminently possible. Other geographers at the same time estimated the size and shape of the earth much more accurately than d'Ailly. He remains important, however, because Columbus enthusiastically adopted his calculations and used them as a basis for his grand scheme.

The geographical ideas of the late fifteenth century were depicted most strikingly by Martin Behaim, in 1492. Behaim's globe presented a view of the world almost identical to that of Columbus. The Americas were totally missing, of course, and Behaim placed Japan far distant from the mainland of Asia and showed the ocean between Europe and Asia strewn with islands. As far as we know, Columbus and Behaim had no contact with one another, but their conceptions of the world, both stemming from the academic geography available at the end of the fifteenth century, agreed almost entirely. Columbus formed his dream of sailing westward toward Asia, as we shall see, during his years in Portugal. By the time Co-

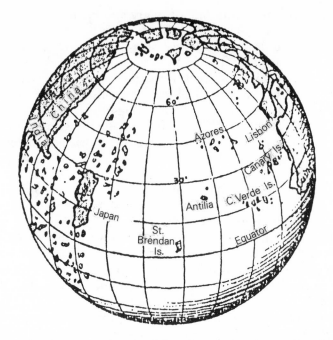

A sketch of Martin Behaim's globe of 1492, showing nothing but a scattering of islands between Europe and Japan. The original globe is in Nuremberg at the Germanisches National Museum. (Map prepared by the Cartography Laboratory, Department of Geography, University of Minnesota.)

lumbus arrived in Lisbon, the Portuguese had had over a half-century's experience in exploring the more obvious sea route to Asia, the one that followed the coastline of Africa. That route offered the best promise of outflanking the Muslim world and establishing a sea route to Asian markets.

The southern seas were initially outside the experience of European mariners, and historians have rightly emphasized the courage required to make those voyages. Slowly and incrementally, an accumulation of knowledge lessened the mystery surrounding the southern seas. Islands far from the coasts of Europe and Africa were discovered and mapped. Ships were developed and adapted to handle the conditions of the ocean sea and the African coast. Even more important, mariners began to know the currents and wind patterns in those areas.

Southward along the African coast, from Morocco to the region of the Senegal River, the predominant winds – the northeast trade winds – blow from the northeast to the southwest. These trade winds

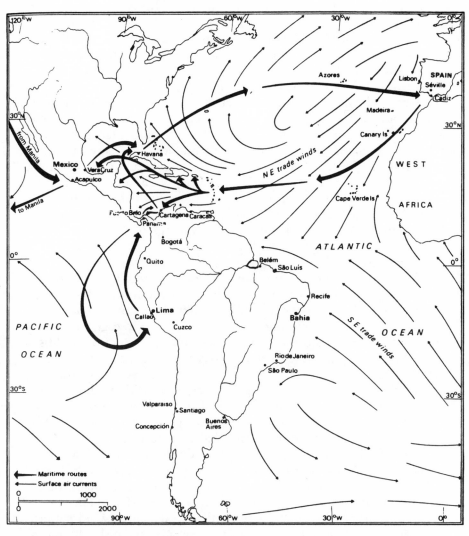

Wind and current patterns in the Atlantic Ocean. (From *The Cambridge History of Latin America*, 2 vols. on *Colonial Latin America*, ed. Leslie Bethell [Cambridge, 1984], 1:343.)

blow across the Atlantic and lead ultimately to the islands of the West Indies. As the Portuguese and Spaniards learned, over the course of the fifteenth century, the northeast winds enabled them to sail easily on a southerly course along the western bulge of Africa and as far out to sea as the Cape Verde Islands and the Canary Islands. Sailing back toward the north was much more difficult. Before the development of the lateen-rigged caravel, it was impossible. In the early fourteenth century, a group of Muslims sailing from Almería in southeastern Spain to a port in Morocco were blown far south along the African coast. They eventually abandoned their ship, although there is no evidence that it was damaged, to make a long and arduous overland trek back to Morocco – presumably because they found it impossible to sail back up the coast.[9] Even with the lateen-rigged caravel, cautious sailors could make only slow progress northward, by tacking back and forth and taking advantage of small daily variations in the wind to gain hard-won progress.

Adventurous sailors found another way. If they tacked out from the African shore and continued northwestward into the open ocean, and if they held that tack long enough, they would find themselves in a region of more favorable winds to carry them home. The "westerlies" – as their name implies – blow from west to east, in the latitude of the Azores and Iberia. Once a ship found them, it could sail home to Iberia without the labor of coastal tacking against a contrary wind. The westerlies were well known by the time of Columbus, and mariners had taken advantage of them since early in the fifteenth century. It is likely that the Azores islands, assumed to have been discovered sometime between 1427 and 1431, were first sighted by ships taking this *volta,* or trajectory, back to Iberia.

South of the equator lay an area of deadening calms called the "doldrums," and still farther south lay a place where winds moved counterclockwise in an elliptical pattern, the mirror image of the clockwise pattern off the northwestern coast of Africa. During the fifteenth century, the Portuguese came to know these wind patterns well and learned how to use them to their advantage. In the meantime, they sought every opportunity to make a profit along the African coast and in the Atlantic islands they claimed.[10]

Europe's increasing knowledge about the heavens and the earth typified the Renaissance, which was not just the rediscovery of ancient wisdom but the rebirth of an all-encompassing curiosity about the universe. Building on ancient wisdom, educated Europeans gradually gained the courage to go beyond received knowledge, correcting ancient scholarship in the light of modern experience. They were acutely aware of living in a new and exciting age, filled with promise for those bold enough to seize the initiative. Scholars of the

Renaissance frequently write about the intellectual curiosity that characterized Europeans in this period, which not only led to advances in astronomy, geography, and other branches of knowledge but also propelled individuals from all levels of the social spectrum to risk their lives in overseas exploration. Perhaps it will never be possible to explain adequately why Europeans took those risks, both intellectual and physical, while other peoples did not, but there is little question that the voyages of discovery owed much to the questing spirit that marked the European Renaissance.

THE WILL TO SUCCEED

It may seem odd to consider Europe's state of mind as a tool of expansion, yet there is a certain logic in doing so. The force of will and the powerful support provided by self-confidence are continually proved effective assets, even in the modern world. Without the confidence to succeed, the best-planned enterprises can fail, but with that confidence success becomes much more likely.

As Iberian mariners gradually refined navigational techniques, enabling them to plot a course beyond sight of the lands and skies they knew, they became increasingly confident about ocean sailing. They knew that with care and skill they could sail out and return home again in those waters, just as they could do closer to home. In short, their intellectual horizons had expanded along with their physical horizons. The ocean sea and its coastlines and islands had been added to the space in which they functioned competently and confidently.[11]

We might say, with many others, that by the late fifteenth century the ocean sea had ceased to be a barrier and had instead become a highway or a bridge to what lay beyond. That is certainly true, but it is equally important to note that the ocean itself had become a space in which Iberian mariners functioned, so that the borders of their home no longer lay at the shores of the Iberian Peninsula. Instead they had been expanded to include the known reaches of the ocean sea. That gave Iberian mariners the confidence to push those borders ever farther, into the truly unknown. An intellectual revolution in geographical familiarity had occurred in the course of a few decades. Once that happened, the process could not be reversed, as long as the will to explore persisted. Many Europeans shared that will, and their governments supported and directed their efforts. The confluence of knowledge, will, technology, and circumstance had set the stage for European expansion.

In sum, on the eve of Columbus's first voyage Europeans possessed both the motives for expansion and the means to achieve their aims. The urge to establish regular contact with Asia had a long and persistent history by the time of Columbus, based on quite practical concerns. The European desire to seek wealth in new trading ventures was coupled with Christian missionary impulses and the hope of outflanking the Muslim stronghold in the Middle East. An intellectual desire to make known the unknown – to discover – played a role as well, but intellectual curiosity alone could not have inspired European exploration. Columbus not only inherited Christian missionary zeal and European fascination with Asia but also the full arsenal of European tools of expansion accumulated over the centuries. As we shall see, Columbus formed a vision of the world that made Asia seem quite close to Europe over the ocean sea, using his own experience and selecting the most congenial opinions from the academic geographies available in his time. The skills he had formed as mariner and merchant gave him the confidence he needed to persevere until he found support for his dream. Ironically, had his calculation of the size of the earth been more accurate, even Columbus might have quailed at the vast distance that really lay between Europe and Asia.

5

Columbus's Early Years in Genoa
and Portugal

D URING COLUMBUS'S LIFETIME, and for more than a century thereafter, no one seemed to doubt that he was an Italian, whose
journeys away from his homeland were spurred by his career as a
mariner and merchant.[1] Then, as the extraordinary importance of his
voyages became clear, Columbus the man was transformed into Columbus the mythic hero, and many strange claims about him began
to surface. The longest-running controversy concerns his nationality
and family background, with many nations and groups claiming him
as one of their own. A writer in England led the parade in 1682,[2]
arguing that Columbus was really from England, although he later
resided in Genoa. Over the centuries writers have spun an unending
series of tales supposedly proving his origin to be French, Spanish,
Catalan, Portuguese, Greek, or some other nationality, all to the understandable irritation of the Italians. The flow of such claims quickened in the late nineteenth and the early twentieth century, spurred
no doubt by the four-hundredth anniversary of Columbus's first
voyage across the Atlantic. The flow of speculation slackened in pace
thereafter, but it never ceased altogether, although every bit of credible historical evidence supported Columbus's Italian origin. Even
today, rarely a year goes by without a new book or article claiming
he was from somewhere else.[3]

A PORTRAIT OF COLUMBUS

Similar confusion surrounds the question of Columbus's physical appearance. As far as we know he was never painted during his lifetime, but several contemporaries mentioned his appearance and demeanor. The earliest description, printed in 1504, noted that Columbus
was "*Genoese, a man of tall and imposing stature, ruddy [rosso], of great
intelligence, and with a long face.*" The description appears in a brief
summary of his first three voyages, attributed to Angelo Trivigiano
(or Trevisan), who knew Columbus in Granada in 1501, when Trevisan was secretary to the Venetian ambassador at Fernando and Isabel's court. He based most of the summary on notes about Columbus's voyages borrowed from Pietro Martire d'Anghiera.[4]

Three decades later, Gonzalo Fernández de Oviedo wrote that Columbus was a man "*of good stature and appearance, taller than middling
and with strong limbs, the eyes lively and the other parts of the countenance*

*of good proportion, the hair very red [*muy bermejo*] and the face somewhat flushed and freckled.*"[5] Bright red hair and freckles would have been unusual in southern Spain and therefore worthy of note. The biography attributed to Columbus's son Hernando, first published in Italian, pictured him as *"well-formed and more than middling stature, of long face and somewhat high cheekbones, without inclining to fatness or leanness. He had an aquiline nose, and light-colored [*bianchi*] eyes, pale skin, and tending to high color. In his youth he had fair [*biondi*] hair, but when he reached the age of thirty years, it all turned white. In eating and drinking and adorning his person, he was very continent and modest.*"[6]

Bartolomé de Las Casas described Columbus in similar terms in the history of the Indies that he drafted from 1527 on, although it was not published until 1875. He noted that Columbus *"in his external person and corporeal disposition was tall rather than of middling height, his face long and commendable; the nose aquiline; the eyes grey-green [*garzos*]; the complexion pale, tending to bright red; the beard and hair, when he was a youth, fair [*rubios*], but which soon became gray with his troubles.*"[7]

The descriptions have a good deal in common and may in fact have borrowed from one another. They picture a strongly built man of more than average height for the time, although what that might mean in modern terms is not clear – certainly no taller than six feet, probably no shorter than five and a half feet. All agree that he was ruddy-complexioned and possibly freckled. He probably had red hair as a young man, which lightened and then turned gray by the time he was thirty – a common pattern for redheads, regardless of the quality of their lives. His face was oblong rather than round, distinguished by an aquiline nose and lively hazel eyes.

The 1893 World's Columbian Exposition in Chicago displayed seventy-one portraits reputedly of Columbus, none that could claim to have been painted from life, and most of them bearing no resemblance whatsoever to contemporary descriptions of him.

In our judgment the most nearly authentic portrait, signed and dated 1512, was painted by Lorenzo Lotto. The Lotto portrait was discovered in Europe in the late nineteenth century and soon gained fame as the most reliable likeness of Columbus. Some scholars initially doubted that the portrait was attributed and dated correctly, but an expert on Lotto's work confirmed its authenticity in 1956.[8] The portrait shows a young man with a high forehead; a face long rather than wide; straight, fair hair; and fair skin. The reputation of the Lotto portrait as a true likeness of Columbus depends not only on its close adherence to contemporary descriptions of Columbus but also on its provenience. Lotto painted the portrait for Domenico

Malipiero, a Venetian senator and historian, on the recommendation of Angelo Trevisan, secretary of the Venetian ambassador to Granada in 1501 and, as we have noted, author of the first published description of Columbus. The connection of the Lotto portrait with Trevisan, and its date of 1512, just six years after Columbus's death, place it closer to its subject than any other depiction known.

Although no one claims that Lotto ever saw Columbus himself, his portrait inspired many other artists. Our particular favorite was painted by the Spanish artist Joaquín Sorolla y Bastida in 1910–11. His *Departure of Columbus from the Port of Palos* was commissioned by an American collector and currently belongs to The Mariner's Museum in Newport News, Virginia. Sorolla must have been aware of Lotto's painting, which caused quite a stir when it was discovered and was officially recognized in Madrid in 1892 as the best available likeness of Columbus. In preparation for his own painting, Sorolla persuaded the duke of Veragua, Columbus's descendant, to model for him. The duke's face may be the one depicted in Sorolla's preliminary oil studies, which are notably different from the final painting.[9] In Sorolla's masterful, full-length portrait, Columbus's features and physique agree quite well with what contemporaries said about him. More importantly, in Columbus's penetrating glance Sorolla has captured the character of his subject with unsurpassed brilliance. (See frontispiece, p. ii.)

COLUMBUS'S ORIGINS AND EARLY LIFE

If Columbus's origins and even his physical appearance have been subject to doubt and conjecture, part of the blame can be laid at the feet of Columbus himself. He rarely wrote about his origins or his family, and there is good cause to believe that he was deliberately reticent, rather than merely shy or too interested in other matters to say much about his family. The reasons probably relate to his powerful ambition for wealth and status. Columbus's family was too humble to do him any good, and the fifteenth century did not necessarily value a man who rose to great wealth and status from humble beginnings.

The few times Columbus mentioned his origins he said he was Genoese, and, despite other claims, every verifiable historical document clearly indicates that Columbus was born in the independent Italian republic of Genoa, in the late summer or early fall of 1451. One interesting possibility, purely speculative, is that he was born on or near July 25, the day of Saint Christopher, his namesake. No

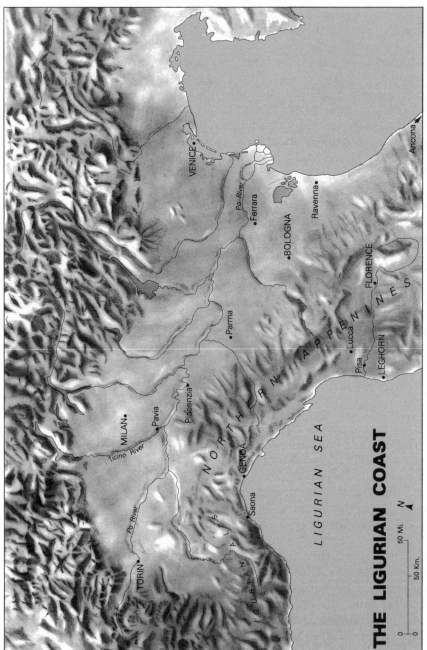

The Ligurian coast of Italy, including the mountainous hinterland behind Genoa. (Map prepared by the Cartography Laboratory, Department of Geography, University of Minnesota.)

one is sure if he was born in the city proper or in some smaller town within the city's jurisdiction. Many contemporary descriptions say merely that he was a Ligurian, using the name for the Mediterranean coastal strip near Genoa.

He would have been known in the Genoese dialect as *Cristoforo Colombo,* but his name is almost always rendered into whatever language an author is using. In English he is *Christopher Columbus,* in Spanish *Cristóbal Colón,* in Portuguese *Christovão Colom,* in French *Christophe Colomb,* and so on. His father Domenico Colombo was a master wool weaver and versatile businessman. Besides Christopher, he and his wife had four younger children: three boys – Bartolomeo, Giovanni-Pellegrino, and Giacomo – and a girl named Bianchineta. The two brothers who would join Christopher in Spain and the New World are usually known by the Spanish or English equivalents of their names: Bartolomé or Bartholomew for Bartolomeo, and Diego or James for Giacomo. We will use the Italian spelling of their names for their early lives and the Spanish spelling for the time after they acquired Spanish citizenship.

Christopher Columbus's family can be traced back to his grandfather, Giovanni Colombo de Mocónesi, born in the late fourteenth or early fifteenth century, in the mountain village of Mocónesi in the Fontanabuona Valley, east of Genoa. The earliest documentary record of the family found so far comes from a notarial contract of apprenticeship. In 1429, when Giovanni was living in the village of Quinto on the eastern outskirts of Genoa, he apprenticed his son Domenico to a cloth weaver named Guglielmo of Brabant, probably an immigrant to Genoa from the Low Countries. Domenico, who was born around 1418, learned his principal occupation during the six years he was apprenticed to Guglielmo. He would later marry and father a son named Cristoforo – the Christopher Columbus of our story.

Domenico's apprenticeship contract offers us one of the first glimpses of the milieu into which Christopher Columbus would be born and thus provides one of our best clues for understanding his early life. The contract shows a good deal of social and spatial mobility by the Colombo family and many of those with whom they associated. Giovanni Colombo left the Genoese mountains to take up residence on the outskirts of the city. When the time came to provide training for his son Domenico, he chose a foreign master, presumably from Brabant in the Low Countries but resident in Genoa. Giovanni's propensity to travel in search of economic opportunity was continued by his son Domenico and later by his grandson Christopher. Evidently such movement was fairly common among weavers. The historian Jacques Heers studied a wide range of Genoese documents from the late 1450s and discovered that most apprentice weavers came from outside the city proper, either from places along the eastern coast or from more distant inland villages. Because weavers tended to be newcomers to the cities where they found work, they often remained marginal to the political and social life of their new urban homes. In response, they formed tightly knit communities of their own that remained close for generations, even when individual families were assimilated into the life of the city.

Domenico Colombo made his living as a weaver during the late 1430s and into the late 1440s. Apparently he prospered. From his training as a weaver's apprentice, Domenico progressed to mastery of his craft. He opened a shop in Genoa and took on an apprentice of his own in 1439 – an orphan named Antonio de Leverone, from a village in the same Fontanabuona Valley were the Colombo family originated. Domenico began to buy income-producing real estate in Quinto (now part of Genoa) and became active on the local political scene as a supporter of the Fregoso faction, one of the political groups that controlled Genoese life. His political loyalty and connections paid off when he was appointed warder or gatekeeper of the Porta dell'Olivella in 1447–8 and again around 1450. In Genoa, as in other European cities, tolls were collected at such gates from outsiders who wished to do business inside the city walls.

Domenico married Susanna Fontanarossa, daughter of a weaver, in about 1445. It was quite common to marry within the same occupation, because that was where business and social ties were strongest. When their son Christopher was born, in 1451, Domenico and his wife were living in Genoa and were prosperous enough to purchase a garden nearby and rent it back to its former owner. In 1455, Domenico moved into a house in the Vico Diritto, where he worked as a wool weaver. Apart from his two appointments as gatekeeper, he does not seem to have held other official posts, which were all tied to the volatile politics of fifteenth-century Genoa. The Genoese factions mirrored the great struggle in Italy and Sicily between the French and the Angevins, on one side, and the Aragonese on the other. The main contention in the fifteenth century was over control of Naples and Sicily. The Fregoso faction in Genoa, to which Domenico Colombo belonged, favored the French and Angevin side, which lost out in the long run. The Adorno faction, and later all the other factions of the city, were linked with the Aragonese. In one of the great ironies of history, Christopher Columbus was born into a family linked to the anti-Spanish faction in Genoa. That may be a reason for his reticence about his family background, once the Spanish crown had become his patron.

Christopher's birth in 1451 came several years after his parents' marriage, assuming that they were married in 1445, but the documents mention nothing about older siblings. In the fifteenth century there seems to have been very little birth control within marriage, but high infant mortality struck at all levels of society. If Christopher had any older brothers or sisters, perhaps they died in infancy. Or perhaps his parents spent time apart after their marriage. Sometimes a man and woman married without setting up a household until some years later. We know quite a bit about the children who were born after Christopher, however. Bartolomeo, slightly younger than Christopher, became his companion and collaborator in later years. His sister Bianchineta married a cheese merchant. We know little about Giovanni-Pellegrino, but Giacomo, born seventeen years after Christopher, was apprenticed at the age of sixteen to a cloth weaver and later joined his brothers in Spain.

Close family ties were important for both sides of the family. When Christopher's mother, Susanna Fontanarossa, sold a piece of real estate in 1469, the notary indicated that nine of her relatives were present at the recording of the transaction, five of whom bore the name Fontanarossa. Even after more than two decades of marriage, she was still definitely part of the Fontanarrosa clan, especially where family property was concerned.

After 1455, Christopher Columbus lived in the upper stories of the house where his father's shop occupied the ground floor. What education he received would have begun at home. In the biography that Hernando Colón presumably wrote of his father, he tells us that young Christopher attended the University of Pavia. That is not true, but we cannot be certain what accounts for the error. One possibility is that Hernando simply misunderstood or embroidered what he heard about his father's early life. The Genoese clothiers' guild, to which Domenico probably belonged, had a school on the street named the Vico de Pavia in Genoa, where the children of guild members could receive an elementary education. There is no evidence that Christopher attended the weavers' grammar school, but if he did Hernando might have inflated the grammar school on Pavia street into the University of Pavia. There are numerous passages in the biography of his father that embellish the family history in a similar way, adding a bit of luster and standing to quite humble reality.[10]

We can assume that the religious instruction Christopher received was Roman Catholic. Both his father and grandfather were landowners, a privilege restricted to Catholics. Moreover, his father could not have engaged in politics or become the warder of the city gate unless he had been a practicing Catholic. The persistent notion that the Colombo family was secretly Jewish or had converted from Judaism has no credible basis in the historical record.[11]

By 1472, when Christopher Columbus was about twenty-one years old, he described himself as a *lanerius,* or wool worker. Some writers find it difficult to understand how he could have been a wool worker, a mariner, a merchant, a bookseller, and perhaps a mapmaker, all before he was thirty. That is hardly surprising in the context of the late fifteenth century, however. As Jacques Heers wrote,

> In Genoa, at this time, no one occupied a narrowly defined profession. Everybody built their fires with whatever wood was available, and used their labor and capital for whatever they could. It seems quite impossible, if one adheres to strict realities, to define a Genoese "merchant" or "financier." In the village, everybody, however modest he might be, however withdrawn from the world of business at first sight, doubtless women and even religious, could give a bale of goods to a traveler headed to a distant eastern port [to sell], could as well buy for a few pounds parts of the public debt or shares of companies, carrying interest and profits. In the same way, the young weaver of Savona or Genoa could carry with him, on a distant voyage, a bit of goods to sell, and bring home a quantity of spices; he could also associate himself [with a voyage] as a clerk.[12]

Moreover, wool weaving in Genoa was not the prestigious profession it was in Florence or Venice. Raw wool entered Genoa from Catalonia and Majorca, from southern France, and from North Africa. The short, coarse fibers of the wool were far inferior to the fine Merino wool of Castile. The weavers of Genoa produced cheap cloth for local consumption and for export to a few markets such as Salerno, Naples, and North Africa. In other words, Genoa gained no renown for its cloth-weaving industry. The weavers had little political importance, and the industry itself was not even old. It had first been introduced only in the mid-fourteenth century by mendicant friars from Lombardy called *humiliati,* and later by weavers from northern Europe – especially the Germanies and the Low Countries – presumably including Domenico Colombo's first master. Although Domenico Colombo prospered as a weaver, he also had his hand in a number of other ventures. By 1470, he was making his living in Savona as a tavern keeper as well as a weaver, and he continued to buy and sell land. By 1483, documents refer to him as a "former" cloth weaver. There is nothing mysterious in his son Christopher's propensity to turn his hand to several different occupations. He was following a tradition common in his city of origin and in his own family.

As Columbus himself wrote in 1501, *"From a very early age I went to sea sailing, and I have continued it until now."*[13] Genoese merchants had created a number of commercial enclaves on the Mediterranean and Atlantic coasts, and it was not difficult for a young Genoese to ship out on one of the many trading voyages they sponsored. His father could have arranged it easily. A small-time entrepreneur such as Domenico – weaver, tavern keeper, and land speculator – would have been accustomed to dealing with the merchant suppliers who brought in the food and drink for Genoa's citizens and the raw material for the city's woolen-textile industry. It would have been a simple task for him to find a post for his eldest son as cabin boy, sailor, or merchant's assistant.

At first the young Columbus probably sailed on short voyages close to Genoa. We know from his own writings that he also went on a longer voyage to Chios, an island in the Aegean then held by the Genoese. Venice periodically fought with Genoa for control of Chios, but for most of the period from the early fourteenth century to the middle of the sixteenth it was under Genoese control. It was held by the Zaccaria family from 1304 to 1329, and then from 1346 to 1566 it was ruled by a Genoese *maona,* or society of shipowners. The members of that particular group became part of a network of fictive kin, all of whom adopted the family name Giustiniani. Paolo Emilio Taviani suggests that Columbus went to Chios in 1474 or 1475, when two Genoese fleets are known to have made the journey. The large fleet of September 1475 included one ship owned by Paolo di Negro and another owned by Nicolò Spinola. Columbus later dealt frequently with both of those men, and he may well have sailed with one of their ships to Chios in 1475.

Although Chios also served as an entrepôt for trade in the eastern Mediterranean, gum mastic was the island's main claim to commercial importance. The mastic bush is widely distributed around the Mediterranean, but in the fifteenth century only Chios produced marketable gum mastic from the plant's resin; its use as a perfume base made mastic highly profitable to the Genoese merchants on the island. (Later, in the Caribbean, Columbus frequently misidentified local plants as mastic in his fever to find opportunities for profit.) On his first voyage across the Atlantic, Columbus would claim that he had previously seen *"all the east and west"* (todo el levante y poniente), and most historians assume that his voyage to Chios lay behind this claim.[14] Although he was clearly stretching the point, Chios could be considered the east or the Levant, especially given its connections to Constantinople and Asia Minor.

Other adventures from Columbus's early days at sea have even more exotic connotations. Hernando Colón provided a quotation from his father that many scholars have found hard to credit. In a fragment of a letter that Columbus supposedly wrote to the monarchs of Spain from the island of Española in January of 1495, he said,

It happened to me that King René (whom God has taken) sent me to Tunis to capture the galleass *Fernandina;* and when I was off the island of San Pietro, near Sardinia, a vessel informed me there were two ships and a carrack with the said galleass, which frightened my people, and they resolved to go no further but to return to Marseilles to pick up another ship and more men. I, seeing that I could do nothing against their wills without some ruse, agreed to their demand, and, changing the point of the compass, made sail at nightfall; and at sunrise the next day we found ourselves off Cape Carthage, while all aboard were certain we were bound for Marseilles.[15]

Several points are remarkable about this statement, assuming that it is authentic. Columbus showed himself to be a skilled enough mariner to command a ship and even to fool his crew when necessary. More interesting, he revealed himself as a loyal servant of René of Anjou, commanding one of the king's corsairing voyages against North Africa. René of Anjou, as a claimant to the kingdom of Naples, was an enemy of the king of Aragón and the leading foreign supporter of the Fregoso faction in Genoa, to which Columbus's father Domenico belonged. If the letter is authentic, Columbus was remarkably bold, daring to tell King Fernando of Aragón that he had sailed against Aragonese interests in his youth – indeed, against the king's own father.[16]

By his early twenties, in any case, Columbus had acquired considerable sailing experience in the Mediterranean, and he had begun to venture into the Atlantic. That he knew the Mediterranean as a mariner is obvious from the set of sailing directions he offered to Fernando and Isabel in a letter of February 6, 1502, describing the sea route between Cádiz and Naples. There is no question, judging from his comments and his detailed account of places and geographical features of the coastline, that he knew the western Mediterranean from personal experience, probably acquired in his early adulthood. In the same letter he discussed sailing directions from Spain to Flanders, but he did so in far more general terms.[17] This suggests that he knew the Flanders run less well, perhaps at secondhand, not as a seasoned mariner on that route. Columbus's long sojourn in Portugal, which probably began about 1476, would broaden his seafaring experience immeasurably, but mostly to the south and west of Iberia rather than to the north.

ARRIVAL IN PORTUGAL

Columbus lived in Portugal for about a decade, a period that was arguably the most formative of his life. He learned enough in those years to believe in the possibility of sailing westward toward Asia – an extraordinary notion for the time, though not unique. As important as Columbus's Portuguese sojourn was, however, we know only the broadest outline and a few basic facts about his life during those years. We do not even know with certainty how and when Columbus reached Lisbon. Hernando Colón, or whoever wrote the early sections of his father's biography, presented a dramatic account of his arrival, which included a nearly miraculous rescue from disaster at sea. The biography tells of a naval battle off the coast of southern Portugal, between Lisbon and Cape Saint Vincent. Columbus was supposedly on a pirate vessel that grappled with one of four large Venetian galleys and caught fire. As the biographer tells it,

> The Admiral, being an excellent swimmer, and seeing land only a little more than two leagues away, seized an oar which fate offered him, and on which he could rest at times; and so it pleased God, who was preserving him for greater things, to give him the strength to reach the shore. However, he was so fatigued by his experience that it took him many days to recover.
>
> Finding himself near Lisbon, and knowing that many of his Genoese countrymen lived in that city, he went there as soon as he could. When they learned who he was, they gave him such a warm welcome that he made his home in that city and married there.[18]

Such drama has all the markings of a scene from a heroic epic – the dashing young hero undergoing a cosmic test of fire and water, only to emerge from a watery grave to rebirth in a new land. It may have happened, or the reality may have been as prosaic as a merchant voyage. We simply do not know. The only source is Hernando's biography, whose early chapters have been strongly challenged. All we know is that Columbus found himself in Lisbon, sometime in the mid-1470s. His younger brother Bartolomeo probably joined him shortly thereafter. Historians used to assume that Bartolomeo was already in Lisbon when Christopher arrived, making his living by selling books and by making and selling maritime charts. Christopher supposedly joined him in that business. Now we know that the historians assumed much more than they knew. There is no clear documentary evidence for Bartolomeo's arrival, for a chart-making business, or for much else.

The documentary evidence that does remain suggests that Columbus continued to make his living from maritime and commercial activities while he lived in Portugal. He expanded his network of personal contacts, sailed on Portuguese and Spanish commercial voyages to Italy, and continued his close association with Genoese merchant companies based in Iberia. He testified in a court case in Genoa, in

1479, that he was acting as an agent of the Genoese merchant Paolo di Negro for a shipment of sugar from Madeira. Many years later, during his second expedition across the Atlantic, he requested that fresh supplies be sent from Spain and that the supply ships detour to Madeira to purchase Madeiran molasses and sugar. His instructions for the purchases reveal complete familiarity with the sugar business on the island.[19]

The documents related to Columbus's mercantile career are few and far between, but they agree with the limited facts we know about his early life, and they also suggest explanations for several points that have long puzzled scholars. One of the puzzles concerns the language Columbus used in his writings. By the 1480s, he could read and write Latin, as is shown by marginal notations he made in books he owned. He used imperfect Castilian for most of his writing, however, and the mistakes he made in spelling and usage seem to come from Portuguese. Why did he not use Italian, or, more specifically, Genoese? Why were his mistakes in Castilian based on Portuguese rather than Italian? If what we suspect about his early life is correct, the answer appears simple: he left home with only a rudimentary education. Hernando Colón said his father went to sea at the age of fourteen, and Columbus himself, in his diary of the first voyage, said he had been going to sea for *"twenty-three years without leaving it for any time worth telling."*[20] Both remarks put his venturing to sea at sometime between 1465 and 1469, when he was in his teens. Presumably Columbus spoke the Genoese dialect from the moment he first uttered a word, but he probably left Genoa knowing little or no written Genoese. If he attended the school for weavers' children on Pavia Street, he would have learned to write commercial Latin, not Genoese.

When he arrived in Portugal, he entered the Iberian trading network, a lively marketplace that included Andalusia, in the southwestern part of the kingdom of Castile, plus much of southern Portugal. People traveled back and forth between the two countries (even in wartime); they intermarried; they borrowed from one another in countless ways. Once Columbus settled into that milieu, he learned the languages that served him best – Portuguese, first, and then Castilian – both of them imperfectly. We sometimes forget that romance languages were much closer to one another in the fifteenth century than they are today, in both spoken and written form. Judging by what is known about how people learn languages, the mistakes Columbus made in writing Castilian are the kind that would logically have come from a knowledge of how to write Portuguese, probably the first written language he had learned. Columbus worked with Genoese merchants who had business dealings in Lisbon, Cádiz, and

Seville and who had been established in Iberia for some time. Written Castilian, even with hints of Portuguese thrown in, would have been the ideal language for that commercial setting.[21] Like other Genoese before him, Columbus made his fortune in Iberia and resided there. Although we can assume that he continued to speak Genoese with his compatriots, he also continued to write in Castilian. That was an eminently logical choice for a man in his position.

During his years in Portugal, his knowledge of spoken Portuguese helped him become assimilated into local society, just as his Genoese identity bound him to the Italian immigrant community already there. It was in that Italian community that he contracted a highly favorable marriage alliance. He had already come a long way from his humble beginnings in Genoa.

MARRIAGE

Most historians present the marriage of Columbus with Felipa Moniz as a match between an ambitious but penniless young man and the impoverished daughter of a noble family down on its luck. On closer examination, the match appears in quite a different light. The family Columbus married into descended from an Italian couple who had moved to Portugal from Piacenza sometime around 1385: Filippo (or Filipone) Pallastrelli and his wife Catalina (or Caterina). Filippo made a fortune from commerce in Lisbon and the northern city of Oporto, and the family name became known to the Portuguese as Perestrelo (frequently spelled Perestrello). In 1399, Filippo became a Portuguese noble. His four children with Catalina all achieved some degree of distinction. The eldest, Richarte (or Rafael), capped a clerical career by becoming prior of the monastery of Santa Marinha in Lisbon. Barred from marriage because of his ordination, he nonetheless had two sons, whom he legitimized in 1423. One of his grandsons later visited China. The two daughters of Filippo and Catalina, named Isabel and Blanca, both became mistresses of dom Pedro de Noronha, the influential archbishop of Lisbon. Between them, these sisters presented Noronha with four children. The youngest child of Filippo and Catalina Perestrelo was Bartolomeu, whose daughter Columbus later married. Filippo arranged for Bartolomeu to be raised in the household of Prince João, son of King João I. Such a position testifies to the distinction that Filippo had attained in his adopted homeland. After Prince João died, Bartolomeu went to live in the household of Prince Henrique, another son of João I.

Bartolomeu's chance at distinction came with the Portuguese settlement of the Madeira Islands, the most important of which are Madeira and Porto Santo. This island group had been known to southern Europeans from the early fourteenth century, but no effort had been made to settle them. The expedition that definitively claimed them for Portugal included Bartolomeu Perestrelo as one of its three captains. As his portion of the conquest, Perestrelo was given the island of Porto Santo for life, but his first two colonizing efforts, in 1418–20 and 1425, failed. Nonetheless, he could hope for better days. In addition to his longtime membership in Prince Henrique's entourage in southern Portugal, he had other connections at the royal court in Lisbon, notably through his two sisters whom we have mentioned, the mistresses of Archbishop Noronha. Noronha legitimized his four children by Bartolomeu's sisters in 1444, evidently signaling a rise in the Perestrelo family's fortunes. In 1446, Prince Henrique made Bartolomeu Perestrelo's captaincy (or grant) of Porto Santo into a heritable office.[22] This evidently gave him the incentive he needed to colonize the island in earnest, and he moved there permanently. Soon Porto Santo began to produce wheat and barley for export to Portugal and Africa.

Bartolomeu Perestrelo married twice. His first wife, Brites Furtado de Mendonza, produced three daughters before she died. The middle daughter, Hizeu Perestrelo, married Pedro Correa da Cunha. Left a widower, Bartolomeu was married a second time, about 1449 or 1450, to Isabel Moniz, member of an important noble family with interests in both southern Portugal and Madeira. Bartolomeu Perestrelo and his second wife lived in Porto Santo and had three children: a son, also named Bartolomeu Perestrelo; an elder daughter, named Felipa Moniz; and a younger daughter, named Violante Moniz.

Bartolomeu Perestrelo died in 1457, leaving his minor son and namesake the rights to Porto Santo. The next year Isabel Moniz sold those rights, for three hundred thousand reis, to Pedro Correa da Cunha, the husband of her stepdaughter Hizeu. The sale appears to have been a caretaker arrangement to protect the family's possession of the island while young Bartolomeu remained a minor. Cunha, a member of the high nobility in Portugal, had been granted the island of Graziosa in the Azores by Prince Henrique. With his wealth and position, Cunha would have been well able to protect Porto Santo against rival claimants. In 1473, when young Bartolomeu Perestrelo was about twenty-three years old and had already served the crown in Africa, he secured royal permission to repurchase his father's rights to Porto Santo from Cunha for the same sum that Cunha had paid for them. Violante Moniz married a Fleming or German named Miguel Moliart, who moved with her to Huelva, in southwestern Spain, by 1485.

Felipa Moniz married Christopher Columbus in 1478 or 1479. Her mother gave Columbus the maps and papers accumulated by her late husband during his career. Assuming that these documents contained information about the seas and winds around the Portuguese possessions in the Atlantic Ocean, they would have been more valuable to Columbus than any ordinary dowry. Columbus and his wife had a son in 1480, whom they named Diogo (Diego). He would witness the dramatic trajectory of his father's career and would have a career of his own in service to the Spanish crown.

By his marriage, Columbus entered a family with connections at the Portuguese court, important ties to Madeira and Porto Santo, a foothold in southwestern Spain, and at least some wealth. It is true that his wife's father had been dead for twenty years, but apparently he had left his family well provided for. Despite the somewhat raffish history of the family's rise to prominence, there is no reason to suppose that they had experienced disgrace or penury. Columbus presumably had achieved some wealth and distinction of his own, or he would not have been able to make such a favorable match. He made good use of his new family connections as he tried to find support for his plan to sail westward toward Asia and India.[23]

THE ENTERPRISE OF THE INDIES

It is impossible to reconstruct all the facets of Columbus's early life, much less his thought. The precise details that we need in order to trace the formulation of his great scheme remain obscure. Nonetheless, by the time of his marriage Columbus had acquired skill, knowledge, and experience that arguably helped to shape his notions about a westward route to Asia. He had learned to command a ship, which meant that he knew something about practical navigation and geography. He had sailed to Portuguese trading stations in parts of the world unknown a generation before, and the papers of his father-in-law probably contributed to his knowledge of the winds and currents of the Atlantic. He had worked with Genoese merchants in the lucrative sugar trade, and he knew the techniques of commerce. Moreover, he had presumably learned about the career of his late father-in-law, who had secured a grant to a newly discovered island and thereafter had administered it profitably. Columbus could easily have gained inspiration from the Perestrelo family's history of wealth and status acquired through royal service in the inlands of the ocean sea.

In addition to practical experience and the inspiration of others, Columbus could draw on his own reading and geographical speculations. The late fifteenth century was the early age of the printed book, when new typesetting techniques made a variety of books available much more cheaply than ever before. Columbus had access to a wide range of notions about the size and configuration of the known world and its peoples, as well as the cosmos beyond, from ancient writers recently reprinted and from recent writers commenting upon them. Using that range of scholarly opinion, Columbus would bolster his notions about the feasibility of sailing westward to reach Asia, trying to impress his would-be patrons with the support of scholarly opinions. But in tracing the likely history of how Columbus's ideas developed, we should keep one cardinal fact in mind: he was wrong. He knew, of course, that the world was a sphere, as did all well-read people, and many others besides. His great error – the one that inspired him to proceed – was his belief that the world was far smaller in circumference than it really is.

So much of the life and career of Columbus remains obscure that we must guard against making unsupported assertion or accepting traditional interpretations of his life and times without proof. This cautious approach is particularly necessary in examining the story of Columbus's long and frustrating search for support. From our modern perspective we know without question that his voyages would be of fundamental importance for the history of the world. Instinctively, we want to side with Columbus and to accuse those who doubted him of stupidity or worse. Yet the future was no more predictable in the fifteenth century than it is now. The learned men who opposed Columbus could not know he would discover a new world, unknown to Europeans, and that his discovery would change the world. They knew only that his proposal to sail westward to Asia flew in the face of much sound geographical knowledge. His notions about the size of the earth were at the lower end of the range of available estimates, and many scholars of the time opted for a considerably larger figure.

Columbus's ideas about the size of the world and the way to the Asian wonderlands of Cipango and Cathy probably did not develop all at once. It seems likely that they evolved in a piecemeal fashion. In the biography of Columbus attributed to his son Hernando, the origins of Columbus's geographical ideas are described as *"natural reasons, the authority of writers, and the testimony of sailors,"*[24] putting Columbus's reasoning ability and scholarship ahead of mere hearsay. The biography consistently embellishes all aspects of Columbus's life to make him appear learned and cultured, which would suit his son Hernando, himself a cultured and wealthy intellectual. In reality, according to many scholars, Columbus read and selected from important writers later, rather than sooner, perhaps even after he went to

Spain, when he had already settled on his plan and was looking to bolster its credibility.

The most important early sources of his ideas were probably far simpler and less impressive: rumors, personal experience, and physical evidence. Even Hernando's biography admitted that Columbus *"was impressed by the many fables and stories which he heard from various persons and sailors who traded to the western islands and seas of the Azores and Madeira."*[25] The biography claims that Columbus had formulated his grand design before hearing the mariners' tales, but it is far more likely that these tales planted the first seeds of his idea. He knew that wealth had been made in new discoveries in Africa and the Atlantic islands, and he knew the honors that the discoverers and governors had received from grateful monarchs. He knew the potential riches that Asia offered. As he heard the stories that merchants and sailors told, of faraway riches and strange peoples and things from the west, he arguable fitted them into a gradually developing design to explain the world – a design that constantly changed, becoming increasingly more elaborate, undergoing changes even after his first discoveries across the Atlantic. But the foundation on which he erected the whole edifice most logically grew from the stories he heard, not from what he had read in academic treatises.[26]

One group of stories concerned physical objects drifting in from the west. A Portuguese ship's pilot, named Martín Vicente, told Columbus that he had pulled from the sea a piece of wood that had been carved but not with iron tools. When he found it he was 50 leagues (185–200 miles) west of Portugal's Cape Saint Vincent, and the wind had been blowing from the west for many days. Vicente assumed that the wood came from unknown islands far out in the ocean sea. Pedro Correa da Cunha, who was married to a half-sister of Columbus's wife, had also encountered a strangely carved piece of wood, driven ashore on Porto Santo while he served as governor there. He had also found pieces of cane plants, unlike any others known to the Portuguese and *"so thick that one joint held nine decanters of wine."* The canes were so strange that Cunha had taken them to court, showing them to the king and speculating that they had come from nearby islands or perhaps even from India. In other words, both Vicente and Cunha believed there were inhabited islands to the west, close enough so that a piece of carved wood might float into Portugal's orbit under certain circumstances. Others told of limbs of unfamiliar species of pine trees floating ashore on the western rims of the islands of Graziosa and Fayal in the Azores. Strange covered boats and canoes, found drifting in the ocean, were assumed to have come from western islands. One famous story reported that the remains of two human beings with strange, broad faces had floated in on the same currents. The unknown winds and currents in the western ocean had previously been a powerful barrier even to adventurous voyagers. By the late fifteenth century, Columbus was not the only one who thought seriously that the barrier might be breached.

Taken together, these stories suggested the strong possibility that inhabited islands lay fairly close toward the west. Even more intriguing, witnesses said they had seen those islands, and some even claimed to have visited them. Columbus collected many stories from people in the Canaries, the Madeiras, and the Azores who asserted that they regularly saw islands to the west and a few who had actually sailed out to find them. In the journal of his voyage in 1492, Columbus said that residents of the island of Hierro, in the Canaries, saw lands to the west each year, and their stories coincided with what he had heard in Lisbon in 1484.[27] Hernando Colón's biography tells us that his father dismissed those stories because their authors had sailed less than 100 leagues to the west and because he thought they had mistaken reefs for islands. Nonetheless, Columbus was clearly fascinated by the possibilities they suggested.

However fanciful the stories of western islands may have been, they coincided with ancient stories of islands in the ocean sea that had proved true in the centuries before Columbus. The Canaries, the Madeiras, the Cape Verdes, and the Azores had all been discovered relatively recently, seeming to confirm both ancient legends and modern firsthand accounts. The discoveries in the fourteenth and fifteenth centuries naturally led to the conclusion that there were more islands yet to find.[28]

Hernando's biography trotted out a string of ancient writers who supposedly influenced Columbus in forming his grand design, including Pliny, Seneca, and Juventius Fortunatus. Medieval tales, such as the story of Saint Brendan's Atlantic voyage with his Irish monks, also played a role. One of the most famous legends concerned the fictional island of Antilia, whose presence was so little doubted that it ended up on many maritime charts, including those of the Portuguese, who showed it as lying west of the Canaries and the Azores. According to legend, Antilia became important to European Christianity in the year 714, when the Muslims were engaged in the first phase of their rapid conquest of the Iberian Peninsula. To escape the Muslim invasion, the story goes, seven bishops loaded ships with their faithful followers and their belongings and sailed to the island. Each bishop founded a city, because of which Antilia was occasionally called the Isle of the Seven Cities. To break all ties with the old world that had fallen under Muslim domination, they burned their ships so none could return.

The legend of Antilia had been embellished, by the late fifteenth century, with the addition of a story that in the time of Prince Henrique (who died in 1460) a Portuguese ship driven off course by a storm had reached an unknown island. Much to their joy the crew found the island to be inhabited by Christians. When the islanders learned that the crew was Christian as well, they asked them to remain until their king could be summoned. Fearing that the king might detain them in order to keep secret the island's existence, the ship's master and his crew fled and returned to Portugal. When their own king ordered them to return to the island, they fled Portugal as well rather than comply. One possible explanation for this tale is that it is a garbled second- or thirdhand account of a Portuguese landing in the Canaries, where Majorcan missionaries had been at work since the fourteenth century, converting numbers of Canarians to Christianity. Whatever the truth of the matter, rumors of a large island to the west of Ireland inspired several voyages that we know about in the late fifteenth century.

Columbus collected stories about these voyages, in Portugal and later in Spain. The crew that went on the voyage of Diogo de Teive included a pilot named Pedro de Velasco, from Palos, who, long afterward, told Columbus of their lengthy voyage southwest from the Azores and their subsequent northward loop to the latitude of Ireland. Because of the land birds they sighted and the condition of the sea, they assumed that land lay fairly close to westward, but the approach of autumn persuaded them to return home instead of searching farther.[29] Other sailors told of similar voyages westward, at varying latitudes. Some had traveled west of Ireland, others west of the Azores, others west of the Madeiras, but all of them were searching for lands beyond the known areas of the ocean sea. The Portuguese crown, which sponsored many voyages of exploration down the African coast, also sponsored attempts to find new lands in the open ocean. One such venture involved a Genoese merchant named Luca di Cazana, resident on the island of Terceira in the Azores. Cazana wrote to his brother Francesco, who lived in Seville, trying to persuade him to invest in the voyage, but Francesco *"jeered at the project."* Luca nonetheless outfitted three or four voyages that sailed 120 to 130 leagues west of the Azores, all in vain. Although he and his partners in the venture never gave up hope, their repeated efforts produced nothing.

The saga of Luca di Cazana has some striking parallels to Columbus's own life. Both stories involved Genoese merchants in the Atlantic islands and the Iberian mainland, a search for new lands, and a request for backing from the Portuguese crown. Hernando Colón mentioned the Azores stories as proof that all others who had sought lands to the west had failed, whereas his father had succeeded. Nonetheless, the stories known to Columbus were also known to countless others, and many were as intrigued as he was by the prospect of lands to the west, between Europe and Asia. In this atmosphere of restless voyaging and speculation, it was only a matter of time before someone put together the evidence from all the tales and conceived of a voyage westward to reach Asia. As far as we know, Columbus was the first, not to conceive the plan, but to persevere until he found backing for it.

Yet for reasons that are not clear, many writers over the past five centuries have wanted to prove that Columbus's grand design was not a triumph of imagination, inductive reasoning, and perseverance. They have argued for a "prediscovery" of America, which made Columbus's 1492 voyage a sure thing rather than a leap into the unknown.[30] One variant assumes that Columbus himself had already been across the ocean and later sought backing merely to secure a proprietary claim to what he had already discovered. Another variant asserts that someone – usually a mysterious unknown pilot – had already been there and had told Columbus what he would find. Among many similar stories, the most poignant has Columbus finding a shipwrecked Spaniard struggling out of the surf at Porto Santo. The Spaniard and his shipmates had supposedly been blown clear across the Atlantic by a storm, but he alone had made it back to the Madeiras. Before expiring, he imparted his secret to Columbus. Las Casas said the story was common on Española in the 1530s; he was inclined to believe it, because the inhabitants of Cuba supposedly had told early explorers that other white and bearded men had come to the islands years before Columbus.[31] Written versions of the prediscovery story go back at least as far as Gonzalo Fernández de Oviedo in 1534, who reported a rumor concerning a Spanish caravel whose crew had run into bad weather and had been blown far to the west, encountering lands inhabited by naked people. Most of the crew died on the return voyage, and the last survivor – fortuitously the pilot – gave Columbus a chart of the new lands. Fernández de Oviedo considered the story to be false, but he acknowledged that it had a wide circulation.[32] Columbus certainly took a map along on the first voyage, and some have assumed that the map was based on, and therefore proof of, a previous voyage. More likely, what he had was a map akin to the Behaim globe, showing nothing but ocean and myriad islands in the sea between Europe and Asia.[33]

Such stories are always used to deny Columbus and his 1492 voyage the importance that history has traditionally accorded them, but the tales have little but wishful thinking and a perverse disregard of historical evidence to distinguish them. Columbus found what would be named North and South America not because he already knew they were there but because he was expecting to find Asia in that same location. His certainty sprang not only from the tales he had heard but also from his experience at sea.

During his years in Portugal Columbus embarked on many voyages, gaining valuable firsthand knowledge about the currents and winds, islands and shorelines, of the ocean sea. His experience of sailing toward the northwest included visits to Ireland and England (probably), Flanders (possibly), and Iceland (plausibly), if we accept some equivocal evidence from his writings. Many of those writings are difficult to interpret, however, even when they are clearly phrased and genuine. For example, at one point Columbus commented on how sailors traveling between Spain and Flanders made use of the changing seasonal winds, but it is not clear if he was writing from firsthand knowledge or hearsay.[34] He certainly went far enough north to have visited both Ireland and England. The best evidence for an Irish landing is a marginal notation made in his copy of Enea Silvio Piccolomini's *Historia rerum ubique gestarum,* which said, *"Men of Cathay came to the West. We have seen many notable things and especially in Galway, in Ireland, a man and a woman with miraculous form, pushed along by the storm on two logs."*[35] Evidence that Columbus also visited England and Iceland is contained in a fragment of a letter that he wrote to Fernando and Isabel from Española in January of 1495. Unfortunately it is preserved only in a partial transcription made by Bartolomé de Las Casas, raising a question about its accuracy and authenticity. The passage reads,

> In the year of 1477, in the month of February, I navigated 100 leagues beyond the island of Tile [Thule], whose southern part is 73 degrees from the equator, and not 63, as some say, and it is not in the line where the West begins, as Ptolemy says, but much more westerly. And to this island, which is as large as England, the English go with merchandise, especially those of Bristol, and at the time I was there the sea was not frozen, although there were tremendous tides, so much so that in some parts they rose twice a day 25 fathoms and they fell the same amount in height.[36]

Interpretations of this difficult passage range from denial that he made such a trip at all to the assertion as fact that he visited Iceland. Taviani makes a persuasive case that the trip to Iceland not only happened but that it was not an unusual voyage for mariners heading westward from England.[37] Perhaps the most striking aspect of the passage is that Columbus openly questioned the received wisdom of Ptolemy. As experience mounted, mariners such as Columbus increasingly questioned aspects of the geography they had read and learned.

Columbus was a practiced observer of natural phenomena, and a single voyage to the latitudes of Ireland would have taught him a great deal about the currents and wind patterns in the North Atlantic. It is reasonable to suppose that he augmented his own observations by talking with other pilots and navigators. If he was paying attention, he might have concluded that a northern route could indeed lead to the west but that it was dangerous and difficult. More promising possibilities lay to the south.

Columbus unambiguously described his experiences in Africa and the Atlantic islands, leaving no doubt that he knew those areas well. Beginning in 1482, he traveled as far south as the fortress of São Jorge da Mina, built on the Gold Coast in Africa, and he returned there at least once more. Sometime between 1482 and 1485, when he left Portugal for Spain, he noted that *"I was in the castle of La Mina of the king of Portugal, which is located beneath the equatorial arc* [i.e., near the equator], *and I am a good witness that it is not uninhabitable, as is said."*[38] During his voyages, Columbus wrote down explicit comparisons between the flora and fauna of the new lands he found and their equivalents in the Old World. Many of these comparisons reveal his familiarity with Africa. On his first voyage to the Caribbean, for example, he wrote that Cuba *"has a great quantity of palms of a different sort from those of Guinea and our own"* and he praised the clear waters and flowing rivers on the Caribbean islands, *"unlike the rivers of Guinea, which are all pestilential."*[39] Moreover, Columbus often used words that the Portuguese had coined in Africa when he was writing about plants, animals, and aspects of native culture in the Caribbean[40] – indirect but persuasive evidence that he had visited Africa during his years in Portugal.

During that same period, Columbus traveled frequently to the Madeiras – both the main island and Porto Santo – and at least once he returned to Genoa. We can assume that on those voyages he carefully observed the winds and currents, storing the knowledge away with his previous experience. Deep-ocean sailors are a special breed. Their survival depends on observing their environment and adapting to it, no less now than in the fifteenth century. The collection of real knowledge and sea lore that Columbus accumulated during his years in Portugal were invaluable as his grand design took shape.

Taviani has suggested that Columbus's knowledge of the prevailing winds and currents was the key ingredient in his plan to sail to Asia and return – that once he had experienced the constant clockwise, elliptical pattern of the prevailing winds of the North Atlantic, he knew the voyage was possible.[41] Perhaps – but that is not to say that his knowledge was complete or flawless. On his outbound voyage in 1492, Columbus chose a nearly perfect trajectory across the

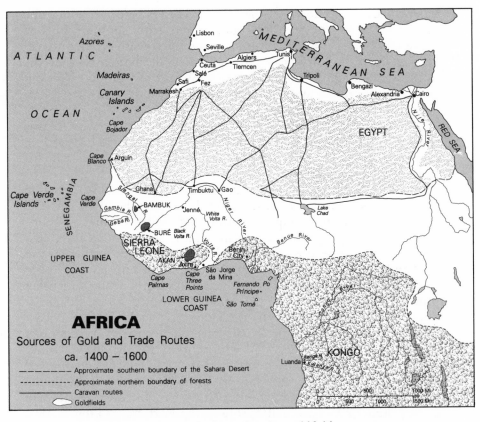

The northwestern coast of Africa, showing goldfields, caravan routes, and important geographical features. (Map prepared by the Cartography Laboratory, Department of Geography, University of Minnesota.)

Atlantic, dropping down to the Canary Islands before heading due west. This is still the preferred sailing route from southern Europe to the Caribbean. On the return voyage, however, he tried to sail due east from the Caribbean and was repeatedly beaten back by the northeast trade winds. Only after several days of fruitless effort did he sail farther north and intersect favorable winds that carried him toward the Azores and Iberia. In other words, there is no simple explanation of how Columbus formulated his plans or why he was so sure they would succeed. Even after he had packaged his startling notions persuasively enough to find backing, many aspects of his project remained subject to chance.[42]

Columbus's access to the Portuguese court presumably increased the store of knowledge he had accumulated from his own personal experience and from the experience of others. At the Portuguese court, all sorts of geographical and cosmological speculations were discussed, as were the most recent exploratory voyages to the African coast and the Atlantic islands. Even if Columbus himself was not in regular attendance at court, his wife's relatives were. Along with other information from the court, Columbus found inspiration in a letter sent to the king of Portugal by the Florentine Paolo dal Pozzo Toscanelli. A typically versatile Renaissance intellectual, Toscanelli was a geographer cum businessman who worked for the Medici bank. Among his other pursuits, he made maps. In 1459, he interviewed several Portuguese who were familiar with West Africa and India, in order to bring their firsthand observations to bear on a world map he was preparing. Toscanelli wrote to the Portuguese king in 1474 that one could reach Quinsai (Hangchow) in China by sailing west for 5,000 miles, breaking the trip with stops along the way at the islands of Antilia and Cipango (Japan). The king did not follow up on Toscanelli's suggestion, which was based in part on Marco Polo's exaggeration of the size of China and of the distance between Japan and the Asian mainland. Nonetheless, Toscanelli's letter was discussed in Lisbon and was common knowledge to those who frequented the court, including – we can safely assume – Columbus's in-laws. Columbus supposedly wrote to Toscanelli himself in 1481, receiving in return encouragement and a copy of the letter and map that had been sent to the king of Portugal in 1474. Whether or not there really was any correspondence between Columbus and Toscanelli – and some doubt it – Columbus clearly knew about Toscanelli and his theories.

Unfortunately, Columbus did not write down his geographical ideas in detail until his third voyage across the Atlantic, so we cannot date their evolution with any precision. The usual tendency among his biographers is to assume that he formulated a full set of geographical hypotheses about the size and configuration of the earth before seeking support at the Portuguese court and that he simply kept trying to sell the same fully developed theory elsewhere after being rejected in Portugal. Nonetheless, it seems more reasonable to suppose that his geographical hypotheses grew incrementally, beginning with the fairly simple idea of sailing westward to reach the Indies and later adding evidence from academic geographers to buttress his case. This scenario is supported – but certainly not proved – by the publication dates of the books in his personal library. His copy of Ptolemy's *Geographia* was published in Rome in 1478; his copy of Enea Silvio Piccolomini's *Historia rerum ubique gestarum* in Venice in 1477; and his copy of Pierre d'Ailly's *Imago mundi* in Louvain between 1480 and 1483. He may or may not have consulted these books before making his case to the king of Portugal, but at least they had been published and were on the market. Columbus's copy of Marco Polo, on the other hand, was a Latin summary published in Antwerp in 1485, and his Pliny (*Historia naturalis*) was an Italian translation, published in Venice in 1489. He may have known other editions of these works before getting his own copies, but he may not have consulted them at all until after his arrival in Spain in 1485.[43]

Columbus made numerous marginal comments in Latin in his copy of Pierre d'Ailly's *Imago mundi,* some that may have been written before he left Portugal in 1485 and others that were clearly written later. One of them – perhaps his most famous marginal note – mentioned his voyages to Guinea, which began in 1482, and explicitly stated how large he estimated the earth to be, and why.

> Note that frequently sailing from Lisbon south to Guinea, I observed the course diligently, as captains and sailors are accustomed, and later I took the altitude of the sun with the quadrant and other instruments many times, and I found that I agreed with Alfragano; that is to say, that 56⅔ *millas* corresponded to each degree. Therefore, one must lend credence to this measure. In consequence we could say that the perimeter of the earth on the equinoctial circle is 20,400 *millas*. The same was found by Master José, physician and astronomer, and many others sent for this single purpose by the most serene king of Portugal. And anyone who measures by the maritime charts can see this, taking the measures from north to south through the ocean, outside of all land, in a straight line, which can well be done beginning in England or Ireland in a straight line toward the south as far as Guinea.[44]

The figure Columbus calculated for the length of a degree along the "equinoctial circle" or the equator – 56.66 *millas* – agreed with many ancient and contemporary sources. Multiplying that figure by 360 degrees produced his estimate of 20,400 *millas* for the earth's circumference. Scholars disagree about the length of the "mile" that Columbus used. Most call it a "Roman" or "Italian" mile, but their estimates range between about 4,810 and 4,860 feet. Even if Columbus's mile corresponded to the larger figure, his estimate for the earth's circumference was equivalent to under 19,000 modern statute miles of 5,280 feet each. The real length of a degree at the equator is 69 statute miles, and the real circumference of the earth is about 24,900 statute miles, or 32 percent larger than Columbus's estimate.[45]

In developing his theory that a westward voyage to Asia was not only possible but practical, Columbus adopted the same erroneous notions from his readings that had influenced Toscanelli and others. With minor variations, they each believed that the continent of Asia stretched some 30 degrees farther to the east than it really does and that Japan lay 1,500 miles to the east of the Asian continent.[46] Following those premises, the open ocean between Europe and Asia shrank to a manageable size, with hospitable islands along the way. On the basis of his sources, Columbus calculated a distance of only 2,400 nautical miles from the Canaries to Japan; the real distance is 10,600 nautical miles. In other words, Columbus chose a set of figures that made his enterprise plausible, and it is hardly surprising that experts at the Portuguese and Castilian courts failed to agree with his premises or with his conclusions. After all, the great Ptolemy had calculated a degree nearly 18 percent longer than Columbus's figure, which would have put Asia much farther away, perhaps out of reach of European ships.[47]

Encouraged by his fortuitous set of miscalculations, Columbus tried first to interest King João II of Portugal in his scheme for a western passage to Asia. He probably requested several ships, as well as provisions. He may also have made the same demands that he later made in Spain: to be ennobled; to be appointed admiral, viceroy, and governor of any lands he discovered; and to be granted a share of all the profits on trade established with those lands.[48] Whatever Columbus's demands, João II refused to support him. It is not clear why. Perhaps Columbus asked too much. Perhaps the king's geographers cast doubt on Columbus's ideas, as well they should have. The Portuguese crown traditionally kept a tight grip on exploration and trade; perhaps the king was not willing to trust a foreigner to do his bidding, particularly not one with the self-confidence and even arrogance that Columbus seems to have displayed at court.[49] The Portuguese ruling house had fostered exploration in the Atlantic for generations, to its great profit, and always under firm royal control. But King João rejected Columbus, at least temporarily, suggesting that he try again in a few years. In the next several years, however, the king allowed at least two other groups of Portuguese mariners to look for new islands to the west.[50]

In the heroic legend of Columbus, the king's actions in rejecting him and later permitting others to explore westward gave rise to the notion of Portuguese treachery. But Columbus was not the only man of his time to believe in the plausibility of finding lands in the ocean sea and a western passage to Asia. The Portuguese court had been briefed by Toscanelli in 1474 and was petitioned by a steady stream of mariners with a dream. It is only in hindsight that we tend to overvalue the vision of Columbus and dismiss the visions of his contemporaries. What set Columbus apart from the others was a single-minded dedication to his grand design, once the first kernel of the idea had occurred to him. He alone was willing to persevere for nearly a decade in seeking support, despite repeated frustrations. If he had any doubts, he stifled them and kept on trying until he succeeded.

6

Columbus in Spain

AFTER THE KING OF PORTUGAL refused to grant his request, Columbus left for Spain, taking his young son Diego with him. Early
in 1485, they arrived at Palos de la Frontera in southwestern Andalusia, and the historical record of Columbus's life becomes clearer
and fuller from then on. We have more certain knowledge of the
seven years he spent seeking support in Spain than for the first thirty-
four years of his life in Genoa and Portugal.[1] Nonetheless, much
remains speculative, and the best we can do is to follow logic and
reasonable assumptions where the documents fail.

A CHANGE OF VENUE

Although neither Columbus nor his early biographers tell us explicitly why he went to Spain, it is not difficult to supply plausible reasons. Assuming Columbus had already developed some ideas about
the wind patterns of the Atlantic, it would make perfect sense for
him to go to Spain. The Canary Islands were controlled by Spain,
and Columbus may well have determined that the Canaries were the
perfect starting place for an Atlantic crossing. Of the four voyages
he made, the first, second, and fourth began in the Canaries, although on the third he went as far south as the Cape Verde Islands
before heading west. Spain also challenged Portugal's lead in Atlantic
exploration. If the Portuguese would not back him, perhaps their
Spanish rivals would.

During the course of the fifteenth century, Spaniards – particularly
Andalusian mariners – had competed with the Portuguese in the Atlantic islands and along Africa's western coast. They had skirmished
over fishing grounds and the lucrative trade in African coastal markets from Morocco south. Their rivalry assumed the status of a real
war with the death, in 1474, of the Castilian monarch Enrique IV,
who left behind a disputed succession. His daughter Juana sought the
throne, with support from part of the nobility and urban leaders in
Castile. Opposing Juana's claim was Isabel, Enrique's half-sister, who
had married the crown prince of Aragón, Fernando, in 1469, without
Enrique's permission. Together Fernando and Isabel won the support of other factions among the Castilian nobility and town governments, and they had the armed support of the crown of Aragón.

Juana's advisers sought a counterweight in Portugal's King Afonso V, who promised to marry Juana and entered Castile to fight for her right of succession.

Fernando and Isabel conducted a small naval war against the Portuguese, pitting Andalusian corsairs against Portuguese shipping in the Atlantic. The decisive battles were fought on land, however, and in the end Fernando and Isabel prevailed. The war and related disputes in the Hispano–Portuguese rivalry were settled through a series of negotiations that illustrates the intricate ties linking Spain and Portugal in the fifteenth century, even in the midst of war. Once peace seemed desirable, Isabel met with Beatriz, the Portuguese duchess of Bragança, who happened to be her aunt, in an effort to open negotiations. The Bragança family had remained neutral in the war of succession, largely out of hostility to Afonso V and his heir Prince João, and they had retained close ties with Isabel. Nonetheless, Afonso was willing to accept Beatriz as his go-between in the early stages of the negotiations. The conversations between Isabel of Castile and Beatriz of Bragança ultimately led to a series of agreements worked out by representatives of Castile and Portugal at the Portuguese town of Alcáçovas, late in 1479. Afonso V and Juana renounced their claims to the Castilian throne, their marriage plans were discarded, and Juana entered a convent. A new marriage alliance was planned between the eldest daughter of Fernando and Isabel and the grandson of Afonso V.

The treaties worked out at Alcáçovas and ratified by Castile in Toledo restored peace between Portugal and Castile. The agreements also contained a definitive settlement of the two countries' African and Atlantic rivalries. By their terms, Castile recognized Portugal's monopoly over maritime traffic along the western shore of Africa, south of the Canaries. Portugal recognized Castile's possession of the Canaries, and Castile recognized Portugal's possession of all the other Atlantic islands so far discovered. The Portuguese also received title to any new lands that might be found, "from the Canary Islands down toward Guinea."[2] In other words, for some five years before Columbus arrived in Spain that country's mariners had been legally barred from the lucrative African trade and the potentially more lucrative sea route to Asia.

COLUMBUS IN THE COUNTY OF NIEBLA

We might expect that a Genoese merchant mariner such as Columbus, accustomed to the exciting atmosphere of Lisbon, would have headed for Seville as soon as he arrived in Spain. As the major port on the Guadalquivir River, Seville was the largest city in southern Spain. The community called Triana, across the river from Seville proper, was home to many of the sailors and ship's masters who provided crews and officers for Spain's Mediterranean and Atlantic expeditions. Moreover, many Genoese merchants and bankers and a smaller number of Florentines and other Italians resided in Seville. They formed part of an Italian community well integrated into Spanish society; many families had been present in the city since its conquest from the Muslims in the mid-thirteenth century.[3]

Instead of going directly to Seville, however, Columbus landed at Palos – an auspicious choice, and almost certainly not an accidental one. The small port of Palos was part of the county of Niebla, property of the duke of Medina Sidonia, who was also its count. Palos would later serve as the embarkation point for Columbus's first voyage. Though overshadowed by the great commerce of Andalusian ports from Seville to Cádiz, the towns of Huelva, Moguer, and Palos on the Tinto and Odiel rivers had a long seafaring tradition. Their citizens specialized in smaller vessels and traded with Portugal and the Canaries. Before the Portuguese–Castilian treaty of 1479 had barred Castilian ships from West Africa, men from the county of Niebla had made many voyages to Portuguese enclaves in Africa; after the treaty some continued to do so without authorization. Niebla could therefore provide good ships, officers, and crew members who were experienced in Atlantic waters.

Not incidentally, Columbus also had family connections in the region and was in need of them at this point in his life. His wife Felipa had died and was buried in Lisbon. Columbus needed a stable home for their young son Diego, and his late wife's sister, Violante Moniz, lived in Huelva with her husband Miguel Moliart. There may well have been another Portuguese in-law living in Huelva at the same time: Pedro Correa da Cunha, husband of Hizeu Perestrelo, Felipa's half-sister. In choosing the Niebla region, with its maritime tradition and his own family ties, Columbus could not have selected a better entry point in Castile.

As the traditional story tells, Columbus walked directly from Palos to the Franciscan friary of La Rábida, high on the cliffs overlooking the Tinto River. Weary from the journey and penniless, he asked at the monastery door for a cup of water for himself and a crust of bread for his small son. As luck would have it, he also found a steadfast supporter for his scheme in the person of one of the friars. The story is a fabrication. Nothing in the sources tells us why he went to La Rábida or even proves that he first visited the monastery in 1485. The historian Antonio Rumeu de Armas does not think Columbus went to La Rábida at all until 1491, because no one there or in Palos knew him when he visited the monastery in that year.[4] His being unknown in 1491 does not preclude the possibility that he had made a short visit in 1485, however. The personnel at the monastery could have changed in the interim, and the townspeople may have had little contact with Columbus as a brief visitor.

If we strip away the romantic veneer from the story of his visit to La Rábida and accept that it occurred in 1485, we might find several reasons for his actions. Columbus was almost certainly not poverty-stricken, but it is logical to assume that he first went to La Rábida as a traveler in search of lodging. Monasteries traditionally offered hospitality to all sorts of travelers, not just to mendicants. Traveling with his young son, Columbus might understandably have preferred a monastic lodging to a room in a rowdy seaport tavern. It is highly likely that Columbus came to the Niebla region seeking his wife's relatives as temporary custodians for his son. He knew they lived in Huelva, but perhaps he did not know exactly where. It is easy to imagine him landing in Palos, having just passed La Rábida on the way into the port, and immediately making his way to the monastery, 3 miles from Palos, where he knew he could find decent lodging for himself and his son. The alternative was to head for Huelva, across the river, where locating Moniz and Moliart might take some time and where the prospect for decent lodging was less secure.

Another possibility is that Columbus had received an introduction to La Rábida in the parish church of Palos, whose priest was also the father superior of La Rábida. It would have been quite natural for Columbus to visit the parish church in Palos the moment he arrived, to give thanks for a safe voyage. He might even have known about La Rábida before he left Portugal and perhaps carried with him an introduction to the Franciscan friars there. Columbus's Franciscan connections in later life are well known. It would be surprising if he had not known Franciscans in Lisbon as well.

Franciscan missionary activities in the Canaries suggest another possible reason why Columbus might have visited La Rábida. Even before the Castilian conquest of the Canaries began, the islands had been the scene of missionary activity, begun by Franciscans from Majorca and later continued by Franciscans from Andalusia. Even though Franciscan activity in the islands was being restricted, La Rábida still had close links with the evangelization of the Canary Islanders. As Columbus sought to gather as much information as possible about the Atlantic and the islands it contained, he might have considered the friars of La Rábida as a valuable resource for the refinement of his plans.[5]

Columbus's decision to leave Portugal when he did, and his choice of Palos and Huelva as his destinations, might also have related to the political situation. The Moniz family, to which Columbus's mother-in-law belonged, supported the Bragança faction in Portuguese politics. In 1483, the duke of Bragança had attempted to assassinate the new king, João II, and take his throne. The plot failed, and Bragança was quickly executed for his treachery. In August of 1484, the duke of Viseu botched another assassination attempt against the king and ended up being stabbed to death himself, probably by the king's own hand. Both conspirators had sought Castilian support. Although Fernando and Isabel would not openly encourage the treason of Bragança and Viseu, they did give refuge to many Portuguese exiles who crossed into Spain in 1483 and 1484 in the aftermath of both failed conspiracies. Columbus's Perestrelo–Moniz relatives may have moved across the Castilian frontier to escape the consequences of their political loyalties. By 1485 Violante Moniz, her husband Miguel Moliart, and perhaps Pedro Correa da Cunha were settled in Huelva, just across the border from the Portuguese Algarve, where the Moniz family owned property.

The biography of Columbus attributed to his son Hernando tells us that he left Portugal secretly, "fearing that the king might seek to detain him."[6] That brief statement, and the fact that King João sent Columbus a safe-conduct when he invited him to return to the Portuguese court in 1488, have led generations of historians to conjecture broadly about the circumstances of his departure. Some say King João feared that Columbus would reveal his knowledge of Portugal's routes to Africa or the implications of the Toscanelli letter. Others say Columbus was deep in debt and fled Lisbon to avoid the wrath of his creditors. The political situation suggests another possibility. In the wake of two failed conspiracies, at least one of which was launched by the political faction to which his in-laws belonged, the chance of obtaining support from the king of Portugal might suddenly have turned bleak. Even if Columbus did not feel threatened personally, he had lost part of his support at court. João II had turned down his project once, and the family connections that Columbus had enjoyed at court had become detrimental. Columbus may well have felt that it was time for a change of venue.[7]

All of this is conjectural, of course. As with so many other aspects of Columbus's life before 1492, the record is incomplete. We do not know for certain why he left Lisbon when he did, but there is no question that he was in the county of Niebla in 1485. Whether or not he visited La Rábida, he quickly contacted his wife's sister Violante and her husband and arranged for them to care for his son while he traveled to the royal court. They had no children of their own and would have been well able to provide for young Diego in his father's absence. Violante rented land in the nearby township of San Juan del

Puerto from the duke of Medina Sidonia.[8] Although there is no evidence that she knew the duke personally, her connection to the foremost aristocrat in southern Spain might have been an advantage to Columbus as he tried to secure an audience at the Castilian court.

Soon after his arrival in Spain, Columbus consulted the Franciscan friar Antonio de Marchena, either in Palos or in Seville. Marchena was ideally placed to help Columbus at court, provided that he agreed to do so; he had powerful friends at court and was rising in the Franciscan hierarchy. Later in 1485, he would become the overseer (*guardián*) of all the Observant Franciscan monasteries in the Sevillian region.[9] Marchena was also an astronomer, who studied the same heavens that guided mariners. Columbus, who never revealed all he knew to anyone, evidently revealed enough to Marchena to convert the knowledgeable friar into his most faithful supporter. Writing to Fernando and Isabel long afterward, Columbus noted his gratitude to Marchena in an otherwise bitter narrative:

> Your majesties know that I spent seven years in the court pestering you for this; never in the whole time was there found a pilot, nor a sailor, nor a mariner, nor a philosopher, nor an expert in any other science who did not state that my enterprise was false, so I never found support from anyone, save father Friar Antonio de Marchena, beyond that of eternal God.

He also noted that *"no person was found who did not hold it to be a joke, except for that father Friar Antonio de Marchena."*[10] Whether the early meeting with Marchena was pure chance or had been arranged by mutual friends, no one knows. Only the result matters: Marchena heard Columbus's plan and became his advocate. When Columbus left for the royal court within a few weeks after arriving in Spain, he bore with him Marchena's letter of introduction to Friar Hernando de Talavera, of the Order of Saint Jerome, at that time prior of the Prado Monastery near Valladolid and confessor to Queen Isabel.[11]

CASTILE AND THE ROYAL COURT

During the early part of 1485 the royal court was in Seville, but in March it moved to Córdoba, where it remained until early September.[12] Castile had no permanent capital city until Felipe II gave Madrid that distinction in the mid-sixteenth century. Earlier monarchs moved from place to place as politics or warfare dictated. The seat of government was wherever the court happened to be. Like most of the monarchies of western Europe, Castile was an amalgam of previously independent kingdoms and counties. It was sound administrative practice for the rulers to move around, making their presence known and felt in the principal cities of their realms.

Fifteenth-century Spain is often portrayed as internally unified but isolated from its neighbors and unprepared to deal with the New World that Columbus and other explorers claimed for it.[13] Such a distorted portrayal makes it impossible to understand how Spain could conquer several empires in the New World, quickly establish its own authority in their place, and become the dominant power in Europe for the next century. A true understanding of this process requires a fresh look – however brief – at the rise of Spain. Long before Columbus, and long before the creation of its empire, Spain was growing economically, spurred by a rise in population, the exploitation of lands reconquered from the Muslims, and widespread trade. Through out the Middle Ages, Muslim Spain had provided a liaison between western Europe and the Islamic world. Once the Reconquest was all but completed, Christian Spain retained that role, benefiting from trade with the Islamic world, Africa, and the Atlantic islands, as well as with the rest of Europe. Enriched by this trade, the Spain of Fernando and Isabel was arguably the most dynamic of Europe's new Renaissance monarchies, but it was far from being united.[14]

There was no "kingdom of Spain" in the fifteenth century and would not be for centuries. Instead, four separate Christian kingdoms and one Muslim kingdom shared the Iberian Peninsula: Aragón, Navarre, Castile, and Portugal under Christian rule, and Granada under Muslim rule. The words "Spain" and *España* are both derived from the Latin *Hispania,* which the Romans had used to designate the whole peninsula that the Greeks had called *Iberia.* Fifteenth-century Europeans used their varying forms of the word "Spain" to designate either Castile or the whole peninsula, except for Portugal. Each Christian kingdom of Spain was further subdivided into regions, and local inhabitants identified with their hometown and their home region much more strongly than with anything larger. Once they were out in the wider world, however, they came to identify themselves as Spaniards, reflecting foreign perceptions of them.

Even after the marriage in 1469 of Fernando, prince of Aragón, and Isabel, claimant to the throne of Castile, and after they both gained their respective thrones, Spain remained divided among several smaller entities, each one the product of geography, topography, environment, and history. The kingdom of Aragón, in the east, included Aragón, Catalonia, and Valencia. The kings of Aragón also ruled a Mediterranean empire that included the Balearic Islands, Sicily, Sardinia, and the kingdom of Naples in southern Italy. West of Aragón lay the small kingdom of Navarre. The kingdom of Castile dominated the peninsula from north to south, with territories acquired from the Muslims during the long centuries of medieval Reconquest. Castile included the northern coastal areas of Galicia, Asturias, Cantabria, and the Basque regions of Vizcaya, Guipúzcoa, and Alava; León and Castile (Old Castile) to the north of the central mountains, and La Mancha and Extremadura (New Castile) to the south; and the kingdoms of Andalusia and Murcia in the extreme south and southeast. The kingdom of Portugal lay to the west of Castile, formed in its own reconquest of territory from the Muslims.

There was nothing inevitable about the creation of modern Spain through the amalgamation of Aragón and Castile. In medieval times, Castilian rulers had made as much effort to secure marriages with ruling dynasties in Portugal as in Aragón. Throughout the fifteenth century as well, Castilian and Portuguese monarchs arranged marriages between their children, as well as marriages with other ruling houses in western Europe. Fernando and Isabel also tried to arrange lasting marriages for two of their daughters with members of the Portuguese royal house. In different circumstances, there could as easily have been a merger of Castile and Portugal as of Castile and Aragón.

The kingdom of Granada, in the southern part of the peninsula, was the last Muslim possession in western Europe in the fifteenth century. Its fate was intimately linked with the project of Columbus; he received the support he needed only after Fernando and Isabel, often called the Catholic Monarchs, had completed the reconquest of Granada and driven out its last Muslim ruler. Queen Isabel moved the Castilian court from Seville to Córdoba, in March of 1485, because she could follow developments in the Granadan campaign more easily from there. Columbus joined the court in Córdoba. His letter of introduction from Friar Antonio de Marchena gave him access not only to Hernando de Talavera, the queen's confessor, but to other members of the court as well. Among persons of influence, Columbus met Friar Diego de Deza, a Dominican who later became archbishop of Seville; Juan Cabrero, King Fernando's Aragonese chamberlain (*camarero*); Alonso de Quintanilla, treasurer of the Santa Hermandad (national militia) and chief accountant of Castile; and – most powerful of all – the cardinal-archbishop of Toledo, Pedro González de Mendoza.

During his first visit to court, Columbus presented a written petition addressed to the Spanish monarchs. Before it could reach them, however, it first had to be considered by the royal council, which summoned Columbus to explain his project in person. When the council rejected his petition, Columbus made an appeal to the monarchs for a personal audience, either directly or through the contacts

Christopher Columbus at the Royal Court of Spain. Lithograph by Mast, Crowell & Kirkpatrick, 1892. (Photo courtesy of the Library of Congress, Washington, D.C.)

he had cultivated at court. In the months during which these events unfolded, Columbus remained at court in Córdoba. The monarchs left for central Castile in early October, establishing residence in Alcalá de Henares, northeast of Madrid, where the court remained during the fall of 1485 and into the winter of 1486. Columbus traveled to Alcalá in late October 1485, and the monarchs probably granted him his first audience on January 20, 1486.[15]

There is no direct documentary evidence to explain why the monarchs agreed to receive Columbus; many writers attribute the audience to the introductory letter Marchena sent to Talavera and to the subsequent contacts Columbus himself made at court. Other possible explanations relate to Columbus's Portuguese experience. Numerous Portuguese exiles were residing at the Castilian court – refugees who, as we have noted, had fled across the frontier after the conspiracies of the dukes of Bragança and Viseu had failed. Columbus's Moniz in-laws were connected to the Bragança faction, and at least one (perhaps two) of his brothers-in-law was already in Spain when he arrived. Either he or they could have contacted more highly placed exiles living at court who could have pleaded Columbus's cause.

Even without such help, which is only conjectural, Columbus had a direct, but slim, connection with the queen herself through his Portuguese in-laws. His father-in-law Bartolomeu Perestrelo had begun his career in the court of Prince João of Portugal, grandfather of Queen Isabel of Castile.[16] Prince João married Isabel of Barcelós, who had lived at the Portuguese court in her youth as the Portuguese extended the frontiers of their knowledge about Africa and the Atlantic. The excitement of those daring voyages, and the profits derived from them, were constant topics of discussion at court, and we can assume that the young woman absorbed both the information and the excitement surrounding her. Following the early death of Prince João, Perestrelo transferred to the household of Prince Henrique, and Isabel of Barcelós remained a widow. In 1447, her daughter (also called Isabel) became the second wife of the aging King Juan II of Castile. When he died, in 1454, he left his widow with two small children: Isabel, the future queen of Castile (born 1451) and Alfonso (born 1453). Their grandmother Isabel of Barcelós moved from Portugal to the small town of Arévalo, on the Castilian plain, to aid her daughter in raising the two children. Attending the child Isabel was another Portuguese woman, Clara Alvarnáez, wife of Gonzalo Chacón, who administered the dowager queen's household. In other words, for the early, formative years of her life Isabel of Castile was raised in a household run by her Portuguese grandmother and mother, no doubt hearing Portuguese spoken and hearing Castilian spoken with a Portuguese accent. Isabel of Barcelós, the grandmother, was an experienced politician, closely linked with the Bragança faction in Portugal. She had observed the bitter infighting among Portugal's high nobility and had witnessed the glory and gold that flowed into Portugal during the first phase of Atlantic exploration, conquest, and expansion.[17]

When Isabel of Castile and Fernando of Aragón first encountered Columbus, the Portuguese inclusions in his spoken and written Castilian would not have seemed strange to the queen. They might even have called up fond memories of her youth in the household of her Portuguese mother and grandmother. Moreover, Columbus was related by marriage to Bartolomeu Perestrelo, who had served her Portuguese grandfather Prince João and later had governed the island of Porto Santo. That Columbus was the widower of Perestrelo's daughter and obviously knew a great deal about his father-in-law's experiences in the Atlantic, may well have inspired the queen's interest and gained her confidence. The ties of affection between Isabel of Castile and Columbus – he always believed her to be a greater benefactor than Fernando – could well have stemmed from his connections with her Portuguese heritage and upbringing.

No direct record of Columbus's first audience with the king and queen has surfaced, but there are indirect reports of what transpired. The chronicler Andrés Bernáldez said that Columbus used a map of the world – possibly one he had drawn himself – to explain his scheme to Fernando and Isabel. It is likely that he quoted frequently and extensively from Ptolemy's authoritative work to buttress his interpretation of world geography, although the evidence for this is only indirect. Later in 1486, King Fernando ordered a copy of Ptolemy's *Geographia* to be purchased for him in Valencia; scholars assume that the king's curiosity about the book was piqued by Columbus's presentation.[18] In any case, Fernando and Isabel were impressed enough to order a special *junta* (commission) to assess Columbus's proposal.

Heading the commission was an able and experienced courtier, Hernando de Talavera, at that time bishop-elect of Avila, and perhaps Columbus's first contact at court. Talavera had handled difficult matters for his sovereigns in the past. In 1479, as prior of the Prado Monastery near Valladolid, he had traveled to Portugal to witness the entry of Juana of Castile, Isabel's defeated rival for the throne, into a convent. About the same time he had headed an inquiry into the status of royal and noble rights in the Canary Islands. Now he was to head the Columbus commission, which included *letrados* (university-educated members of the royal court, mostly lawyers); *sabios* (men learned in astronomy and cartography); and mariners. We do not know in detail the deliberations of this *junta,* but at some point Columbus displayed a map of the world and seems to have promised that he would find land within 750 leagues (under 3,000 miles) across the ocean sea from Spain. Whatever arguments Columbus put forth, the commission rejected them totally during its meetings in November and December of 1486 and January of 1487, passing their findings along to the monarchs. The biography of Columbus attributed to his son Hernando tried to minimize the miscalculations and geographical errors explicit in Columbus's scheme. The biographer even went so far as to suggest that Columbus was merely seeking new islands west of those already discovered, rather than a western route to Asia. But ample evidence shows that Columbus was indeed proposing to sail westward to Asia, which he judged to be fairly close to Europe.

Despite the discouraging report of their commission, the Catholic Monarchs were not willing to dismiss Columbus out of hand. Although they never explicitly mentioned why they eventually decided to back him, one obvious explanation was economic. The riches of Asia, unquestioned by those who knew their Marco Polo, were attractive in themselves. For Castile in the 1480s they were particularly appealing as possible substitutes for African gold. Direct Spanish access to the gold markets of West Africa and to an eastern route to

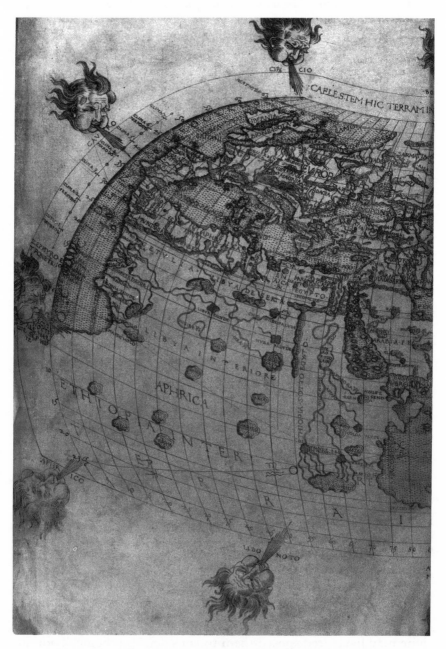

Western Europe and Africa, from Ptolemy's *Geographia* (Florence: Nicolaus Laurentii, 1480-82). When Columbus met with Fernando and Isabel in 1487, he may have shown them a similar map. Note that Africa is represented as a giant landmass extending westward into the South Atlantic, making the Portuguese dream of sailing around Africa to India impossible. (Photo courtesy of the James Ford Bell Library, University of Minnesota.)

India around Africa were prohibited by the terms of the agreements that had ended five years of war with Portugal in 1479. Moreover, Castile had long received an indirect but regular supply of African gold in the form of tribute payments from the kingdom of Granada. When Columbus came to court, in 1486, Fernando and Isabel were in the middle of a long war of conquest against Muslim Granada. They foresaw that the end of that war would also mean the end of their golden tribute payments. If Columbus was right, direct trade with Asia could compensate for their loss of access to African gold and their exclusion from the still hypothetical route around Africa to India.

Beyond economic concerns, Columbus's scheme dovetailed neatly with the religious ideals of Reconquest and religious unification that would culminate in 1492 with the defeat of Muslim Granada and the expulsion of Spain's Jews. Long before 1492, many at the Castilian court hoped to carry the Christian advance farther into lands under Muslim control. If Castile could drive the Muslims from Spain after seven centuries, perhaps anything was possible, even the end of Islam altogether. Columbus's project suggested a link between a westward voyage to Asia and an assault on Islam. In the prologue to his diary of the first voyage, he mentioned the Great Khan as a possible ally.[19] Later in the diary he reminded the monarchs that he had urged them "to spend all the profits of this my enterprise on the conquest of Jerusalem."[20] His scheme had the potential to tie together and accomplish the dreams that European merchants, monarchs, missionaries, and mystics had held since the end of the Crusades. An established sea route to Asia would surely produce great riches, and it might also lead to an alliance with the Great Khan against the Muslims and an unprecedented opportunity to spread the Christian message. Many Christians in Columbus's time believed that their faith should be preached to all peoples and that Jerusalem should be regained in order to prepare the way for the Second Coming of Jesus. How much Columbus agreed with these millenarian views before 1492 is not clear. From his second voyage (1493–96) until the end of his life, however, his acceptance of millenarian and apocalyptic prophesies became intense and firmly held.

Fernando and Isabel had their own immediate struggle with Islam close at hand when Columbus first approached them in 1485. That alone may have predisposed them to consider his scheme seriously, despite questions about the accuracy of his geography. Whatever their motivations may have been, Fernando and Isabel began authorizing modest grants for Columbus's living expenses and for travel to and from the court. Their first grant (for 3,000 maravedis) was made in May 1487, while Columbus was residing in Córdoba, where the court had returned. A second grant, for the same amount, followed on July 3. In August, Christian forces recaptured Málaga, and Fernando and Isabel summoned Columbus to attend them at court in the royal encampment outside the city, sending him 4,000 maravedis for the journey. Considering that a Spanish ship's pilot earned about 2,000 maravedis a month, these were quite generous subsidies.

During the siege of Málaga, a dramatic episode had taken place that may have influenced Fernando and Isabel in Columbus's favor. The Castilian besiegers were encamped in tents on the outskirts of the city. One night, Castilian forces under the duke of Cádiz surprised a party of one hundred fifty Muslims trying to bring arms and gunpowder into the city and captured about half of them. One of the prisoners told the duke that he would reveal a sure plan for taking the city if he were taken to the king. The duke agreed to take his prisoner to see the king, but – incredibly – allowed the still-armed Muslim to slip away. He entered a tent where a richly dressed couple was playing chess, and, believing them to be the king and queen, pulled a scimitar from beneath his cloak and attacked them. Guards quickly arrived and killed the attacker, and his body later was hacked to pieces and catapulted over the walls into Málaga. In the aftermath of that stunning breach of security, the royal bodyguard was strengthened to two hundred.[21]

The woman in the tent, who suffered nothing worse than damaged clothing, was Beatriz Fernández de Bobadilla, the marchioness of Moya, keeper of the queen's wardrobe and her close confidante. Beatriz was married to Andrés de Cabrera, who had won Isabel's undying gratitude for having turned over the crown treasury of Segovia to her on the death of Enrique IV, thereby assuring her financial base for the civil war that followed. Several historians have suggested that the marchioness intervened on Columbus's behalf with the queen, who could not easily deny a small favor to her old friend and ally, especially after the scimitar attack.[22] The available documents do not reveal why Beatriz Fernández de Bobadilla would have favored Columbus, but her chess partner on the night of the attack, seriously wounded, may have played a role. His name was Alvaro de Portugal; as brother of the executed duke of Bragança, he was the most prominent of the Portuguese exiles living at the Castilian court in 1487. Among the other Bragança exiles in Castile were several of Columbus's Moniz in-laws. Columbus may possibly have used those connections to request another audience at court.

Whatever the reason, Fernando and Isabel summoned Columbus to Málaga, where they held out a slight possibility of helping him later, perhaps after the war with Granada had ended. Despite the negative reaction of their commission, they could not be sure that

Columbus's scheme was impossible. By stringing him along, they prevented him from taking his project elsewhere until they had the time and money to deal with it. Columbus applied for support several more times, while the war still continued, and the monarchs not only treated him courteously but gave him additional grants. Neither totally rejected nor fully supported, he was kept in a kind of limbo, his frustration growing as time passed.

BEATRIZ ENRÍQUEZ DE ARANA

Columbus's personal life at this stage in his career is worth considering briefly, because both his domestic arrangements and his business affairs affected his later life. Columbus spent a great deal of time in Córdoba, because the queen was using that city as a frequent base while the war with Granada continued. During his time in Córdoba, Columbus established a romantic liaison with a young woman named Beatriz Enríquez de Arana (or Harana).[23] No documents found so far tell us how the lovers met. Beatriz was an orphan living in Córdoba under the care of her cousin, Rodrigo Enríquez de Arana, a widower, who had married as his second wife Lucía Nuñez, who owned looms for the production of linen and woolen cloth. Most writers who have dealt with Beatriz suggest that Columbus must have met her through the Genoese pharmacists Lucián and Leonardo de Esbarroya, whose shop was a popular meeting place. One could also imagine that Columbus the weaver's son first noticed the weaving machinery in her family's house and thereafter noticed the young woman living there with her relatives. Whatever the circumstances, Columbus established a liaison with Beatriz and, late in 1487, conceived a child with her. She bore a son, named Hernando, in August 1488.

Hernando was a natural son, born to parents who had no impediment to marrying if they wished. Columbus was a widower, and she presumably was a single woman. Nonetheless, they never married. The reason is not clear, but we can assume it related to Columbus's lofty ambitions. Marriage to a low-born orphan would do nothing to enhance his prestige and would surely impede his search for noble status. The stigma did not affect their son, however, nor discourage Columbus from providing for Beatriz financially, although they did not even live together regularly. Early in 1493, after returning from his first transatlantic voyage, he gave Beatriz an annual income of 10,000 maravedis, and in 1502 he gave her another annuity for the same amount. In his will Columbus instructed his son Diego to care for her as if she were his own mother, and the rest of her life seems to have been spent in comfortable circumstances. She sold two houses in Seville, in 1519, for 52,000 maravedis, a sizable sum. And in 1521, two years before she died, her son Hernando sent her money via Genoese agents.

In many ways Columbus treated Hernando in the same way as he treated his first-born, legitimate son Diego, securing positions for both boys as pages to Prince Juan, the heir of Fernando and Isabel. Diego became Prince Juan's page by virtue of a royal letter patent (*albalá*) dated May 8, 1492.[24] Hernando joined him early in 1494.[25] By then the younger boy would have been six years old, and the historian Juan Manzano suggests that the fact of becoming a royal page effectively legitimated him.[26] In later life, Hernando converted himself into a gentleman-scholar, building upon his father's book collection to create the great Biblioteca Colombina in Seville. The library's collection is one of Hernando's lasting monuments. The other is the biography of Columbus attributed to him. Although the trustworthiness of the biography is open to doubt, it unquestionably demonstrates a son's love and admiration for a famous father. It is fitting that Hernando constructed his monuments with the printed word, for at the time when he was born his father may have been earning his living by selling books. Columbus also made use of the wealth of printed material available in the late fifteenth century as he planned his voyages and speculated on religious matters.

The scant information we have concerning Columbus's employment during this period comes from contemporary authors. Las Casas said that Columbus made navigational charts and sold them.[27] The court chronicler Andrés Bernáldez said that Columbus sold printed books and conducted this business throughout Andalusia, especially in Seville.[28] Printing by the new method using movable type was spreading throughout Europe, and Seville was at that time the most important center for Spanish book production. The city also served as a distribution center for books imported from Italy and Valencia by Italian merchants.[29] With Columbus's background as a merchant and his connections in the Italian community of southern Spain, he might easily have found a job with another Italian merchant selling printed books.

Columbus's prime vocation, of course, was maritime discovery, and his major occupation in the 1480s was to secure funding for his scheme. Events in Portugal quickened the competition for support. In 1487, Bartolomeu Dias set out to find the southern tip of Africa and, by extension, the Indian Ocean and the long-desired sea route to Asia. Also, between March 1486 and March 1487 Fernão Dolmo (Ferdinand van Olmen) and João Afonso de Estreito planned to sail from the island of Terceira in the Azores, under a Portuguese license, to discover "islands and lands" to the west.[30] King João II of Portugal increasingly concerned himself with exploration and discovery. In addition to sending naval expeditions to the west and south in search of the passage to India, he sent espionage agents overland, to the eastern Mediterranean and beyond, to find Prester John. With Portuguese probes directed east, south, and west, and with the westward expedition having failed, João II's attention turned again to Christopher Columbus.

Whether because Columbus had written him or on his own initiative, João II wrote a cordial letter to Columbus, addressed to Seville.[31] The king urged Columbus to visit him in Lisbon and gave him a safe-conduct for the round trip. Columbus's actions are not documented explicitly during this period, but it seems clear that he traveled to the Spanish royal court with his letter from the Portuguese king. When he set out, the court was in Valencia (March 4 to mid-April 1488); he probably traveled eastward and saw someone at court, either in Valencia or after the court had moved to Murcia. Whoever he contacted must have been impressed with the letter, for on June 16, 1488, Columbus received a subsidy of 3,000 maravedis from Fernando and Isabel. Nonetheless, he still seems to have accepted João II's invitation.

Columbus may have been in Córdoba for the birth of his son in August of 1488; he was surely in Seville in October of 1488. Historians are divided about whether he visited Lisbon thereafter, but in a marginal note in his copy of d'Ailly's *Imago mundi* Columbus says that he was there when Dias returned from Africa:

> Note that in this year of '88, in the month of December Bartolomeu Dias tied up in Lisbon; [he was] that captain of three caravels that the most serene king of Portugal had sent to Guinea to measure the land. And he told the most serene king of Portugal how he sailed 600 leagues beyond what had been sailed before, that is to say, 450 to the South and 250 to the North [sic], as far as a promontory he called the Cape of Good Hope, which supposedly is in Asesinba. In this place he found that by the astrolabe it was 45 degrees from the equator, the most remote place was 3,100 leagues from Lisbon. The voyage itself he drew and wrote down on a sailing chart, to present it before the eyes of the most serene king. *In all this I was present.*[32]

Whether or not Columbus was in Lisbon when Dias arrived, he would soon have learned about the voyage, and it might easily have plunged him into despair. He had failed to secure backing from either Portugal or Spain, and the discoveries of Dias at the tip of Africa meant that the Indian Ocean was probably not landlocked; the long-sought passage to India was now only a matter for another Portuguese expedition to accomplish. Columbus's options seemed to be narrowing. His brother Bartolomeo had been in England, trying without success to interest King Henry VII in the enterprise. It is possible that one of the Columbus brothers had already made overtures to France, and Bartolomeo was soon to travel there. Columbus apparently considered going to France himself. If he was ever to find the royal support he craved, he had to move quickly.

The historian Juan Manzano thinks that Columbus approached the duke of Medina Sidonia and the duke of Medinaceli at this juncture. Las Casas also wrote that Columbus discussed his project with both of those men, but the available documentation does not enable us to say when.[33] Both dukes were prominent members of the greatest and richest of the noble houses of Castile. Both had strong interests in shipping and maritime trade. Either could easily have mounted an expedition on the small scale that Columbus had in mind. Yet it seems Columbus had not approached them earlier, although he might have done so via several possible avenues: through the mediation of Italian merchants in Seville; through his connections at La Rábida and in Palos; or through the contacts he had made at the Spanish court. If Columbus did not approach either Medina Sidonia or Medinaceli until four years after his arrival in Spain, the reason may well lie in his search for status and power. Although Columbus eagerly sought wealth and fame, these were not enough for a man of his burning ambition. He wanted status, in the medieval and Renaissance sense – hereditary nobility, such as his late wife's family had acquired in Portugal. He could secure that exalted status for himself and for his heirs only through royal favor. This motivation would explain his direct approaches to the monarchs of Portugal and Spain and his indirect approaches to the rulers of England and France through his brother Bartolomeo. After marking time in Spain for four years, with only vague promises and occasional stipends to show for his efforts, and after Dias's successful return from the edge of the Indian Ocean, Columbus may have been willing to consider other ways of obtaining the funds he needed.

He probably first approached Enrique de Guzmán, duke of Medina Sidonia and one of the richest noblemen in Spain. Through inheritance he was also count of Niebla, which fostered his strong interest in Atlantic shipping. The ships he owned competed with the Portuguese in African ventures, and he had important interests in the Canaries and the Mar Pequeña (Little Sea), the Spanish nickname for the part of the Atlantic that lies between the Canaries and the African coast. Medina Sidonia could easily have backed Columbus, but when approached he declined to do so. Manzano speculated that Medina Sidonia refused because he knew too much: he certainly had been at court during its sojourn outside Málaga. He may even have been present at the moment when the royal commission recommended against accepting Columbus's proposal.

Rejected by Medina Sidonia, Columbus approached Luis de la Cerda, the fifth count and the first duke of Medinaceli. He was also the lord of Puerto de Santa María, an important town on the northern side of the Bay of Cádiz. The duke's mother, Leonor de Mendoza, was a niece of the powerful cardinal-archbishop of Toledo, Pedro González de Mendoza, whom Columbus had met at court. Medinaceli was quite willing to help with Columbus's plans and provided him with room and board in Puerto de Santa María for a considerable period.[34] The duke and his guest worked out an agreement by which Medinaceli would provide between 3,000 and 4,000 ducats – a generous sum, equal to 1.1 to 1.5 million maravedis – to pay for three ships, their crews, provisions for a year, and trade goods. One detail remained. Medinaceli had to be sure that the king and queen truly were not interested in sponsoring Columbus. In recent years, the monarchs had become much more involved in Atlantic ventures and more concerned to keep such ventures under royal control. To back a voyage without their approval was no longer possible, even for a nobleman as rich and powerful as Medinaceli. When Medinaceli wrote to the queen, she summoned Columbus back to court.[35]

During the summer of 1489, Columbus traveled to another town near the frontier with Muslim Granada, Jaén, where the court then resided. He may have been present in July when two Franciscans from the Church of the Holy Sepulcher in Jerusalem arrived with a message for Fernando and Isabel from the sultan of Egypt. The sultan warned them to stop the war against the Muslims in Granada, who were his brothers in faith. Because the sultan's lands included Palestine and Jerusalem, with Christians among their population, he was in an especially strong position to urge Fernando and Isabel to tolerate the continued presence of Islam on the peninsula. The sultan was politic enough to choose Christian friars as his envoys, but his request could be read as a veiled threat to Christians in Jerusalem. If Columbus witnessed or heard of the sultan's message, its implications can only have strengthened his commitment to the reconquest of Jerusalem, which he often mentioned in his later writings.

At the end of the 1480s, the main concern of Fernando and Isabel was to end the war in Granada victoriously. Despite the emissaries from the Muslim world, they were determined to gain control over the last vestige of Islamic power in western Europe, and they conducted complicated diplomatic maneuvers to that end, as well as pursuing the war. Their negotiations with Columbus were much less important. Nonetheless, the monarchs and their officials were careful to keep Columbus's hopes alive and to discourage him from making any deal with Medinaceli. They absolutely refused to commit any resources to his scheme while the war with Granada continued, but they offered Columbus the possibility of support once hostilities ceased.

Columbus sustained his hope for a bit longer, but in the early fall of 1491 he seems to have decided that the Spanish monarchs would never support him – either that, or he was hoping to increase the pressure on Fernando and Isabel by threatening to leave. He went to La Rábida in 1491 with the expressed intention of embarking for France. Columbus arrived at La Rábida alone, and he was unknown to the people of the town of Palos and to the friars at the monastery. Columbus told his story to the current warden (*guardián*) of La Rábida, Juan Pérez, a former official of Queen Isabel.[36] Obviously intrigued, Pérez called in a physician of Palos, a man of some scientific knowledge, to question Columbus about his theories, his proposal to Fernando and Isabel, and their postponements. Columbus worked his charms as a salesman one more time, winning over both Pérez and the physician.

Pérez proved to be a powerful intermediary. He wrote to Queen Isabel requesting further reconsideration of Columbus's proposal and an audience for himself. She responded within two weeks, granting official permission for Pérez to come to court. Traveling on a rented mule, Pérez joined the court at Real de Santa Fe, the royal military encampment outside the city of Granada. There he made a forceful argument in Columbus's favor. Pérez's visit came at an opportune time. The Muslims had just signed an agreement promising to turn Granada over to the Catholic Monarchs the next year; with the end of the long Granadan campaign in sight, Isabel ordered Columbus to return to court, sending him the sizable sum of 20,000 maravedis in florins to pay his expenses.

Once Columbus reached Santa Fe, his proposal underwent a new inquiry, conducted by a "council composed of the most eminent men" of the royal court, augmented by experts in law, astronomy, and navigation, and once again presided over by Hernando de Talavera. Disastrously for Columbus, the council confirmed the judgment of the earlier commission: his proposal did not impress a panel of experts. A witness to these events, Miguel Toro, testifying in a lawsuit in 1514, was asked whether *"it was public knowledge and well known that before the Indies were discovered . . . many wise men and letrados and mariners said that it was not possible"* that they would discover the Indies. Toro replied that he had *"heard many people express the contents of the question while he was in the Real de Granada."*[37] The decision of the council, however well-founded, was the final blow for Columbus. He set out on the road for Córdoba, the first planned stop on his journey to France. After seven weary years, he abandoned hope of securing support for his scheme and his ambitions in Spain and headed off to find it elsewhere.

Then King Fernando stepped in. Up to that point, Queen Isabel had been in charge of the negotiations with Columbus, with her confessor Talavera coordinating most of the necessary staff work. For reasons unstated in the documents, the king ordered Talavera and Deza to see if something could be arranged after all. Years later, Fernando would remember his crucial action when he said, in 1508, *"It was I [who was] the principal cause why those islands were discovered."*[38] The queen was finally persuaded by Luis de Santángel, an Aragonese who was manager of the king's household accounts (*escribano de ración*). Santángel's argument was eminently practical: backing Columbus would be a cheap gamble, with comparatively little risk for a potentially great reward. The opportunity should be seized; if not, Columbus would go to a foreign power, which would reap all the potential benefits if the gamble paid off. Isabel agreed and sent out a royal guard (*alguacil de corte*) to find Columbus and escort him back to court. He was 2 leagues north at the bridge of Pinos, on his way to Córdoba, when the rider reached him. He turned back to Granada and into the pages of history.

His joy might have been tempered had he realized that the royal couple had not necessarily been converted to his way of thinking. Instead, they were willing to risk a relatively small sum to keep any potential profit from the hands of their rivals. In a letter of May 1493, just after Columbus's return from the first voyage, Pietro Martire d'Anghiera said flatly that Columbus finally got his ships through strong negotiating, because the Catholic Monarchs did not really believe him. And Columbus's own son Diego admitted that the rulers had provided support despite their lack of faith that the venture would succeed.[39]

Meanwhile at court the talk turned to the question of where to find the money to outfit the voyage. The royal treasury was dangerously drained. By the next year the monarchs would have to pay over 24 million maravedis to the Muslims for relinquishing Granada. The biography of Columbus attributed to his son Hernando reported that Isabel offered to pawn her jewels for the Columbus venture.[40] If she actually made such an offer, it would not have been the first time she had raised money in that way. In 1491, some of her jewels were already pawned and had been for two years. She still had others available, but pawning them turned out to be unnecessary. Luis de Santángel solved the dilemma by promising to find the money, which he did by shifting funds among various government bodies. The money came in the first instance from the treasury of the Santa Hermandad, the national organization overseeing the rural militias of Castile. Talavera was joint treasurer of the Hermandad, and as its income passed into his control he used it to pay the expenses of preparing Columbus's small fleet. Later the Hermandad was reimbursed from other government funds.[41] Deficit financing and fiscal maneuvering were not invented in the twentieth century.

With the money secured, the final details could be arranged. Columbus presented a proposal (*memorial*) with his demands for compensation, and his contract with the crown was worked out in a series of negotiations held in the house of Isabel's secretary Fernando Alvarez. Juan de Coloma acted for the monarchs, and Juan Pérez acted for Columbus. The final document that emerged from their discussions, called the Capitulaciones de Santa Fe (Capitulations of Santa Fe), followed a standard form of agreement or contract in fifteenth-century Castile, with specific points arranged in separate paragraphs or chapters (*capítulos*).

We know very little about the negotiations that produced the Capitulations of Santa Fe, but by their terms Columbus secured impressive concessions from the crown. The monarchs agreed to grant him noble status, together with the offices of admiral, viceroy, and governor general, in all the islands and mainlands that he might claim for Castile in the Atlantic. These royal gifts would become effective only after the discoveries and the claims were made. A royal letter of April 30, 1492, spelled out what Columbus would receive in return for his discoveries. The letter also offered more detail than the capitulations themselves on the offices and noble status he was to receive, which were to remain hereditary in Columbus's descendants. The capitulations had been signed some two weeks earlier, on April 17, 1492. The original versions are no longer extant; the earliest version available is contained in the confirmations issued by the crown in Barcelona in 1493, after Columbus had returned from his first voyage.

The first sentence of the confirmation of 1493 somewhat confusingly refers to the successful completion of the first voyage and to the second voyage then being planned. Afterward, the original capitulations are copied. Columbus and his heirs would hold the office of admiral of the islands and continents he would discover. He would be viceroy and governor general for all the discoveries, with the right to nominate the governor of each island. The offices of viceroy and governor general were not to be hereditary in Columbus's family, however; he would hold those offices at the pleasure of the crown. Regarding profits from the venture: after deductions for expenses, one-tenth would go to Columbus, and nine-tenths would go to the

crown. The agreement also cited the rights and obligations of Columbus as admiral. In modern times, the title "admiral" usually ap-
plies to a naval officer in charge of a fleet. In the agreements negotiated with Columbus, however, a better translation of *almirante* would
be "chief judge of the admiralty court," for Columbus, as admiral,
received the right to judge all disputes arising from commerce in the
lands that he discovered. Finally, Columbus could if he wished invest up to one-eighth of the cost of any "ships outfitted for trade and
business." If he did so, he would be entitled to a proportionate share
of any profits made.[42]

Interestingly enough, the agreement made no mention of Asia.
This omission led some historians, early in this century, to suggest
that Columbus never intended to go to Asia at all but only to discover new lands.[43] Among the documents Fernando and Isabel gave
Columbus for the voyage, however, was a letter of introduction to
the Great Khan. Moreover, on his first voyage he took with him an
interpreter who knew (among other languages) some Arabic, which
was understood in many parts of India and, presumably, would be
understood in East Asia as well. That the articles of agreement did
not mention Asia explicitly probably reflected a Castilian desire to
avoid the appearance of encroaching on the Portuguese monopoly
on new discoveries in the Atlantic south of the Canaries and toward
Africa. The agreements of Alcáçovas in 1479 had explicitly barred
Castile from such ventures. During his first voyage, Columbus carefully sailed due west from the Canaries and was reluctant to deviate
to the south. He may well have been instructed in this by the crown.

The total cost of the voyage was projected at 2 million maravedis.
It is impossible to reconstruct all of the financial arrangements for
the voyage. According to Las Casas, Columbus contributed 500,000
maravedis to the venture, but it is not altogether clear where he might
have got that sum. For years he had been living on his income from
business dealings, with periodic supplements from the crown. For a
capital outlay of such magnitude he might well have needed to borrow, but from whom? Recent research suggests that he borrowed
from Italian merchants, notably from the Florentine Juanoto Berardi,
a slave trader since at least 1486 and a man who remained closely
linked to Columbus until Berardi's death in 1495. In his will he said
he had been dealing with Columbus for three years. Thus Berardi is
the likely source of at least part of the 500,000 maravedis that Columbus contributed to the voyage. The Catholic Monarchs contributed 1,140,000 maravedis out of the funds Santángel shifted from
the Santa Hermandad. One million maravedis were to go toward the
general expenses of the voyage, and 140,000 maravedis comprised

Columbus's salary as captain general (*capitán mayor*) of the fleet.[44] The town of Palos was obliged to put up the rest of the money, as we will discuss in the next chapter. With the agreements duly signed and the finances settled, Columbus was ready to begin preparations for the long-awaited voyage.

7

The First Voyage

AFTER THE CONCLUSION of his negotiations with the crown, Columbus left Granada on May 12, 1492. On the way to the southwestern coast he detoured through Córdoba to see Beatriz Enríquez de Arana and their son Hernando and persuaded Beatriz's cousin, Diego de Arana, to join his expedition as marshal (*alguacil mayor*) of the fleet. Columbus arrived in Palos, where his fleet was to be outfitted, sometime before May 23. Even though Palos proved very important for his enterprise, we are not sure why that particular town had been selected, rather than some other Andalusian port. From Columbus's point of view, the most likely reason lay in the connections he had formed in the area defined by the Tinto and Odiel rivers, where Huelva, Palos, and Moguer formed an economic unit. Columbus's sister-in-law and her husband still lived in Huelva, where Columbus and his son Diego had previously stayed. Besides, in his visit to the area in 1491 he had become friendly with Friar Juan Pérez and his brother Franciscans at La Rábida. Their influence, especially Pérez's, might be needed in raising a crew among the tightly knit communities of mariners that defined the region.[1]

Experienced masters, pilots, and sailors were certainly available in all three ports. Many of them had sailed down the African coast in the days before the treaties of Alcáçovas-Toledo had prohibited Spaniards from sailing south of Cape Bojador. Above all, they made a living from Atlantic fishing, sustaining themselves and their families in the coastal tuna fisheries, or *almadrabas,* that had been in operation for centuries. In the early fifteenth century, fishermen from the Atlantic ports of Andalusia began to fish the banks along the African coast between the Canary Islands and the Sahara Desert. With this new source of supply, fish became not only an important component of the Andalusian diet but a major contributor to the area's commercial prosperity as well. In Palos, fishing and shipbuilding were sustaining activities of the working population. When some tuna fishers from Palos violated the royal prohibition on venturing south of Cape Bojador in 1491, the town's penalty was to pay for two caravels for the crown's use.[2] Fernando and Isabel assigned those caravels to Columbus's expedition, making Palos a logical choice for the embarkation point.

Another circumstance made Palos attractive from the crown's point of view. In the spring of 1492, the larger ports of Seville and Cádiz were filled with ships taking Spanish Jews into exile. July 31 marked the deadline (later extended for nine days) for the departure of Jews who chose to keep their religion rather than convert to Christianity and remain. Similar expulsions had occurred in England in 1295 and in France in 1306. The rising tide of ethnic and religious hostility caught up with Spain in 1492, adding an ironic twist to Columbus's preparations. While he searched for Spaniards willing to brave the unknown on his expedition, another group of Spaniards was being forced into unwilling exile.

Palos had first been settled in the 1380s and by the time of Columbus had some three thousand inhabitants. It was owned by a three-part consortium of nobles: Pedro de Silva, count of Cifuentes, with his brothers and sisters, owned half the town; Pedro de Zúñiga, count of Miranda, and Enrique de Guzmán, duke of Medina Sidonia, owned the rest. In June of 1492, Queen Isabel bought the Silvas' half of Palos, including the port. This purchase, which entailed an expenditure of 16 million maravedis at a time when the treasury was already strained, was part of a conscious maritime strategy. Royal support for Columbus formed part of that strategy, as did the crown's assumption of direct control over the final conquests in the Canaries. Fernando and Isabel had begun their reign without control of any southern port, with the notable exception of the inland city of Seville on the Guadalquivir River. Not only Palos, but all of Andalusia's Atlantic ports were in the hands of nobles when Isabel became queen of Castile. Rodrigo Ponce de León controlled Cádiz and Rota. The duke of Medinaceli held Puerto de Santa María. Sanlúcar de Barrameda, Chipiona, and Huelva belonged to the duke of Medina Sidonia, and Moguer was under the Puertocarrero family. Fernando and Isabel's purchase of half of Palos was only part of their effort to acquire Atlantic ports. Around 1480 they had built a totally new port – Puerto Real – on the shoreline of the Bay of Cádiz controlled by Jerez de la Frontera, a royal city. With the end of the Granadan war in early 1492, they acquired Almería, Málaga, and the rest of the Mediterranean ports formerly controlled by the Muslim kings of Granada. In January of 1493 they took over Cádiz, following the death of Rodrigo Ponce de León, compensating his family with the town of Casares, near Ronda, and a payment of 10 million maravedis.[3] Columbus's voyage and other Atlantic ventures would be anchored securely in ports controlled by the crown.

THE SHIPS AND CREW

On May 23, 1492, Columbus and Friar Juan Pérez from the monastery of La Rábida went to the church of San Jorge in Palos for a public meeting. There the town clerk (*escribano*) read a royal proclamation announcing Columbus's voyage to an impressive assembly of local officials. The document stated that the monarchs had appointed Christopher Columbus as captain general (*capitán mayor*) of an armada of three caravels – as it turned out, two small caravels and a larger *nao* – to sail to certain parts of the ocean sea, avoiding Mina and its trading region on the African coast, which were reserved by treaty to the Portuguese. In support of the expedition, the officials of Palos had to pay for the use of two caravels with their crews and provisions for two months. The balance of the rental fee would be borne by Columbus and his financial backers. The crown would pay the ships' crews four months' salary in advance. After hearing the proclamation, the local officials affirmed that they would make sure the royal will was carried out. Columbus then went to the nearby town of Moguer, where he published another royal proclamation, this one calling for the people of Andalusia to allow him to purchase the equipment and provisions he needed for the voyage.

In fairly short order, Columbus requisitioned two caravels in Moguer on Palos's account, using the royal decree as his authority. One was the *Santa Clara,* built in Moguer and commonly called *Niña* after its owner Juan Niño. The other was the *Pinta,* owned by Cristóbal Quintero. Columbus himself chartered the third vessel, a *nao* called the *Santa María,* built in Galicia and often referred to as *La Gallega.* Its owner was Juan de la Cosa, born in Santoña on Castile's northern coast and resident in Puerto de Santa María.[4] Columbus had probably met him several years earlier when he was a guest of the duke of Medinaceli, the lord of that port.

Requisitioning the caravels and chartering the *nao* were simple business transactions; persuading officers and sailors to sign on as crew proved to be much more difficult and complicated. At first Columbus had little success, even with the help of the Franciscans of la Rábida. Only after he struck a deal with a prominent local shipowner named Martín Alonso Pinzón did the crew begin to take shape.

At the time, Pinzón was a man in his early forties. He had owned ships and traded in the Mediterranean and the Atlantic for most of his adult life. He had visited Lisbon and the Canaries, and he had probably been to Guinea as well. Like many other mariners, he occasionally engaged in piracy as well as legitimate trade. For example, in 1479 he seized a vessel from Ibiza loaded with wheat and took it to Palos to sell. Unfortunately for him, local authorities confiscated the load, but his reputation as the best-known shipowner in the region hardly suffered from the experience. When Columbus first tried to raise a crew, Martín Alonso was at sea, delivering a cargo of sardines to Rome. Years later, in the court cases embroiling the Columbus and Pinzón families and the crown, witnesses recalled him with admiration. One said that he *"was eager and held to be a very wise man expert in the matters of sailing, and that he was a rich and well-connected man and one of the principal ones that there were at that time in Palos, and there was no one else so renowned as Martín Alonso Pinzón."*[5]

His family had wide maritime connections, and Martín Alonso's two sons were carrying on the family tradition. The elder son, Arias Pérez Pinzón, born about 1470, was in Palos when the 1492 fleet left; thereafter he traveled to Flanders and was back in Bayona (in Galicia) in time to meet his father, who was returning from the newly discovered island of Española. Juan Martín Pinzón, the second son, was born about 1475. He too was in Palos when the 1492 expedition left and sailed to Madeira soon after his father's return. In other words, the Pinzón family seemed quite at home in Atlantic waters.

The younger brother of Martín Alonso Pinzón, Vicente Yáñez Pinzón, was born in the early 1460s. Local people regarded him, like his brother, as a distinguished and honorable person. The historian Gonzalo Fernández de Oviedo considered Vicente Yáñez *"one of the best-spoken men of the sea whom I have seen and who best understood his art."*[6] Nonetheless, like his brother he may have dabbled in piracy. A Catalan account in 1477 related that a *"Vicens Anes Pinsón, from the town of Pals,"* commanded a caravel engaged in piracy along the coast of Catalonia, in company with two caravels from Seville. Vicente Yáñez Pinzón would have been no more than about seventeen years old in 1477, and there is no conclusive proof that the pirate named was one and the same with the younger brother of Martín Alonzo Pinzón; nonetheless, many historians have assumed that was the case.[7] Trade, war, and piracy were often interchangeable in the fifteenth century.[8] Whatever the truth of allegations of piracy against the Pinzones, they had learned their considerable maritime skills in the pirate-infested waters that surrounded Spain.

Sometime in June of 1492, Martín Alonso returned to Palos from Rome.[9] With encouragement from the Franciscans of La Rábida, he then began to negotiate with Columbus. It seems clear from the documents that Columbus made his agreements with the Pinzón brothers only after concluding negotiations with the Spanish monarchs at Santa Fe. In other words, a prior agreement with the Pinzones was not the reason he chose Palos.[10] Fragmentary evidence suggests the nature and contents of the discussions between Pinzón and Columbus, who seems to have made his pitch on the basis of Toscanelli's letter and map. He produced a sailing chart – either Toscanelli's or his own adaptation of it – and extolled the riches of Japan in the manner of Toscanelli and Marco Polo, by saying that the temples and royal houses were roofed with gold.[11]

Columbus and Pinzón met at least once in the house of an old mariner named Pedro Vázquez de la Frontera, who lived in Palos and had a history of his own in Atlantic exploration. Forty years before, he had sailed with the legendary Portuguese Diogo de Teive in search of lands to the west. Starting from the island of Fayal, in the Azores, they had sailed southwest for about 150 leagues (560–600 miles), observed the sea grasses of the Sargasso Sea, turned back toward the Azores, there discovered the western islands of Flores and Corvo, and then sailed north to the latitude of Cape Clear in Ireland. Vázquez encouraged Columbus and Pinzón to try the venture and not to fear the grasses, which were harmless if disconcerting.[12]

Martín Alonso was impressed by Columbus's presentation and the corroboration provided by Vázquez. He threw in his lot with the mariner from Genoa, promising by the royal crown that neither he nor his relatives would return to Palos without discovering land to the west.[13] Martín Alonso accepted command of the *Pinta* from Columbus and persuaded his brother Vicente Yáñez Pinzón to join the expedition as captain of the *Niña*. Together, the Pinzón brothers took responsibility for raising the crew.

Despite his local reputation, Martín Alonso still faced a difficult task. Many local seamen needed to be convinced of the wisdom of the venture before signing on. The reasons for their reluctance and the effect this had on the composition of the final crew have been variously interpreted, but two misguided notions should be laid to rest at once. The first asserts that because all sailors believed the earth was flat they feared sailing off the edge by going too far west. The notion that everyone but Columbus believed in a flat earth seems to be a modern misconception. Its origins are unclear, but they may stem from the "T-O" maps. In showing the land masses of the Old World at the center of a circle and surrounded by a band of ocean, the T-O maps attempted to present three-dimensional reality in a two-dimensional medium – the flat paper or parchment of a book or map. Modern writers without a sense of historical cartography may have seen the T-O maps as evidence of belief in a flat earth. We can only speculate. In reality, educated people all over Europe knew the earth was spherical; the knowledge had been commonplace for a thousand years. Even people without much formal education could observe proof of a spherical earth. A farmer walking to market watched for the steeples of the town to appear on the horizon and gradually "rise" into view. A sailor long at sea watched for the first sight of land in the same manner. It took very little imagination to know that the earth was a giant sphere and that every road and ocean curved over its external skin. Although we cannot exclude the possibility that some ignorant Europeans thought the earth was flat, presumably the experienced sailors whom Columbus and the Pinzones tried to enlist knew otherwise. They also had sufficient knowledge of Atlantic sailing to regard voyages into the deep ocean without terror. Yet voyages far beyond the familiar space of the eastern Atlantic did hold real terrors. The sailors of Palos and Moguer disliked the uncertainties of a new route, without a guarantee of being able to return safely, let alone of finding anything worthwhile. The sailors who declined to go with Columbus and the Pinzones clearly preferred to let others be in the vanguard of exploration.

One of those who stayed behind was Pedro Arias, who later testified that even though Martín Alonso Pinzón asked him to go he did not want to, because it was an uncertain thing at the time. He was far from alone in that opinion. Many believed that there was no land to be found a safe distance to the west. Juan Rodríguez de Mafra, who said he was in Palos when the first fleet was being prepared, also said that he declined to enlist *"because it was a vain thing and he thought they would not find land."*[14] Bartolomé Colín, who in fact signed up but backed out before the voyage began, summed up the local attitude by saying that people commonly believed and said *"that there was no land in that part of the world, because it had been sought from Portugal many times"* and that Columbus's effort would come to nothing.[15]

The second misconception about Columbus's crew members relates to the first. Because the best sailors feared falling off the edge of the flat earth, the story goes, the crew had to be signed on from condemned criminals, who, presumably, were desperate enough to take the risk. In fact, of approximately ninety men who accompanied Columbus and the Pinzones on the first voyage in 1492, three had come directly from the public jail. One of the men had been charged with murdering the town crier of Palos, and the other two had been charged with breaking the accused out of jail. They were evidently not considered a threat to public safety and were granted a shortened sentence if they would sign on for the voyage. Although three in ninety hardly qualifies as an expedition of jailbirds, the fact that criminals were signed on at all testifies to the difficulties of filling the crew.

Once the Pinzón brothers agreed to support Columbus, they worked vigorously to overcome local misgivings about the voyage. Martín

Alonso was the chief recruiter and made his pitch on the basis of the riches to be gained. Years later a witness recalled Martín Alonso saying, *"Friends, come on, make this journey with us, instead of moping around being miserable; make this journey, for with the help of God we will discover land, for according to rumor we will find houses roofed with gold and everyone will come home rich and fortunate."*[16] Although Pinzón may have known the Asian stories already, it is more likely that Columbus was his source for this obvious echo of Marco Polo and Toscanelli. With the vigorous recruiting of Martín Alonso and other members of his family, preparations shifted into high gear. Columbus and the Pinzones began signing up crew members on June 23, and within a little over a month they had filled the rosters. By then the three vessels were ready to sail and loaded with enough provisions to last for a year.

We know a good deal about the crew members who finally sailed on the voyage, thanks primarily to the work of a remarkable American named Alice Bache Gould. An independent scholar from a wealthy intellectual family in New England, she spent decades researching the life histories of the men who dared to join Columbus and the Pinzones.[17] The men whose lives she chronicled represented a cross section of maritime society in southwestern Spain in the late fifteenth century.

On board the flagship, named *Santa María* and nicknamed *La Gallega* for its Galician origins, forty men served. Thirty-seven of them have been identified. Christopher Columbus acted as the flagship's captain, as well as the captain general of the small fleet of three vessels. Juan de la Cosa, the ship's owner, served as its master for the voyage, keeping track of rations and equipment and performing the general administrative duties aboard ship. Peralonso Niño, from the Niño family of Moguer, served as pilot, although Columbus actually set the course and Niño merely carried out his orders. Diego de Arana, cousin of Columbus's lover Beatriz, served as *alguacil* or marshal, presumably responsible for keeping order among the men in the fleet. The flagship also carried a notary named Rodrigo de Escobedo, a surgeon named Juan Sánchez, and an interpreter named Luis de Torres. Torres knew several languages, including a bit of Arabic, which, it was hoped, would enable him to communicate with people across the ocean, especially in Asia. Torres happened to be a converted Jew, but no particular significance should be attached to that fact. It is sometimes claimed that Torres was chosen because the secret purpose of the voyage was to find a new homeland for the Jews of Europe. There is no proof whatsoever to support this claim. No doubt his language skills alone made Torres a desirable member of the expedition. If anyone who knew Chinese or Japanese could have been found in Spain, Torres probably would have been replaced. In addition to these men, the flagship carried eight additional officers, eleven able seamen, ten apprentice seamen, and a page, plus another three men whose names and duties have not been discovered.

The larger of the two caravels was called *Pinta,* although it may have had a more formal saint's name as well. Martín Alonso Pinzón served as its captain, with his brother Francisco Martín Pinzón as its master. The ship's owner, Cristóbal Quintero, accompanied the expedition (albeit reluctantly) as an able seaman, and Cristóbal García Sarmiento was ship's pilot. In addition, the *Pinta* carried four other officers, ten able seamen, and eight apprentice seamen, for a total of twenty-six men.

The smaller caravel, named *Santa Clara* and nicknamed *Niña,* was captained by Vicente Yáñez Pinzón, the third Pinzón brother to accompany the expedition. Juan Niño, who owned the ship and for whom it was nicknamed, served as its master. The pilot was Sancho Ruíz de Gama. Four other officers, eight able seamen, six apprentice seamen, and three other men whose positions are unknown, made up the total of twenty-four men on the *Niña.* Significantly, the owners of all three ships chose to accompany the expedition, no doubt anxious to keep a close eye on their property, as well as to share in any good fortune that came their way. And the notable presence of the Pinzones confirms that their recruitment efforts were sincere. Overall, the men on the expedition had ample experience of ocean sailing and had been toughened by years at sea. Their compensation for the voyage was standard for the time: the masters and pilots earned 2,000 maravedis per month, the sailors earned 1,000, and the apprentices 666. All together, salaries accounted for 250,000 maravedis of the 2 million maravedis that the expedition cost.

Surprisingly, for all we know about the crews, we know almost nothing about the ships. In fact, the relative numbers of crewmen on the *Santa María,* the *Pinta,* and the *Niña* provide some of the only firm evidence we have about the size of the ships themselves. Two other pieces of evidence help a bit. An Italian named Michele de Cuneo, who accompanied Columbus on his second voyage and wrote a lively account of their activities, mentioned in passing that the *Niña* was about 60 *toneladas.*[18] Assuming this was the same *Niña* that sailed in the 1492 expedition, we at least have an estimate for the smallest ship in the fleet. Recently, other information has been found for the rigging and life history of the *Niña.*[19] The only other evidence discovered for the 1492 fleet is a remark by a writer nearly a century later that Columbus's ships were small, with the largest *"very little larger than 100* toneladas.*"*[20] We also have some information about the rigging and equipment of the ships from comments that Colum-

Carrack or *nao* of the late fifteenth century, the ship type of Columbus's flagship *Santa María,* shown with a typical ship's boat. (From Bernhard von Breydenbach, *Peregrinatio in Terram Sanctam* [Mainz: E. Reuwick, 1486]. Photo courtesy of the James Ford Bell Library, University of Minnesota.)

bus made in the on-board diary of the voyage. For example, we know that each ship carried or towed a small launch or boat for going ashore and for communicating between the ships at sea. Using these bits and pieces of evidence, plus what is known or assumed about other ships of the time and about the meaning of a *tonelada,* scholars have tried to estimate the sizes and configurations of the *Santa María,* the *Pinta,* and the *Niña.*

Without getting into the technicalities of those arguments, we can be sure at least that all three ships were fairly small for ocean voyaging. The largest, *Santa María,* was a *nao,* probably fairly typical of merchant vessels of the time. It would have carried square sails on a foremast and a mainmast, with topsails for each one, and a triangular lateen sail on a mizzenmast at the rear of the ship. Given the estimate of just over 100 *toneladas,* and the size of the crew, this ship was probably no more than 19.2 feet in maximum width or beam, and no longer than 38.5 feet along the keel and 57.7 feet on the lower of its two decks. The depth in the hold, measured from the lower deck down to the floor laid on top of the keel, was probably no more than 9.6 feet. These are all gross estimates, based on the general shape of merchant *naos* of the time, but they would have resulted in a ship measuring about 108 *toneladas,* according to official Spanish formulas for measuring ships.[21] The caravels *Pinta* and *Niña* were somewhat smaller, at about 75 *toneladas* and under 60 *toneladas* respectively. We estimate the *Pinta*'s dimensions at a maximum of 17.6 feet wide, 42.2 feet along the keel, 55.1 feet in length, and 7.6 feet in depth of the hold beneath its one deck. The *Niña*'s measurements would have been similar, at no more than 15.9 feet wide, 38.5 feet along the keel, 49.8 feet long, and 6.8 feet deep. The *Pinta* was rigged like the *Santa María;* the *Niña* would begin the voyage rigged with two lateen sails.

The date of departure for the little fleet was set for the early morning of August 3, a Friday. August 2 was an important religious holiday for the region, the feast of Nuestra Señora de los Angeles (or Porciúncula), the patroness of the monastery of La Rábida. There could be no question of missing the event, given the importance of La Rábida and its Franciscans to the region and to all on board the three ships.[22] An hour before dawn on August 3, the three ships left Palos, headed down the Tinto River past La Rábida on the left bank and then into the Atlantic. The first leg of their voyage was an easy sail that would take them to the Canary Islands. Tradition has it that on the same morning that Columbus's small fleet left Palos, a group of ships carrying the last of Spain's Jews into exile also sailed from Palos. The year 1492 marked the last medieval expulsion of Jews from western Europe, even as it marked the discovery of the New World of the Western Hemisphere.

THE CANARY ISLANDS

Columbus's choice of the Canaries as the real starting point for the Atlantic crossing was either his greatest stroke of luck or the proof of his genius as a mariner. Columbus himself was silent on the matter, but the islands are ideally suited as a point of departure for transatlantic sailing, even today. Those with little faith in Columbus's seafaring skills might believe that he chose the Canaries fortuitously, only because they were under Castilian, rather than Portuguese, control. He knew that his commission from the Spanish crown would guarantee help from royal officials in the Canaries to reprovision and to make any repairs that might prove necessary. Following this logic, one could argue that if Columbus had sailed under Portuguese sponsorship, he might have tried to start from the Madeiras or – even worse – from the Azores. But Columbus knew the winds and currents of the eastern Atlantic fairly well. He also knew that Portuguese expeditions trying to sail west from the Azores had all been forced back by head winds. In other words, Columbus's experience in the Atlantic suggests that he chose the Canaries for nautical, not political, reasons. Those who believe in Columbus's genius are tempted to think that he had full knowledge about Atlantic wind patterns before the first voyage. In our judgment, such an interpretation assumes too much. Columbus believed that Japan lay directly west of the Canaries, and he knew that the fall and winter winds usually blow from east to west in that latitude. He gambled on his assumption that the prevailing winds would carry him across the Atlantic to Japan at the latitude of the Canaries. His actions on the return voyage, however, suggest that he had not mastered the full implications of the elliptical wind patterns in the Atlantic, as we will see.

On the voyage to the Canaries, the *Pinta* had handling problems and twice suffered damage to her rudder. Columbus suspected sabotage on the part of Gómez Rascón and Cristóbal Quintero, *Pinta*'s owner, who had not wanted to go on the voyage. Columbus also was upset because he could not aid the *Pinta* without endangering his own ship, but he trusted Martín Alonso Pinzón to carry on capably. Columbus left Martín Alonso and the *Pinta* off the island of Gran Canaria while he took the other two ships to the island of Gomera to top off their provisions. After the *Pinta*'s repairs were completed, she joined the others at Gomera. The *Niña* had not been handling well either, so she was rerigged at Gomera, from a two-masted lateen to a three-masted combination of square and lateen sails, like the other two ships.

With last-minute preparations made, water barrels filled, and firewood and fresh meat loaded on, the fleet was ready to set sail. Columbus reminded his fellow officers and the crew about the royal instructions he had received – to go exploring directly to the west without deviating to the south – and issued his own, standing fleet orders. He warned the men that they should not expect to find land before they had gone 750 leagues (2,800–3,000 miles). To make sure that they did not come unexpectedly upon reefs or islands, after they had gone 700 leagues they would no longer sail all night but stop at midnight and resume their voyage the following dawn.[23] In ordinary sailing conditions, the three vessels would be scattered over a large area, due to their varying sailing characteristics. The *Pinta* was the fastest of the three, and both caravels were faster than the *Santa María*. Columbus ordered the two caravels to close up with his flagship twice each day, at dawn and sunset. In addition to exchanging general information, they could compare their readings of the wind and sea, as dawn and sunset were generally best for long-distance sightings. At other times a cannon shot would signal the ships to assemble, and the first ship to see land would fire a cannon and raise a flag to the top of the highest mast. With everything ready, a little over a month after having left Palos, the fleet began its voyage into the unknown, on September 6, 1492, from the island of Gomera.[24]

ACROSS THE ATLANTIC

After losing sight of Hierro, the last island in the Canaries, on September 9, they sailed along the northern edge of the belt of northeast trade winds. Columbus and the ships' pilots navigated by dead reckoning, using direction, time, and speed to plot their course and position. That meant determining direction by compass, time by a sand-clock marking the half hours, and speed by eye and feel. Columbus kept a diary of each day's events, carefully marking down his estimate of the distance traveled. In the prologue of the diary he also promised to keep a maritime chart indicating the lands the expedition encountered. Unfortunately, the original diary and chart have disappeared. All that remains is an abstract of the diary, made by Bartolomé de Las Casas. Las Casas often summarized Columbus's entries in the diary, rather than quoting them directly, and he was not a mariner. There are many puzzling passages in his summary, probably attributable to Las Casas's unfamiliarity with the sea. Even when he said he was quoting Columbus directly, we cannot be sure he quoted accurately. And even if he quoted accurately, Columbus's peculiar spelling and sentence structure clouded the meaning in many places. For all these reasons, any conclusions based on the abstracted diary about the course and speed of the voyage are impossible to prove.[25] Only if the original diary is found some day will we be able to analyze it seriously. Until then, all we have is Las Casas's flawed abstract. Fortunately, an excellent new edition of the abstract has recently been published, with a transcription of Las Casas's manuscript in Spanish and a good translation in English on facing pages.[26] By paying attention to the language, a careful reader can begin to sort out the parts by Las Casas and the parts by Columbus.

According to Las Casas, Columbus made two sets of calculations for the distance traveled, in order to deceive the crew into thinking that they had sailed less far than Columbus knew they had. Periodically in his summary of Columbus's diary, Las Casas reported that the admiral made two estimations of distance, one for himself and one for the crew. This notion of a "false log" passed into the mythology of Columbus and is mentioned in virtually every discussion of the 1492 voyage. Nonetheless, the false-log theory does not make sense. Columbus would have had to fool not only the sailors on his own ship but also the captains, masters, and pilots on the other two ships, all of whom were presumably experienced navigators. On several occasions during the voyage, the pilots of all three vessels compared their calculations, and there is no hint that Columbus had to persuade them to accept his figures. A much more likely explanation for the dual calculations is simply that Las Casas misunderstood the diary. Instead of making a false log for the crew, Columbus first calculated the distance traveled by a method he had learned as a young mariner; then he calculated the equivalent in terms the crew understood. A similar situation arises when modern travelers move back and forth between countries that use miles and those that use kilometers. In figuring the distance they have gone, travelers tend to start with the system they know better and then calculate the equivalent in the other system, if need be. The mysterious and slightly sinister false log that Las Casas postulated may be no more mysterious than that, and not sinister at all.[27] We cannot know for sure until and unless the original version of the diary is found.

The voyage was rather short – just thirty-three days from the Canaries to the Caribbean – and mainly uneventful. The little fleet encountered good weather, mainly calm seas, and remarkably little dissension. From September 16 on, Columbus said, they encountered fair weather akin to April in Seville, an evocative phrase for anyone who has ever experienced the warm, soft days of spring in Andalusia. Also in mid-September they first encountered the sea grasses of the Sargasso Sea, which they had been warned not to fear by the old mariner back in Palos. Instead of fear, they felt hope, believing the Sargasso grasses to be plants torn from nearby land. During such a quiet and uneventful voyage, there was time to watch the sea and sky carefully for signs and portents. Officers and crew alike closely noted each sighting of birds, identifying them and indicating whether they were seabirds or land birds, for they believed that land birds would not be far from land. They were all aware that the Portuguese had followed flights of birds to locate previously unknown islands. In fact, journal entries from September 16 on record a steady stream of signs that the men on board interpreted as indicating nearby land, including – in addition to the birds – whales and dolphins at sea, and crabs on the surface of the Sargasso grasses. Nevertheless, Columbus believed the mainland to lie due west and was unwilling to lose time beating around looking for islands.

Life on board ship cannot have been pleasant by modern standards.[28] On the *Santa María,* forty men lived and worked together in a cramped space, and conditions were similar on the two caravels. Only the chief officers would have had enclosed quarters for sleeping and stowing their belongings. The rest of the men would have simply staked out some corner as their own, trying to stay out of the way of lines and tackle for the working of the ship. Sanitary facilities were almost nonexistent. For bathing, a bucket of water could be hauled out of the sea, if anyone were so inclined. For toilet facilities, a seat suspended over the edge of the ship sufficed. Presumably, fastidious passengers might prefer the privacy of a bucket, but lifelong sailors probably did without such niceties.

The abstracted diary of the voyage says nothing about living conditions on board, but there is no reason that Columbus would have mentioned them, even in his original diary. Like other experienced mariners, he accepted the crowding, the discomfort, the poor food, and all the rest as the price one paid for going to sea. In fact, most of what we know about shipboard life in the early days of ocean travel comes from accounts written by reluctant landsmen who were passengers on those voyages, not by mariners. The shipboard diet would not have differed much from the diet on land, except that ship's biscuit (twice-baked small loaves of bread) would have been the staple instead of fresh bread. Legume stews with salted meat and fish, presumably seasoned with onions, garlic, and olive oil, constituted the main meal of the day at sea as they would have on land. The main difference was that on land fresh meat and fish would have been more common. At sea, only salted and dried foods lasted long enough to be carried in quantity. Ships provisioned in Andalusia would carry local white wine, which traveled much better than fresh water, as a major source of calories and good morale. A few exotic items such as raisins, almonds, and eggs would be carried as special curatives for anyone who fell sick. Fresh water and some fresh food would usually be the last supplies taken on board before a voyage. Nonetheless, after a relatively short time at sea, fresh food and water would begin to spoil. Even biscuit and other dried foods would absorb the moist air and unavoidably decay, especially in warm weather. If vermin got into the supplies, as they almost invariably did, the decay proceeded even more rapidly. By the end of any voyage that lasted more than a week or two, everyone on board must have longed for fresh, appetizing food in place of the questionable fare they were forced to eat. The landsmen noticed these things more than the mariners, but even experienced crews could become irritable and anxious after several weeks at sea. This was all the more true on Columbus's first voyage, when they sailed uncharted seas, long out of sight of land.

For over two weeks, until about the twenty-second of September, the winds were so regular and the seas so calm that the crew began to complain. They feared that those conditions meant that there would never be favorable or sufficient winds to take them back to Spain. On the twenty-second, Martín Alonso Pinzón on the *Pinta,* asked for Columbus's chart, which indicated certain islands. After studying the chart for several days, Pinzón, was convinced that they were in the vicinity of the islands. He shared his conclusions with Columbus on the twenty-fifth and returned the chart to him by means of a line stretched between their two ships. Columbus also began to calculate their position on the chart, with the help of his pilot and other sailors on the *Santa María.*

That very evening, Martín Alonso Pinzón called out from the poop of the *Pinta* that he saw land, to the great excitement of all three crews. In thanks and relief, the crews said the "Gloria in excelsis deo," probably adding it to the regular prayers that they said every day at nightfall. Several men climbed the masts and rigging and confirmed the sighting. Columbus believed the land to lie about 25 leagues (under 100 miles) off to the southwest, and the fleet changed course to approach it. The next day, with breezes sweet and soft, and with the sea as calm as a river, they had to admit disappointment. The men and their leaders had seen a mirage, and in their eagerness to find land they had persuaded themselves that it was real.

Resuming their westward course, the ships sailed for several more days, until on October 3, Columbus believed they had gone beyond the place where he had charted islands. Nonetheless he was determined to press on westward toward what he considered to be the mainland of Asia. He probably did this in large part to maintain his authority over the captains and their crews. He had told them to expect land due west of the Canaries. Allowing side excursions in search of islands would diminish the aura of certainty that he had been at pains to project.[29] On October 6, Martín Alonso Pinzón asked Columbus to change course to the southwest, which caused Columbus to suspect that Pinzón wanted to seek Cipango and its golden roofs. Although Columbus believed that they had gone beyond most of the islands, perhaps even beyond Cipango, he insisted in continuing due west.

On that same day, Columbus faced his first near-mutiny when the men of the *Santa María* began demanding a return to Spain. Many times Columbus had told the crew they should start looking for land at 700 leagues and should expect to sight land at 750 leagues (no more than 3,000 miles). By October 6, according to the pilots of all three ships, they had gone 800 leagues. In response to the complaints of his crew, Columbus decided to consult the other captains and ordered a cannon fired to signal the other ships to close up with his. When they had assembled, Columbus told the other captains about his crew's desire to return and asked them for their opinions. Their responses, as recalled by witnesses in legal cases years later, were wholly supportive of continued exploration.

Vicente Yáñez said they ought to go on for 2,000 leagues before returning. Martín Alonso's response to Columbus's question was variously remembered. In one version, when told that the crew of the *Santa María* was near revolt he advised Columbus: *"Your lordship should hang a half dozen of them or throw them in the sea, and if you don't dare to, my brothers and I will come alongside and do it, for an armada that sailed with the mandate of such high princes cannot go back without good news."*[30] Another version had him saying: *"Onward, onward, for this is an armada and embassy of such high princes as our lords the monarchs of Spain."*[31] One witness remembered Martín Alonso appealing to the mariners' pride, saying, *"God will grant us the victory to discover land, for God would never want us to return in such shame."*[32] Still another witness recalled a more philosophical response: *"Remember, your lordship, that in the house of Pedro Vázquez de la Frontera I promised you that neither I nor any of my relatives would return to Palos before we found land, so long as the people were healthy and had provisions; now then, what is lacking? The people are healthy, the ships new, and we have plenty of provisions. Why do we have to go back? Whoever wants to can go back, but I want to go on, for I have to discover land or die in the attempt."*[33]

Even accurate firsthand observations dim over time, and some witnesses were reporting secondhand information from participants on the voyage and had not actually been there themselves. The testimony as a whole was also somewhat tainted, given the circumstances in which it was recorded. Years after the voyage, witnesses were asked to testify on behalf of the Pinzón family or the crown in a series of lawsuits related to the Columbus family's claims to land and titles. The Pinzón family and lawyers for the crown all wanted to enhance Martín Alonso's role in the first voyage and diminish the part that Columbus had played. Witnesses were presumably selected for their favorable inclinations. Nonetheless, it seems safe to assume that on October 6 Columbus faced a restive crew on his flagship. When he sought the opinion of the other captains, both of them immediately and strongly backed continued exploration.[34]

On October 7 the crew of the *Niña*, which had sailed ahead of the others, gave the signal that land had been sighted: they raised a flag at the top of the mainmast and fired a cannon. But the sighting proved illusory. When the ships came together that evening at sunset, no one had been able to verify a landfall. As the ships approached their sunset rendezvous, however, all present noted multitudes of birds flying toward the southwest. They interpreted this phenomenon in two ways, both of which reinforced the idea that land was near. Either the birds were flying home to sleep for the night, or they were migrating in anticipation of the approaching winter in the north. The latter interpretation may have been correct. Early October is the height of the autumn migration of birds from North America southward to the Caribbean and South America.

Impressed by the huge flocks and mindful of Portuguese discoveries made by following birds, Columbus agreed to deviate from his westward course and sail west-southwest for two days. From the evening of the seventh they followed that course, with calm seas and favorable winds. All along, they kept monitoring the kind and number of birds they saw and carefully watched where the birds were heading. On the evening of the ninth, they were still on the same course but had not sighted land. The wind shifted, and they changed course toward the west once again. In the spare but hopeful words of the abstracted diary, *"All night they heard birds pass."*

On October 10, Columbus again turned away from a straight westward course to sail west-southwest. The diary does not comment on this course change, although Columbus had initially promised to deviate from his westward course for only two days. A laconic notice in the diary provides a possible reason for the new compass direction: the crew had begun to complain vocally about the length of the voyage and the failure to find land. According to the diary, Columbus tried to encourage his men, reminding them of what they had to gain and of his determination to continue the voyage until they found the Indies. Nothing more about the incident appears in the diary's abstract.

From other accounts, the grumbling on October 10 appears to have been much more serious. The masters of all three ships and the Pinzón brothers, who had been quick to support a continuation of exploration as recently as October 6, now turned against Columbus. No doubt reflecting the rising anxiety of their crews, they expressed the fear that the nearly continuous winds blowing from east to west might make it impossible to return home at that latitude. After all, that had been the chronic and well-justified fear in West African exploration for centuries. Columbus could only answer that God had given them the weather to take them this far and he would give them proper weather to get back home. That rather weak defense suggests that he did not yet understand the North Atlantic wind patterns. Unconvinced that the matter should be left entirely in God's hands, the mutinous crewmen began to rattle their weapons, but Columbus urged them to reconsider. They could easily kill him and his loyal officers, he told them, but they could never hope to escape royal justice back at home. He proposed a compromise. They would continue on their westward course for two more days (or three or four;

accounts vary). If they still had not found land at the end of that period, they would turn back. The Pinzones and the other officers accepted the compromise easily, returning to their ships and persuading their crews to continue the voyage.[35]

After their near-mutiny of the day before, on October 11 the crew needed surprisingly little encouragement. All day they seized on everything they saw as a portent of an imminent landfall. They identified land birds. They eagerly scrutinized the flotsam in the ocean: a cane, a stick, a plank, another stick seemingly worked by iron, and still another covered with barnacles. At the evening rendezvous Columbus set the course again to the west. From all the signs, he was convinced they were approaching land. When the men of the *Santa María* assembled at sunset to say the "Salve Regina," he told them to keep a good lookout from the forecastle. He reminded them that the monarchs had promised a life annuity of 10,000 maravedis to the first man to sight land, and he himself would donate a silk jacket to the lucky fellow. Evidently Columbus had abandoned his earlier order not to sail past midnight. Two hours after midnight, on October 12, with the *Pinta* sailing ahead, the weather cleared. In the moonlight one of the sailors on the *Pinta*, Juan Rodríguez Bermejo, saw a white sand beach and land beyond it. After his shout of *"Land! Land!,"* the *Pinta*'s crew raised a flag on its highest mast and fired a cannon.

As Columbus later told the story, he had sighted land before the sailor in the *Pinta*, when he saw a faint light, late on the evening of October 11. He asked Pero Gutiérrez, the royal steward, to confirm the sighting, and Gutiérrez saw it too. Columbus also asked Rodrigo Sánchez, the fleet's royal overseer, to confirm the sighting, but he was unable to do so. Uncertain of what he had seen, Columbus did not signal the other ships. On the basis of his recollection of the events of October 11, he later claimed the reward for himself and saved the price of a silk jacket as well. He may have regretted his behavior, however, because he assigned the annuity to Beatriz Enríquez de Arana rather than keep it for himself.

When the three ships drew together on the early morning of October 12, land was clearly visible, but wind blowing them toward the island made the officers wary of approaching more closely until daylight. Fearing unseen rocks and shallows, the three ships hauled down all their canvas except the mainsails and tacked back and forth offshore until the eagerly awaited dawn. They had found land and had proved that there were more islands in the ocean sea. They also believed they were on the verge of establishing direct contact with Asia, its rich spice markets and its houses roofed with gold. Instead, they were a few short hours from one of the most fateful human encounters in all of history, a meeting between peoples previously unknown to one another. Columbus and the Pinzones believed they were somewhere close to the legendary Cipango. They had no idea that their landing the next day would take place on an island in the Bahamas and that the Japan they sought was still half a world away.

8

Columbus and the New World

FIRST CONTACT

ON THE MORNING of October 12, 1492, Europeans made their first verified contact with Americans since the time of the Vikings, five centuries before. The day is still known in many parts of the world as the anniversary of Europe's discovery of America, but the men involved thought they were about to step ashore in Asia. As their ships approached the island, they could see naked people on the beach, watching their progress.

Columbus assembled a landing party, which rowed to the beach in the *Santa María*'s launch. Columbus carried the royal banner. The Pinzón brothers, as captains of the two caravels, carried the flags Columbus had ordered for all three ships, which bore a green cross in the center and on either side the letters *F* and *Y,* each surmounted by a crown, to signify King Fernando and Queen Isabel (sometimes spelled "Ysabel" in those days). When they reached the shore, Columbus had the party assemble in the presence of Rodrigo de Escobedo, the fleet's notary, and Rodrigo Sánchez de Segovia, who was the royal overseer (*veedor real*). He then spoke the standard proclamation for taking possession of land for the crown and named the island San Salvador, in honor of Jesus Christ, the Holy Savior of the Catholic faith. By these acts, Columbus fulfilled the conditions necessary for him to become Admiral of the Ocean Sea. He had found land and claimed it for his sponsors.

What the local inhabitants, who called the island Guanahaní, thought of all this is not recorded. If they had been able to understand the language, they would probably have been somewhat puzzled by the proceedings. Their land, after all, was presumably already under the lordship of their own chieftains. The location of Columbus's first landfall has been vigorously debated over the past century, with most scholars agreeing that it was the Bahamian island currently named San Salvador and formerly named Watling. In the 1980s, the controversy was revived by several amateur and a few professional scholars, who offered alternatives to the San Salvador thesis. In November of 1986, the *National Geographic* magazine published an attractively presented set of articles arguing for the small island of Samaná Cay. Using Las Casas's abstract of Columbus's diary, computer projections, and various other attention-getting devices, they claimed to

Columbus Landing on Guanahaní/San Salvador, according to a late sixteenth-century interpretation. (From Theodore de Bry, *Reisen in Occidentalischen Indien* [Frankfurt, 1590–1630]. Photo courtesy of the James Ford Bell Library, University of Minnesota.)

have solved the matter. The flawed abstract of the diary offers no conclusive proof of the landing site, however. The hundreds of islands in the Bahamas and its neighboring chains that resemble descriptions in the diary make the question of the first landfall an intellectual dead end for most serious scholars. Without Columbus's original diary, the issue cannot even be addressed adequately, let alone solved. The controversy will no doubt persist, but it has almost no real significance, even if it is someday sorted out. The real significance of the voyage lies elsewhere, in the first encounter of Europeans and inhabitants of the Western Hemisphere since Viking times and in the far-reaching consequences of that encounter. For these more general matters, rather than the specific details required to reconstruct Columbus's navigational course, Las Casas's abstract of the diary can be useful.[1]

The landing on the island of Guanahaní marked the last moment of the voyage that corresponded to Columbus's plan, although he had no way of knowing that yet. Until then, he must have felt fairly confident that everything he had predicted and every hope he had held were coming to pass. After leaving the Canaries a little over a month before, the fleet had followed a westward course, with only minor variations and generally good weather. Spirits and morale had been high, for the most part, and the grumbling toward the end had been overcome by persuasion and compromise and by the abundant signs indicating land nearby. Finally, the fleet had reached land in approximately the location predicted. Columbus was sure they had landed on an island off the coast of the Asian mainland, having inadvertently bypassed Cipango. There was no reason at first for him or anyone else to doubt the underlying assumptions of the expedition.

GREAT EXPECTATIONS

Still, nothing they observed about the island matched their mental image of Asia as described by Marco Polo and Toscanelli. No great ships had appeared. They did not see populous and prosperous cities with houses and temples roofed with gold. Their first reaction was to continue the search. In the history of the expedition, and especially in Columbus's actions, we can trace several processes at work as exploration of the islands proceeded. Because Columbus dominates the documentary record, we know less about the other men on the voyage, but his observations, as summarized by Las Casas and bolstered by other evidence, can stand as a general description of their experience. On one level, Columbus and his colleagues acted as geographers, naturalists, ethnographers, and anthropologists. They observed and remarked upon the natural beauty of the islands they found. They also tried hard to understand the people they encountered, to observe their society, and to find methods for communicating and trading with them. On another level, Columbus and his colleagues pursued their entrepreneurial agenda, driven to find wealth one way or another.

In search of wealth, Columbus simultaneously followed two avenues of approach, which he mentioned again and again in his diary. Until fairly late in his reconnoitering of the Caribbean on the first voyage, he believed he would soon come upon the rich Asian ports that he had set out to find. At the same time, he constantly looked for gold, natural products, and other commodities that could be traded profitably. As time passed and he failed to find golden-roofed temples or anything else resembling Marco Polo's Asia, this latter approach came to occupy the center of his attention.

Columbus's model for seeking out local commodities was the experience of Portuguese expansion in Africa. Like the Portuguese, he hoped to establish contact with centers of trade and set up fortified trading posts. The best example of such an arrangement was the Portuguese trading post and castle at Mina on the African Gold Coast. Columbus had been there, and he knew how the fortress at Mina operated. He also knew how the Portuguese had strengthened their commercial presence in Africa. They traded European items for local products, they learned about local centers of large-scale trade, and they negotiated agreements with local rulers to ensure their continued presence. That approach worked well, given coastal West Africa's decentralized kingdoms and fairly simple trading networks. Columbus well knew, from reading Marco Polo, that the scale and complexity of trade in Asia was a quantum leap from the African situation. He had expected to find Asian trade in the Caribbean; instead he found a situation more akin to the African variety but much less developed.

That discouraging realization did not come to him immediately, however. In sailing around the Caribbean in search of Asia, Columbus followed Portuguese precedents, contacting local inhabitants and their leaders, trying to gain their confidence and learn the location of their trading centers. As evidence of the fleet's commercial intentions, various trade goods had been brought along that had been popular in Africa: glass beads, small bells, and so on. Columbus also saw to it that the fleet carried samples of Asian spices, so that they could be compared with native plants in the lands they visited. His ultimate goal was to locate the great Asian trading centers that Marco Polo had made famous in Europe.

Eventually Columbus was forced to admit that large-scale commerce did not exist on the islands he had found. Although there was an extensive interisland trade among the local people, it was not large enough for European merchants to tap into profitably. Even worse, Columbus had to face the fact that the great commercial cities of Asia were not in the immediate vicinity. He would have to revise his plans and improvise for the rest of the voyage. Faced with the reality of the Caribbean islands, his thoughts would turn to colonization as a way to make the islands profitable. The Castilians and the Portuguese had created prosperous colonies in the Atlantic islands. Columbus had personal knowledge of how he might accomplish the same result. He had, after all, married into the family that governed the Portuguese colony of Porto Santo, and he had lived in the Madeiras and visited the Canaries. He knew that European settlement and the introduction of commercial plants and livestock could turn newfound islands into profitable enterprises. The evolution in Columbus's goals from Asian trade to African trade to island colonization would occur gradually over the course of three months, marking the partial triumph of experience over expectations.

EXPLORING THE CARIBBEAN

In the first days on Guanahaní/San Salvador, however, Columbus and his companions still had great expectations, and these were only encouraged by their reception from the local inhabitants, who seemed friendly and interested in communicating and trading with them. No sooner had Columbus and his men finished their ceremony claiming possession of the island than they turned their attention to the people who had assembled to watch them. The first thing Columbus mentioned was an exchange of goods, noting the friendliness of the local people and their desire to communicate with the newcomers and exchange goods with them. In an entry in the diary dated October 11, but actually describing events on October 12, Las Casas quoted Columbus as saying,

> in order that they would be friendly to us – because I recognized that they were people who would be better freed [from error] and converted to our Holy Faith by love than by force – to some of them I gave red caps, and glass beads which they put on their chests, and many other things of small value, in which they took so much pleasure and became so much our friends that it was a marvel. Later they came swimming to the ships' launches where we were and brought us parrots and cotton thread in balls and javelins and many other things, and they traded them to us for other things which we gave them, such as small glass beads and bells.

The exchange of goods may have had a quite different meaning to Caribbean people than to Old World merchants, but neither side had any way of knowing this. Columbus viewed the exchange as the start of a fruitful commerce, though his pleasure was tempered by the suspicion that these were not the wealthy Asians he had sought. His disappointment seems obvious when he described them as *"people poor in everything."* Their most striking characteristic was their nakedness. Next was their hair, described as straight and coarse as a horse's tail, and short, except for a long piece in the back which was left uncut. Columbus noted that they painted themselves in black, red, or white; some painted their whole bodies, others just portions, and some just their noses. In the beginning, Columbus offered no explanation for this practice. Later, on December 24, he reported that they did so for protection from the sun. That is a plausible enough explanation for people who lived in a tropical climate without clothing to shield them, but it is not clear if Columbus had been told this or if he was just guessing. Other possibilities are that the paint had a magical or religious significance or simply that it offered some pro-

Indian paddling a small dugout canoe. (From Gonzalo Fernández de Oviedo y Valdés, *La historia general y natural de las Indias* [Seville: Juan Cromberger, 1535]. Photo courtesy of the James Ford Bell Library, University of Minnesota.)

tection against the ferocious mosquitoes and other biting insects in the tropics. With his usual tendency to minimize the negative aspects of his discoveries, Columbus had nothing to say on the subject of mosquitoes. By contrast, participants on later voyages wrote bitterly and at length about the voracious insect pests they encountered.

Columbus was also struck by the skin color of the islanders. Assuming that he was near India, he called them Indians, noting that they were not black, like Africans, but rather the color of the Canary Islanders. He added, *"Nor should anything else be expected since this island is on an east-west line with the island of Hierro in the Canaries."*[2] Like many of his contemporaries, Columbus seems to have believed that skin color varied according to distance from the equator; the farther north toward the pole, the lighter the skin tone. After describing the people, Columbus described the boats they made of hollowed logs and tree trunks. Some were small enough to be paddled by a single man, whereas others could carry a crew of forty to forty-five. To describe the boats, he first used the Portuguese word *almadía* (dugout), a term that had been applied to the native boats of West Africa. Later he learned the local term *canoa* and used it thereafter. He told how the men paddled their boats with oars resembling bakers' paddles and moved swiftly and skillfully through the water. We know the people he first encountered and described were Tainos, members of the widespread tribes of the Arawak language group that inhabited lands ranging from the Amazon through the Caribbean. In his first impressions of them, Columbus was acting much as an anthropologist does, describing and categorizing a people according to the background and expectations that he brought to the encounter.

These anthropological observations quickly gave way to the search for Asia and its fabled wealth. Columbus noted that some of the islanders had pierced noses in which they wore small pieces of gold. It was not much, but it might be a clue leading toward the golden roofs of Cipango. He reported on October 13 that *"by signs I was able to understand that, going to the south or rounding the island to the south, there was a king who had large vessels of it and had very much gold. . . . And so I will go to the southwest to seek gold and precious stones."*

Before leaving Guanahaní/San Salvador, Columbus reconnoitered the northern part of the island, where he found a reef-enclosed harbor which he grandly claimed could hold *"as many ships as there are in the whole of Christendom."*[3] He also noted an ideal spot where a fort could be built, and he continued to comment on harbors and good defensive sites throughout the voyage. The Portuguese had found few good harbors on the African coast, and they – like Columbus – were well aware that harbors and fortresses were the keys to successfully establishing trade in remote outposts. In Africa and later in Asia, the Portuguese maritime empire would be defined by its network of harbors and fortresses, especially Mina in West Africa, Hormuz on the Persian Gulf, Goa on the western coast of India, and Malacca on the strait separating the Malay Peninsula from the island of Sumatra. Columbus's grandiose claims for the natural endowments of Guanahaní/San Salvador and other islands seem designed to reassure his patrons that he had found valuable lands, which could be developed and defended efficiently. In the first days after the landfall, hopes were high, and Columbus and his companions were eager to continue their explorations.

Columbus intended to take samples back to Spain of everything he found that could be traded or otherwise turned to profit. Unfortunately, that included people. The men he encountered on Guanahaní/San Salvador were not very warlike, he noted. They had no metal weapons and were so ignorant of swords that they grabbed them by the blade and cut themselves. Fifty Europeans could dominate the island, Columbus asserted, and, although not apt warriors, the islanders would nonetheless make good servants. In the diary entry describing the events of the first day of the encounter, Columbus expressed his intention to take six islanders with him from Guanahaní; the entry for October 14 indicated that he actually took seven. He planned to take them back to Spain, where they could be converted to Christianity and taught the Castilian language, before returning with subsequent expeditions as interpreters. In this plan, Columbus was following the model that Franciscan missionaries had pioneered in the Canaries and that the Portuguese were continuing to use in Africa. Although Columbus did not say so explicitly, the captured islanders would also serve as proof of his reaching a distant land with exotic peoples. Columbus clearly intended to treat his captives well, but he never seemed to doubt that he had the right to hold them against their will. This would gain him the dubious distinction of being the first European slaver in the Western Hemisphere.

Before sailing from Guanahaní/San Salvador, Columbus asked his Indian informants about nearby islands. They named over a hundred for him and said the islands were in fact numberless. Columbus elected to head for the largest island they named, which turned out to be some 7 leagues (26–28 miles) from Guanahaní/San Salvador. Sailing on October 14, the fleet arrived at the island the next day and spent another day exploring the coastline. A landing party took formal possession of the island on October 16, giving it the name of Santa María de la Concepción. The Indians they encountered were similar to those on Guanahaní, peaceable and fairly friendly. But none liked being held captive. Two of the men Columbus had taken with him from Guanahaní took the opportunity to escape from the ship off Concepción.

About ten in the morning on October 16, the fleet departed for another island, which Columbus named Fernandina. In midpassage from Concepción to Fernandina, the fleet overtook a lone Indian in a canoe making the same journey. Columbus brought him aboard the *Santa María* and learned a bit more from him about the interisland trade. The man was paddling toward Fernandina after having left San Salvador and visiting Santa María. In other words, he had followed the same trajectory as Columbus's fleet, just a bit ahead of them, until they overtook his canoe. Astonishingly, he was carrying a small basket with Castilian trade goods: a string of small glass beads and some small Castilian coins, which had obviously been inserted into the local trading network as soon as Columbus's men had bartered them. Local inhabitants were not only spreading European goods but also the knowledge of an alien presence in their islands and a new source of trade goods. The man in the canoe had not encountered the Europeans before, only their goods, and yet he was able to communicate with them when he came on board the *Santa María*. In the four days since Columbus's landing on October 12, communication and trade had been established between the inhabitants of the old and the new worlds, but the fruitful encounter was still very different from what Columbus had hoped.

He continually praised the lush vegetation of the islands, which in the fall of the year were still as green as Castile in the spring. He

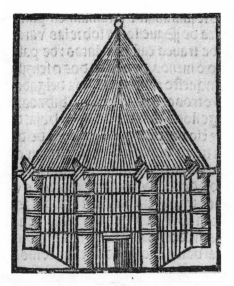

Hut used by natives of the Caribbean. (From Gonzalo Fernández de Oviedo y Valdés, *La historia general y natural de las Indias* [Seville: Juan Cromberger, 1535]. Photo courtesy of the James Ford Bell Library, University of Minnesota.)

marveled at the variety of plants, admitting that he could not identify many of them. But he also noted that all he could find of commercial value was aloe, which, as it turned out later, he had misidentified.[4] By the time the fleet reached the fourth island – Samoet to the Indians, dubbed Isabela by Columbus – he had accepted that the small islands had little to offer in economic terms. As beautiful as they were, they were home to simple people who lived in small and scattered villages and had little gold or other trade goods that would be attractive to Europeans. The diary entry for October 19, addressed (like much of the diary) to Fernando and Isabel, said, *"I am not taking pains to see much in detail because I want to see and explore as much as I can so I can return to Your Highnesses in April, Our Lord pleasing. It is true that, finding where there is gold or spices in quantity, I will stay until I get as much of it as I can. And for this reason I do nothing but go forward to see if I come across it."* Columbus's plans were guided by information from native islanders. He did not credit all of what he thought he heard, *"from not understanding them well and also from recognizing that they are so poor in gold that any little bit that the king may wear seems much to them."* Still, he was impressed with what they told him about the island called Cuba, *"which I believe must be Cipango according to the indications that these people give of its size and wealth."*[5] So on to Cuba

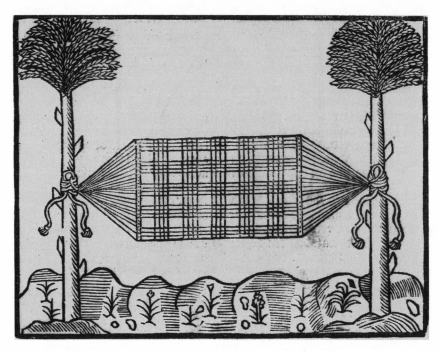

Hammock used by natives of the Caribbean. (From Gonzalo Fernández de Oviedo y Valdés, *La historia general y natural de las "Indias,"* [Seville: Juan Cromberger, 1535]. Photo courtesy of the James Ford Bell Library, University of Minnesota.)

they sailed, in search of the riches of Cipango. Following directions supplied by the Indians, the fleet followed a southwesterly route to a string of flat and sandy islands that Columbus appropriately called the Islas de Arena, or Sand Islands. From there they continued south-southwest toward the northeastern shore of Cuba.

CUBA

Columbus's descriptions of Cuba began on October 28, with phrasing so similar to earlier diary entries that the result was a cliché: *"that island is the most beautiful that eyes have ever seen: full of good harbors and deep rivers. . . ."* He was filled with great hopes at the beginning of his exploration of Cuba, which he renamed Juana. His guides from Guanahaní/San Salvador told him Cuba had ten large rivers and was itself so large that canoes could not circle it in twenty days. They also told him there were gold mines and pearl beds on the island. In his ignorance and enthusiasm, Columbus also believed the natives were telling him that ships from the Great Khan visited Cuba and that a powerful local king maintained his seat nearby. He therefore sailed northwest along the Cuban coast in search of the river that would lead to the king's court. In planning his approach to the king, Columbus followed precedent from the Portuguese in Africa. He would send emissaries with presents for the king and a copy of a letter from the Spanish monarchs. To lead the expedition he selected a sailor who had participated in the same sort of mission in Africa.[6]

By November 1, Columbus had convinced himself that Cuba was part of the mainland, despite what the locals had told him. He believed that he was only about 100 leagues from Zayto and Quinsai, cities figuring prominently on European maps of Asia. On the second of November, he made up his embassy, consisting of Rodrigo de Jerez (presumably the man with African experience), the linguist Luis de Torres, and two Indians, one from Guanahaní and one a local resident. Evidently the Indians believed that by participating in the embassy they would win the right to return to their homes. The embassy carried strings of beads to exchange for food during the six days allotted for the journey. They also carried samples of spices to compare with what they might find, and Columbus instructed them carefully on what to say to the king once they arrived.

After sending off the four-man embassy, Columbus had a crew spend the next several days investigating their surroundings and careening the ships for recaulking. Various crew members identified plants they found as cinnamon, aloe, and mastic, but even though Columbus was keen to find lucrative commodities and made many misidentifications of his own, he rejected the purported cinnamon, while accepting the other two. The plants of the island were impressive in their own way, including varieties of beans unlike those of Europe, and the versatile cassava. The Europeans also marveled at large cotton trees, which they supposed could be harvested in all seasons.

Efforts to gain information from the local Indians seemed promising to Columbus and his men. In retrospect, we can trace the obvious mutual misunderstandings between these two very different groups of human beings. Columbus showed his samples of cinnamon and pepper to the local Indians and also showed them gold and pearls. To everything shown them, they responded that it could be found to the southeast. In that direction, in a place they called Bohío, or so the Europeans understood, there were people who wore gold on their necks, ears, arms, and legs. A trading center with large ships also lay to the southeast, or so they thought. All this seems to have been wishful thinking on the Europeans' part, based on a nearly total misunderstanding of what the Indians were telling them. The Europeans also believed they were hearing stories of one-eyed men and cannibals with the faces of dogs.

On the night of November 5, the embassy returned from the interior. They had found a village of about fifty houses but no sign of a large city anywhere nearby, or any king. Nonetheless, when the villagers were shown samples of pepper and cinnamon, they too replied that large amounts could be found to the southeast. By the sixth of November, Columbus determined to go southeast to continue his search for the large ships of the khan. They were clearly not to be found in this part of Cuba. Nor were the people any different from those he had previously encountered. They went about nearly naked, the women covering their genitals with a small piece of cotton cloth. *"And they are very respectful and not very black, less so than Canarians."* They could be taught to accept Christianity, if missionaries who knew their language thoroughly were sent among them, Columbus noted. Either consciously or unconsciously, Columbus was echoing the policy that had served the Franciscans well in the Atlantic islands: language was the key to cultural understanding and the only sure route to conversion. Nevertheless, he had decided that the local inhabitants were no longer worth his time and trouble. With the careening of the vessels completed, he planned to sail off to the southeast toward what he envisioned as the center of the Asian trade.

As if to warn of disappointment to come, contrary winds came up, and the fleet could not get away until November 12. The entry in Columbus's diary for that day is particularly long and revealing. In words addressed to Fernando and Isabel, Columbus revealed his attitudes regarding missionary activity, the search for wealth, and relations with the Indians. He saw no difficulty in converting the natives to Christianity, in part because (so he thought) they had no bad habits to overcome. Las Casas quoted Columbus as saying,

These people have no religious beliefs, nor are they idolaters. They are very gentle and do not know what evil is; nor do they kill others, nor steal; and they are without weapons and so timid that a hundred of them flee from one of our men even if our men are teasing them. And they are credulous and aware that there is a God in heaven and convinced that we come from the heavens; and they say very quickly any prayer that we tell them to say, and they make the sign of the cross, ✠. So that Your Highnesses ought to resolve to make them Christians: for I believe that if you begin, in a short time you will end up having converted to our Holy Faith a multitude of peoples and acquiring large dominions and great riches and all of their peoples for Spain.

Once again, Columbus's optimism and his will to succeed led him to color reality in the rosiest possible hues, failing to see that the people he had met were human beings, with as much variety in their behavior as any other group of human beings.

He went on to offer wholly exaggerated accounts of the financial opportunities in the islands. Gold was to be found in *"a very great quantity,"* and precious stones, and pearls and infinite spiceries. Until then, he had seen only small amounts of personal jewelry worn by the islanders, and he had no idea where they had obtained it. He had seen no precious stones, no pearls, and no spices. He was confident he had found mastic, but when his men tapped the "mastic" trees, no sap could be drawn. Even that did not deter him; he reported that the trees must have been out of season. Cotton he had certainly seen, throughout the islands. In his optimistic boosterism, he asserted that profit could be made from cotton without even having to transport it to Spain. It could be sold in *"the big cities belonging to the Grand Khan, which doubtless will be discovered, and to many other cities belonging to other lords who will be happy to serve Your Majesties. . . ."* Yet more was at stake than mere profit. Columbus had to justify the faith that the sovereigns had shown in him. He had to find the riches of Asia and the multitudes of potential Christian converts, because he had promised to find them.

Columbus knew that he needed Indian interpreters, both for the immediate voyage at hand and for the future conversion of the local people to Christianity. A canoe had approached his ship on November 11, and five young men had come aboard. Columbus quickly had them seized as additional future interpreters. He realized that they might not serve willingly, however, for his diary recalled the bad luck of the Portuguese, who had brought men from Guinea to Portugal, treated them well, given them gifts, and taught them Portuguese, only to have them disappear when they were taken back to Africa. Columbus thought he had the perfect solution to avoid such ungrateful behavior: he would bring local women along with the men. *"And later I sent men to a house which is west of the river, and they brought back seven head [sic] of women, counting young ones and adults, and three small children."* He hinted that the women would also serve as concubines for his crew, saying that they would teach his men their language, *"which is identical in all of these islands of India."* He revealed another piece of his knowledge of Africa here, by contrasting what he believed to be the single language of the Indies with the many languages of Guinea.

The story did not end there, however. On the night of November 12, *"the husband of one of these women and the father of three children, one male and two female,"* came alongside the ship in a canoe; *"and he asked me to let him go with them and he implored me greatly: and all of them were consoled by him, for they must all be related, and he is now a man of 45 years."* Las Casas quotes nothing more of the story, but we may assume that the new arrivals stayed on board.

The fleet spent several days coasting and investigating harbors in eastern Cuba, but they found nothing that even hinted at the riches of Asia. Ironically – and perhaps predictably – Columbus's descriptions of the physical setting became more elaborate and more exaggerated as his hopes faded of finding the hub of Asian trade. On November 14, he reported seeing countless beautiful islands, all heavily forested, and he described the mountains of eastern Cuba as the highest in the world. He was certain he had reached Asia, for he thought that *"these islands are those innumerable ones that in the maps of the world are put at the eastern end."* Exploring yet another excellent harbor, on the sixteenth, he seems to have faced reality a bit more squarely when he noted that *"a fortress could be built there at little cost if at some time in that sea of islands a notable trade should develop."*

When asked about gold and the Great Khan, the local inhabitants almost always had responded in terms that Europeans took as indicating that they lay to the south or southeast. Columbus and his men understood that southeast of Cuba lay rich islands, and the richest was named Baneque. On the evening of November 21, Martín Alonso Pinzón took the caravel *Pinta* and headed east toward the island of Baneque, without the admiral's permission. Thereafter Martín Alonso and his crew were on their own, and Columbus had no indication of when, or if, they would ever return. The records we have from the first voyage, especially Columbus's diary, provide much more colorful details than the prosaic sources we have for Pinzón's adventures. We know from testimony in court cases filed years afterward that he sailed eastward from Cuba and reached the island that Columbus would later rename Española (Hispaniola). At the time of his departure, Pinzón shared Columbus's opinion that Cuba was the Asian mainland and that Cipango lay to the east. Later, both believed Española was Cipango. Pinzón explored Española and even named a river after himself. When Columbus learned of this violation of the chain of command, he was so angry that during his second voyage he prohibited settlement on "Martín Alonso's river." Pinzón took a crew inland on Española for three days and traded for gold with the natives. In fact, trading for gold may have been the principal reason that Pinzón bolted; Columbus had prohibited any trading outside his auspices.[7]

Meanwhile, Columbus had decisions to make. On November 25 a new tone appeared in the diary, with the first entry admitting that European enterprise, and not trade alone, would be necessary to produce wealth from the islands Columbus had found. In eastern Cuba he came upon a grove of magnificent pines, tall and straight. Columbus deemed them suitable to provide masts and planking for the ships of Spain and noted that they were located where a water-powered sawmill could easily be constructed. Slowly but inevitably Columbus's approach to the islands was shifting from the trading-post model of African exploration to the settlement and colonization model of the Atlantic islands.

The departure of Pinzón raised another set of concerns for Columbus. He still had two ships, even if one of them was under the command of Martín Alonso's brother Vicente Yáñez Pinzón, and therefore potentially unreliable. Nonetheless, Columbus was in no immediate danger and continued his leisurely reconnaissance of the Cuban coast. He did worry, however, that Martín Alonso might sail back to Spain alone and seize the glory for the discoveries. In the diary entry for November 27, Columbus seemed anxious to cover himself in case he was not the first to return home; his thoroughness would make up for any lack of speed. As Las Casas summarized,

> He was delaying more than he wished because of the desire and delight that he had and received from seeing and looking at the beauty and freshness of those lands wherever he entered. . . . He says that it seemed to him that one might not wish to leave that place. He kept telling the men who were in his company that, in order to report to the sovereigns the things they were seeing, a thousand tongues would not suffice to tell it or his hand to write it; for it seemed to him that it was enchanted.

The imagery of paradise was reinforced by Columbus's assertion that no one had been sick or even had a headache on all three ships, except for one old man with a long-term problem with kidney stone.

But this Garden of Eden still had to yield a profit. The region should be settled extensively, Columbus advised, because of the variety of products available to be traded in Europe. Once settlements and trade had been established, Spain could do a profitable business in the islands. To leave no doubt that piety and profit went hand in hand, Columbus also recommended that only Catholic Christians be allowed to trade with or settle in the Indies, writing that *"the beginning and the end of the enterprise was the increase and glory of the Christian religion."* Once again, Columbus discussed the religious future of those he had dubbed Indians, emphasizing that they had no false religion and predicting their quick and easy conversion to Christianity, once missionaries knew the local language.

The problem of language loomed large among Columbus's preoccupations. Early on, the Europeans had assumed a higher degree of mutual understanding than in fact existed, but by November 27 Columbus was feeling frustrated by his lack of fluency. *"I do not know the language, and the people of these lands do not understand me nor do I, nor anyone else that I have with me, them."* Just as Columbus's observations about the commercial possibilities of the islands were too optimistic, his gloomy assessment about language was too pessimistic. Regular and increasingly reliable communication seems to have been growing between the two groups, although frequent misunderstandings occurred. Belying his own words, Columbus mentioned that Spaniards in one landing party had urged a group of natives not to be afraid, speaking in the local language, *"because they knew a bit of it through association with those they brought with them,"* as Las Casas summarized the encounter. Clearly, some rudimentary understanding was developing on both sides.

By the fifth of December, the expedition had reached the eastern tip of Cuba. Still assuming that Cuba was the Asian mainland, Columbus designated the eastern promontory (now Cape Maisí), as Cape Alpha and Omega,[8] the beginning and the end of Asia. Sailing east the next day they reached a large island that Columbus called Española, and he named a harbor on the island the Puerto de San Nicolás, because he arrived there on December 6, the feast day of Saint Nicholas.

ESPAÑOLA

On Española, Columbus was still charmed by the landscapes and the vegetation, and he still eagerly cataloged the items that might make for profitable commerce. Nonetheless, for the short term he eagerly sought gold, hoping to find enough before his return voyage to please his royal sponsors. It seems clear that the example of the Gold Coast in Africa still inspired him. The inhabitants of Española were first encountered by a small party that Columbus put ashore with instructions to investigate the interior. They returned on December 13 with reports that the people they met were more handsome and better built than those on the other islands, in addition to being lighter in skin color than any others. Columbus initially could not credit these descriptions, but when he had a chance to make his own observations he changed his mind. Writing on December 16, he reported that the people of Española were naked and the most handsome people yet encountered. They were also *"very white, for if they went about clothed and protected themselves from the sun and wind they would be almost as white as people in Spain."* Just as he described Española as the most fertile and the most beautiful of the island paradises he had visited, adding hyperbole to hyperbole, Columbus described its inhabitants as *"plump and brave and not weak like the others."*

At this point in his explorations, Columbus abandoned his insistence on finding the trade of the Great Khan and also abandoned the Portuguese model of the trading-post system. Instead, on December 16 he outlined what he considered a suitable colonial policy for the islands he had discovered, similar to the policies of Portuguese and Castilian colonization in the Atlantic islands.

> May Your Highnesses believe that these lands are so greatly good and fertile, and especially this island of Hispaniola, that there is no one who can tell it; and no one could believe it if he had not seen it. And you may believe that this island and all the others are as much yours as Castile; for nothing is lacking except settlement and ordering the Indians to whatever Your Highnesses may wish. Because I with the people that I bring with me, who are not many, go about in all these islands without danger; for I have already seen three of these sailors go ashore where there was a crowd of Indians, and all would flee without the Spaniards wanting to do harm. They do not have arms and they are all naked, and of no skill in arms, and so very cowardly that a thousand would not stand against three. And so they are fit to be ordered about and made to work, plant, and do everything else that may be needed, and build towns and be taught our customs, and to go about clothed.

Contrary to what many authors have claimed, Columbus invented nothing when he called for settlement. He merely invoked the policies that had succeeded in the Atlantic islands. He had not abandoned his hope for a gold trade, trusting that God would lead him to its source. He does seem to have given up hope of finding gold mines, however, perhaps because he thought mining technology was beyond the skill of the islanders.

As Christmas approached, the men of the *Santa María* and the *Niña* explored the northwestern coast of Española, and Columbus made contact with various local chieftains. In his description of the islanders and their leaders, Columbus anticipated all of the noble-savage mythology of the New World that would color European attitudes well beyond the eighteenth century. On December 18, he described the arrival of a young king who ruled about 5 leagues away from the fleet's anchorage. The king, whose name does not appear in the sources, arrived in a litter carried by four men, and Columbus praised his dignity and the ceremony with which his people bore themselves. He thought the Spanish monarchs would have approved of these people and their bearing, *"even though everyone went about naked."* The king came aboard ship and met Columbus in the sterncastle, where he was eating. Columbus offered the king food and then exchanged gifts with him. The king gave Columbus a belt and two thin bits of worked gold; Columbus reciprocated with the coverlet from his own bed, a flask of orange-flower water, some red shoes, and a length of amber beads that he wore around his own neck. Columbus then showed the king a Castilian coin with the likenesses of Fernando and Isabel. Always eager to embellish, Columbus put a speech into the mouth of the young king praising the Spanish sovereigns. Unfortunately he spoiled the effect in the next sentence by confessing that he had actually understood little of what the king said.

The auspicious beginning of Columbus's stay on Española was also spoiled soon thereafter when disaster struck the fleet. On Christmas eve, the *Santa María* went aground on a bank off the northern coast of the island. Although this was the moment of greatest drama in the entire trip, Columbus reported it laconically in the diary, perhaps because it represented an unadorned loss for the expedition, one that could have been prevented by greater vigilance on his part. Several routine precautions in caring for the ship had been relaxed, perhaps because of the holiday, setting the stage for the tragedy. First, Columbus had taken the word of sailors who had surveyed the bay for safe anchorages – something he had not done before – rather than checking the situation himself. Compounding error with error, that night the tiller was under the control of a ship's boy rather than an experienced helmsman. Columbus cannot be blamed for that violation of the standing rules. The ship's master and owner Juan de la Cosa bore responsibility for allowing the helm to be operated by an incompetent crew member.

The *Santa María* went aground suddenly. The boy's cry of anguish awakened Columbus, who quickly analyzed the situation. His first thought was to have the ship's boat tow the larger vessel to deeper water, and he gave that order to the master when he appeared on deck. The master took a party in the boat, but instead of attaching a towline they made for the safety of the *Niña*, whose officers quite rightly refused to let them board. As Columbus watched his men rowing away in the boat, he ordered the *Santa María*'s mainmast to be cut down and thrown overboard in a desperate attempt to lighten the vessel. It was too late. The tide was running out, and, as the ship stood higher and higher out of the water, her planking opened and broke apart. In what must have been a bitter moment, Columbus then abandoned his flagship and took his crew to the *Niña*, where they waited for the dawn.

In the clear light of day, there was nothing to be done but salvage what they could from the wreck, but they lacked the manpower to do it on their own. Before dawn Columbus had sent a party ashore to carry a message to the local ruler, King Guacanagarí, whose town was 1½ leagues away. The king immediately sent his people in large canoes to help in the unloading and donated some houses to the Europeans for the storage of their goods and equipment.

Columbus's attitude toward the local people displayed a curious but understandable ambivalence. He placed armed guards around the clock to guard the storage houses, but in his words to the Catholic Monarchs he called the Indians a loving people, docile and without greed. On that dismal Christmas Day, with his flagship lost and the *Pinta* elsewhere, he could still write,

> And I assure Your Highnesses that in the world there are no better people or a better land. They love their neighbors as themselves, and they have the sweetest speech in the world; and [they are] gentle and are always laughing. They go about as naked, men and women, as their mothers bore them, but may Your Highnesses believe that among themselves they have very good customs, and the king [observes a] very wonderful estate in such a dignified manner that it is a pleasure to see everything.

There was no choice but to leave a portion of the fleet's crew on Española, because they could not all travel home on the *Niña*. On the day after Christmas, preparations began for their stay. Guacanagarí, their impromptu host, arrived at dawn. He and Columbus shared a ceremonial meal and then toured the area together. Columbus described the king as an impressive figure. *"In his table manners, his urbanity, and* [his] *attractive cleanliness, he quite showed himself to be of noble lineage."* Nonetheless, Columbus lost no time in trying to impress him with the strength of the Europeans' weapons. He had a Turkish bow and arrows brought out and demonstrated for the king and followed that by a demonstration of the gunpowder weapons they had available, the lombard (a small cannon) and the spingard (a heavy muzzle-loading gun with a flared mouth). At the same time he ordered his men to begin building a fortress. In this as in so many other actions, Columbus was consciously replicating the methods of the Portuguese in Africa. His hosts on Española may have loved their neighbors as themselves, but Columbus was keen to do everything he could to protect the men he was forced to leave behind. If the friendliness of the locals turned to hostility, his men would be in dire peril.

As preparations proceeded for leaving the settlers, Columbus's diary entries combined practicality with religious speculations. In the crisis caused by the loss of his flagship, many of Columbus's deepest emotional and intellectual traits came to the fore. Despite objective circumstances, on December 26 he reiterated in the strongest possible terms that profit could be made in the new lands, probably to persuade his royal backers, but possibly also to persuade himself. He stressed the passivity of the local inhabitants, even as he reported on the fort he had ordered his men to build. He seemed anxious to persuade himself that his men would be safe in an alien land.

In his anguish after the shipwreck, Columbus saw the will of God behind his predicament. He interpreted the wreck as a sign that he should further explore the area and found a settlement. Once a trade in gold had been developed, he urged Fernando and Isabel to remember his suggestion to use the profits for the conquest of Jerusalem, the time-honored goal of Christian crusaders and millenarians alike. Many contemporary Franciscans were coming to believe that the kings of Spain were ordained by God to carry out that worthy task and to preside over the conversion of the world's peoples to Christianity. The universal empire of Spain would thereby usher in the end of the world and the Second Coming of Christ. Columbus's Franciscan connections were already well established before his first voyage, and they strengthened in his later years, even as he befriended members of other religious orders. His subsequent contacts with friars and clerics helped to intensify his religious convictions and his own millenarian and apocalyptic beliefs.

Although Columbus accepted the shipwreck as God's will, he was also anxious to deflect blame from himself for that incident. He reported that the *Santa María* was not a good ship for exploration to begin with – too slow and not sufficiently maneuverable – and that he would not have used it if the people of Palos had fulfilled their obligation to the crown to provide the necessary ships. (Columbus had evidently forgotten that their obligation had been fulfilled with the two caravels.) Even so, the ship might have been saved after the wreck *"if it had not been for the treachery of the master and of the men, all or most of whom were from [his] region [in Spain]. . . ."* For all the self-serving tone of Columbus's remarks, it is difficult to disagree with him on that point.

After the loss of the *Santa María*, Columbus was ready to return to Spain. The fleet had accomplished a great deal already, and with only one ship left another disaster could prove insurmountable. Columbus still feared that Martín Alonso Pinzón might sail for home on the *Pinta* and steal his glory. Columbus's resolve to begin the return voyage hardened when Guacanagarí told him on December 27 that the *Pinta* had been sighted. The king quickly sent a canoe to search for it, and Columbus sent a sailor along with the Indians.

Columbus was leaving thirty-nine men behind on Española, in the settlement he called La Navidad, commemorating its birth in the shipwreck of the *Santa María* on Christmas Day. Those remaining would be under the authority of Diego de Arana (the cousin of Columbus's mistress), Pero Gutiérrez (a royal official), and Rodrigo de Escobedo (a notary). The men seemed to be relatively secure. They had their fortress, built with some timbers from the wreck. They believed they had the friendship and support of King Guacanagarí. Nonetheless, to reinforce earlier lessons Columbus ordered war games to be staged. Among other things, he had a lombard shoot a hole through the wrecked hull of the *Santa María*. Then he had the departing crew and the remaining settlers stage a mock battle, all designed to impress the locals with the power of European fighting skills. There is no way to know how the display was interpreted by its intended audience, however.

On January 4, Columbus left shore with a favorable wind and worked the *Niña* eastward along the northern coast of Española, which he had persuaded himself was Cipango. On January 6, a lookout saw the *Pinta* sailing toward them. The caravels approached one another (somewhat warily, we might suspect) and anchored together for the night. Martín Alonso Pinzón came aboard the *Niña* and offered a series of excuses for having left the company, all of them unpersuasive. Columbus, seething inside, nonetheless hid his anger so as not to endanger their return voyage. Pinzón told Columbus that the *Pinta* had first sailed to the island the natives called Baneque (now called Great Inagua), but they had failed to find gold there. They had also gone to Española and had been conducting a lively gold trade before they rejoined the *Niña*.

The *Pinta*'s reappearance seems to have persuaded Columbus to explore a bit farther. The newly reassembled fleet coasted eastward along Española, and in the course of their exploration they encountered the first hostile islanders of the voyage. The Europeans put them to flight after a brief skirmish. Columbus believed they had finally met the Caribs, enemies of all the islanders they had met until then, fierce and widely believed to be cannibals. The fleet sailed away from Española in search of the island of the Caribs, but less than a day out the winds blew favorably for a direct return to Spain. Perhaps rethinking the merits of chancing another hostile encounter, and with the crews grumbling about the poor condition of the *Pinta* and the *Niña*, Columbus took advantage of the wind and decided to set a course straight for Spain, northeast by east.

THE RETURN VOYAGE

The return voyage presented a sharp contrast to everything the expedition had experienced thus far. The idyllic weather, the favorable winds, the exciting discoveries, and the good health that had sustained the spirits of the admiral and his crews until then were replaced by increasing difficulties. They could not find the proper wind, and Columbus at first persisted on a direct course toward Spain, although he was bucking the northeast trade winds in so doing. Only when he finally took the ships farther north did they find the winds to take them eastward without resistance. Columbus probably knew the easterly wind patterns before he left Spain, but he found the westerlies only by trial and error.

To add to their worries, the *Pinta* was sailing badly and needed a new mast. Columbus could not resist noting in his log that Martín Alonso Pinzón should have spent part of his time in the Indies cutting and mounting a new mast, as Columbus had done for the *Niña,* rather than searching for gold. They had left Española with not much to eat except bread and wine and the sweet potatoes (*ajes*) they had got from the Indians. Columbus had intended more extensive provisioning while exploring other islands, but the abrupt decision to head for home changed his plans. The periods of calm encountered on the homeward voyage were worrisome, but at least the men could fish at those times. Worse, they could not be sure where they were. In addition to Columbus, there were four qualified pilots on the *Niña* alone. Comparing notes on February 6, Vicente Yáñez charted the ships south of the Azores and west of Madeira, whereas Bartolomé Roldán had them south of the Azores and west of Porto Santo.[9] By the tenth of February, all four pilots believed they had passed the Azores, although Columbus believed they were still on the approach.

On the fourteenth of February, after two days of increasingly heavy weather, a storm broke over them in earnest. As the boiling seas heaved the small ships around, the *Pinta* could no longer hold her position and was blown out of sight. To boost morale on the *Niña,* Columbus ordered a lottery held to request divine intervention in their plight. The men put chickpeas into a bag, one of them marked with knife cuts in the form of a cross; the man who drew the marked chickpea would make a pilgrimage to the monastery of Guadalupe in Extremadura and donate a five-pound wax candle in thanks for their safe deliverance. Columbus was the first to draw and picked out the marked chickpea. Then another lottery was held, promising a pilgrimage to Santa María de Loreto in the Papal States if the ship were saved. This time a sailor drew the lot, and Columbus promised to pay the expenses for his trip. A third lottery called for a vigil and a mass in the church of Santa Clara de Moguer. Again Columbus drew the marked chickpea. Afterward the whole crew vowed to go in their shirtsleeves to the first shrine to Saint Mary they could find after their next landing.

The storm was terrifying, as Atlantic storms frequently are in winter. In addition to praying for divine aid, Columbus did what he could to improve their chances. The *Niña* was sailing badly, in part because she carried no ballast. They had unloaded as many of the supplies as possible before leaving their mates at La Navidad. Columbus had intended to reballast the ships at the Carib island they were seeking when they decided to head directly for Spain instead. To make up for the missing ballast, Columbus had the crew fill the empty wine and water barrels with seawater and by that expedient somewhat stabilized the vessel.

In the heightened emotions inspired by the storm, Columbus revealed a bit more of himself in the diary than he had done before. He was fearful that he would die and leave his two sons orphans. But he was probably less afraid of dying than of failure. If he died and Martín Alonso Pinzón survived and reached Spain, Pinzón would steal the glory for the discoveries. That was a particularly galling possibility to Columbus, because he wanted to show everyone that he had been right all along. As Las Casas summarized the diary entry for February 14, Columbus chided himself for his fears, attributing them to his *"small faith and loss of faith in Divine Providence."* He also reminded himself that *"since earlier he had entrusted his destiny and dedicated all of his enterprise to God,"* he should have faith that God would see him safely to the conclusion of his mission.

In his desperation to claim the credit that was his due, Columbus wrote as much about the voyage as he could on a parchment addressed to Fernando and Isabel. He prepared the message secretly and then wrapped the parchment securely in a waxed cloth. Ordering a barrel brought to him, he placed the packet inside and had the barrel thrown into the sea. The crew assumed the packet and the barrel had something to do with an act of piety and were spared the alarm of knowing that the admiral doubted they would survive.

Almost miraculously, on February 15 they sighted land, but they had no idea where they were. The pilots and sailors made wildly varying estimates of their position, proving only how confused and lost the storm had left them. Some thought they had sighted Madeira, others the Rock of Sintra near Lisbon, and others still that they were off Castile. Columbus thought they were in the Azores, or so he said when that turned out to be true. In an odd passage summarizing the diary, Las Casas says that Columbus claimed to know for certain they were near the Azores and congratulated himself and thanked the Lord that he had charted so well. Las Casas also noted in the entry for February 18 that Columbus had *"pretended to have gone a greater distance to confuse the pilots and sailors who were charting their course so that he would remain the master of the route to the Indies, as*

in fact he does, since none of them showed on their charts his true route,
because of which no one could be sure of his route to the Indies."

It is difficult to know what to make of this passage. It may be an
accurate summary, or it may be yet another incidence of Las Casas's
failure to understand nautical matters. The biographers of Martín
Alonso Pinzón provide some support for the notion that Columbus
had a superior understanding of the route. They suggest that Pinzón
rejoined the admiral on January 6 only because he did not trust himself to find the way home alone.[10] Following that logic, his subsequent separation from the *Niña* during the storm may not have been
accidental; once the fleet had found the westerlies, Pinzón may simply have used the storm as a pretext for going his own way again.
On the inbound as well as on the outbound voyage, Las Casas's notion that Columbus kept a false log is nearly impossible to credit.
The false information Columbus supposedly disseminated – too short
outbound and too long inbound – would have produced an enormous discrepancy in the estimate of the distance traveled each way.
Surely someone would have noticed, if not at the time then later in
the volumes of testimony generated by the lawsuits over Columbus's estate. In order to resolve this and many other strange passages
in the summarized diary, we can only hope that the original diary is
found one day. In its absence, we do not accept the notion of a false
log.

Contrary winds kept the *Niña* from anchoring until the eighteenth
of February, when local residents told them they had reached the
island of Santa María in the Azores. On the evening of the eighteenth, a delegation from the captain of the island came to give the
Niña fresh provisions and a message that the captain himself would
appear the next day. Columbus sent half his men ashore the next
morning in their shirtsleeves to fulfill their collective vow of a pilgrimage to the first shrine they saw dedicated to the Virgin. Columbus planned to go with the rest of the crew when the first group
returned. Despite the welcoming words of the day before, however,
the captain of the island arrested the shore party and threatened the
others still on the *Niña*. Columbus shouted that he was the Admiral
of the Ocean Sea and that he still had enough men to sail to Seville
and alert the Spanish monarchs about the outrage being perpetrated.
The captain shouted back that in Portuguese territory letters from
the Spanish monarchs had no validity; in any case, he added, he was
acting on orders from the Portuguese king. Columbus then threatened to seize a hundred captives on the island and take them to Castile. With the weather still bad, half his crew detained on shore, and
no safe harbor, Columbus had the ship head out to sea once again.

At that point, still hindered by bad weather and with only three real sailors among those still on the caravel, Columbus drew on religious speculation to explain the real world. He expressed astonishment about the bad weather, contrasted with the excellent weather they had enjoyed in the Indies. Recalling that bad weather had also plagued them the previous August on the way to the Canaries from Spain, he speculated that in the Indies they had approached the terrestrial paradise. As proof, Las Casas said Columbus noted on February 21 that *"venerable theologians and wise philosophers"* had placed the terrestrial paradise at the end of the Orient, where the climate is most temperate, and that the Indies he had found were *"the end of the Orient."* Columbus's view of the world blended biblical prophesy and direct observation without any apparent contradiction. Despite his long experience as a merchant and mariner, his religious mysticism would often lead him to see what his religious beliefs prepared him to see.

The *Niña* returned to the island of Santa María on the twenty-first of February, for either Columbus did not want to leave his men stranded, or he believed he could not reach the mainland with the remaining crew. The captain of the island had softened his attitude somewhat and sent a delegation to the ship to examine Columbus's credentials. Evidently persuaded of the vessel's good faith, the captain released the launch and the shore party, who returned to the *Niña*. Columbus and his crew sailed along the coast of Santa María looking for a place to take on firewood and stone for ballast. After several days of fruitless searching, however, they caught a favorable wind on February 24 and headed for Spain.

Storms continued to bedevil the *Niña*. On the third of March a squall nearly tore the sails from the masts. It was again time for divine supplication, and Columbus held another chickpea lottery. The man chosen would go as a pilgrim in shirtsleeves to Santa María de la Cinta in Huelva. Again Columbus drew the lot, and one suspects that he had a trick or two (or perhaps a marked chickpea) up his sleeve. The men also vowed collectively to fast on bread and water the first Saturday after they reached land. Fierce wind and seas came from two directions, lashing the ship and placing all on board in mortal danger. With their sails nearly gone, they proceeded under bare poles through torrential rain and lightning. On the evening of the third they saw land, but it was too dangerous to approach at night, and they had all they could manage to stay out at sea. By dawn they recognized the Rock of Sintra, near the mouth of the Tagus River leading to Lisbon. With no hope of going anywhere else, they sailed into the river and anchored at Restelo, an outer harbor of the Portuguese capital.

When they reached land, the crew realized just how fortunate they had been to escape destruction. The townspeople of Cascais had been watching them all morning in earnest prayer, and after they anchored people approached them marveling at their success in reaching land. The sailors of Restelo told them that the winter had been the stormiest in memory and that in Flanders twenty-five ships had been lost.

Columbus wrote the king of Portugal, asking for permission to take the ship to Lisbon to reprovision. A large Portuguese royal ship was also anchored at Restelo. On March 5 its master, Bartolomeu Dias de Lisboa, approached the *Niña* in an armed boat and asked Columbus to accompany him and report to the ship's captain and other officials on board.[11] Columbus replied that he was the admiral of the monarchs of Castile and that he did not have to leave his ship to report to anyone. Dias replied that Columbus could send the *Niña*'s master to give the report, but the admiral refused even that request, insisting on his dignity. Finally the Portuguese master came aboard the *Niña* to examine Columbus's papers. After he reported back to his ship, his captain *"with great ceremony, and with kettledrums, trumpets, and horns sounding gaily, came to the caravel and talked to the Admiral and offered to do all that he commanded."*

The king of Portugal was at that time staying outside Lisbon. He requested that Columbus join him there. Perhaps nursing old wounds for his rejection years before, or perhaps suspicious of the king's intentions, Columbus was reluctant to go. Nonetheless, he acceded to the king's request and was courteously received by the king and later by the queen. King João II heard the report of Columbus's discoveries and speculated that the new lands might belong to him, because of his treaty agreements with Castile. Columbus said he knew nothing about the treaty but that his orders had been to avoid Guinea and Mina and that he had done so.

Las Casas, in his *Historia de las Indias,* added details about the interview that appeared in neither the *Diario* nor in Hernando Colón's biography, most notably concerning the Indians Columbus brought with him. During the interview, João had a container of dried beans (*habas*) placed on a table before him. Then he ordered one of the Indians to arrange the beans in the form of a map of the islands Columbus had visited. The Indian quickly arranged the beans to indicate Española, Cuba, and the Bahamas. As if by accident (Las Casas portrays King João as devious and scheming), João disarranged the bean map. Later he asked another Indian to make another map with the beans, and the man quickly remade the main features of the first map and added many more islands. Las Casas added a dramatic climax to the scene, almost surely fictional but effective nonetheless.

Then the king, understanding clearly the greatness of the discovered lands, and the riches that had already been imagined in them, not being able to hide the great pain which he felt . . . for the loss of such inestimable things, which through his own fault he had let slip through his hands, with a loud voice and an impulse of anger against himself, beat his fist upon his chest saying: "Oh, man of poor understanding, why did you allow such an enterprise of such importance to get out of your hands?"[12]

Whether King João made such an outburst or not, he ensured that every honor was shown to Columbus. The matter of what lands belonged to whom would take another year to sort out.

On March 13, 1493, with its reprovisioning completed, the *Niña* sailed for Andalusia. Two days later the ship and its weary crew crossed the bar at Saltés and anchored at Palos, the harbor they had left on August 3 the year before. Later that same day, Martín Alonso Pinzón brought the *Pinta* into Palos harbor, having landed first at Bayona in Galicia on the northwestern coast. Columbus's momentous first voyage to the Western Hemisphere was over, but neither he nor any of the men who accompanied him knew where they had been or what their experience would ultimately mean.

9

Conquest and Colonization: Spain in the Caribbean

W HEN COLUMBUS RETURNED to Spain in the spring of 1493, he believed he had accomplished his dream of reaching Asia by sailing westward from Europe. True, he had not found the populous cities and the thriving trade Marco Polo had described. True, he had been forced to abandon his original intention of establishing a trading factory and had founded an unplanned colony instead. Still, despite the absence of golden-roofed temples and harbors filled with ships, and despite the presence of naked natives in place of richly clad Chinese merchants and courtiers, Columbus was determined to wrest every ounce of profit and prestige from the lands he had discovered. He remained supremely optimistic and determined to convey his optimism to his patrons in Spain.

Columbus's efforts at manipulating opinion in Spain about his triumph began even before the voyage was over, when he had sealed a message into a barrel dropped into the water off the Azores, hoping that it would eventually reach Spain. That desperate gesture shows Columbus's passion to be honored as a great explorer, even if the honor were posthumous. Once he had safely come to shore, his biographers tell us that he dispatched other letters from Lisbon. Presumably he sent one letter to Fernando and Isabel, but if so it has been lost, along with any others he may have written. His letters from Lisbon must have been circumspect, given the need for security, and it is not implausible that they were intercepted. When he got back to Palos, he wrote again, presumably telling the sovereigns that he would await their reply in Seville. And, from either Palos or Seville, he probably sent them a full report of his voyage.

We can only speculate, because no letter reporting the voyage in Columbus's own hand has been discovered. The only report available is the so-called letter to Luis de Santángel, which exists in the Archive of Simancas but not in Columbus's hand. Scholars now think that the Santángel letter is a revised version of a lost Columbian original, doctored by royal officials at the behest of Fernando and Isabel, who were in Barcelona when the original letter arrived. In the revised version, it formed the basis of numerous printed editions that circulated throughout Europe.[1]

We will deal a bit later with the question of how and why the monarchs presumably had the Santángel letter altered. Even if we accept that Columbus was not its sole author, the letter still sketched the general outlines of his first glimpse of lands in the western ocean and continued the tone of unbridled optimism that appeared in the diary of the voyage. The letter began with the story of Columbus's island discoveries, which he named in descending hierarchical order, first after his divine sponsors, then after his human sponsors. The first island he named for the central figure of Christianity – Jesus Christ, the Holy Savior (San Salvador). The second he named for Mary the mother of Christ, Santa María de la Concepción. The next three he named for the Spanish royal family: Fernandina for King Fernando; Isabela for Queen Isabel; and Juana for the monarchs' son and heir Prince Juan. Last of all, the island where he confidently expected to find gold he named the Spanish island, La Isla Española.

Echoing the religious and secular legends that formed part of the consciousness of Columbus and other Christian Europeans of his time, Columbus presented these islands as a combination of the terrestrial paradise described in the Bible and a secular wonderland of untapped wealth. In his description, the islands of the Caribbean sounded even better than the fabled Orient. All of the islands, he said, were inhabited by peaceful and gentle people, who were as naked as the day they were born and had no skill with weapons. Willing to trade anything they had for European trifles, they could easily be put to work and converted to Christianity. Presumably they would accept their new masters peaceably and thus be protected against enslavement. But there were other native tribes, known as fierce fighters and cannibals, who would have to be conquered and could then be enslaved for profit. In appearance they were like the gentle Indians, but they wore their hair long like women and used bows and arrows instead of spears. Columbus knew that his audience was familiar with stories of monsters and variant human races. Educated Europeans had been reading about strange, semihuman creatures for centuries, in works ranging from Isidore of Seville in the seventh century to John Mandeville in the fifteenth. They would expect something similar from Columbus, and he did not disappoint them. In his letter to Santángel, Columbus confided that although he had encountered no monstrous races he had heard stories about them. In eastern Cuba he had been told that there were people born with tails. Somewhere east and south of Española there was reportedly an island with hairless people and incalculable amounts of gold; and the island of "Matininó" supposedly contained an Amazon society, where women warriors with copper breastplates lived alone without the regular company of men.

Monstrous races of men, from a Spanish edition of John Mandeville's book of travels. The title page from this 1531 edition indicates that the book has been updated to include the Indies. (From Sir John Mandeville, *Libro de las maravillas del mundo* [Valencia, 1531]. Photo courtesy of the James Ford Bell Library, University of Minnesota.)

As for the potential profits to be made, Columbus exaggerated mightily, knowing that his reputation and his future success would depend on the profitability of the lands he had discovered. The islands were *"fertile to a limitless degree,"* he announced, blessed with harbors *"beyond comparison with others which I know in Christendom."* Cuba, he claimed, was larger than England and Scotland and had eastern mountains higher than those in the Canaries. Española, whose coastline he described as longer than that of the Iberian Peninsula, was beautifully wooded and contained fair fields. The human population was numberless, the land afforded vast amounts of spices, and the interior possessed *"great mines of gold and other metals."* Columbus announced that on this marvelous island he had founded a large town, La Navidad, *"in the best position for the mines of gold . . . and for [trade] with the mainland . . . belonging to the Grand Khan, where there will be great trade and gain."* He said nothing of the shipwreck that had forced him to establish the colony and nothing about the low-lying position of the land that made it unsuitable for long-term settlement.

The letter concluded with a litany of profitable commodities available in the islands. Columbus promised the monarchs as much gold as they desired. He wrote of spices and cotton, *"as much as their highnesses shall command";* mastic, *"as much as they shall order to be shipped";* aloe wood, *"as much as they shall order to be shipped";* and slaves, *"as many as they shall order to be shipped and who will be from the idolaters."* He reported that he thought he had found rhubarb and cinnamon as well, and he confidently promised that *"I shall find a thousand other things of value."*

Several conclusions emerge from reading this letter, which presents Columbus's expedition in the best possible light. Above all, it is a tissue of exaggerations, misconceptions, and outright lies. Columbus had found no gold mines. He was mistaken when he identified mastic and aloe. The rhubarb and cinnamon he thought he had found would turn out to be mistakes as well. His geographical and topographical assertions were even more wrongheaded. Cuba is not bigger than England and Scotland, Española has a much shorter coastline than the Iberian Peninsula, and the mountains of eastern Cuba are not as tall as those in the Canaries. The only local items that had real commercial potential were cotton and the Indians themselves, and fifteenth-century Europe had limited demand for cotton and slaves. The summary of the on-board diary suggests that Columbus had given up hope of finding the Great Khan and rich Asian commerce in the immediate vicinity of the islands, yet Columbus's letter to Santángel reported that La Navidad was perfectly placed to benefit from that commerce.

Obviously Columbus had inflated the evidence to support his main contention – that he had found new lands of boundless wealth and numerous peoples apt for Christian conversion. He emphasized and exaggerated the positive features, minimized or omitted the negative features, and exuded energy and optimism. Whether or not he really believed what he wrote, he proved once again that he was one of the greatest salesmen of his time. His self-serving use of evidence and his powers of persuasion had already carried him far from his relatively humble origins. His unshakable confidence had enabled him to approach the most powerful monarchs of his time and to win the support of Fernando and Isabel. He had also won the support of knowledgeable people as diverse as Friar Antonio de Marchena, Luis de Santángel, and the Pinzón brothers. Within a few days of meeting Columbus, Martín Alonso Pinzón, that tough and canny entrepreneur, had exhorted the sailors of the Tinto River ports to stop moping and join a voyage that would surely find the golden roofs of Cipango.

Clearly, Columbus the masterful salesman could inspire a wide range of people to want what he had to sell. But in selling his vision of the Indies, he promised too much and implied that success would come quickly. His glorified descriptions of the islands, which he may sincerely have believed to be near the terrestrial paradise of the Bible, embellished reality in powerfully evocative terms for those with a classical and Christian education. He created an image of the Americas before contact with Europeans that still glows five hundred years later. Like Columbus's audience, sophisticated humanity continues to long for a terrestrial paradise, unspoiled and endlessly bountiful. Columbus's arcadian imagery would betray him when it became apparent that treasures were not to be gained for the asking and that extracting profits would be extraordinarily difficult. When reality intervened, Columbus needed the practical skills of a manager and administrator; not only did he lack those skills, but he seemed to lack the temperament to develop them. Columbus's enterprise of the Indies, so long in the planning, would quickly outgrow his abilities. Over his protests, the Spanish monarchs would eventually remove him from control, in part because he oversold what he had discovered.

But all that was in the future. In 1493, Columbus and his seven Taino companions were the toast of the continent. Even before he made his way to the royal court, versions of his letter were coming off printing presses all over Europe, spreading his fame and aiding the Spanish effort to secure papal recognition for Castilian control of the islands in the western ocean. The first edition of the letter, in the original Castilian, was published in Barcelona at the beginning of April 1493, some two weeks before Columbus himself arrived there. An Aragonese cleric, Leander del Cosco, translated it into Latin, and before the year was out three editions had been printed in Barcelona, the same number in Paris, and other editions in Antwerp and Basel. Giuliano Dati produced a much-embellished and rhymed version in Italian that was published in Rome and Florence in 1493.[2]

Just as Columbus crafted his report to his own advantage, the monarchs and their advisers tailored it to suit their interests. By treaty and papal bull Spain had sovereignty over the islands of the Canaries already discovered and yet to be discovered. Several small but significant fictions formed part of the Santángel letter as we know it, apparently designed to show that the islands Columbus had discovered were near the Canaries and in fact part of the same chain. First, the letter stated that the entire voyage had taken twenty days, whereas it had really taken thirty-three days after leaving the Canaries. Second, the location of the new islands was put at 26 degrees north latitude, identical to that of the Canaries. Española in fact is located between 18 and 20 degrees north latitude. Columbus's logbook put Española at 34 degrees north and Cuba at 42 degrees north latitude, safer from the standpoint of the treaties with Portugal but not close enough to the Canaries to be useful as propaganda. The figure in the Santángel letter was clearly a politically motivated fabrication. Finally, the letter was dated at sea, on February 15, "sobre las Yslas de Canarya" (off, or near the Canary Islands), when in fact on that date Columbus estimated that they were among the Azores. If these fictions associating the Columbian discoveries with the Canaries aided the Spanish campaign at the papal court, all to the good. If they helped to disguise the true locations and sailing directions from the Portuguese, even better.[3]

THE TREATY OF TORDESILLAS

The altered Santángel letter was part of the shrewd diplomacy of the Spanish monarchs, designed to ensure that the lands Columbus had claimed for them would stay in their possession. By the terms of the agreements of Alcáçovas-Toledo in 1479–80, the Portuguese had a presumptive claim to new discoveries in the Atlantic south of the Canaries, as King João II had reminded Columbus in 1493. Beyond those agreements, the pope had issued a bull, in 1481, called *Aeterni regis,* granting the Portuguese a monopoly on navigation south of the Canaries and west of Africa. (A papal bull was a charter granted by the pope, called a "bull" because of the official seal, or *bullarum,* it bore. A bull is designated by the first words of its text.) Because the language and the substance of both the 1481 bull and the bilateral agreements of 1479–80 recognized Portuguese interests in the Atlantic, Fernando and Isabel turned to the pope to support their claims to the lands discovered by Columbus. The altered letter to Santángel was part of their overall strategy to influence the pope.

Even before Columbus arrived in Barcelona, they dispatched envoys to the papal court and to the king of Portugal regarding their claims. Luckily for Spain's interests, the pope at the time was Alexander VI, a member of the Borja (spelled Borgia in Italy) family of Valencia in the kingdom of Aragón. Because Spain was too valuable an ally for the papacy to alienate, Alexander VI issued four bulls in 1493 advancing Castilian claims in the Atlantic. In the first two, the pope granted Castile sovereignty over all lands discovered or to be discovered in the area Columbus had explored. The third, *Inter caetera,* dated May 4, 1493, drew a north-south line 100 leagues (375–400 miles) west of the Azores and the Cape Verdes. The Portuguese would hold sway east of the line. West of the line, the Castilians received the pope's grant of all islands and mainlands discovered or to be discovered toward the west and south, in the direction of India or any other direction, so long as the lands were not held by a Christian prince or king prior to 1493. Thus far, Portuguese interests had not been openly challenged.

The fourth bull, *Dudum siquidem,* changed the situation by extending Castile's sphere to lands discovered along the western or southern route, "whether they be in western parts, or in regions of the south and east and of India." João II of Portugal, whose kingdom's efforts at overseas exploration were focused on India, protested. Well aware of where his interests lay, the pope would nui rescind his support for Spain, so João approached Fernando and Isabel directly. After due deliberation, Portugal and Castile agreed to the Treaty of Tordesillas, signed in 1494. This crucial document redrew Pope Alexander VI's dividing line at 370 leagues (1,380–1,480 miles) west of the Azores and the Cape Verdes. Thus the Portuguese gained ratification of their African claims and the African route to India (plus Brazil, as it turned out). Castile gained an undiluted claim to what would become its empire in the Western Hemisphere.[4]

The flurry of diplomatic efforts touched off by his discoveries had little to do with Columbus. They began while he was in Andalusia, far from the royal court in Barcelona, and they concluded while he was on his second voyage.

TO THE ROYAL COURT

In the spring of 1493, Columbus remained in Andalusia, waiting for a response from Fernando and Isabel. From Palos he headed for Seville, after a detour to Puerto de Santa María with Juan de la Cosa to settle accounts for the loss of de la Cosa's *Santa María*.[5] Along the way, and later in Seville, Columbus and the seven Tainos who accompanied him attracted crowds. Bartolomé de Las Casas, as a teenager, saw the Indians at their lodgings in Seville, near the Arch of the Images leading to the Church of San Nicolás.[6]

Columbus had lived in Seville occasionally before 1492; thereafter he made it his principal base during his sojourns in Spain. He rented houses in the Calle Francos and cultivated a large social network that included family members, business associates from among the Florentine merchant community in the city, and local Franciscan and Dominican friars. Columbus seemed to enjoy having family and friends, especially family, around him. Shortly after returning from his first voyage across the ocean, he arranged to bring his sister-in-law Violante Moniz and her husband Miguel Moliart from Huelva to join him. He provided a home for them by asking Fernando and Isabel for a house in Seville that had been confiscated from one of Spain's expelled Jews. They obliged. In Seville, Violante maintained a home for Columbus and his son Diego, in between the admiral's voyages and when Diego was free from his duties as a page at the royal court. Eventually, Columbus's brothers Bartolomeo and Giacomo, two nephews from Genoa (Gian Antonio and Andrea), and three other siblings of his late wife all joined his entourage in Seville.[7]

When Columbus received the royal invitation to attend Fernando and Isabel at court, he headed across Spain for Barcelona, accompanied by the Indians and green parrots from the exotic lands he had discovered. The trip was a well-planned public relations bonanza. People crowded into the towns he passed, prompted by news of his intended itinerary and attracted by the novelty of his accomplishment.[8] Nothing could have spread the news more effectively about the Indies and their reported riches. Together with the printing of his letters, Columbus's stately progress from one corner of Spain to the other created a tidal wave of excitement about the lands and peoples across the ocean.

Columbus must have been very satisfied with the reception he received, and he was surely pleased with the response from Fernando and Isabel. Even before he reached court, the salutation of their letter of welcome indicated that they were disposed to confirm the promises made to him in the agreements of Santa Fe. The letter was addressed to *"don Cristóbal Colón, nuestro Almirante del mar Océano, e Visorrey y Gobernador de las islas que se han descubierto en las Indias"* (Sir Christopher Columbus, our Admiral of the Ocean Sea, and Viceroy and Governor of the islands that have been discovered in the Indies).[9] Acknowledging the successful completion of his voyage, Fernando and Isabel implicitly fulfilled their promises to Columbus by their salutation and later officially confirmed them in Barcelona.

Columbus's arrival in Barcelona in mid-April was tumultuous.

Through thronged streets he proceeded to the royal court, where Fernando and Isabel had arranged to receive him in the impressive Gothic throne room of the counts of Barcelona. He approached the rulers, knelt, and kissed their hands, as required by etiquette and custom. They rose and treated him with great honor, kissing his hands and inviting him to sit on the dais with them, their behavior demonstrating extraordinary favor. There he told them about his voyage and introduced the seven Indians he had brought with him, who served as representatives of the gentle islanders who longed to embrace Christianity. A solemn mass of thanksgiving concluded the welcoming ceremony.

In the weeks following that initial interview, public processions and private banquets in Barcelona continued to honor Columbus.[10] It was presumably at one of these banquets that the famous episode of "Columbus's egg" took place. As told by Girolamo Benzoni in 1572, another guest at the feast challenged the importance of Columbus's voyage by suggesting that anyone might have done the same. Columbus responded by taking an egg and asking if anyone could make it stand on end. After various guests had tried and failed, Columbus took the egg and set it down sharply on the table, crushing the shell slightly and leaving the egg standing in place. The moral of the story was clear for all to see: tasks that look difficult or even impossible become easy once someone has found the way to master them.[11] There is no proof that the episode of Columbus's egg ever happened, of course, but apocryphal stories have lives of their own, precisely because they demonstrate truths that transcend the specific event.

During the time that Columbus and his entourage remained in Barcelona, the Indians who accompanied him were all baptized, with the king and his heir Prince Juan acting as godfathers. The most prominent new Christian was a relative of Guacanagarí, who received the baptismal name of Fernando de Aragón after his royal sponsor. Another was baptized Juan de Castilla, receiving the name of his sponsor the prince. Columbus's most faithful interpreter received the Christian name Diego Colón, after Columbus's own first-born son.[12] The agreements between Columbus and the crown received royal confirmation as well. As an extraordinary sign of royal favor, beyond what was contained in written agreements, the monarchs allowed Columbus to place the lion of León and the castle of Castile – part of the royal insignia – on his own coat of arms. His brothers benefited as well. Bartolomeo and Giacomo both became members of the hereditary nobility of Castile, with the right to use the term *don* before their names. Because they are usually referred to as Bartolomé and Diego in the Spanish documents that chronicle

Banquet depicting the story of "Columbus's Egg." (From Theodore de Bry, *Reisen in Occidentalischen Indien* [Frankfurt, 1590–1630]. Photo courtesy of the James Ford Bell Library, University of Minnesota.)

their lives thereafter, we will use those spellings of their names from now on. In Barcelona, Columbus undoubtedly reached the pinnacle of his fame, if not of his fortune. Yet, ironically, Barcelona and the crown of Aragón as a whole would have little to do with the new lands, which had been claimed by Columbus for Castile and would remain as solely Castilian possessions.

Ever since he had lost his flagship at Christmas and been forced to leave thirty-nine men on Española, Columbus had been anxious to embark on a second voyage in order to relieve those he had left, to settle Española on a more secure basis, and to continue his exploration. The monarchs were in full agreement with the need for a second voyage. While Columbus was still in Barcelona, they appointed a team in Seville to make the preparations. Fernando and Isabel were vitally concerned for the welfare and conversion of their new subjects across the ocean. On May 29, 1493, they issued a set of instructions for the operation of the new settlement in the Indies that began with a statement urging good treatment of the Indians and their in-

Coat of arms adopted by Columbus in 1502. He had used variations of this design earlier. (From John Boyd Thacher, *Christopher Columbus: His Life, His Work, His Remains* [New York, 1903–4].)

struction in and conversion to Christianity. The clerical team appointed to carry out the Christian mission was under the leadership of Bernardo Buil, a former Benedictine monk who had become a preaching friar. The royal instructions called on Columbus to secure the best caravels and crews available in Andalusia for the voyage and continued with an outline of how they expected the enterprise to be run – as a royal monopoly. All goods coming or going across the ocean were to be registered in a customhouse in Cádiz. Everyone going to the Indies had to swear homage to Fernando and Isabel. All private trade was forbidden. The settlers were to be salaried employees who would be given their wages at regular musters, under the watchful eyes of officials of the crown and the admiral. The only trade permitted would be royal trade orchestrated by Columbus. For his position as admiral, Columbus would receive one-tenth of the profits from all trade. In addition, he could invest in up to one-eighth of the trade goods, in return for one-eighth of the eventual profits.[13] Fernando and Isabel seemed determined to keep a tight rein on their colonial enterprise, obviously attempting to duplicate the Portuguese model of overseas trade.

Columbus left Barcelona in the middle of June to return to Seville, taking with him a number of courtiers who wished to participate in his second expedition. During the overland journey, he may have made a pilgrimage to the shrine of Guadalupe in the hills of upper Extremadura, fulfilling the promise he had undertaken in the worst moments of the return voyage.[14] Although we have no explicit proof that Columbus visited Guadalupe, the chances are good that he did. He was a strongly religious man, as well as a mariner who shared the sailors' superstitions. He had won the chickpea lottery to make the pilgrimage for them all, and to neglect this duty would have offended the heavenly protector who had saved them from the storm. When he named one of the first islands that he found on the second voyage Guadalupe, he said he was making good a promise to the monks of the Extremaduran monastery who had asked him to do so. He was also making a gesture to the monarchs who employed him; Fernando and Isabel were staunch patrons of Guadalupe and spent much time there. The Virgin of Guadalupe would be associated with the Spanish conquests in mainland America as well, as the patroness of the Extremaduran conquistadors Cortés and Pizarro. Her veneration would be assured when a Mexican farmer said the Virgin of Guadalupe appeared to him in 1531; thereafter, her shrine became the most important place of pilgrimage in Mexico.

PREPARATIONS FOR THE SECOND VOYAGE

For the rest of his life, Columbus would find himself torn by the multiple responsibilities thrust upon him by the need for colonization and administration of the Spanish settlements in the Caribbean. Columbus was a complex man who had become a master mariner and navigator, a capable merchant, a religious visionary, a self-educated scholar of cosmography and the classics, and a gifted salesman. Now that his initial venture had been completed, he was called upon to master several other skills. He had to command a mixed complement of sailors, merchants, soldiers, farmers, clerics, and gentlemen-adventurers. He had to deal with the Castilian bureaucracy. He had to plan settlements and govern them. Columbus was always more interested in continued exploration than in the humdrum satisfactions of careful administration, and the new tasks constituted a challenge that he was unwilling or unable to meet. Although at first his inadequacies were masked by the competence of royal bureaucrats working with him, they became increasingly apparent as time passed.

The royal team outfitting the armada for the second voyage was headed by don Juan Rodríguez de Fonseca, member of an influential family, who in 1493 was archdeacon of Seville. Before his death in 1524, he rose, through a series of clerical appointments, to become bishop of Burgos for the last ten years of his life. Throughout their reign, the Catholic Monarchs entrusted Fonseca with the preparations for their armadas, and he seems to have justified their trust. Las Casas disapproved of Fonseca, however, in part because Fonseca repeatedly disagreed with Columbus. More generally, Las Casas disapproved of a bishop acting in the capacity of a royal purveyor; somewhat grudgingly, he described Fonseca as *"very competent for worldly business, outstanding at recruiting soldiers for sea armadas, which was more a task for a Biscayan than for a bishop."*[15]

The news of the first voyage spread so quickly and made the Indies seem so alluring that Fonseca and Columbus had no difficulty in finding about twelve hundred men to go on the second voyage. The initial plan for a trading post (*factoría,* in Castilian), or a series of them, had been abandoned as soon as it became apparent that large-scale production and trade did not exist in the islands. The preparations for the second voyage foresaw a modified version of the trading-post model, with the admiral exercising full control of all transactions, in the name of the crown. The settlers would be salaried employees who would obtain gold through trade with the islanders and provide support and protection for the enterprise as a whole. Consequently, the settlers included artisans and farmers in addition to soldiers and gentlemen-adventurers. According to Las Casas, they carried with them plants and animals for establishing agriculture and husbandry on a European model in the Indies: horses and cows, goats and sheep, wheat for planting, and seeds for garden vegetables and for citrus and apple trees.[16]

In Cádiz a large fleet of seventeen vessels was assembled, including three *naos: Colina, La Gallega,* and a new flagship *Santa María,* nicknamed *Mariagalante* (not, of course, the *Santa María* that had been wrecked off Española on the first voyage). The owner and master of Columbus's flagship was Antonio de Torres, a man with connections at court who also enjoyed Columbus's confidence. In addition to the *naos,* there were ten *carabelas redondas,* two lateen-rigged caravels, and other smaller vessels. On September 25, 1493, the fleet

Departure for the second voyage, with a fleet of seventeen ships. The engraving is from Caspar Plautius, *Nova typis transacta navigatio* [N.p., 1621]. The right-hand portion, showing Fernando and Isabel in Spain and the three ships nearest to them, is often used erroneously to illustrate the departure for the first voyage. (Photo courtesy of the James Ford Bell Library, University of Minnesota.)

departed from Cádiz for the Canaries, with Columbus's two sons Diego and Hernando watching until it was out of sight. Columbus was feeling slightly ill as the crew and passengers embarked, and he consequently failed to inspect the horses and arms brought aboard by the soldiers. That lapse in vigilance would cause problems later.

The fleet reached Gran Canaria on October 2 and stayed in port for a day to repair a leaking ship. By October 5 they were anchored at Gomera, where they topped off their provisions before beginning the Atlantic crossing. In addition to other supplies, at the last minute someone brought eight live pigs on board. Las Casas would later claim that these early transatlantic passengers formed the foundation stock of all the pigs in the Indies.[17] Michele de Cuneo, a Genoese who wrote the most gossipy of all the accounts of the second voyage, related that the stop at Gomera was not all serious business. *"If I told you how many celebrations, cannon shots, and salutes we made here, it would take too much space; and this was done in honor of the mistress of the place, because once our Admiral had been greatly in love with her."*[18] From this passing remark, romantic historians have woven a tale of blazing passion between the admiral and the female governor of the island, Beatriz de Bobadilla.[19] The truth of the matter, like many other aspects of Columbus's personal life, has not been found in the documentary record.

A prolonged calm kept the fleet from leaving the Canaries until October 13, a year and a day after the first expedition's landfall on Guanahaní. Columbus set his course west by south, not a direct route toward Expañola but an appropriate one for visiting the islands he expected to find to the east and south of Española. The ocean crossing was even quicker than on the first voyage, but still the passengers and crew groused about Columbus's order to keep on short rations until sighting land. Except for a four-hour storm, they experienced good weather throughout the voyage and sighted two islands on November 3. The first Columbus named Dominica, after the Latin word for "Lord God," and the second he called Santa María la Galante for his flagship, which he evidently found more pleasing than the ill-fated *Santa María* of the first voyage.

No diary by Columbus remains for the second voyage, but we have a letter he wrote to the Spanish monarchs, as well as vivid accounts left by other members of the expedition. The firsthand, hardheaded testimony of witnesses other than Columbus provides a sharp contrast to the admiral's own sentimental hyperbole. One of the fullest accounts comes down to us from Diego Alvarez Chanca, a physician from Seville who sailed with a royal commission as the fleet's doctor. Dr. Chanca, as he is usually called, wrote a long letter to the municipal council of Seville recounting the events of the voyage. The other important account was written by Michele de Cuneo, Columbus's friend from Savona, on the Ligurian coast near Genoa. He addressed his letter to a fellow Genoese, Hieronymo Annari. Although Chanca's letter can be considered official, in the sense that he wrote to public officials, both letters are valuable correctives to the admiral's overblown descriptions. Unlike Columbus, they had no reason to embellish what they saw. They were charmed by the scenery, but their accounts of the people of the islands and their customs contradicted Columbus's glowing accounts in many respects.[20]

Chanca's first description of a deserted village on the island named Santa María la Galante reported the discovery of human arm and leg bones in the houses, presumably the remains of a cannibal feast. Later, on Guadalupe, an island christened when the fleet arrived on November 4, Dr. Chanca reported the seizure of a number of Caribs and their captives, who fled to the Europeans for deliverance from the Caribs. The women captives were especially grateful to be rescued and secretly told the Europeans which of the islanders were Caribs and which were not. After this incident, Chanca and the other commentators began drawing a distinction between the Caribs, or cannibals, and the *"Indians,"* who were not cannibals and feared the

Caribs. From then on, some of the complexity of New World societies began to color their narratives.

Chanca was horrified by what he and his colleagues learned from the women they rescued. He described the Caribs as *"bestial"* and indicted their treatment of conquered peoples.

> These people raid the other islands and carry off the women whom they can take, especially the young and handsome. They keep them in service and have them as concubines, and they carry off so many that in fifty houses no males were found, and of the captives more than twenty were girls. These women also say that they are treated with a cruelty which appears to be incredible, for they eat the male children whom they have from them and only rear those whom they have from their own women. As for the men whom they are able to take, they bring such as are alive to their houses to cut up for meat, and those who are dead they eat at once. They say that the flesh of a man is so good that there is nothing like it in the world, and it certainly seems to be so for, from the bones which we found in their houses, they had gnawed everything that could be gnawed, so that nothing was left on them except what was too tough to be eaten. In one house there a neck of a man was found cooking in a pot. They castrate the boys whom they capture and employ them as servants until they are fully grown, and when they wish to make a feast, they kill and eat them, for they say the flesh of boys and of women is not good to eat. Of these boys, three came fleeing to us, and all three had been castrated.[21]

Chanca's matter-of-fact reporting of these horrors leaves little doubt of their authenticity.[22]

After leaving Guadalupe, the fleet sailed north, west of what are now called the Leeward Islands, which Columbus named from the Christian pantheon, some for Mary and others for the saints, including one for his own namesake Saint Christopher (San Cristóbal, now Saint Kitts). On the fourteenth of November, the expedition anchored on the island Columbus named Santa Cruz, known since its later French occupation as Saint Croix. There they had an encounter with the local Caribs that developed into a bitter fight. One day the Europeans saw a canoe approaching, with a party of three or four Carib men and two Carib women. They had two Indian captives aboard and had recently castrated them, the Europeans later learned. The Europeans gave chase in a ship's boat, and the Caribs met them with arrow shots, wounding several men, one of whom later died. The Europeans captured or killed everyone in the canoe; one Carib with a lance wound was left for dead in the water; when he was seen trying to swim away, he was hauled on board the ship and beheaded by the Europeans.[23]

That was the first major skirmish recorded between Americans and Europeans since the Skraelings and the Vikings had clashed five centuries earlier. It foreshadowed the shape of things to come, and it had been anticipated by the unrecorded strife on Española between the islanders and the Europeans Columbus had left behind on the first voyage. In the aftermath of the engagement, Michele de Cuneo related a sordid tale of his own, emblematic of the age-old relations between conquering men and conquered women. Cuneo had been in the ship's boat and participated in the skirmish.

> When I was in the boat I took a most beautiful cannibal woman, whom the lord Admiral made a gift of to me; and having her in my berth, with her being nude according to her customs, the desire to enjoy myself with her came over me; and wishing to put my desire to work, she resisting, she scratched me with her fingernails to such a degree that I would not have wished then that I had begun; but with that seen, to tell you the end, I grabbed a leather strap and gave her a good chastisement of lashes, so that she hurled such unheard of shouts that you could not believe. Finally, we reached an agreement in such a manner that I can tell you that in fact she seemed to have been taught in the school for whores.[24]

These two incidents in the same day interjected a harsh note of reality into the admiral's sanitized version of the encounter between two very different societies. The presence of outsiders had added a new element to local politics and provoked a mixed response, depending on whether the local people saw the outsiders as aggressors or potential allies. When fighting broke out, the outcome of the struggle depended on which side had the most power. Women, treated as prizes by locals and outsiders alike and lacking power, adapted to the changing situation as best they could. Although Columbus and the rest of the expedition did not know it yet, the same drama had already been played out at La Navidad, as it has been played out countless times throughout human history.

Leaving Santa Cruz on November 15, the expedition headed north for the chain of islands that Columbus named in Spanish the "Eleven Thousand Virgins," to commemorate the legend of Saint Ursula. The chain is known today as the Virgin Islands. The fleet coasted along the southern shore of the island that the Indians called Boriquén or Borinquen and which Columbus named San Juan Bautista. In time the island came to be called Puerto Rico for its earliest port city.

On November 22 the fleet reached a large island, which the Indian guides who had accompanied Columbus to Spain and back declared was Española. Because Columbus had seen only the mountainous part of Española on his first voyage, he found it hard to believe that the flat island he saw before him could be the same. He was later persuaded, however, and by the twenty-seventh the fleet reached Caracol Bay, where the *Santa María* had been lost eleven months before. Disturbing portents had already confronted the expedition regarding the fate of the original colonists. Near Monte Cristo, elsewhere on Española, Columbus had investigated possible sites for settlement, because he knew La Navidad was ill situated for long-term colonization. During the reconnoitering, shore parties encountered three badly decomposed corpses. One was bound around the neck, another around the feet, and the third had been bearded. No one on the fleet had ever seen a bearded Indian, so they concluded that the body belonged to one of the men Columbus had left at La Navidad.[25]

One night, as the fleet coasted toward Caracol Bay, canoes approached the ships, and the Indians in them asked for the admiral. After his ship had been indicated, they paddled up to it and asked to see Columbus. When he came on deck, they asked that his face be lighted so they could recognize him. Satisfied that he was the admiral they had been seeking, they said they were emissaries of Guacanagarí. Coming on board the flagship, they presented Columbus with a golden mask. They had another for the captain of the *Niña* on the first voyage, Vicente Yáñez Pinzón, but he had not joined the second expedition.

When asked about the thirty-nine Europeans at La Navidad, Guacanagarí's emissaries said they were all fine, except for those who had died of sickness and others who had got into quarrels. It turned out that those categories included the whole garrison. They had aroused hostility by seizing gold and other goods and by assembling harems of local women. One after another, they had been killed by the Indians. Guacanagarí was terrified that Columbus would hold him responsible and stayed in bed feigning a leg wound. He had not been responsible for the deaths, but he had been unable to prevent other chiefs and their men from killing the Europeans.

Once the full horror of the situation became clear, Columbus was even more concerned to found a suitable settlement. Taking the fleet back east along the coast, with great difficulty in the face of the steady trade winds, he found a location near where he believed that gold would be found and broke ground in early January 1494 for La Isabela, named in honor of the queen. For all his brave talk on the first voyage about noble sites for mighty cities, Columbus again chose poorly in founding La Isabela, locating it on a flat plain, a mile away from the nearest fresh water. Nevertheless, he began by laying out a grand classical grid of streets. Michele de Cuneo reported the more modest reality. *"Here we made two hundred houses, which are as small as hunting cabins back home and are roofed with grass."*[26]

The European settlers soon began to fall ill. Dr. Chanca put their sickness down to three reasonable causes: they had been on short rations during the voyage, because no one could be sure when they would find land; they had been forced to labor on the construction of La Isabela; and they had experienced a change in climate. Taken together, these changes would have been enough to cause anyone to sicken. They seem to have been suffering from malnutrition. Little of the imported seed brought along on the voyage had been planted, and that had not had time to mature. As a short-term expedient, Columbus ordered a flour mill built and then had the remaining seed grain ground for food. Dr. Chanca noted that the local fish were good, even better than in Europe, but they had to be eaten immediately or they spoiled. Recent research suggests that the settlers may have developed Reiter's syndrome, characterized initially by dysentery and later by arthritic conditions, especially of the lower joints; inflammation of the eyes, and even blindness; and a penile discharge. Its cause is a tropical bacillus named *Shigella flexneri,* and it is spread by unsanitary food handling.[27]

Columbus sent Alonso de Hojeda (sometimes spelled Ojeda) to reconnoiter the country in January, taking forty men with him. Hojeda was well known at the royal court as a client of the duke of Medinaceli and had captained one of the caravels on the second voyage.[28] He returned by the end of the month from a successful exploration of the island's interior with large nuggets of gold. Even though Columbus wanted to gather more gold to send back to Fernando and Isabel, he had no choice but to send most of the fleet back to Spain immediately for additional supplies. Columbus's fine plans for the second voyage were already going badly wrong, and he may have felt the need to present his version of the situation to Fernando and Isabel as soon as possible. His report (dated January 30, 1494) was structured like a legal deposition, or an official *relación* of the expedition's progress and problems. Its bearer had to be as carefully selected as its wording, and Columbus chose Antonio de Torres for the delicate task of carrying the written report and presenting an oral version of it to the monarchs. Torres was an ideal emissary, because of his connections at court: his sister had been the nurse (*ama*) of Prince Juan and could gain access to the monarchs for him. Columbus gave Torres a detailed set of instructions, indicating point by point what he should say in the royal audience. Fortunately for the historical record, both Columbus's instructions and the royal responses to them survive.[29]

The instructions reveal what Columbus thought he had accomplished and what he judged necessary to ensure the success of his plans. As usual, he took great care in presenting the best case possible to his audience. Torres was first instructed to kiss the royal hands and feet, in a classic gesture of obeisance and respect. Then he was to tell the monarchs, first of all, that ample evidence of spices could be seen from the shore on Española, and that Hojeda had reported finding rivers full of gold, in incredible amounts, during his scouting expedition to the interior of the island. The glowing prologue with these extravagant claims was an obvious exaggeration, similar to Columbus's earlier reports about the lands he had claimed for Castile. Despite the vast quantities of gold supposedly available, Torres was to tell the monarchs that the colonists would have to construct mines to extract it and that the crown should recruit miners, especially from the mercury mines at Almadén, to travel to Española. Indirectly, Columbus was warning the sovereigns that they should not expect quick returns on their investment.

Not surprisingly, given the annihilation of the original garrison, Columbus also retreated from his earlier confident reports about the gentle nature of the Indians. Even though he still called them *"very simple and without malice,"* he reported placing guards on duty day and night and ordering the construction of a wall around the Spanish settlement. He next mentioned a plan to build a fort to hold the gold until it could be loaded on ships for the voyage to Spain. As long as the Europeans remained watchful, Columbus assured Fernando and Isabel, the Indians would never attempt an assault, suggesting that a lack of care had led to the destruction of the garrison at La Navidad.

Columbus reported that his men were falling ill, which had prevented his sending more gold, but that their maladies were nothing to worry about. The change in air and water had sickened them, and when they received the Spanish food he was requesting they would recover. The dependence on Spain for provisions would be only temporary in this most beautiful of lands, he assured the monarchs. When the wheat and vines he had brought began to flourish, *"there will be no need of Andalucía or of Sicily,"*[30] two proverbially rich agricultural regions. At the moment, however, the situation was difficult. Poor casks had allowed most of the wine to leak away, and much of the salted meat turned out to be bad. Columbus asked the monarchs to send wine and wheat, biscuit, and salted meat to tide the expedition over. Among other items, he requested raisins, almonds, sugar, honey, and rice – foods that would continue to be part of Spanish dietaries for the sick for centuries to come. They were considered delicate and easy to digest, as well as serving as ingredients for many medicines. To assure the provisioning of these vital supplies, Columbus instructed Torres that if Fernando and Isabel were not in Seville when he arrived, he should give some of the gold to merchants for the needed supplies. The merchants could later present the gold to the monarchs and be compensated for it. Columbus also requested sheep and lambs, calves and young heifers, male and female asses, and mares.[31] It must have been clear by then that the islands lacked domestic animals altogether, both for food and for hauling power. Like so many other things, they would have to be imported by the colonists.

Columbus presented an elaborate scheme to increase the imports of livestock to the islands by establishing a regular trade, with royal permits and licenses, and royal inspectors on each ship to make sure the animals were not diverted away from the official colonies. Columbus knew the sharp practices of traders in Africa and the Atlantic islands and was anxious to prevent similar chicanery in the islands under his jurisdiction. He suggested that the funds could be raised to pay for the imports by exporting human slaves, one of the few salable items readily available in the islands:

> Payment for these things could be made . . . in slaves, from among these cannibals, a people very savage and suitable for the purpose, and well made and of very good intelligence. We believe that they, having abandoned that inhumanity [of cannibalism], will be better than any other slaves, and their inhumanity they will immediately lose when they are out of their own land.[32]

With the Torres fleet, Columbus had sent between twenty and thirty Indians, presumably cannibals. They were sold as slaves as soon as they reached Seville. If we are to believe Columbus, their slavery could be justified not only by their defiance of the Europeans but also because it was for their own good. Columbus instructed Torres to tell the monarchs,

> it is thought here that to take some of the men and women and to send them home to Castile would not be anything but well, for they may one day be led to abandon that inhuman custom . . . of eating, men, and there in Castile, learning the language, they will much more readily receive baptism and secure the welfare of their souls.[33]

Columbus also thought the capture of cannibals would make a positive impression on the Indians who were their mortal enemies.

The royal couple was in Seville when Torres arrived in the late spring of 1494. Despite all the rhetorical effects Columbus deployed to create a fine impression, the unsettling news from the islands seems to have aroused suspicions in the minds of his royal patrons. Sickness among the colonists and the lack of native domestic animals in the new colony could not be blamed on Columbus, nor had he been responsible for the provisioning, but the monarchs may have suspected a lack of care in his overall management of the expedition. It had just barely arrived, and already the basic requirements of life were in dangerously short supply. Moreover, Columbus had clearly neglected his duty by failing to inspect the troopers and their equipment before they were loaded. Fernando and Isabel had ordered twenty mounted troopers to be recruited from among the members of the Granadan branch of the national militia, or Santa Hermandad. They and the other armed men of the expedition had arrived in Seville well mounted and well armed, but Columbus never inspected them as they embarked. *"I did not see to it, because I was a little indisposed."*[34] Only when he reached Española did he realize that the troopers had sold their good horses and purchased cheap nags for the voyage, pocketing the difference in price. They and many other armed men had done the same with their weapons. Columbus estimated that the fighting men lacked one hundred cuirasses, one hundred harquebuses, one hundred crossbows, and a considerable amount of powder and shot.

It was clear from his report to the monarchs that Columbus could not control the troopers. Even when they were sick or when they refused duty, they would not allow anyone else to use their horses. Columbus proposed buying their horses, bad as they were, so that the expedition as a whole would get at least some use out of them. That must have seemed an astonishingly weak suggestion to Fernando and Isabel, skilled commanders who had brought a rebellious nobility under control in Castile and successfully waged a five-year battle against the Portuguese and a ten-year war against the Muslims. Columbus seemed unable to manage the resources given him, and he certainly seemed unable to command anyone outside a ship's crew. His version of events almost always blamed someone else when things went wrong. In the report sent with Torres, he complained about the behavior of many of the men who had come with him, failing to recognize that as the head of the expedition he was supposed to command obedience, not complain about its absence. His skills as a mariner supported his leadership at sea; they did not help him on land.

Whatever doubts they may have had, the monarchs responded generously to Columbus's requests in the spring of 1494, with a few notable exceptions. They rejected out of hand his proposal to buy the troopers' horses. Instead, Columbus was told to remind the troopers of their duty and force them to relinquish their horses when ordered to do so. If the horses suffered injuries, Columbus was to compensate the troopers who owned them, but under no circumstances was he to buy their horses. The monarchs deferred comment on Columbus's scheme to enslave New World cannibals to pay for European livestock. Isabel was very concerned about the possibly unjust enslavement of her new subjects, cannibals or not. She and Fernando told Columbus that he should combat the cannibals when the need arose and try to convert them to Christianity, but in the islands, not by bringing them to Europe.

COLUMBUS RESUMES EXPLORATION

After Antonio de Torres departed for Spain on the resupply mission, Columbus himself made an expedition into the interior of the island of Española in March of 1494 to seek gold. He left his brother Diego in charge of the settlement at La Isabela. Columbus led five hundred men into the interior, and their adventures and complaints were dispassionately recorded by Michele de Cuneo:

> . . . we spent twenty-nine days with terrible weather, bad food, and worse drink, but for the ardent desire for gold we all kept ourselves strong and daring. On the round trip we crossed two very wide rivers . . . by swimming; and the one who did not know how to swim had two Indians who floated him across. The Indians for affection and for some trinkets carried our clothes, arms, and everything . . . across on their heads. . . . In short time we made a wooden fort, impregnable to the Indians, called Santo Tomás, which was about 27 leagues from our village. Many times we made tests in those rivers, but no one ever found a single grain of gold.
>
> Therefore we ended up discontented with the Indians of that place, who all told us that the gold was in the control of the king Goacanaboa, who was found about 2 leagues away from our fort. As we were in the fort, many Indians of up to 10 leagues around came to see us as a wonder, carrying the gold they had, which they traded with us, so that we gathered up gold worth about 2,000 *castellanos*. . . . In addition, . . . trade was also done in secret and against instructions and orders . . . in the amount of some 1,000 *castellanos*. . . . Almost all [the guilty Europeans] were discovered, and those who were found at fault received a good chastisement: some they cut their ears and others the nose, which was painful to see.[35]

Immediately after his return from the interior, Columbus was ready to explore further. The mundane chores of administration bored him, and inland forays were not much better when they failed to yield gold in massive quantities. Accordingly, on April 24 he sailed from the settlement at Isabela for Cuba, which, after several vacillations, he had decided was a peninsula of the Asian mainland. Once again he left Diego in charge. His small fleet consisted of the original *Niña*, which also made the second voyage, and two smaller vessels, the *San Juan* and the *Cardera*, all three suitable for coastal exploration. On the twenty-ninth, they landed at the eastern cape of Cuba (which Columbus had named Cape Alpha and Omega on the first voyage) and performed the formal ceremony claiming the land for Castile.

Through May and into June of 1494, the fleet explored the southern coast of Cuba, without finding anything resembling Asia. Acting on information the Indians provided, Columbus took a detour to the south and came upon Jamaica. After finding hostile Indians and no gold, he returned to Cuba. By early June, about 50 miles from the western end of Cuba, he believed that he had reached the Gulf of Siam or the Malay Peninsula. He fantasized about completing the first circumnavigation of the world by sailing on farther west to work his way back to Spain. As his son Hernando put it, *"had he had plenty of food, he would have gone on to return to Spain by way of the East."*[36] The chronicler Andrés Bernáldez wrote that Columbus told him he thought he could make such a trip. Because Bernáldez wrote before the Americas were recognized as a barrier to the Pacific, he also considered such a trip plausible. According to Bernáldez, Columbus thought

> he had reached a point very near the Golden Chersonese [the Malay Peninsula]. . . . And there he formed the opinion that, if he were fortunate, he would be able to return to Spain by the East, coming to the Ganges and thence to the Arabian Gulf, and afterwards by way of Ethiopia, and afterwards he would be able to come by land to Jerusalem, and thence to Jaffa, and to embark and enter upon the Mediterranean Sea and thence come to Cadiz. The voyage could certainly be made in this way, but it would be very dangerous by land, since they are all Moors from Ethiopia to Jerusalem. But he could nevertheless have gone by sea and have gone from there to Calicut which is the city that the Portuguese have discovered [in India], and in order not to go by land but by water always, he would have had to return by the same Ocean Sea circumnavigating all Libya, which is the country of the negroes, and to go by the route by which the Portuguese come with the spice of Calicut.[37]

To confirm his perceptions, Columbus had his men attest and swear in writing that this Cuba, or Juana, was the mainland and could not possibly be an island. They were further required to affirm Columbus's erroneous reckoning that they had coasted Cuba for 335 leagues

(1,250–1,340 miles), that they had never heard of an island so large, and that they had no doubt it was the mainland.[38] This strange exercise could not change reality, but it could prolong Columbus's claim to have discovered the western route to Asia.

Then, because his supplies were dwindling fast, Columbus headed back to Española and the colony at Isabela. The return voyage along Cuba's southern shore was difficult, because the ships had to sail in shoal waters, eastward against the prevailing winds. Columbus then sailed for Jamaica, where he explored the island's southern shore, and on the nineteenth of August the little fleet left Jamaica for Española. Arriving at the end of the month off the southern coast, they had to ride out a hurricane, hiding behind an island Columbus had named Saona, in honor of the hometown of his companion and fellow Genoese Michele de Cuneo. Columbus became ill shortly thereafter, probably suffering from exhaustion, overexertion, and poor food. His officers took the fleet back to Isabela. When they arrived on September 29, Columbus had to be carried ashore.

Good news awaited them. Several months earlier, Columbus's brother Bartolomé, whom he had not seen for several years, had arrived. Bartolomé had been in France at the time of the first voyage and had been unable to reach Spain before the second expedition set sail, although both he and Diego had been made *hidalgos* (minor noblemen) at Columbus's grand reception at Barcelona. When Bartolomé finally reached Spain early in 1494, Fernando and Isabel appointed him captain of the small relief fleet that Juan Rodríguez de Fonseca was outfitting in Seville. Bartolomé set sail with two or three caravels and reached Española on June 24, 1494, carrying the much-needed supplies.[39] Any good news was welcome to Columbus, because conditions had gone from bad to worse at Isabela. Diego had proved to be even less effective as an administrator than Columbus, and discontent was running so high that disillusioned settlers had seized several caravels and sailed home to Spain without permission. Two years after Columbus had first crossed the ocean, the route was becoming well enough known to make transatlantic voyages possible for many experienced mariners, not just Columbus or the Pinzones.

Before the end of 1494, Antonio de Torres returned from Spain with another relief fleet and an invitation for Columbus from the Catholic Monarchs. They expressed pleasure with his work and his expertise and asked him to return to Spain to advise them on their negotiations with Portugal.[40] Columbus declined their request, but things might have gone better for him later had he accepted. Just possibly the monarchs were trying to ease Columbus honorably out of the administrative duties that did not suit his skills. A few years later they would not be so careful of his feelings.

In February of 1495, Antonio de Torres took a fleet back to Spain once again, and Columbus was determined to send with him proof that the colony was showing a profit. Consequently he organized a mass roundup of Indians, intending to send many of them back to Spain to be sold. His justification was one that was currently being used to justify enslavement in the Canary Islands: the islanders were at war with the Europeans. Whether in the Canaries or in the Caribbean, the indigenous peoples were considered subjects of the Castilian crown, and thus, in ordinary circumstances, protected against enslavement. Only if they warred against the Europeans could they be seized and enslaved, as captives in a "just war." By the time Columbus's second expedition arrived in the Indies, some of the people of Española had certainly turned hostile toward the Europeans, but that was beside the point. The monarchs wanted a moratorium on slaving until the situation could be clarified, and, unfortunately for all concerned, Columbus did not realize it. He and his men marched through the island with horses, dogs trained for warfare, and harquebuses, taking captives as they met resistance. Of the sixteen hundred persons captured, only five hundred fifty would fit on board the ships Torres was preparing for the voyage. At Columbus's order, about six hundred fifty were allotted to European settlers; the remaining four hundred he released. The released captives responded to their unexpected freedom with a mixture of relief and terror, which was obvious from Cuneo's report: *"among them were many women with infants at their breasts; in order to be better able to flee from us, for fear that we would capture them again, after abandoning their infants on the ground to their fates, they fled in desperation. And they fled so far that they ended up seven or eight days from our little village, Isabela, beyond mountains and great rivers."*[41]

The native population was already declining, due to the effects of disease as well as to casualties in battle, and Columbus's slaving expedition only made the situation worse. Relations between Europeans and Indians continued to deteriorate during 1495, as Columbus responded to growing hostility toward Europeans and their property. In March he fought and won a pitched battle in the interior of Española. To reward his men and protect his battlefield gains, he instituted a system of forced labor on the island, assigning natives to work for the settlers. He also ordered the construction of scattered forts to protect Spanish interests. By 1496, the island's people had been reduced to obedience. The explorers and settlers had become conquerors, and their erstwhile hosts had become enemies to be vanquished.

Back in Spain, those opposed to Columbus were spreading stories about his misdeeds, and the crown began to listen. The most vocal critics, at least according to Las Casas, were among the disillusioned

Battle between cannibals and Spaniards in the Caribbean. (From Caspar
Plautius, *Nova typis transacta navigatio* [N.p., 1621]. Photo courtesy of
the James Ford Bell Library, University of Minnesota.)

settlers returning from the second voyage. Some had gone back with
one or the other of Torres's relief fleets; others had left for Spain at
the end of September 1494, on the return voyage of the caravels that
had brought Bartolomé Colón to Española. Among the latter were
the missionary Bernardo Buil and Pedro Margarite. They and others
informed the monarchs that the whole enterprise was a joke (*era burla*),
that there was no gold on Española, and that the expenditures of the
crown would never be recovered. Their main complaint seems to
have been directed at the strict control Columbus and his lieutenants
strove to maintain over the colonists. Spaniards were familiar with
their own traditions of Reconquest, in which settlers in a newly acquired territory individually received grants of land and collectively
received a municipal charter giving them certain rights of local self-
government. The system Columbus and the Spanish monarchs were
trying to maintain in the Indies, with official trade conducted by
salaried employees, did not appeal to them.[42]

Contemporary supporters of Columbus, as well as his modern
apologists, often accuse his critics of envy or blame the mindless
hostility of the Spanish colonists toward a foreigner. There was much
more to it than that, however. Columbus had made himself a target
of discontent by overselling the virtues of the islands and their inhabitants. He had told of an idyllic setting, with bountiful lands sure to
enrich all Europeans who ventured there and simple people living

Lurid portrayals of encounters between Europeans and natives in the New World became the stock-in-trade of many European artists. In the background of a famous engraving by Theodore de Bry, one group of cannibals butchers and roasts captured Spaniards. In the foreground, another group pours gold down the throat of a bound Spaniard, presumably showing contempt for the lust of gold that drove many European explorers. (From Theodore de Bry, *Reisen in Occidentalischen Indien* [Frankfurt, 1590–1630]. Photo courtesy of the James Ford Bell Library, University of Minnesota.)

much as Adam and Eve had lived before their expulsion from the Garden of Eden. It took no more than a realistic view of the situation to call everything Columbus had said into question and to make the colonists feel betrayed as well as disillusioned.

On the second voyage Dr. Chanca reported on the Caribs as bestial cannibals, differentiating them from the more tractable Indians. Michele de Cuneo, on the other hand, lumped all the islanders together in a general condemnation of their style of life.

> They live just like beasts; when they are hungry, they eat; they have intercourse openly whenever the feeling moves them, and aside from brothers and sisters, all the rest are common property. They are not

jealous, and it seems to me they are a cold and not very libidinous people, which perhaps comes from their bad diet. From what we have seen in all the islands where we have been, both the Indians and the cannibals are great sodomites, not knowing, I suppose, whether they are doing good or evil.[43]

Cuneo's observations made it clear that the Indies were a far cry indeed from the Garden of Eden.

THE CROWN TAKES CHARGE

Despite disquieting reports coming from returned colonists, Fernando and Isabel responded generously to the colony's need for domestic livestock. On April 9, 1495, they ordered Fonseca to send the expedition six mares, four male and two female asses, four calves and two heifers, two hundred hens, eighty sows, and twenty hogs, plus rabbits and sheep. For the protection of the Spaniards and their goods, mastiffs would also join the expedition. In response to the immediate and long-term need for feeding the colony, the monarchs also instructed Fonseca to recruit a number of specialists, including mining engineers, farmers, vegetable gardeners, an ironworker, two barrel makers, a bow maker, and someone who knew how to construct a mill. Fonseca was also to recruit a team of fishermen for the colony, together with fishing boats to be built in Seville.[44]

There is no doubt that Fernando and Isabel were committed to making the colony self-supporting as soon as possible. Nonetheless, trying to direct a colonization plan across the ocean in a part of the world unknown to them two years before, they needed reliable administrators. At home they trusted Fonseca, a competent man from a well-known family. In the Indies they had trusted Columbus, whom they knew as masterfully persuasive. As reports reached them that the Indies and their peoples were not as Columbus had presented them, they began to doubt his veracity. Much distressed by these reports, the Spanish monarchs appointed Juan Aguado, a royal household official, to investigate. Aguado had accompanied Columbus on his second voyage, commanding one of the caravels, and had returned to Spain with Torres in February 1495. Among his other new duties, Aguado was charged with ensuring that the provisions supplied to the colony were distributed fairly and that the planting of wheat was done properly. Fernando and Isabel told him to do nothing, for the moment, about slavery or the slave trade, because a royal commission of theologians, canon lawyers, and other learned men was in the process of examining the question in detail.[45]

In October of 1495, Aguado arrived on Española with a royal commission to investigate the charges made against the viceroy and the governor – in other words, against Columbus and his brother Diego. Aguado was appalled by what he found. In addition to alarmingly high deaths among the natives, the number of colonists had been greatly reduced by disease and desertion, many men having simply abandoned the colony and sailed home with ships returning to Spain. Perhaps galvanized into action by Aguado's investigation, Columbus decided to return to Spain. He sailed in March 1496, leaving his brother Bartolomé in charge of the colony and giving him the title of *adelantado*. The post of *adelantado,* roughly translatable as "frontier governor," had been used often during Spain's medieval Reconquest to hold land newly conquered by Christian forces. The Spanish crown would use *adelantados* frequently as colonization efforts proceeded in the Indies, and the right of appointment generally resided with the crown. Nonetheless, Fernando and Isabel would overlook Columbus's presumption in appointing Bartolomé to the office and confirm his appointment after the fact.

Columbus took only two vessels with him, the faithful *Niña,* now completing her second transatlantic round trip, and the *India,* a small caravel cobbled together from the timbers of two wrecked ships. Perhaps looking for a shortcut, Columbus tried a trajectory eastward from the Leeward Islands, considerably to the south of his first Atlantic return, a choice that forced him into a long and wearying trip, fighting head winds all the way. The choice of this inefficient route provides further support for the idea that Columbus was still learning the winds and currents that led back to Iberia. His fleet first sighted land north of Cape Saint Vincent in Portugal, and on June 11, 1496, Columbus arrived in the port of Cádiz. His crew was ill, their *"faces the color of saffron,"* perhaps from tainted seafood.[46] The illness of the crew was a somber foreshadowing of a homecoming that would be far different from Columbus's triumphal reception three years earlier. Nonetheless, the political situation in Europe conspired to sustain his position of authority a bit longer.

10

Coercion and Commerce: The Birth of Empire

B Y THE TIME COLUMBUS RETURNED from his second voyage in early
June of 1496, Fernando and Isabel knew that immediate profits
from his overseas ventures would not be forthcoming. Nonetheless,
they would still support plans for another major voyage, largely because of foreign policy considerations. The Portuguese were outfitting Vasco da Gama's attempt to reach India, and Henry VII of England was sending Jacobo Caboto (John Cabot), another Italian
adventurer, to find a northern route to Asia. The Spanish monarchs
may not have known about Cabot's voyages,[1] but certainly they were
apprehensive about direct Portuguese competition in overseas trade.
This was not the time to abandon Columbus or his schemes.[2]

As soon as Columbus landed in Cádiz, he wrote the monarchs,
telling them of his arrival and of his eagerness to report to them in
person. At that point Fernando and Isabel were in northern Castile,
preoccupied with diplomatic negotiations involving their relations
with France and the marriages of two of their children. While awaiting their invitation to come to court, Columbus traveled from Cádiz
to his home in Seville, after dispatching Peralonso Niño with an immediate return fleet for Española. Fernando and Isabel wrote him on
July 12, giving him permission to join them when he wished.[3] The
royal couple's daughter, Princess Juana, was on the verge of embarking for Flanders and her marriage to Philip the Handsome, heir to
the Habsburg possessions. Anxious to be of service, Columbus wrote
Queen Isabel a letter (no longer extant) advising her on voyages to
Flanders, and she responded graciously, thanking him for his concern and his expert advice. King Fernando was in Catalonia and would
not rejoin the queen and the court in Burgos until late October. Columbus traveled northward to Burgos in late October or early November of 1496 to report on his progress and solicit further support.
The court would remain in Burgos until the spring of 1497, and he
would remain with it.

Columbus had begun dressing like a Franciscan friar by this point
in his life. The chronicler and cleric Andrés Bernáldez described Columbus's costume as being the same color as an Observant Franciscan's robes, with a similar cut, bound at the waist by a Franciscan
cord.[4] Dressed in this modest clothing, suggesting voluntary poverty and self-abnegation, and accompanied by Indians carrying rich

and exotic wares, Columbus was at his persuasive best. Hernando Colón, who lived at court as a page of Prince Juan, described his father's formal report to the monarchs:

> he presented a great quantity of things and specimens that he brought back from the Indies, including various birds, animals, trees, and plants, as well as such implements and things as the Indians have for their use and pleasure: many masks and belts with plates of gold set in place of eyes and ears; and gold dust in its natural state, fine or large as beans and chickpeas and some the size of pigeon eggs. Later this was not regarded as remarkable, for they found nuggets weighing more than 30 pounds, but at that time it was held to be a wonderful thing, and to portend what the future might bring, so the Catholic Sovereigns accepted it with rejoicing as a great service.[5]

Bernáldez saw the wares as well and interpreted the images very differently. *"The admiral then brought many things from there . . . crowns, masks, belts, collars and many other things made of cotton, and in all the devil being depicted in figures of cats or owl faces. . . . It was believed that . . . [the Indians] were idolaters and held the devil for their lord."*[6] Still, Bernáldez acknowledged that the monarchs were pleased to see such strange things. Perhaps they did not perceive the same symbolism that he did. Pietro Martire d'Anghiera was impressed by the metal samples he saw in Medina del Campo a year later, including a mass of gold as large as a man's fist and a piece of pure tin so heavy that he could not budge it unassisted.[7]

If Columbus could inspire Fernando and Isabel, despite the opposition of others at the court and in the face of disquieting news from the Indies, the monarchs also knew how to handle Columbus, as they had shown in the past. He wanted to return quickly to the Indies, and they had already promised support for the voyage. Nonetheless, events intruded. They told him, with regret, that all their available cash was being spent on the marriage ceremonies for Prince Juan and Princess Margarita of Austria and on the defense of Catalonia against France. The cost of the next voyage could be covered by the gold being brought back on the ships of Peralonso Niño – in other words, continued exploration in the lands across the ocean would have to pay for itself.

When Niño arrived in Cádiz on October 29, 1496, he handled relations with the court badly. First, he wrote to the monarchs and to Columbus asking to be rewarded for bringing back a large quantity of gold. That he would ask for money at a time of constraint was one mark against him. Niño's report of the amount of gold he carried raised royal hopes that their financial pinch would soon be eased, but he irritated the monarchs further by his delay in reporting to court. Instead of coming immediately to Burgos, where Fernando and Isabel were awaiting the gold he brought and where Columbus was awaiting news of the colony in the letters Niño carried, he went home to Moguer and did not travel to court until the end of December. By then, Las Casas wrote, the monarchs were greatly annoyed at waiting, and Columbus was "as though hung from a tenterhook" because of the delay in getting letters from his brother. When the gold brought back was far less than expected, and when it turned out that Niño's projection of profits from the voyage had included estimated proceeds from selling the Indians he carried as slaves, the monarchs were even more annoyed.[8] The circumstances surrounding Peralonso Niño's return reflected poorly on Columbus as well, causing many at court to doubt his tales and promises of riches in the Indies.

The monarchs may have doubted Columbus as well, but they were far too astute to break with him. Better to let him wait until the political situation in Europe had clarified. Their excuses were valid enough – a lack of ready money and insufficient time to consider his plans fully. Both Fernando and Isabel were concerned by a French siege of the fortress of Salcés, near the Catalan border, which occupied Fernando's full attention for the time being.

EVENTS ON ESPAÑOLA

Before his return from the second voyage, Columbus, as we noted, had appointed his brother Bartolomé as *adelantado,* with authority over Española. The situation of the European settlers was already tenuous before Columbus left, and conditions deteriorated under his brother's administration. Columbus had instituted a policy of tribute paying by the Indian communities, who were to provide a certain amount of gold periodically to Columbus, as their new overlord. If a community were located far away from the gold-bearing streams, its inhabitants could substitute cotton or spices. Las Casas reported the specifics in these terms: Columbus imposed a tribute *"on all those living near the mines, everyone from fourteen years up, each three months, [of] a Flemish hawk's bell . . . full of gold, . . . and all the other people who did not live near the mines would contribute with an* arroba *[ca. 25 pounds] of cotton per person."*[9] Las Casas's reference to mines was anachronistic; there were none yet. Because the Indians collected gold by hunting for nuggets and did not know how to mine or pan for it, there was almost no possibility of expanding output sufficiently to meet the quotas.

Shortly before Columbus had left Española, the settlers at Isabela had found gold in another area, across the mountains in the southern part of the island. The admiral had little time to do more than name the area San Cristóbal before he returned to Spain. After his departure, the *adelantado,* Bartolomé Colón, devoted considerable attention to it. He had a series of forts or way stations built to connect Isabela with the new gold field and established a new port, Santo Domingo, on the southern shore of Española. It was located in a good harbor at the mouth of a river and was surrounded by fine, arable land. Moreover, the routes from Santo Domingo to the gold fields passed over moderate terrain. All these advantages marked Santo Domingo as superior to Isabela, which Columbus had founded and settled with colonists on the second voyage.

As Bartolomé Colón shifted his attention to the gold regions and Santo Domingo, he began stripping Isabela of whatever useful equipment and supplies he could move, angering the settlers and making it more difficult to collect tribute from the Indians. This led to a revolt against the authority of the Columbus brothers. Francisco Roldán, whom Columbus had left in charge of Isabela, led the revolt, arming the European settlers and recruiting Indian allies by promising them an end to the tribute system. Bartolomé was unable to pacify Roldán and his supporters, who were not even the most disgruntled settlers. Those had left already. During the two and a half years before Columbus returned, Bartolomé was able to capture the two principal caciques of the island and round up a number of Indians to be shipped to Europe as slaves. But he was unable to make the tribute system work, and he was unable to bring down Roldán. That would be the situation facing Columbus when he finally returned.[10]

PREPARATIONS FOR THE THIRD VOYAGE

By early April 1497, the royal wedding had taken place, and Fernando and Isabel were ready to turn their attention back to Columbus. They reconfirmed all his titles – admiral, viceroy, and governor general – on April 23. He also persuaded them to rescind the permissions to other explorers that they had issued on April 19, 1495. For the time being, Columbus's exclusive rights were secure, but he still had no funding for a third voyage. His preparations were further delayed by administrative difficulties. Fonseca, newly named bishop of Badajoz, would need to be replaced as the official in charge of preparing fleets to the Indies. The monarchs chose Antonio de Torres, Columbus's friend, experienced in Indies voyages and well connected at court through his sister, the former nurse of Prince Juan.

Indians panning for gold, using European methods. (From Gonzalo
Fernández de Oviedo y Valdés, *La historia general y natural de las Indias*
[Seville: Juan Cromberger, 1535]. Photo courtesy of the James Ford
Bell Library, University of Minnesota.)

But Torres made unacceptable demands on the crown, and the monarchs withdrew his commission and reappointed Fonseca. For the
long term, that was bad for Columbus, because he had never got on
well with Fonseca. For the short term, it delayed preparations further, because all the royal orders issued in Torres's name had to be
rewritten to substitute Fonseca's. Not until July 21, 1497, were the
revised documents ready.[11]

Another set of royal orders prepared between April and July set
out directives for Columbus's colonial administration. First, the orders confirmed several previous decisions. Bartolomé Colón was
formally appointed *adelantado*[12] and given permission to found a new
town on the southern coast, which of course he had already done.
The necessity of confirming appointments and actions after the fact
illustrated a persistent problem that governments in Europe would
continue to face in their overseas empires. Fewer than five years into
the colonial period, it was already apparent that events and people
across the ocean could not easily be controlled from Europe. Administrators on the spot would often exceed their authority and ask for
approval later. If their gamble paid off, the crown had little choice
but to give its belated permission for actions that had already happened.

Far preferable was to give permission in advance. In the summer
of 1497, the monarchs approved the future appointment of administrators for the colonies. Columbus received authority to hire enough
new people to bring the total on the royal payroll up to three hundred
thirty. These were to include forty mounted troopers, one hundred
foot soldiers, thirty sailors, thirty apprentice sailors, twenty gold

workers (neither the Europeans on the island nor the Indians knew the techniques of placer mining), fifty farmers, ten vegetable gardeners, twenty artisans of different skills, and thirty women.[13]

Royal orders also specified the supplies that were to be carried, both for new settlers on the third voyage and for the settlers already on Española. Tools included hoes, spades, pickaxes, sledgehammers, and crowbars. The inclusion of millstones and other equipment would allow the settlers to construct additional mills. Enough oxen, mares, and asses were to be taken to make up twenty yokes of draft animals for cultivation. Fernando and Isabel were obviously providing for a self-sustaining agrarian colony that would produce food for those in gold-mining ventures, the primary aim of the colony. As the monarchs decreed,

> It seems to Us that the gold found in the Indies should be coined into Granadan *excelentes* . . . because by doing this, deceit and fraud related to the gold in the Indies can be avoided; and We order you to take with you the necessary persons, dies, and equipment to make these coins, and We give you full power for this, provided that the coins made in the Indies conform to the regulations We are now ordering to be drawn up. . . .[14]

Fernando and Isabel also demonstrated concern for the indigenous inhabitants of the islands who had come under their rule. The first provision in their instructions for the admiral enjoined him to work for the conversion of the Indians and to arrange for clerics and priests to serve the spiritual needs of both Indians and Europeans. They also confirmed the tribute system that Columbus had instituted, even including his plan to have the Indians wear a brass or lead coin suspended from a cord around their necks, to be marked each time they paid their tribute. The monarchs also gave Columbus authority to grant land in the colony to those who agreed to occupy it for a four-year period, *"giving to each one the fields, woods, and streams you think he should receive in accord with his personal merit, the services he has performed for Us, and his social condition and manner of life."*[15] That decree set the legal basis for the distribution of land, or *repartimiento,* in the colonies. The New World *repartimiento* was similar to the system of land distribution that medieval Castilian rulers had used to resettle and defend territory reconquered from the Muslims. Nonetheless, it marked a significant shift from the modified trading-post system that Columbus and the crown had first attempted in the islands, with settlers as salaried employees. In response to changing circumstances, the crown was gradually formulating the policies that would define the Spanish Empire in the New World. Permanent, self-sustaining colonies would be needed to develop the economic potential of the lands claimed for Castile. To attract and retain colonists, the crown would abandon the fortress and trading-post model pioneered by the Portuguese in Africa. Instead, Fernando and Isabel would shift to the model of settlement that had proved successful during the reconquest of Castile and the ongoing colonization of the Canaries: land grants and local self-government managed by town councils. The crown would retain overall authority, regulate trade, and provide the structure of government and the rule of law.

In the latter half of 1497, tragedy struck the royal family and delayed final preparations for Columbus's third voyage. The heir and only son of Fernando and Isabel, the recently married don Juan, died on October 4, 1497, leaving a pregnant widow, doña Margarita. The best hope for an undisputed inheritance of the kingdoms of Castile and Aragón lay with her unborn child. At the end of the year, Margarita delivered a stillborn daughter, plunging the royal court into a year-long period of mourning. Don Juan's death brought changes in the Columbus family as well. On November 11, 1497, having left court for Seville, Columbus sent both his sons to live at court as pages of the queen, presumably at her invitation. Since 1492, Diego Colón had been a page of Prince Juan. Hernando had received an identical position some time later. They had been living at court on and off since 1494. Now they would be there indefinitely, as constant reminders of the admiral's ties with Queen Isabel.[16]

THE THIRD VOYAGE, 1498–1500

Royal agreements had provided for eight ships to be sent to the Indies with Columbus.[17] Two of them were readied before the others and sailed ahead of the main fleet that Columbus would command. The remaining six were divided into two contingents. The first, comprising one *nao* and two caravels, would be at Columbus's disposal to use for exploration. The other contingent, with three caravels, carried provisions for Española and had authorization to carry three hundred men and thirty women as additional colonists, if they could be recruited. That proved more difficult than it had been for the second voyage; the news from Española was not good. To entice settlers, the crown offered pardons to all prisoners – except those guilty of major crimes such as treason, heresy, smuggling, counterfeiting, and sodomy – if they would join the expedition. Eventually, ten pardoned murderers signed up, the only criminals among approximately two hundred twenty-six members of the third expedition. Misinterpretation of this recruitment effort for the third voyage probably spawned the story that the men who accompanied Columbus on the first voyage were all criminals, a claim that was patently untrue of any of the voyages.[18]

Preparing the fleet took longer than Columbus had expected; he chafed at the delay and blamed Fonseca for it. In his agitated state of mind, Columbus lost his temper and actually got into a brawl with Jimeno de Briviesca, an armada official in Seville. Briviesca had evidently been making disparaging remarks about the Indies enterprise as the preparations proceeded. When he repeated his comments just before the fleet departed, Columbus attacked, kicking him and pulling his hair and causing him considerable injury. The admiral worried so much about the possible long-term consequences to his career from the incident that he mentioned it in a report to Fernando and Isabel, asking them to intervene in the investigation on his behalf.[19]

In the meantime, the combined fleet took on provisions at Seville and prepared to depart. Late in May of 1498, it floated down the Guadalquivir River to Sanlúcar de Barrameda to pick up Columbus, and on May 30, 1498, the third voyage began. Sailing together, the six ships of the fleet stopped in Madeira before heading for Gomera in the Canaries. There the two contingents separated, with the three caravels bound for Española departing directly from Gomera, while Columbus took his three ships farther to the south.

Columbus's route may have related to the notion that gold and other luxuries were to be found in hotter regions near the equator. Many of Columbus's contemporaries believed that metals grew and matured under certain conditions, that gold was metal that had fully matured, and that it grew best under the influence of the sun.[20] Columbus got encouragement for these notions in a letter from Jaime Ferrer de Blanes, a widely traveled lapidary and cosmographer who had advised cardinal Pedro González de Mendoza on geography shortly after Columbus's first voyage and had consulted with the Spanish monarchs themselves during discussions leading to the Treaty of Tordesillas. In August 1495, he wrote to advise Columbus that

> near the equator are the great and costly things, such as fine stones and gold and spices and drugs. And this is what I can say about it because I have much experience in the Levant, in Cairo and Damascus, and because I am a lapidary and I always like to investigate the regions from which those [stones] come, and what clime or province bears them; and the best that can be understood from many Indians and Arabs and Ethiopians is that the largest part of the good things come from very hot areas, where the inhabitants are black or dark [*negros o loros*]. Therefore, according to my judgment, until Your

Lordship finds people like that, you will not find an abundance of such things; even though of all this, Sir, you know more sleeping than I waking.[21]

Aiming for a southerly crossing of the Atlantic, Columbus traveled first to the Cape Verde Islands. From there, he headed west across the ocean on July 7, reaching an island off the northeastern coast of South America on the thirty-first. Along the southern shore of Trinidad, as Columbus named the island, the fleet anchored and sent a party ashore at what is now called Erin Bay, to reconnoiter and collect fresh water. Sailing north thereafter, they encountered the northwestern tip of Trinidad and saw to the west the mountains of the Paria Peninsula, in today's Venezuela, the first Columbus landfall on the continental shores of the Western Hemisphere. On further exploration, the fleet reached the mouths of the impressive Orinoco River. From the quantity of fresh water flowing from the Orinoco, Columbus deduced, not that they had reached a vast continent but that they were near the Bible's earthly paradise. Holy Scripture, he wrote, stated that the terrestrial paradise contained the sources of the four great rivers of the world: the Ganges, the Tigris, the Euphrates, and the Nile. Columbus thought he was near that paradise or somewhere very like it, *"for I have never read or heard of so great a quantity of fresh water so coming into and near the salt. . . . And if it does not come from there, from paradise, it seems to be a still greater marvel, for I do not believe that there is known in the world a river so great and so deep."*[22]

In speculating about his discoveries, Columbus revealed some of his more eccentric geographical notions. In one famous passage, he speculated on the irregularity he thought he had noted in the supposedly spherical shape of the earth:

I have always read that the world, land and water, was spherical, and authoritative accounts and experiments which Ptolemy and all the others have recorded concerning this matter, so describe it and hold it to be, by the eclipses of the moon and by other demonstrations made from east to west, as well as from the elevation of the pole star from north to south. Now, as I have already said, I have seen so great irregularity that, as a result, I have been led to hold this concerning the world, and I find that it is not round as they describe it, but that it is the shape of a pear which is everywhere very round except where the stalk is, for there it is very prominent, or that it is like a very round ball, and on one part of it is placed something like a woman's nipple, and that this part, where this protuberance is found, is the highest and nearest to the sky, and it is beneath the equinoctial line and in this Ocean sea at the end of the East.[23]

Columbus believed that the earthly paradise was located at the peak of the protuberance he described and that he would come as close as possible by sailing south of the equator. *"Not that I believe that to the summit of the extreme point is navigable, or water, or that it is possible to ascend there, for I believe that the earthly paradise is there and to it, save by the will of God, no man can come."*[24]

This is the earliest document that has been found in which Columbus explicitly mentioned the sources for his theoretical knowledge of geography and his critique of those sources based on experience. Much of the world was still unknown, and some European geographical notions about the habitable parts of the world had already been challenged by the discoveries of Columbus and of the Portuguese in Africa. Moreover, to Columbus and his contemporaries, Holy Scripture was not just a religious text but a valid source of knowledge about the world. Consequently, Columbus's speculations about the earthly paradise and his blending of the Bible, Ptolemy, and his own experience would not have seemed as odd to his intended audience as they seem to us. Nonetheless, in Columbus's descriptions and speculations, he often allowed theory to color his version of reality.

After briefly exploring the coast of Venezuela, where the expedition encountered pearl beds and pearl fishers, Columbus sailed on to Española. Although much exploring remained to be done in the region, only six years after his first voyage into the unknown he had mapped the Caribbean well enough to know his way around and to find Española without difficulty, even after crossing the ocean by a different route. Considering what awaited him, he might have been better off had he got lost.

RETURN TO ESPAÑOLA

Columbus found chaos and crisis on Española. Some of the colonists had mutinied, the Indians were up in arms and mightily sick of tribute payments and of the undisciplined hoard of Europeans in their midst, and neither Bartolomé nor Diego Colón had been able to maintain order among them. Columbus himself had little better luck once he arrived. The rebellion of Francisco Roldán still had not been settled, and in addition to Roldán's supporters a large number of disaffected settlers were ready to abandon the colony. Columbus gave them permission to leave and provided free passage home, allowing each settler to take a slave with him.

In reporting to the crown, Columbus continued to exaggerate the promise of the colony, even as he reported on Roldán's uprising. The contradictions between Columbus's reports and reality – or, at least, reality as described by the disillusioned settlers and suggested by the rebellion itself – must have been disquieting. Fernando and Isabel may not have challenged Columbus's geographical musings, but other information in his letters did not coincide with what they knew and with what they planned for the Indies.

One troublesome issue was slavery. The caravels that brought Columbus's letters also brought about three hundred former settlers and an equal number of slaves. That slaves were still being taken contravened the crown's evolving policy on native subjects; the queen was furious and ordered the intended slaves freed. Hurting Columbus's cause even more, in another of his letters he proposed to send as many slaves as could be sold in *"Castile and Portugal and Italy and Sicily and the islands of Portugal and of Aragón and the Canaries"* and an equally valuable quantity of brazilwood.[25] Obviously Columbus was acting in total disregard of royal policy. Adding insult to injury, he pointedly reminded the monarchs of his devoted service. Self-assured as ever, Columbus blamed those opposed to him for any small errors that might have been observed in his conduct. After complaining that those who doubted him *"talk about me worse than a Muslim without giving any reason for it,"* he boasted that *"Our Lord, who knows my intention and the truth of everything, will save me as he has done until now, because until today there has not been a person opposed to me with malice whom He has not punished. . . ."*[26]

He concluded the letter with a typically Columbian piece of hyperbole. In describing Española, where Indians were being killed and enslaved, where Europeans were starving or giving up as settlers, and where no one had yet made a profit, he still used the same exaggerated sales pitch, this time with overtones of religious fanaticism.

> it is obvious that Our Lord gave [the land] miraculously and which is the most beautiful and the most fertile under heaven, in which there is gold and copper and many kinds of spices and a quantity of brazilwood. . . . And I believe from the needs of Castile and the abundance of Española, a large population will have to come from there to here, and the capital will be in Isabela, where the beginning was, because it is the most ideal spot and better than any other in the land, as should be believed because Our Lord took me there miraculously, for it was impossible to go on or go back with the ships. . . .[27]

The monarchs had enough information from other sources to recognize the basic falsity of the admiral's reports, even with two miracles in one paragraph. It was commonly known at court that Isabela had proved a disastrous site for a town and that Bartolomé Colón had moved the settlement to Santo Domingo, taking everything from

Isabela that he could. Even with Columbus's parting gift of a slave, each of the returning settlers was a potential source of complaint against the government of the admiral and his brother. Columbus did not help himself by going on to say that tales told against him at the court originated from his enemies, caused by envy of *"a poor foreigner; but in everything He who is eternal has helped and is helping me, He who has always been merciful with me, a very great sinner."*[28]

Fernando and Isabel decided to launch an investigation. Ironically, at the height of his trouble with Roldán Columbus had requested an investigating judge, and Francisco de Bobadilla had been designated. The monarchs decided to increase Bobadilla's power, granting him the use of extraordinary measures to restore authority, not for Columbus's sake but for the sake of the colony and the crown. Brother of the queen's confidante Beatriz Fernández de Bobadilla, the marchioness of Moya, Francisco de Bobadilla was a commander in the military order of Calatrava, one of the associations of knights who took modified monastic vows and dedicated their lives to warring on the infidel. In Castile the knights were landholders skilled in estate management and the direction of agricultural workers. As a commander of Calatrava, Bobadilla could be expected to bring years of military and executive experience to his post in the Indies. As a further demonstration of their loss of faith in Columbus, Fernando and Isabel began again to license other voyages of exploration, implicitly rescinding their concession of exclusive rights to Columbus. They were to permit eleven such voyages during the remainder of Columbus's lifetime. Most went to the South American mainland and were led by some old companions of Columbus, including Vicente Yáñez Pinzón, Alonso de Hojeda, and Juan de la Cosa, and others including Amerigo Vespucci, whose name came to be applied to the entire hemisphere.[29]

While the monarchs were commissioning an investigation of his administration, back on Española Columbus had finally been able to solve many of the problems facing the colony, although not on terms that were likely to please the crown. Roldán and his supporters had ended their rebellion in exchange for the right to form their own communities and to requisition the use of labor services from Indian communities. Columbus's instructions from the queen authorized him to make land grants to individual Europeans according to their merits, if the grantees would live on their grant, build a house, and farm the land. In settling with Roldán and rewarding his own followers, Columbus exceeded his authority by making a very different sort of concession – granting the labor services of a chief and his people. The grantee could move the people wherever he wished and make them do whatever he wished. In other words, the system of

Amerigo Vespucci exploring the River Plate. Woodcut, ca. 1505. (Photo courtesy of the James Ford Bell Library, University of Minnesota.)

repartimiento, which had originated as a land grant in medieval Castile, was coupled in the Indies with a grant of labor services, forerunner of the *encomienda* system, in which Indian laborers were "commended" (that is, assigned) to a landholder, who had the right to part of their labor.

In settling his differences with Roldán, Columbus had created the foundations for a damaging pattern of European overlordship and Indian labor service in the Indies. Combined with European diseases and warfare, the systems of *repartimiento* and *encomienda* would cause great disruption in the early sixteenth century, contributing to the disintegration of many native communities.

HOME IN CHAINS

Even though Columbus had settled with Roldán and his supporters by the time Bobadilla arrived in the harbor of Santo Domingo on August 23, 1500, additional challenges had arisen to Columbus's government. The admiral and the *adelantado* were out in the countryside putting down minor rebellions and sending European captives back to Santo Domingo, where Diego Colón was administering jus-

Spanish rebels being hanged under the administration of Columbus and his brothers. (From Theodore de Bry, *Reisen in Occidentalischen Indien* [Frankfurt, 1590–1630]. Photo courtesy of the James Ford Bell Library, University of Minnesota.)

tice. Bobadilla had his first view of the situation while still on board ship, waiting for a favorable tide and wind to enter the harbor. From the deck of his vessel he could easily see the corpses of seven rebels hanging from prominent gallows, and he soon learned that five more were awaiting execution. This shocking news must have seemed proof of a government gone badly wrong. When he landed at last, Bobadilla acted decisively. He seized control of Santo Domingo, confiscated Columbus's goods, arrested Diego Colón, and demanded that the admiral and the *adelantado* also surrender to him. In October 1500, he sent them home ignominiously in chains.

The captain of the vessel offered to remove the chains, but Columbus, with stubborn pride, refused. He may have visualized the impact such a spectacle would have in Spain. The hero disgraced by changeable fortune formed one of the standard motifs of classical and Renaissance drama, and the image of Columbus in chains has continued to excite the imagination of poets, artists, and writers even to our own day. Columbus used the enforced idleness of the voyage to write a letter of lament to doña Juana de Torres, the sister of his friend Antonio de Torres and the former nurse of Prince Juan. In writing to her, Columbus knew the contents of his letter would reach the king and queen, without risking royal displeasure by directly questioning royal authority. Upset and despondent, Columbus comforted himself with the certainty that he had been chosen by God to carry out his great mission.

> Most Virtuous Lady: If it is something new for me to complain of the world, its custom of mistreating me is of very old standing. A thousand battles have I fought with it, and I have withstood all until now when neither arms nor wit avail me. With cruelty, it has cast me down to the depth. Hope in Him Who created all men sustains me; His succor has been always very near. On one occasion, and that not long ago, when I was deeply distressed, He raised me with His divine arm, saying: "O man of little faith, arise, it is I, be not afraid."
>
> I came with such earnest love to serve these princes, and I have served with a service that has never been heard or seen. Of the new heaven and of the new earth, which our Lord made, as St. John writes in the Apocalypse, after he had spoken of it by the mouth of Isaiah, he made me the messenger and He showed me where to go. In all there was incredulity, and to the queen my lady He gave the spirit of understanding and great courage, and He made her the heiress of all, as His dear and very loved daughter. I went to take possession of all this in her royal name. All wished to cover the ignorance in which they were sunk, hiding their little knowledge by speaking of difficulties and expense. Her highness on the contrary approved and supported the enterprise as far as she was able. Seven years were spent in discussion and nine in performance. Remarkable and memorable events took place in that time. Of all this, there had been no conception.
>
> I came to be, and I am, such that there is none so vile as not to dare to insult me.[30]

He predicted that by the time he returned to the mainland, the local pearl fishers would have collected a bushel basket (*fanega*) of pearls for him, but for the most part the letter concerned the injustices and damage he had suffered. This was the opening salvo in Columbus's campaign for restoration of his titles and honors, and he asked for inquiries to be made so that justice might be done. Similar complaints of ingratitude and injustice would color his writings for the rest of his life. Taken by themselves, without allowing for the great wealth he was accumulating for himself and his heirs, his complaints have led to the persistent view that Columbus died impoverished, neglected, forgotten, and bitter. In fact, he was only bitter. Amid the complaints, Columbus did make one effective point in his favor: that he should not be judged by the standards of European governors, but rather as a frontier captain fighting a *"warlike and numerous"* foe. He had abandoned all pretense that the Indians were gentle and malleable souls.

> At home they judge me as a governor sent to Sicily or to a city or two under settled government, and where the laws can be fully maintained, without fear of all being lost; and at this I am greatly aggrieved. I ought to be judged as a captain who went from Spain to the Indies to conquer a people, warlike and numerous, and with customs and beliefs very different from ours, a people, living in highlands and mountains, having no settled dwellings, and apart from us; and where, by the will of God, I have brought under the dominion of the king and queen, our sovereigns, another world, whereby Spain, which was called poor, is now most rich.[31]

In his letter to Juana de Torres, Columbus mentioned more than once *"a new heaven and a new earth,"* echoing the Apocalypse of Saint John from the biblical Book of Revelation: *"And I saw a new heaven and a new earth: for the first heaven and the first earth were passed away; and there was no more sea."*[32] Some writers have used this phrase as evidence that Columbus realized he had not reached Asia, but a new continent instead. His other writings make clear, however, that he thought this new heaven and earth was a hitherto unknown part of Asia. When he wrote to Fernando and Isabel in 1498 that the Orinoco River was near the terrestrial paradise, he located it quite specifically: *"it is beneath the equinoctial line and in this Ocean sea at the end of the East,"* that is, close to the equator and at the eastern extreme of Asia, precisely where the world maps of his time placed it. To make his point as clearly as possible, he added, *"I call that 'the end of the East,' where end all the land and islands."*[33] In the draft of a letter to Pope Alexander VI in February 1502, which he may or may not have actually sent, Columbus repeated his assertion that Cuba was the mainland of Asia and that he had sailed along it for 333 leagues.[34] Moreover, when he wrote to Fernando and Isabel in preparation for his fourth voyage, he asked permission to take two or three Arabic translators with him, as Las Casas reported, *"because he always held the opinion that having passed this our mainland, if a sea passage were found, he had to come across people of the Great Khan or others who spoke that language or a bit of it."*[35]

ROYAL JUSTICE

Columbus sent his letter to doña Juana, and perhaps a similar one to the monarchs, from Cádiz, where he arrived in November 1500.

Fernando and Isabel immediately ordered him released from custody and summoned him to court in Granada in December. They even granted him expense money for the trip. When he arrived at court, in the same city where his grand scheme had finally gained their support, the king and queen received him warmly, assuring him that his imprisonment had been ordered without their knowledge or consent and promising him that all would be settled to his satisfaction. Eventually Fernando and Isabel allowed Columbus to keep some of his titles and all of his property, but the titles would henceforth be empty of authority. Never again would they let him serve as viceroy or governor. They also delayed in granting him permission for another voyage. Although the pathetic spectacle of Columbus in chains had touched their hearts, they were well aware of the charges of maladministration that had led to his arrest by Bobadilla.

During the period between the third voyage and the fourth, as Columbus sought to regain royal favor, he worked on two important compilations of documents. He would use both of them to justify his actions and sustain his legal and moral claims to primacy in the development of the Indies. The first was his *Book of Privileges,* a notarized collection of royal agreements, orders, and letters bearing on Columbus's relations with the crown. The collection begins with a copy of documents relating to the privileges of the admiral of Castile, which had served as the model for Columbus's title of Admiral of the Ocean Sea. The most important documents follow next: the agreements of Santa Fe of April 1492 and their confirmation the next year after the successful first voyage. The remainder of the *Book of Privileges* consists of copies of other royal documents dealing with Columbus and the Indies. He had begun the collection before his third voyage and had other documents notarized in Santo Domingo. With his arrest by Bobadilla, and with his hard-won royal concessions in jeopardy, Columbus needed a complete and authoritative documentary base for the litigation that almost surely would follow. He enlisted notaries in Seville to make a complete set of the documents; when they were finished, he sent two copies to Genoa and a third to the Carthusian monastery of Santa María de las Cuevas near Seville.[36]

One of the monks at Las Cuevas, Gaspar de Gorricio, collaborated with Columbus on the other important compilation he produced between his third and fourth voyages: the *Book of Prophecies.* In it Columbus assembled a collection of biblical passages, writings of church fathers, and the work of modern writers such as Pierre d'Ailly. The passages chosen were an eclectic mixture indeed, apparently selected for their presumed relevance to Columbus's discoveries, the need to take Christianity to all parts of the world, and the reconquest of Jerusalem. The *Book of Prophecies* reveals Columbus's increasing preoccupation with apocalyptical speculation, which had already begun to color his official communications with the monarchs.[37]

Meanwhile, the king and queen appointed a new governor for Española, Nicolás de Ovando, a noble from a small town in Extremadura who had been raised in the royal court with the late Prince Juan. He had joined the Franciscan order as a tertiary (lay brother) and was a knight-commander of the military order of Alcántara. On September 3, 1501, the monarchs named him governor of the islands and mainland (*tierra firme*) in the Indies, except for the "islands" controlled by Alonso de Hojeda and Vicente Yáñez Pinzón. The royal orders reveal how little was known about the lands across the ocean in 1501. By *tierra firme* they referred to Cuba, which Columbus persisted in identifying as part of the mainland of Asia. The "island" possessions of Hojeda and Pinzón were really part of the mainland of modern Venezuela. At the same time, the monarchs revoked franchises for the collection of gold that had been issued by Bobadilla and reclaimed the crown's share of gold established by Columbus. They further ordered that all of Columbus's possessions in Española be restored to him.

Ovando sailed for the Caribbean in February 1502 with a large fleet of thirty-two ships, commanded by Antonio de Torres. The ships carried twenty-five hundred sailors, soldiers, and settlers, enough for a fresh start at the colonization venture botched by the Columbus brothers. Columbus was not allowed to accompany the fleet, but he could and did send an agent, Alonso Sánchez de Carvajal, to recover the money Bobadilla had seized from him. A month after Ovando's fleet sailed, Fernando and Isabel finally agreed to grant Columbus permission for a new fleet under his command.

It was no coincidence that they gave Ovando plenty of time to establish his authority in the colony before letting Columbus return. In the construction of empire, Ovando was their first really effective deputy in the Indies.[38] The monarchs had already granted licenses to other explorers besides Columbus. From the extent of the lands already explored and the size of their indigenous populations, Fernando and Isabel realized that a large bureaucratic structure would be needed to govern the territories properly. Such a government could not rely on talented entrepreneurs such as Columbus beyond the initial phase of exploration. It had to be staffed by trained officials, loyal to the faraway authority of the crown, who expected their rewards to come from the crown. As Columbus had found, and as he had demonstrated by his own behavior, men tended to slip the restraints of law and loyalty when they were far from the seat of government.

Over the course of the year 1501, the colonial administration of the Catholic Monarchs began to take shape. Already they had appointed Ovando as their new governor. In September they made additional appointments: Diego Márquez as overseer (*veedor*), Francisco de Monroy as factor, Rodrigo Alcázar as gold founder and marker (*fundidor y marcador de oro*), and Adrián Pérez as chief justice of the Indies (*alcalde mayor de Indias*). The next month, they appointed Rodrigo de Villacorta as treasurer of the islands and mainland. They negotiated contracts with Antonio de Hojeda, Vicente Yáñez Pinzón, and Diego de Lepe for new voyages of discovery. They secured papal approval to collect church tithes in the Indies. They issued orders prohibiting their Indian subjects from having European weapons.[39] The Spanish Empire was gradually coming into being, following well-established patterns dating from the Reconquest and reaffirmed in the Canaries. In the evolution of Spain's American empire, Columbus was now only one among many.

THE FOURTH VOYAGE, 1502–1504

Once he received the monarchs' approval and support for a fourth voyage, Columbus left Granada in October 1501 for Seville, where he began his preparations for outfitting the fleet. On his fourth voyage Columbus proposed to explore west of a line stretching from Cuba to the northeastern mainland of South America, in an area that had hardly been explored by previous European voyages. He assembled a fleet by buying four small, shallow-draft vessels, suitable for exploring shallow bays and rivers. Two caravels of 70 *toneladas,* the *Santa María* and the *Santiago de Palos,* were joined by two even smaller *navíos,* the *Gallega* and the *Vizcaína,* of 50 *toneladas* each. Recalling earlier triumphs, Columbus and his thirteen-year-old son Hernando traveled on the *Santa María* as flagship of the fleet; Diego Tristán served as captain, with Ambrosio Sánchez as master and Juan Sánchez as pilot. The *Santiago de Palos* carried a captain from Seville, Francisco de Porras, whose brother Diego de Porras was the fleet's notary. Francisco Bermúdez served as the ship's master, and Bartolomé Colón sailed as one of its passengers. The *navío Gallega* was captained by Pedro de Terreros, with Juan Quintero as master. The *Vizcaína* had a Genoese as its captain: Bartolomeo de Fieschi, called by the Spanish Bartolomé de Fiesco. Altogether the fleet carried only one hundred thirty-five persons, underscoring its primary mission as an exploring expedition rather than a colonizing venture.

The historian Manuel Ballesteros was struck by the number of Genoese included – eight, in addition to the admiral. Samuel Eliot Morison was struck by the low average age of the crews. There were fifty-six apprentice seamen between the ages of twelve and eighteen in the fleet and only forty-three seamen over the age of eighteen, roughly 32 percent of the crew. A typical Indies fleet a century later would carry 50 to 60 percent adult seamen, and a war fleet would carry 60 to 70 percent adult seamen and gunners.[40] The young crew suggests that Columbus was no longer able to attract the best seamen that southern Spain had to offer; presumably they were off on exploratory voyages of their own or maintaining the regular links between Santo Domingo and Cádiz. His ships were not of the best quality either, as we shall see.

The fleet assembled in Seville on April 3, 1502, and sailed downriver to dock in Cádiz for final preparations. They sailed from Cádiz on May 9 and cleared the harbor two days later. On the way to the Canaries they stopped at the Moroccan port of Arzila, where a Portuguese garrison had just beaten back a Moroccan siege. In Arzila they met some kinsmen of Felipa Moniz (Columbus's late wife) before sailing for the town of Las Palmas on the island of Gran Canaria, where they arrived on May 20. Departing five days later, they crossed the Atlantic, *"without having to touch the sails,"* as Hernando Colón would later write. Some historians doubt that Hernando wrote the early sections of his father's biography, but there is no doubt that he wrote the description of the fourth voyage from personal experience. His wonder at the world his father had claimed for Spain permeates his descriptions of the lands and peoples he saw as an adolescent.

The fleet reached land at the island of Matininó (now Martinique) on June 15. After sailing through the Antilles, the ships arrived at Española on June 29, although Columbus had been expressly forbidden to go there. To underline the fact that he lacked all authority on the island, Fernando and Isabel had ordered him to avoid Española on his outbound voyage, over his vigorous protests. They conceded only that he could make a short visit in passing on the return voyage.

Columbus's aggrieved state of mind may have led him to blatantly defy royal orders, but there were practical concerns as well. The *Santiago* had sailed very poorly across the ocean, and Columbus hoped to sell it and buy another in Santo Domingo. His visit to Española turned out to be more dramatic than he had planned, however. Columbus knew that Governor Ovando was about to send a fleet home, and as he neared the island he realized that a hurricane was brewing just as the fleet was about to leave. Having experienced one hurricane in the Caribbean on his second voyage, which he rode out between the southern shore of Española and the island of Saona, and having experienced the fringes of another, Columbus wanted to tell Ovando of the approaching storm and also to use the harbor at Santo Domingo as a haven for his own ships.

Hurricane in the Caribbean. (From Theodore de Bry, *Reisen in Occiden-talischen Indien* [Frankfurt, 1590–1630]. Photo courtesy of the James Ford Bell Library, University of Minnesota.)

Anchoring offshore, Columbus sent a message about the storm to Ovando, who refused to believe him and ordered the fleet to depart; he also refused Columbus permission to land. The hurricane struck, just as Columbus had predicted, sinking twenty-five ships in the fleet dispatched by Ovando. Among those killed were Columbus's faithful friend Antonio de Torres, his old adversary Bobadilla, the Indian cacique Guarionex, and the rebel Roldán and most of his followers. Only three or four ships survived the storm, and the one that made it back to Spain, ironically was the *Aguja,* which carried 4,000 pesos of gold belonging to Columbus. If Columbus had ever entertained doubts that God was on his side, the hurricane and its aftermath laid them to rest.

Once the hurricane had passed, Columbus and his men rested in southern Española. Thereafter they spent most of the remainder of the voyage along the coast of Central America. Heading first toward the mainland, they reached a small group of islands off the coast of Honduras. While exploring one of the islands, called Guanaja, they spotted a huge canoe coming from the north. Though made of a single tree trunk like other Caribbean canoes, this was the biggest any European had yet seen. With twenty-five paddlers, it was eight feet wide and as *"long as a galley,"* with a pavilion in its center roofed with palm fronds. The covered pavilion sheltered women and children, as well as baggage and trade goods. Hernando Colón, still short of his fourteenth birthday, was fascinated by the trade goods:

> cotton mantles and sleeveless shirts embroidered and painted in different designs and colors; breechclouts of the same design and cloth as the shawls worn by the women of the canoe, being like the shawls worn by the Moorish women of Granada; long wooden swords with a groove on each side where the edge should be, in which were fastened with cord and pitch, flint knives that cut like steel; hatchets resembling the stone hatchets used by the other Indians, but made of good copper; and hawk's bells of copper and crucibles to melt it.[41]

This cargo comprised the most sophisticated native manufactures the Europeans had yet seen. The canoe had been coming from the north, very likely from Yucatan, as Hernando later speculated, but even the impressive canoe and its cargo did not deter the admiral from his southward quest along the continent in search of an ocean passage to the west. He knew that he could easily reach the home of the canoe traders by sailing directly west with the wind from Cuba, and he assumed there would be a later occasion to do so.

Arriving at the mainland, Columbus formally claimed it for Castile and spent over two months of difficult sailing to reach the end of the northern shore of Honduras. After that he and his companions made good time down to Panama, where they had been led to believe a strait existed. Not finding one, they explored the region and decided to establish a small settlement on the river they christened Río Belén, the River of Bethlehem, in the region called Veragua. Columbus planned to leave his brother Bartolomé in charge of the settlement; the *Gallega* would be left with him to break up for building materials, since its sailing days were over. The local Indians had other ideas, however. Their attacks succeeded in making it so unpleasant for the would-be settlers that they abandoned the effort. Leaving the worn-out hulk of the *Gallega,* Columbus decided to return to Española with the remnants of his fleet.

Dissatisfaction began to surface among the crew about that time. The voyage had been difficult, to say the least. Because of Columbus, they had been refused landing rights at Santo Domingo. They had ridden out a major hurricane. They had suffered losses in skirmishes with the Indians of Panama. Now, before they had accomplished anything, it seemed to many men in the fleet that Columbus was planning a voyage directly back to Spain, for so they interpreted his easterly course along the shore of Panama. Another of the caravels, the *Vizcaína,* had been fatally damaged by the shipworms of the warm Caribbean waters and had to be abandoned at Portobelo. Finally, on May 1, 1503, Columbus turned his two remaining vessels toward the north to set a course for Española. By the twelfth they had reached the numerous islands they called Jardín de la Reina (Queen's garden), south of Cuba.

The ships were so full of worm holes by then that three pumps had to be worked constantly on each vessel to keep them afloat. The added labor severely strained the crews, who were already on short rations because supplies were running out. To make matters worse, one night during a storm the ships collided, damaging both of them. By then the caravels could barely pass as seaworthy. After reprovisioning at a Cuban Indian village, they made for Jamaica. Española, the only island with Spanish settlements, lay out of reach. The trajectory would have required constant beating against the wind, and their sinking ships could never have made the trip. By continual pumping they were able to reach Jamaica, arriving with water almost up to the decks. The crews kept the ships afloat just long enough to pick out a reef-enclosed harbor. Columbus had the caravels brought up close together and sailed straight toward land to ground them. Once grounded, they were lashed together and shored up so they would remain upright. The men built cabins on the decks and castles fore and aft, designed to be a safe home until rescue could be arranged. This makeshift wooden fortress, a crossbow shot from shore, in water that rose nearly up to the deck with each high tide, would be Columbus's home for nearly a year. Friendly Indians in the neighborhood were eager to trade with the Europeans, but Columbus tried as hard as he could to keep his men on the ships, in order to avoid conflict with the local people.

Columbus and the other leaders of the expedition discussed their options. They could not count on a chance sighting by a passing ship to rescue them. They had neither sufficient tools nor skilled artisans to build a proper ship, and a makeshift vessel would be of no use against the winds and currents running from east to west. The best hope was to seek rescue from Española by sending a message with Indian canoes. They had lost all the ships' boats in a series of mishaps that started with the hurricane.

For the crossing from Jamaica to Española, they collected two suitable canoes and recruited ten Jamaicans and six Europeans for each of them. Captained by Diego Méndez de Segura, the fleet's chief clerk, and Bartolomeo de Fieschi, a Genoese, the crews would paddle the canoes to Española. Once there the plan was for Méndez to travel to Santo Domingo to arrange the rescue. Fieschi would return to Jamaica to let the marooned Europeans know that Méndez had arrived safely and that help was on the way. Bartolomé Colón took a party to accompany the canoes to the eastern end of Jamaica and watched until they paddled out of sight. Their marooned shipmates would hear nothing from the rescue party for eight months.

Columbus had great difficulty restraining the men who remained with him. Shortly after the new year began, the Porras brothers – Francisco and Diego, captain of the *Santiago de Palos* and the fleet's notary, respectively – led a mutiny. Seizing all ten of the Indian canoes Columbus had collected, they set out, intending to paddle to Española. On the way they plundered Indian villages, confiscating food and telling the Indians to apply to Columbus for compensation. Their attempts to reach Española came to nothing, however, and the mutineers had no choice but to start back toward Columbus's settlement.

While the mutineers were gone, relations between Columbus's loyalists and the local Indians deteriorated. The locals, clearly aware of the dynamics of supply and demand, began to supply less food and to demand higher prices for it. At that point Columbus used his powers of persuasion to pull off a desperate, brilliant trick. From the astronomical tables he carried for navigation, he knew a lunar eclipse was due shortly, and he summoned local Indian leaders to meet with him on the day before the eclipse. He told them that his men were Christians, servants of a God in heaven who punished the wicked and rewarded the good. God had punished the wicked men who followed the Porras brothers by not permitting them to paddle to Española. God was now angry with the Indians for asking high prices for scarce provisions. God would send a sign of that displeasure and a portent of the punishments he had in mind for them. He told them to watch the rising moon that night, and they would see the sign. As Hernando later recalled it:

> at the rising of the moon the eclipse began, and the higher it rose the more complete the eclipse became, at which the Indians grew so frightened that with great howling and lamentation they came running from all directions to the ships, laden with provisions, and praying the Admiral to intercede with God that He might not vent His wrath upon them, and promising they would diligently supply all their needs in the future. The Admiral replied that he wished to speak briefly with his God, and retired to his cabin while the eclipse waxed and the Indians cried all the time for his help. When the Admiral perceived that the crescent phase of the moon was finished and that it would soon shine forth clearly, he issued from his cabin, saying that

Battle between Columbus and Spanish mutineers on Jamaica. (From Theodore de Bry, *Reisen in Occidentalischen Indien* [Frankfurt, 1590–1630]. Photo courtesy of the James Ford Bell Library, University of Minnesota.)

he had appealed to his God and prayed for them and had promised Him in their name that henceforth they would be good and treat the Christians well, bringing provisions and all else they needed. God had now pardoned them, in token of which they would soon see the moon's anger and inflammation pass away. Perceiving that what he said was coming true, they offered many thanks to the Admiral and uttered praises of his God as long as the eclipse continued. From that time forward they were diligent in providing us with all we needed, and were loud in praise of the Christian God.[42]

Finally, eight months after Méndez and Fieschi had left, a caravel arrived from Governor Ovando. The captain relayed the governor's compliments and gave them a side of salt pork and a barrel of wine. He said the governor was sorry, but no vessel large enough to take them all was then available. The caravel's captain did report that

Méndez was in Santo Domingo trying to charter a rescue vessel; then he sailed away as suddenly as he had come. With rescue imminent, Columbus tried to reduce the mutineers to obedience. They resisted, but a pitched battle brought them into line. When Diego Méndez finally brought a caravel from Española, they all left Jamaica together for Santo Domingo. Méndez's story, which was printed in Europe and enjoyed great fame, told of an arduous canoe passage to Española, during which many of the Indian paddlers died. Once on Española, he and Fieschi had proceeded east along the coast. Then they went inland to meet Governor Ovando, who was engaged in a pacification campaign and insisted that Méndez remain with him until it was completed. In the end, it was seven months before Méndez could reach Santo Domingo and secure a ship.[43]

From Santo Domingo, Méndez despatched a letter Columbus had written in Jamaica to the monarchs in Spain. Composed in the depths of despair, much of the letter was rambling and incoherent, filled with stories of religious visions and grandiose plans for the reconquest of Jerusalem. Complaining bitterly of poverty and ill-treatment at the hands of his enemies, Columbus beseeched his royal patrons for restoration of all his titles and honors. In recalling events at the Belén River, he described waiting at sea without a ship's boat, helplessly watching while his brother beat off an Indian attack on shore. Under these conditions of extreme stress, he reported having a dream-vision. Nowhere are his delusions of grandeur and his self-definition as God's chosen instrument more clear.

> I toiled up to the highest point of the ship, calling in a trembling voice, with fast-falling tears, to the war captains of your highnesses, at every point of the compass, for succor, but never did they answer me. Exhausted, I fell asleep, groaning. I heard a very compassionate voice, saying: "o fool and slow to believe and to serve thy God, the God of all! What more did He for Moses or for His servant David? Since thou wast born, ever has He had thee in his most watchful care. When He saw thee of an age with which He was content, He caused thy name to sound marvellously in the land. The Indies, which are so rich a part of the world, He gave thee for thine own; thou has divided them as it pleased thee, and He enabled thee to do this. Of the barriers of the Ocean sea, which were closed with such mighty chains, He gave thee the keys; and thou wast obeyed in many lands and among Christians thou hast gained an honorable fame."[44]

The voice went on to compare Columbus to the heroes of the Bible, suggesting that his trials were only a preparation for greater things to come. Modestly, Columbus concluded the passage by claiming he did not know whose voice he had heard. He then added a long dissertation on gold and suggested that the mines in Veragua, Panama, were the same as the mines of Aurea, which the Bible says provided King Solomon with the means to build the original Temple of Jerusalem.

Then Columbus returned to his recurring theme of the reconquest of Jerusalem, which was prophesied to precede the end of the world, and pledged himself to help that reconquest. Since 1501, Columbus had adopted a cryptic signature, whose central element was "Xpo Ferens": "Christo Ferens," or Christ-bearer.[45] In 1500, when Juan de la Cosa drew the first map of the islands that Columbus had discovered, he included a figure of Saint Christopher carrying the Christ child across a swollen stream. In the medieval legend, the muscular Christopher felt the child become almost unbearably heavy by the end of the journey. When the child revealed his divine identity to the man who had carried him, he also revealed the reason for his extraordinary weight: in carrying Christ across the water, Christopher had also borne the weight of the world. Columbus seems to have identified with Saint Christopher, his holy namesake, and to have accepted the awesome burden of bearing Christ, or Christianity, across the water. Perhaps he was inspired by Juan de la Cosa's map, but the idea could as easily have come to him independently. The legend of Saint Christopher was perfectly suited to Columbus's sense of his own worth and his acceptance of enormous burdens to accomplish exalted aims. The letters that form the rest of Columbus's signature have been the subject of endless and unprovable speculation, but there is no question that by 1501 he had come to see himself as an instrument in God's hands, as the Christ-bearer.

> Jerusalem and Mount Sion are to be rebuilt by the hand of a Christian; who this is to be, God declares by the mouth of His prophet in the fourteenth psalm. Abbot Joachim said that he was to come from Spain. St. Jerome showed the way of it to the holy lady. The emperor of Cathay, some time since, sent for wise men to instruct him in the faith of Christ. Who will offer himself for this work? If Our Lord bring me back to Spain, I pledge myself, in the name of God, to bring him there in safety.[46]

Columbus was suffering from poor health that had begun to affect him from the time of the second voyage. He underwent bouts of extreme pain in his lower extremities, sometimes accompanied by inflammation of the eyes that rendered it impossible for him to read. These symptoms were ascribed at the time to gout, but modern scholars suspect arthritis or Reiter's syndrome.[47] It is possible that his physical torments contributed to his increasingly bleak mental outlook.

Whatever its motivation, such a letter would not inspire Fernando and Isabel to place its writer in charge of an empire. There is no question of the devotion of the Catholic Monarchs to Christianity; Isabel in particular was famous for her piety, which had undoubtedly helped draw her to Columbus. Nonetheless, both monarchs were also shrewd politicians and administrators. It is hardly surprising that they refused to reinstate Columbus to any official position in the empire. Columbus's disturbed rantings on the fourth voyage would guarantee his continued exclusion from power, if not from wealth.

Once Columbus and his crew had been rescued from Jamaica, he had Méndez's caravel repaired in Santo Domingo and chartered another as well to sail home. Most of the men who had embarked on the fourth voyage decided to remain on Española; only Columbus's family members and close associates chose to accompany him. Their trials were still not over, however. Hardly 2 leagues out of port, the mainmast split on the caravel that Méndez had chartered. Columbus sent it back to port and continued his journey with a single vessel. With bad luck continuing, the mainmast on that vessel also split – into four pieces – and the admiral and the *adelantado* jury-rigged a new mast from a lateen yard. A storm later caused the foremast to spring loose. The crippled ship limped into Sanlúcar de Barrameda, at the mouth of the Guadalquivir River, on November 7, 1504, a date that marked the end of Columbus's career at sea.

He went upriver to Seville to rest, hoping for a summons to report in person to the monarchs. But Queen Isabel was gravely ill and would not recover; she died on November 26. Over the centuries, various writers have claimed that Columbus's fortunes waned with the death of Isabel, his great patroness, implying that King Fernando was responsible for the crown's withdrawal of support from Columbus. Yet even had Isabel lived longer, it is difficult to imagine any circumstance that would have induced her to trust Columbus to administer her empire, or even a small part of it. Before she died, the queen had realized that full recognition of the titles and offices promised to Columbus before the first voyage – admiral, viceroy, and governor of the lands he found – would fatally weaken royal control in the new colonies. His proposal to enslave and sell the natives had also angered her. She considered the natives subjects of the crown, not to be enslaved except in exceptional circumstances, and her successors followed those guidelines. The Castilian crown was reasserting control at home in the late fifteenth century, after decades of disorder; as much as possible the queen tried to extend the same control and orderly government to the new lands added to her realm.[48] From the point of view of the crown, Columbus's incompetence as an administrator and his open disobedience of royal orders provided a perfect opportunity to recapture the initiative in the Indies. The same thing would probably have happened in any case, however.

No government would have allowed Columbus's privileges to stand, once it became clear how much was at stake.

LAST YEARS

Defying reality, as he had often done, Columbus spent the rest of his life lobbying vigorously to have all his grants and titles restored. Even without them he was a wealthy man, but he felt betrayed and slighted, which left him unable to enjoy his achievements. That the Spanish crown was unwilling to grant Columbus all he wished cannot be blamed on royal ingratitude or on Castilian resentment of Columbus's Genoese ancestry. Columbus had forfeited his claim to royal preferment by badly mismanaging the Española settlement and by breaking his agreements with the crown on numerous occasions. In a larger sense, the business of discovery and colonial settlement had quickly grown too large for any one man to manage, however skilled he might have been. During Columbus's later years, many other voyages set out for the new-found lands, most sponsored by the Castilian crown but some sailing without any official support or even permission. Swiftly as the crown moved to establish control over the new colonies, it never altogether succeeded. The powerful lure of trade and plunder in the Caribbean drew men across the Atlantic in increasing numbers, with and without permission. It took the most experienced and loyal administrators that Castile could muster to assert royal control under those circumstances.

Political events in Spain did not work in Columbus's favor either. After the death of Queen Isabel, the crown of Castile passed not to Fernando but to the couple's oldest surviving child, Juana, married to Philip of Habsburg. Fernando, who of course was still king of Aragón, suggested that Columbus submit his claims against the Castilian crown to arbitration, but he refused, and by the time Juana arrived in Castile, he was already near the end of his life.

Columbus died in Valladolid in 1506, surrounded by his loving family, a rich but dissatisfied man. With the perspective of nearly five centuries, we can appreciate his great accomplishments more than most of his contemporaries could, and, ironically, more than he did himself. Still believing that he was close to Asia, Columbus had discovered a New World unknown to Europeans, exploring many of the larger islands of the Caribbean and long stretches of mainland in Central and South America. And he had set in motion a chain of events that, even in his lifetime, had begun to alter human history on both sides of the Atlantic. Eventually, their effects would spread throughout the world.

11

The Post-Columbian World

T HE POST-COLUMBIAN WORLD is, of course, the modern world. Its increasingly interdependent and interconnected societies began to be linked together in the late fifteenth century, following Spanish voyages to the west and Portuguese voyages southward and eastward to Asia. After those early voyages, there has never been a time when the major civilizations of the world have lost contact with one another, never a time when major events could have only local consequences. From the diverse and isolated worlds on the face of the earth in the late Middle Ages, a single world has been woven together by merchants and missionaries, colonists and conquerers, imperialists and idealists. Columbus placed the world on the path leading toward global interdependence, with enormous consequences – both good and ill – for the peoples of the world.

BEYOND COLUMBUS

Most of the consequences of his voyages were unforeseen in 1506 when Columbus died, not knowing how far Asia really lay from the lands he had explored. Even though Vasco da Gama brought the first Portuguese fleet from India into Lisbon some five years before Columbus died, Europeans still did not know the size of their world or how long a journey separated the Caribbean from the civilizations and commerce of Asia. Their ignorance would not be dispelled until 1522, when Juan Sebastián del Cano brought the remnant of Ferdinand Magellan's fleet back to Spain to complete the first circumnavigation of the globe. During its Pacific crossing from South America to Guam, Magellan's fleet was out of sight of land for four months, and the crew nearly starved, as well as suffering from scurvy and a variety of other ailments. With the fleet's arrival in Asia, then India, then Africa and Europe, the true extent of the land and water surfaces of the globe began to be known, just thirty years after Columbus's first voyage.[1]

By the time of Columbus's second voyage, caravels were shuttling between Cádiz and Española with trade goods, initiating the famous *carrera de Indias* that maintained regular trade across the Atlantic for over three centuries. By the second half of the sixteenth century, a global system of commerce had developed. The commodities exchanged over long distances still tended to be of high value. Given the distance and cost involved, they could not have been otherwise. Yet the global network created in the decades after 1492 would gradually expand to include quite ordinary items of daily consumption, and the modern world of global interchange and instantaneous global communication would be created.

The initial step in that process seems insignificant – Columbus's brief voyage westward across the Atlantic. Undoubtedly someone else would soon have taken that step, even if Columbus had never lived. By 1500, two other routes to the Western Hemisphere had been pioneered, far to the north and south of Columbus's route. John Cabot claimed what is today Labrador and Newfoundland for the king of England in 1497. And in 1500, Pedro Alvarez Cabral discovered Brazil with a Portuguese fleet, after sailing into the southwestern Atlantic in search of ideal winds and currents to let him round the southern tip of Africa. Whether his route so far to the west was accidental or an intentional test of the limits of the Treaty of Tordesillas is a matter of debate. Regardless, the preferred Portuguese trajectory for reaching the Cape of Good Hope required a long southwesterward swing out into the Atlantic; inevitably, a Portuguese pilot slightly off course would have sighted Brazil.[2]

Columbus was not as innovative as his supporters often claim. Closer connections throughout Eurasia and Africa were developing long before his time, and his fascination with Asia was a logical extension of many earlier commercial and missionary ventures. He inherited the traditions of Mediterranean commerce, and he learned about sailing in the eastern Atlantic by following routes pioneered by mariners from Portugal and Castile. His geographical knowledge synthesized biblical and academic knowledge that had existed, in many cases, for centuries. Columbus's innovation lay in combining that knowledge with speculation to postulate something new: that one could reach Asia fairly easily by sailing west. Even though he was not the first or the only man of his time to think so, he was the first to turn his speculation into reality. Once Columbus had shown the way, many others were eager to try their luck in the western ocean. They did not know the full identity of their destination, but they knew how to get there and back.

SPAIN'S AMERICAN EMPIRE

Spain's hope of establishing a network of profitable trading bases in "the Indies" began to fade while Columbus was still alive. Fernando and Isabel licensed nearly a dozen other westward voyages of exploration to look for the Asian mainland. Of course they failed to find it, but explorers, soldiers of fortune, missionaries, and settlers continued to stream across the Atlantic in the wake of Columbus.

To protect royal interests and extend some vestige of law and order in their overseas colonies, Fernando and Isabel sent royal governors and bureaucrats across the ocean as well. In 1503, they established the Casa de Contratación (House of Trade) in Seville, to supervise emigration, transport, and trade with what Europeans would continue to call the Indies. In setting up a colonial administration, the government drew on centuries of European experience in dealing with lands conquered, settled, and brought under the rule of law. They also followed more recent precedents set during the Reconquest of Spain from the Muslims and the Castilian conquest of the Canary Islands. Aragonese experience in ruling southern Italy and Portuguese experience in its outposts in Africa, the Azores, and the Madeiras also provided precedents for the colonial government in the Caribbean. Spain began to create a functioning colonial empire surprisingly quickly. Without being aware of the centuries of European history that had prepared Spain for ruling and settling new lands, it would be easy to see that empire as an improvisation, unplanned and almost accidentally created. There is a grain of truth in that observation. Fernando and Isabel had not planned to *found* a huge land-based empire; they had planned to *find* the fabled empires of Asia. Nonetheless, when China and its neighbors proved elusive, they moved quickly to organize and exploit the lands Columbus had claimed, with all the tools of bureaucracy and military organization available to them. Not far into the sixteenth century, what had begun as a search for a new trade route to Asia had turned into the Spanish Empire.

The changes resulting from the process of conquest and colonization during Columbus's lifetime pale in comparison with those that followed. Using the Caribbean islands as a base from which to explore the coastline of the Americas, Spaniards soon established contact with mainland peoples and eventually with the powerful empire of the Aztecs in the central Valley of Mexico. Many of these expeditions were financed from the profits of trade based in the Caribbean; explorers no longer had to rely on European merchants and governments to support them.

A Spanish expedition left from Cuba in 1519 under the leadership of Hernán Cortés, who disobeyed orders from the governor who had sent him and founded a town called Veracruz on the Mexican coast. Marching inland from there, the expedition met many peoples who resented Aztec power. The Tlascalans and some of their neighbors were pleased to welcome the newcomers, hoping to use them in their

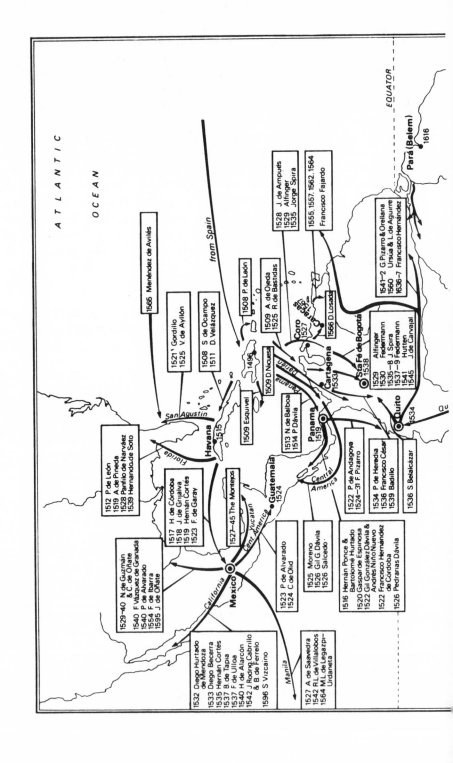

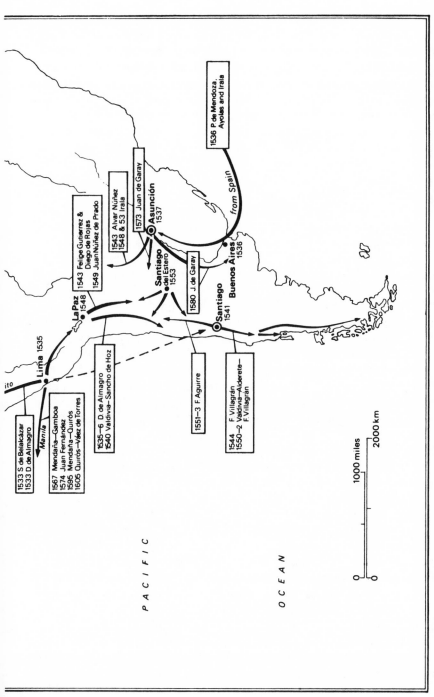

Spanish voyages of exploration in the sixteenth and early seventeenth centuries. (From *The Cambridge History of Latin America*, 2 vols. on *Colonial Latin America*, ed. Leslie Bethell [Cambridge, 1984], 1:150–1. Reprinted from Francisco Morales Padrón, *Historia general de América*, 2d ed. [Madrid, 1975], pp. 336–7.)

own struggle against the Aztecs. Cortés and his several hundred men initially approached the Aztec empire peacefully, fully aware that they were outnumbered and vulnerable, and held together by Cortés's inspired and intelligent leadership. The Spaniards formed alliances with the Aztecs' enemies before the initial contacts with the Aztecs degenerated into hostility. Backed by their local allies, the Spaniards were able to conquer the vast Aztec empire with surprising ease.

Earlier generations of historians wrote stirring accounts of the Spanish conquests in the New World. To account for the rapid success of the *conquistadores,* they trotted out such explanations as the assumed natural superiority of the white races, although this was tempered in the works of Protestant historians by their antipathy toward Spain and Catholicism. More recent explanations of the conquest discard assumptions that European warriors enjoyed any racial superiority over their American counterparts. Instead, historians now stress the disadvantages that thousands of years of isolation had wrought in the Western Hemisphere. Chief among those disadvantages was the lack of advanced metallurgy and other technology in the New World, which the Old World had developed over several thousand years. In any battle, regardless of the numbers on each side, the stone weapons of the Aztecs were no match for the iron, steel, and gunpowder of the Europeans. Many of the Spaniards also rode horses, a totally unfamiliar beast to the Indians. Although the importance of horses to the success of the conquest has often been overrated, they clearly had some ability to frighten native armies, as well as providing the Europeans with greater mobility and striking power.

Cultural differences seem to have played a role in the Spaniards' victory as well. Aztec rulers had heard about the Spanish newcomers long before they saw them, but they had a limited context in which to place them. Isolated for millennia from the Old World, the peoples of the Western Hemisphere knew only themselves and their gods. The Europeans, by contrast, were aware of a wide range of human societies in the Old World. Columbus had recognized immediately that the people of the Caribbean were not like the people of Europe, the eastern Mediterranean, or North Africa. They were also different from Marco Polo's Asians and from the black Africans Columbus had known in his travels. Instead, he compared the people of the Caribbean to the Canary Islanders, which gave him and his companions a ready-made context and a set of expectations about how they would behave in a variety of situations. Neither the Tainos and Caribs of the Caribbean nor the Aztecs and their tributaries on the mainland had a similarly broad experience of human differences. The Spaniards must have looked quite alien to them, and Spanish clothing and tools also differed substantially from their own and seemed in many ways superior. There was no obvious way either to define the Spaniards or to predict how they would behave. Arguably, the limited cultural experience of the Aztecs put them at a disadvantage in dealing with outsiders.

In battle, the Aztecs fought to capture their enemies for slavery or religious sacrifice; the Spaniards, like other Europeans, generally fought to kill. This difference inevitably favored the Spaniards. A moment's hesitation in hand-to-hand combat with an armed Spaniard would cost the Aztec warrior his life. Aztec interpretations of the conquest developed the belief that the Spanish arrival represented the return of gods the Aztecs had spurned in their rise to power. Logically, warriors who saw the Spaniards as vengeful gods may have lost their will to defend themselves, allowing the Spaniards an easy victory. As appealing as this interpretation is, many historians now think that the idea of Spaniards as returning gods was a legend created after the conquest, rather than before, as an attempt to explain the catastrophe of defeat by resorting to divine intervention. Technological and cultural differences were sufficient, without the legend, to settle the outcome of the struggle, despite the military skills of the Aztecs in their own cultural context.

The Spanish conquest of Mexico in 1519–21 was an archetypal clash of civilizations, filled with drama and human tragedy, but it was not unique. A decade later in 1532–3, the story was repeated in Peru, when Francisco Pizarro conquered the empire of the Incas with only one hundred sixty-eight men. Similar scenarios unfolded in many other parts of the Western Hemisphere in the sixteenth century.[3] Nevertheless, the human wars of conquest in the Americas caused less destruction than another conquest at a microscopic level: the onslaught of Old World diseases and parasites against populations previously unexposed to them.

DEMOGRAPHIC CATASTROPHE IN THE SIXTEENTH CENTURY

Because of its isolation, the Western Hemisphere was free from many diseases that were widespread and endemic in the Old World. These probably included influenza, smallpox, measles, malaria, bubonic plague, and perhaps even the common cold. When they were introduced to what epidemiologists call the "virgin soil" of the Hemisphere, Old World diseases struck the native population with devastating force. Scholars reconstructing the demography of early colonial Latin America are unable to determine combination of diseases caused the Indians to succumb in such large numbers. Medical diagnosis was not well developed in the sixteenth century, and the records commonly lump diseases together in such a way as to make it almost impossible to sort out the nature of a given epidemic. What is clear, however, is that great human mortality and suffering resulted from the introduction of Old World diseases to the Western Hemisphere and that smallpox was the chief killer.[4]

Smallpox had existed since ancient times in the Old World, but variants of the disease differed widely in their incidence and effects. The best evidence we have suggests that a mild form of the disease (*Variola minor*) predominated in Europe before the seventeenth century. Because smallpox is highly contagious in a densely settled population, nearly everyone in Europe caught it, mostly in childhood, but only about 1 percent died. European writers often discussed the disease as a predictable, and even a salutary, part of childhood, rarely mentioning that it could occasionally kill. Those who survived any variant of smallpox acquired lifelong immunity, which explains why successive epidemics disproportionately infected children – the only group without immunity. The severe form of the disease (*Variola major*) seems to have surfaced a few times in Europe before the seventeenth century, but it did not displace the mild form until the seventeenth century. Then it became a serious scourge, returning at regular intervals with enough virulence to kill 10 to 30 percent of its victims and to disfigure those who survived with severe facial pockmarks.

Many Spaniards, like other Europeans, had survived smallpox and other Old World diseases as children, and the individuals who crossed the Atlantic were generally young and vigorous. Those without immunity could and did fall victim to epidemics in the New World, but the *conquistadores* as a whole were not vulnerable to wholesale epidemic mortality from Old World diseases. Moreover, their numbers could be replenished by new arrivals from Spain. It is not clear to medical historians which variant of smallpox crossed the Atlantic with them. Some argue for the mild form of the disease, because of its widespread dominance in Europe. Why *Variola minor* would strike the native inhabitants of the Western Hemisphere with such force remains a puzzle. Some suggest that the limited gene pool in preconquest America had made a large number of people especially vulnerable even to the mild form of a new disease. Other scholars argue that because the disease killed 20 to 30 percent or more of the natives who became infected, the deadly form of smallpox must have been the variety introduced from the Old World, either from Europe or from Africa. Medical historians have no clear answer to these puzzles.[5]

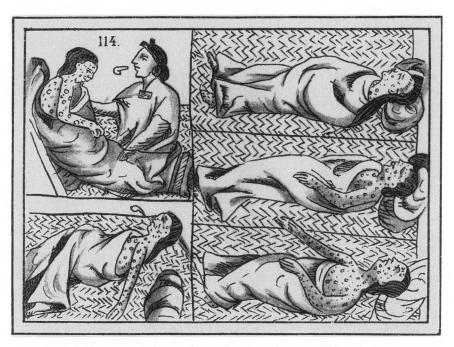

Indians in Mexico suffering from smallpox. (From the *Florentine Codex*. Peabody Museum, Harvard University.)

Without question, the worst possible combination of circumstances left almost no escape for the native population of the Western Hemisphere, once new diseases arrived in their midst. Women of childbearing age and adult males succumbed along with children and the elderly, since at first no one had acquired immunity. This meant that deaths during the acute phase of an epidemic could not be balanced by an increased birthrate once the crisis had passed. Adding to the disruptions caused by conquest and disease, the new political and economic structure imposed by the conquerors uprooted many people from long-established patterns of social organization and forced them to work in mines and in unfamiliar agricultural activities. Even though the Spanish bureaucracy tried to change only what was necessary to secure and maintain authority, their reorganization disrupted the fundamental bases of indigenous society, at least for a time. Those who fell ill often had no community network to support them. Many historians used to argue that cultural despair contributed to the inability of native peoples to resist disease during and after the conquest. Some now question the notion of cultural despair and look instead at how the remaining native community responded to the combination of military defeat, social disruption, and cata-strophic epidemics. The discussion of native adaptations to the co-lonial regime is related to an ongoing debate about population num-bers before and after the conquest.

No population records were kept in the Americas before the con-quest; Europeans did not begin to keep systematic records until quite some time after they arrived, and then only for areas under their control. Unquestionably, native populations suffered a demographic catastrophe after Europeans arrived in the Western Hemisphere, but the magnitude of that decline remains in dispute. Estimates for the preconquest population vary widely, even though most of them are based on the same documents. Typically, scholars select figures for the late sixteenth century they think are more or less reliable and work backward to estimate the earlier population. Based on these methods, the preconquest population of the Western Hemisphere as a whole has been estimated at anywhere from about 14 to 20 million to over 100 million. By 1650, it stood somewhere between 4.5 and 10 million.[6] Current scholarship tends to discount high estimates of the preconquest population as wildly exaggerated. The newer figures are based in part on growing knowledge about the economies of the Western Hemisphere before 1492. Hunting and gathering food, or growing it in limited areas, simply would not have supported the inflated numbers estimated by some earlier historians. Even the densely settled civilizations in Mexico and Peru had limits to their popula-tions, based on the carrying capacity of the land. The most compre-hensive history of world population to date estimates the population from Mexico south to the tip of South America at 14 million people before contact with Europeans and their diseases.[7] If that estimate is correct, then we must discard high estimates for North America as well, where the population was generally very sparse and where al-most no documentary evidence exists. Current estimates for Amer-ica north of Mexico range from 1 million to as high as 15 to 20 million, with the figures still hotly debated.[8]

The best-studied regions are the Caribbean, the Valley of Mexico, and Peru. The island of Española, the principal scene of early Euro-pean activity in the Caribbean, may have experienced the most dra-matic decline in population. By 1570, only a few hundred natives remained, from a preconquest population estimated between fifty to sixty thousand and several million. Recent scholarship favors the lower end of the range. Estimates for central Mexico show a similar diver-gence in overall figures but an agreement that sharp declines fol-lowed the conquest. About 1 million native inhabitants were counted in 1605, the remnant of a preconquest population estimated between 4.5 million and 25 million.[9] Estimates for preconquest Peru range between 2 to 3 million and 12 to 15 million. One recent study argues for 9 million before the conquest and eight hundred fifty thousand in 1600.[10] The estimates will change as scholars make new discoveries and offer new interpretations of old data. Nonetheless, two generalizations can be stated with assurance: first, the demographic history of certain regions is, and will likely remain, far better known than others; second, there was a massive population decline after the conquest.

The Spaniards had not deliberately caused such devastating losses to the native population and witnessed the horrifying epidemic mortality with puzzlement and anguish. No episode in Spanish (or Portuguese) colonial history has come to light equivalent to the story of General Jeffrey Amherst in North America. A commander of British forces attempting to end the Indian uprising called Pontiac's Rebellion in 1763, Amherst tried to infect the rebels with smallpox by sending them contaminated blankets.[11] The Spaniards inadvertently introduced smallpox and other diseases and worsened their effects by wars of conquest and the disruption of native societies. They did not, however, aim for the annihilation of the native population. Quite to the contrary, they wanted a large native population to convert to Christianity and use as a labor force.

LABOR SUPPLY IN COLONIAL SPANISH AMERICA

The first policy established by Queen Isabel regarding the native population claimed them as vassals of the crown of Castile and therefore barred their enslavement. By 1495, however, the crown conceded that natives captured in a "just war" could be enslaved, and Spaniards were allowed to purchase captives held as slaves by other native groups. A thriving slave trade in native Americans soon developed throughout the Caribbean and the adjacent mainland. In fact, the original plans for Cortés's expedition to Mexico, as conceived by the governor of Cuba who authorized it, was to seek gold and slaves, not conquest or settlement. At the same time, the Spanish government began to intervene on behalf of the natives. The Laws of Burgos in 1512 prescribed fair treatment for Indians in the Spanish colonies, though their enforcement was nearly impossible in the chaotic situation of the early conquest period. Bartolomé de Las Casas and other Spaniards strongly advocated greater legal protection for the native population. During the reign of Carlos I of Spain (Emperor Charles V) from 1517 to 1556, several laws limited the ability of colonists to enslave natives or practice other forms of forced labor. Nonetheless, laws prohibiting Indian slavery – and laws generally –

were difficult to enforce in the New World. Colonists who wanted to evade them could use a variety of pretexts. Attempts to use Amerindians as slaves were not especially effective, however, in part because of continuing epidemic losses among the native population.

A second effort to marshal labor looked to models developed in Spain during the Reconquest and in the Canaries, designed to hold conquered lands and to provide for the Christianization and pacification of the local population. The name *encomienda* described the system in both the Old World and the New, although in practice the systems differed considerably on opposite sides of the Atlantic. The most obvious difference was that the Old World *encomiendas* were grants of land or the rents from land, with responsibilities for the inhabitants already living there. In the New World, *encomiendas* were typically grants of labor service to those who already held land. The laborers did not necessarily reside nearby. All of the variants of *encomienda* shared one essential characteristic, however. They defined relationships in which the crown contracted with private parties to exercise official functions – defense, social control, Christianization, and so on – in return for some kind of financial reward. By giving private citizens a stake in the settlement and economic development of frontier areas, the crown could govern a much larger area and a much larger population than its own officials could manage. *Encomiendas* had proved valuable in extending government authority in the Old World. The New World variant of the *encomienda* system proved effective at first but eventually led to serious problems.

Early *encomiendas* in the New World typically assigned labor services from an entire native village under its own chief to a Spanish colonist. The natives "commended" owed specified labor services, and the Spanish *encomendero* had certain responsibilities for their assimilation into the colonial system. Problems arose when many settlers mistreated the people commended to them and began to act as if their *encomiendas* were hereditary landed estates rather than a grant of labor services. In addition, in many cases declining populations reduced the value of the original grants of labor service. As the native population plummeted, some *encomenderos* became responsible for grouping survivors in central villages and providing for their religious education, in effect reconstituting village life disrupted by epidemics. The Spanish notion of civilization placed great emphasis on the social structure of town life and communal religious worship, for natives as well as Spaniards. The crown and royal officials in Spain, made aware of abuses by a long series of complaints by Spanish settlers and missionaries on the spot, began to curtail the settlers' authority over the indigenous population. Native slavery was declared illegal in the New Laws (*Nueva Recopilación*) of 1542, which also curtailed the power of *encomenderos* and rescinded the *encomiendas* of settlers who had been involved in civil war in Peru. Moreover, all *encomiendas* were to revert to the crown when their holders died, and no new ones were to be assigned. These laws so angered settlers in Peru that they rebelled, and in the violence the region's first viceroy was killed. His successor chose not to enforce the laws, and the crown eventually allowed two or more generations to inherit *encomiendas* before they reverted to the crown. Time accomplished what strict legality could not: nearly three-quarters of the income from *encomiendas* in central Mexico had passed to the crown by 1570, as *encomenderos* died without heirs. Once in royal hands, the *encomiendas* were administered by crown officials appointed for short terms. A similar process occurred in Peru. In far-flung areas of the empire, *encomiendas* were allowed to survive, presumably because they threatened neither royal authority nor royal income.

The need for labor to develop the colonial economy was addressed in the last half of the sixteenth century by a system called *repartimiento*. The word itself means "distribution" and was used to describe a variety of arrangements. Columbus had assigned chiefs and their tribes on Española to Spanish settlers as laborers and had called the system *repartimiento,* but it was rather different from the later assignment of native labor on the mainland. In the latter system, which followed traditions of forced labor in the Aztec and Inca empires, Spanish settlers were provided with native workers on a rotational basis from nearby communities, as a kind of tax. Each labor draft served for two to four months. The system was called *repartimiento* in Mexico and *mita* (the name of the old Inca system) in Peru. Spanish settlers were expected to provide decent working conditions for the laborers and to pay them a specified wage. The type of work varied with the local economy: agriculture, mining, road construction and maintenance, and textile production were the most common assignments.

As the colonial economy grew, the shortage of labor was increasingly met by free wage labor, along with the importation of slaves from West Africa. Free wage labor had become dominant in the Andean mines by the late sixteenth century and had mostly replaced forced labor in Mexico by about 1630. By the seventeenth century, colonial Spanish America generally relied on the free wage labor of native workers (*naboríos*) and those of mixed race (mestizos and mulattos), supplemented by the slave labor of African blacks, forced migrants whose numbers eventually reached into the millions. The progression from Indian slavery, to coerced labor, to a mixed system of free wage labor and imported slave labor in the Americas followed the pattern that had unfolded in the Canary Islands, and for similar reasons: the impact of warfare and disease, the need for labor to de-velop the colonial economy, and the cumulative influence of law and administration.[12]

Passage of laws did not end abusive treatment of the Indians over-night, but it made a start. One of the great ironies of Spanish history is that the work of Bartolomé de Las Casas and other Spanish re-formers became a powerful weapon in the hands of Spain's enemies in the sixteenth century and beyond. Las Casas had begun his adult-hood as a *conquistador* and *encomendero* but later became a Dominican friar and a tireless advocate for the native population. He called for the importation of black African slaves to spare the Indians, even though late in his life, and not in print, he recognized the moral blindness of substituting the coerced labor of one group for another. The evidence he marshaled to goad the crown into protective legis-lation came from the first three decades after Columbus's 1492 voy-age, during the chaotic and lawless time when the Caribbean settle-ments were the farthest frontier of European civilization. Las Casas collected horrendous cases of brutality and indiscriminate pillage and murder from the 1510s and 1520s, sometimes exaggerating them. He presented his *Brief History of the Destruction of the Indies* to Emperor Charles V in 1540 as part of a crusade for reform. Understandably, because his work was designed as propaganda he told only the neg-ative parts of the story, ignoring evidence of peaceful contacts and intermarriage between Spanish colonists and the native population, and ignoring as well the increasing spread and effectiveness of the rule of law in the colonies during the 1530s. By the time his cam-paign succeeded, the lawlessness he had chronicled had been replaced in large part by a stable colonial administration.[13]

Dutch rebels fighting for their independence from Spain after 1568 discovered Las Casas's report and printed it. Spain's other enemies in Europe eagerly adopted Las Casas's polemic as well, some in-spired by Protestant zeal against Catholicism and others by fear of Spain's imperial power in Europe and envy of its rich overseas em-pire. The popularity of Las Casas fanned the flames of anti-Spanish sentiment in sixteenth- and seventeenth-century Europe and spawned what has been called the "Black Legend" of Spanish colonialism and Spanish civilization as a whole. In many ways the legend still sur-vives, in the unexamined prejudices of popular writers and even in the work of trained historians. As Eric Wolf commented,

> Pleaders of special causes ascribed the decimation of the Indian popu-lation to Spanish cruelty, but the Spaniards were neither more nor less cruel than other conquerors, past or present. . . .
> The chief factor in this disaster appears to have been not conscious

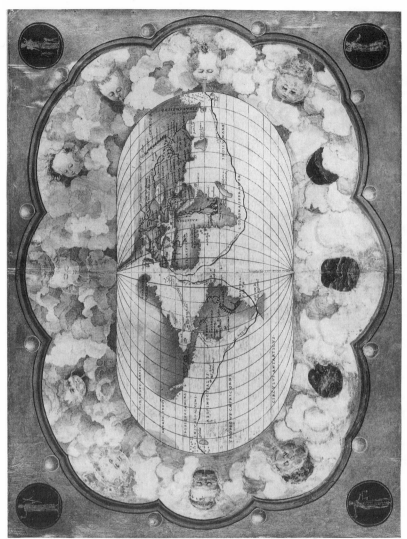

World map drawn for Emperor Charles V by Battista Agnese (Venice, ca. 1544), showing the route of Magellan's circumnavigation of the globe. (Courtesy of the John Carter Brown Library at Brown University.)

maltreatment of the Indian but the introduction of new diseases to which the Indians were not immune. The Spaniards did not want to kill off the native population – just the opposite, in fact – they wanted to put them to work. In their attempt to do so, they encountered difficulties that convinced them that native labor was not well suited for the most lucrative ventures they proposed for the New World. One of the greatest difficulties, from the colonists' viewpoint, was that the Spanish imperial government took measures intended to protect the Amerindians from exploitation. These measures were never totally effective, but they reflected the humanitarian impulses of the home government and hindered the colonists who tried to extract the maximum labor possible from the Amerindians.[14]

In the short term, the Spanish conquest devastated the peoples of the New World – demographically, politically, and culturally. In the longer term, the native population stabilized and began to recover, and a new civilization arose to replace the ones that had been destroyed. This new civilization combined peoples, laws, customs, and governmental systems from Europe, Africa, and the Americas, ultimately creating a New World in fact as well as in name.

THE EFFECT OF THE AMERICAN CONQUESTS ON EUROPE

Europe and the rest of the Old World felt much less dramatic effects from the clash of civilizations begun by Columbus. In exchange for the devastating diseases introduced to the New World, the Old World evidently contracted only syphilis, a venereal disease. Syphilis spread with epidemic fury in the aftermath of Columbus's first return voyage in 1493, largely through sexual contact but also through the skin by contact with the lesions of victims of the disease in its active phase. Transmitted to Italy by 1493, and elsewhere in Europe almost as quickly, syphilis seems to have made its way to India, and even to China, as early as 1505.[15] Its rapid progress shows, ironically, that the trading networks of the Old World were fairly efficient links, even before the voyages of exploration greatly expanded their scope.

Despite the advent of syphilis and other immediate results of the voyages, it is widely acknowledged that Europeans did not fully comprehend the reality of the New World until nearly a century after Columbus's first voyage. At the root of this lingering incomprehension lay a European view of the universe that had not known the New World and its peoples existed and consequently had not allowed for them in its systems of law, religion, and intellectual outlook. Educated individuals at the court of Charles V might realize the magnitude of the discovery – Francisco López de Gómara, secretary to the conqueror Cortés, called it *"the greatest event since the creation of the world"*[16] – but ordinary Spaniards and others had trouble knowing just what it meant. Without having seen the New World for themselves, they could not absorb it into their consciousness.

The precise geographical location of the New World in America, and its vast extent, became known to Iberian mariners through a series of extraordinary voyages. The dozen or so expeditions that sailed across the Atlantic during Columbus's lifetime were followed by others, fanning out along the coasts as the explorers gained confidence in unfamiliar waters. As one piece after another of the coastline was explored, they were mapped and studied in Seville. In many ways the crucial voyage was the circumnavigation of the globe begun in 1519 by Ferdinand Magellan, a Portuguese in Spanish service, and completed after Magellan's death by the Basque Juan Sebastián del Cano in 1522. During the years when Cortés conquered Mexico, Magellan's voyage proved just how far Mexico was from Asia. Another vast ocean separated the lands Columbus had found from the ones he had sought. In 1529 another Portuguese working for Spain, the cartographer Diego Ribero, produced a remarkable map of the world, summarizing the knowledge gained by Iberian exploration in the previous thirty-five years. On Ribero's beautiful "Carta Universal," all of Africa, the eastern coastline of North America, and nearly the full coastline of South America were fairly accurately mapped. India, Asia, and the Pacific were less accurate, and many areas were left blank. The relationship between "New Spain" (Nueva España), recently conquered by Cortés, and Asia remained unknown, even in official circles.[17]

Outside Iberia, even officials did not have access to detailed maps of the lands beyond the seas, in part because those maps were often considered state secrets. Moreover, when monarchs presented maps to one another as ceremonial gifts, the geographical features were not necessarily represented accurately. A map was a political statement in the rivalry among nations; geographical features might be sized to indicate their importance rather than their true configurations. Only slowly and incrementally did the shape of the real world become known. If Ribero illustrated what was known in 1529, the small globe made by Caspar Vopell Medebach in 1543 showed how much was still not known, at least in northern Europe. One realizes with a jolt that Medebach placed Mexico ("Messigo") and other Spanish colonies on the same land mass with China. In other words, he conceived the Americas as a huge peninsula attached to Asia, rather than as two separate continents, thousands of miles east of Japan.[18]

To assimilate the reality of the New World and its peoples took

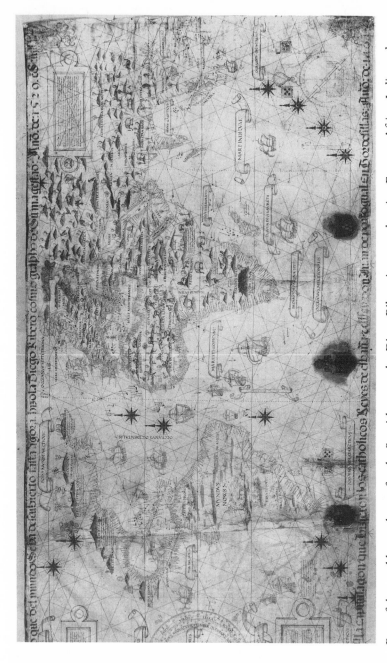

Part of the world map drawn for the Spanish crown by Diego Ribero in 1529, showing Europe, Africa, India, and part of Asia in the Eastern Hemisphere, plus the mapped parts of the Western Hemisphere. (Biblioteca Apostolica Vaticana, Rome.)

Spaniards nearly a century, and other Europeans even longer. At first, many writers compared the Indians of the New World to figures from classical Greek and Roman mythology, as if they represented an unspoiled and nobler version of the European past. Only gradually did they recognize that the peoples of the New World were very different from the peoples of the Old World, even if they held certain traits in common. To govern and Christianize them, which Spain recognized as a clear duty resulting from the conquest, Spaniards first had to understand them. This led bureaucrats, clerics, and other intelligent observers to study various aspects of New World cultures. Some aspects the Spaniards found uninteresting, such as many varieties of Amerindian art. Other aspects they found profoundly offensive, such as human sacrifice, cannibalism, homosexuality, bestiality, and other sexual practices. What really interested them were New World systems of government, land tenure, taxation, and social organization. At least among the major New World empires, bureaucratic and societal organization had a familiar shape, which the Spaniards could compare and contrast with their own ways of doing things. Knowledge about government and society had an obvious practical value, as Spain created a bureaucratic structure to govern its growing empire.

In the course of defining New World peoples, Spaniards had to define themselves as well and to reexamine their role within God's universal plan for mankind. Because the New World peoples were clearly part of creation, they had a place in God's plan, which could only be ascertained by studying them in relation to the other human groups on earth. The first observer to put all the pieces together was José de Acosta. His *Natural and Moral History of the Indies,* published in 1590, examined a wide range of evidence about the New World's peoples, defining them as capable of receiving God's grace, and civilized in some ways. In other ways, he found them less advanced than Europeans or Asians. For example, many of the native inhabitants did not live in large civilizations but in small tribal groups, which appeared disorganized and therefore barbarous to European observers. Acosta's scale of gradation from barbarism to civilization reinforced the European notion of progress in human affairs and imposed a duty on the Spanish conquerors to help the New World's peoples progress toward civilization and a knowledge of God. The Spanish quest to understand the reality of the New World ultimately strengthened some of their own beliefs, even as the moral issues raised by the conquest cast others into doubt. Overall, in approaching an understanding of the New World and its peoples, Spaniards and other Europeans experienced a renewed sense of the worth of Christian civilization and its place in God's design.[19]

Spain's colonial empire in the Americas strengthened the monarchy at home in a variety of ways. For one, the expanded need for trained administrators created an array of lucrative jobs. As a result, ambitious nobles and commoners found an acceptable outlet for their energy overseas, relieving some of the pressures within Spanish society. This safety valve contributed to the relative social peace in Spain during the sixteenth and seventeenth centuries, a time in which nearly every other country in Europe was beset by social and political unrest, and some were beset by widespread rebellion and even regicide.

Moreover, tax revenues from the New World provided additional funds for Spain's ambitious European foreign policy, serving to extend the reach, if not the grasp, of Spanish ambitions. In the late sixteenth and early seventeenth centuries, Spain championed the Catholic Reformation and fought nearly continual wars to defend the lands inherited by Charles V and his successors. Although revenues from the American empire generally provided only about 11 percent of the annual income of the Spanish crown, and never more than 20 percent, New World revenues provided the crucial margin that made such high expenditures thinkable, if not always affordable. Ultimately, the overextension of its resources would cause the downfall of Spanish power in Europe, and many historians have blamed the empire and its windfall of wealth for luring Spanish monarchs into disaster. For over a century, however, New World wealth helped to bring Spain to the pinnacle of power at home and abroad. Even when that power faded in Europe, the overseas empire remained in Spanish hands, a reminder of past glories that would last into the nineteenth century.[20]

INCURSIONS INTO THE IBERIAN EMPIRES

Other countries felt the lure of the New World as well, attracted by the vast wealth filtering through Spain. By the late sixteenth century, France, England, and Spain's own rebellious subjects in the Netherlands were trying to break into the Spanish Empire, refusing to accept Spanish claims to a monopoly on trade with its colonies. These incursions into the Americas – called "piracy" when they were forbidden by their home governments, and "privateering" when they were not – put great pressure on Spanish defenses. At least part of the overextension that brought about the end of Spanish hegemony was due to the need to defend the colonies against foreign attackers and interlopers.

By an extraordinary effort during the late sixteenth and seventeenth centuries, Spain managed to keep intruders out of the heart of its empire, from the mainland of Mexico and Central America to the tip of Tierra del Fuego. Except for a few toeholds on the coasts and on Caribbean islands, would-be rivals were pushed northward beyond the effective limits of Spanish authority, settling along the eastern coast of North America and only slowly pushing their way inland in their own colonial adventures.

Elsewhere, European rivals encroached on the Portuguese trading empire in Africa, Asia, and Brazil. Through the sixteenth century, Portugal concentrated its efforts on seaborne trade with Asia and Africa, on the other side of the world from the Spanish Empire in the Americas. Even while Portugal and Spain shared a monarch, between 1580 and 1640, their two empires remained legally separate. Nonetheless, Spain's enemies also attacked the Portuguese empire from the late sixteenth century on, and Portuguese and Spanish forces were combined to fight Dutch incursions into Brazil in the 1630s. Portugal managed to oust the Dutch from Brazil in the mid-1650s, in the midst of its rebellion against Spain, but it could not avoid losing control of its far-flung empire in Asia. Ironically, as the Iberian phase of expansion reached its limits, Columbus's goal finally came to pass. After two decades of effort, Spain conquered the Philippine Islands in 1565 and established a trading colony in Manila, with access to the rich markets of Asia. Thereafter, Spanish galleons carried Mexican and Peruvian silver from Acapulco across the Pacific to Manila and returned with the Asian silks and spices eagerly sought by the wealthy Spanish colonial elite.[21] What Columbus had vainly attempted in the Caribbean was eventually realized in the South China Sea. By 1650 European expansion overseas included the Dutch, the French, and the English, as well as the Portuguese and the Spanish, encompassing ever-wider areas within a global trading network.

THE GLOBAL MIGRATION OF PLANTS AND ANIMALS

The economic consequences of the European expansion that began with Columbus affected aspects of life as mundane as the daily diet of ordinary people and as exotic as the structure of international trade and finance. Beginning with the mundane, a partial listing of ordinary plants and animals native to the Old World or the New, and now known to both, hints at the pervasiveness of transoceanic borrowing (see Table).[22] Europeans, on the eve of Columbus's voyages, sustained themselves with a diet based on cereal grains, especially wheat, which supplied most of their calories. Sources of protein included meat, game, fish, eggs, milk products, and legumes (often

Exotic plants and fruits depicted in the late sixteenth century, as the Dutch began to take over the Portuguese empire in Asia. (From Jan Huygen van Linschoten, *Itinerarium, ofte Schip-vaert naer Oost ofte Portugaels Indien* . . . [Amsterdam, 1623]. Photo courtesy of the James Ford Bell Library, University of Minnesota.)

called the "meat of the poor"). The complex vegetable proteins provided by a combination of wheat and legumes, or rice and legumes, supplemented the complete proteins found in animal products. Every region had its characteristic cereal grains, and traditional diets centered on them. The wheat bread of the Mediterranean, the rye bread of Germany, and the oat porridge of Scotland shaped each local cuisine as a reflection of the region's climate and soil. The availability and variety of vegetables and fruits depended on the climate and type of soil in each area as well. The Mediterranean region, poor in many ways, nonetheless grew a wider range of fruits and vegetables than did more northerly regions. Especially in winter, the lack of fresh fruit in central and northern Europe contributed to a variety of health problems, including scurvy. Although this dread disease, caused by a lack of ascorbic acid in the diet, gained notoriety on the long sea voyages that characterized European expansion, it undoubtedly existed beforehand. Many of the peoples of central and northern Europe must have suffered prescorbutic symptoms, on the borderline of scurvy, during winter.

Origins of typical plants and animals

OLD WORLD

Cultivated Plants		Domesticated Animals
wheat	radish	horses
rye	onion	cattle
oats	olive	pigs
rice	European melons	sheep
soybeans	citrus and other fruits	goats
chickpeas	banana	asses
peas	wine grapes of various kinds	camels
other legumes	almonds and other nuts	chickens
cabbage	coffee	dogs
cauliflower	sugarcane	cats
salad greens		

NEW WORLD

Cultivated Plants		Domesticated Animals
potato	pumpkins	llama
sweet potato	pineapple	alpaca
maize	guava	guinea pig
beans of various kinds	papaya	turkey
Chili peppers of various kinds	avocado	Muscovy duck
tomato	peanut	chicken (perhaps)
manioc (cassava)	tobacco	dog
squashes	cocoa	

Source: Alfred W. Crosby, *The Columbian Exchange.*

Some items of the European diet, such as wine, were not essential to health, even if they were thoroughly embedded in the diet, culture, and economy of many regions of Europe. Still other foods, such as coffee and sugar, were available in quantity only in the eastern Mediterranean, and coffee drinking cannot be documented even there much before the late fifteenth century. European crusaders in the late Middle Ages had acquired a taste for sugar during their sojourn in the East, and its cultivation was introduced to the Atlantic islands by European colonists in the fifteenth century.

The animals of the Old World supplied more than just protein. Some of them provided labor for agriculture, transport, and industrial processes such as milling. Animal power, coupled with widespread use of the wheel, meant that civilizations in the Old World required relatively less human labor than civilizations in the New World. Moreover, the domestication of a wide range of animals in

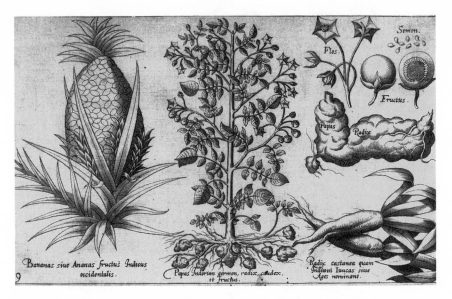

Pineapple, potatoes, and other exotic plants from the Western Hemisphere. (From Caspar Plautius, *Nova typis transacta navigatio* [N.p., 1621]. Courtesy of the James Ford Bell Library, University of Minnesota.)

the Old World had probably contributed to the domestication of a wide range of diseases, shared in variant forms by humans and the animals they lived with. For example, smallpox and cowpox were related diseases shared between humans and animals, and cowpox would figure prominently in the development of a vaccine against smallpox in the eighteenth century.

In the New World, complex vegetable proteins played a major role in assuring a balanced diet. Maize (often known in the United States as "corn" or "Indian corn"), in combination with beans or other legumes, supplied the complete proteins essential to health. Maize was particularly important to diets in the densely settled civilizations of Mexico and Central America, but it was widely consumed in North America as well. The potato supplied substantial calories and nutrition in the highlands of South America, the home of the Inca Empire. Elsewhere, sweet potatoes, manioc (cassava), and squashes held a prominent place in the daily diet. Pineapples, guavas, and other fruits supplied ample amounts of ascorbic acid and other nutrients, as did tomatoes and chili peppers.

The most important dietary shortage in the Western Hemisphere was animal protein. The New World as a whole had few domestic animals, either for food or for labor. Small dogs and various kinds of fowl did not begin to provide the protein that domesticated cattle and pigs could have. Wild game, especially the characteristic deer, bison, elk, and caribou of North America, played a crucial role in the diet and overall economy of native peoples, but they had to be hunted, at great cost in time and energy. Fish and shellfish were not available everywhere. Llamas and alpacas in the mountains of South America provided fiber for weaving and some animal power for transport, but their contribution to New World civilizations did not compare with the contributions of Old World animals. The limited types of domestic animals in the New World, coupled with the lack of the wheel, also meant that indigenous economies had to rely almost exclusively on human labor.

Once contact was established between the Old World and the New, the characteristic crops and animals of each area began to be interchanged, consciously, and yet without a sense of the effect they would have in a new environment. European pigs multiplied astonishingly fast in the New World, in an atmosphere almost devoid of predators. Las Casas told the story that the ships on Columbus's second expedition reprovisioned at Gomera before starting the Atlantic crossing and took on eight pigs at the last moment. He remarked in awe about their – obviously exaggerated – ability to propagate: *"From these eight sows have multiplied all the pigs which until today have been and are in the Indies, which have been and are infinite."*[23] Cattle and sheep, horses and asses did likewise, spreading across the landscape and often usurping land formerly used for farming. With the catastrophic decline in the human population of the New World, vast tracts of land were converted to open pasture, sometimes on soil that needed careful nurturing to remain fertile. The results were mixed. Domesticated animals greatly increased the mobility, productivity, and dietary protein of the local populations; at the same time, unrestricted grazing could severely damage the soil by denuding it of natural foliage. Domesticated animals introduced by Europeans changed Mexico fundamentally. Already by the 1540s there were too many animals in the areas heavily settled by human populations. Livestock ranching was encouraged to move ever farther northward, in an extension of the colonial frontier that produced its own distinctive and independent culture. The start of a domestic woolen cloth industry and a growing export trade in hides and tallow, all based on European livestock, came to characterize the vast area called New Spain (Mexico).

European food crops had less effect than imported animals in New Spain but much greater effect in South America, in what the Spanish called the Viceroyalty of Peru. Originally, Spanish settlers had imported familiar staples of their diet, such as wheat and wine, from home, but transport costs raised the price of these commodities to prohibitive levels in New World markets. Despite efforts from Spain to monopolize the production of dietary staples, the fertile areas of what is today Peru and Chile produced wine grapes, wheat, and other European products in abundance by the seventeenth century.

Europeans also adopted American foods, some more readily than others. Sailors in Spanish fleets as early as Columbus's first return voyage became accustomed to eating sweet potatoes and cassava bread on their homeward voyages,[24] as well as to more exotic items such as sea turtle, which they compared in taste and texture to the veal they knew at home.[25] In broader terms, however, the most important New World foods introduced to Europe were undoubtedly potatoes and maize.

Potatoes, introduced to Europe by Spaniards before the mid-sixteenth century, could grow in wet, cold climates where it was difficult to produce a reliable wheat harvest year after year. They eventually flourished not only in the British Isles, Poland, Germany, Russia, and other northern European countries but also in the cold, wet regions of northern Spain, in parts of France, and elsewhere in southern Europe. This is not to say that they were adopted overnight. Profound social and economic changes, such as changes in traditional diets, generally take decades or even centuries to develop. Many European peasants resisted the potato at first. Learned men had determined that it was related to the poisonous nightshade plant, and, indeed, its uncooked eyes are toxic to humans. The strange shapes and colors in which some potatoes grew also caused suspicion among a cautious and ignorant peasantry. Only gradually did the merits of the potato as a food crop overcome the reluctance of ordinary people to try it. Potatoes produced a high yield on small plots of land. Where its culture spread, the potato multiplied the available food supply enormously and may have encouraged young couples to marry and establish families earlier than time-honored custom allowed. This had far-reaching implications for the expansion of the European population in the eighteenth century, the beginning of sustained population growth in Europe.[26]

Maize had a similar career. A crop of almost magical reproductive qualities, it could produce high yields on lands that discouraged other crops. Columbus himself took it to Spain, and by the time of his third voyage he was able to say that there was much of it growing in Castile.[27] The Spanish and Portuguese introduced maize to Africa and Asia as well in the sixteenth century, but it took several centuries to become an important staple of the human diet, mostly for the poor. By the eighteenth century it had gained a permanent place around the globe as a food for human beings and for livestock. In regions where wheat and other grains had always been scarce, maize – like the potato – allowed the expansion of the human population on lim-

Maize from the Western Hemisphere. (From Giovanni Battista Ramusio, *Delle navigationi et viaggi . . . ,* [Venice, 1556–83]. Photo courtesy of the James Ford Bell Library, University of Minnesota.)

ited amounts of land, a development that has been a distinctly mixed blessing for the modern world.

Several other crops, less important than staples in human consumption, became very important to the development of the European economy. Coffee and sugar, Old World crops of debatable nutritional value, and tobacco and cocoa, New World crops of similarly questionable merit, share the distinction of contributing to the store of wealth in Europe and to the eventual rise of mass markets and industrialization.[28] Sugar, long considered to have medicinal value, was priced beyond the reach of ordinary consumers in the Middle Ages. Its availability began to increase and its price to fall when it was introduced to the Atlantic islands and grown on large plantations with coerced labor. Transplanted to the New World and grown commercially by slave labor, it became cheap enough to figure in the diet of quite poor people by the seventeenth century.[29] Coffee, also reserved for the rich in former centuries, developed into an important cash crop in the New World and in Asia, with a price low enough to attract a mass market. Tobacco, a New World crop to begin with, soon found an audience of dedicated addicts in Europe. The hysteria of booming tobacco prices in Europe in the early seventeenth cen-

Coffee plant and beans, shown with a grinder, pot, and cup used to prepare and drink the brew. (From Philippe Dufour, *Traitex nouveaux & curieux du café, du thé et du chocolate* [Lyon, 1688]. Photo courtesy of the James Ford Bell Library, University of Minnesota.)

tury encouraged a heavy investment in its production in the New World for the international market. And New World cocoa became a fashionable drink in Europe at all levels of society. The mass market for these products in Europe fueled the expansion of trade and trading profits in the seventeenth and eighteenth centuries, in the same way that the seaborne spice trade with Asia had expanded profits in the sixteenth century.[30]

Long-distance trade, which had relied in past centuries on the high profits made from mostly low-bulk luxury goods, began to rely instead on the profits from a high volume of low-priced goods. Trade could expand in both volume and extent in a manner undreamed of in the fifteenth century. Increased agricultural production and productivity in Europe also played an important role in the expanding economy of the late seventeenth and eighteenth centuries. Overall,

Sugar mill in Brazil, 1640, drawing by Frans Post. (Musées Royaux des Beaux-Arts de Belgique, Brussels.)

the combination of agricultural progress and expanding markets and profits from trade helped to lay the basis for the Industrial Revolution in Europe from the mid-eighteenth century on.[31] The voyages of Columbus and the plants and animals exchanged in the wake of the historic contact he initiated played a crucial role in the process that led to the modern world economy, characterized by interdependent global trade.

INFLATION AND THE MONEY SUPPLY

Money and credit arrangements underlay the great expansion of trade, and here too the discovery of the New World contributed importantly to their development. Spaniards brought back gold, pearls, jewels, and – above all – silver from their American colonies, starting in the fifteenth century and reaching a peak in the early seventeenth. Altogether it has been estimated that between 1500 and 1650 some 181 tons of gold and 16,000 tons of silver arrived in Europe from the Spanish colonies. And that is only the amount legally registered, from which the crown extracted a hefty tax. Smuggling added an unknown quantity to the total of precious metals imported from the New World. Many historians think that the amount smuggled was no more than 10 percent in the sixteenth century but rose much higher in the seventeenth century.[32]

Viewed in one way, gold and silver are themselves commodities, which are produced by investment in land, labor, and capital and can be exchanged for other commodities, such as food and manufactured products. Viewed in another way, their use as money makes gold and silver the intermediaries of exchanges, setting the value of goods in the marketplace. The value of those goods, defined by their price in silver or gold, is affected not just by market demand but also by the amount of money in circulation. A restricted money supply tends to hold prices down; an expanded money supply allows them to rise more easily if market demand increases. Europe on the eve of its overseas exploration is thought to have had a limited supply of money, which internal silver mines could only partially ease. The rise in population that began about 1450 increased market demand for food, manufactured goods, labor, and nearly everything else. Consequently, prices tended to rise, but with a limited money supply they did not rise as high and as fast as they might have done otherwise.

A scholarly argument much in vogue until a few decades ago held that the enormous flow of New World bullion into Europe was primarily responsible for the great rise in prices that occurred in the sixteenth century.[33] Recently scholars have provided a much more detailed explanation. When large amounts of gold and silver began arriving in Spain in the mid-sixteenth century, the increased money supply allowed prices to rise. Eventually, a large part of the imported bullion flowed out of Spain to pay the costs of trade and empire. The effects of bullion imports therefore spread all over Europe, increasing the supply of money, allowing prices to rise, and affecting local economies in a variety of other ways.[34]

Some scholars have judged the European price rise of the sixteenth century to be so large and influential that they have called it a "Price Revolution." Others have questioned the effects and even the existence of dramatic price rises in particular areas. In Spain, prices rose fivefold in about one hundred years, not a dramatic rise compared to hyperinflation in certain periods and places in the twentieth century but disturbing and probably without precedent in the sixteenth century. Yet even in the case of Spain, the effects of the price rise are still debated by scholars. Did it mean that the economy was growing, or did the bullion simply allow prices to rise without promoting growth? Were the common people better off because of rising wages or worse off because of rising prices? What did inflation mean for the overall shape of the Spanish economy? We know that Spain's political power in Europe declined in the seventeenth century. What role, if any, did inflation play in that decline? Similar questions arise as historians try to sort out the effects of inflation elsewhere in Europe, and the debates are not likely to be settled soon. What most agree upon is that bullion from the New World expanded the money supply and fueled international trade and warfare, both of which had

Depiction of how rolled tobacco leaves are ignited and smoked. (From André Thevet, *Les singularitez de la France antarctique* [Paris, 1557]. Photo courtesy of the James Ford Bell Library, University of Minnesota.)

important consequences in Europe and the wider world. Much of the New World bullion eventually found its way to Asia, to pay for trade goods and the cost of maintaining overseas empires. Historians are still trying to attach figures to these flows of bullion on a worldwide scale and to assess their effect on the growth of a global marketplace.[35]

BANKING AND CREDIT

In another way as well, the aftermath of Columbus's voyages contributed to the evolution of world trade. Credit and banking arrangements in medieval Europe assumed a fairly short time to complete a cycle of trade and clear merchants' account books of outstanding debts and credits. To finance trading voyages, a medieval merchant might borrow money to buy goods, or he might join with partners to share the risks and potential profits. For example, several merchants might invest in sending a ship carrying Venetian cloth to Alexandria in Egypt, where spices could be bought for the return voyage. Even in peacetime, such ventures were risky and could go wrong at several points. Spreading the risk became the prime goal of cautious merchants. Larger groups of associates might come together as insurance underwriters, each one signing up to guarantee the safe arrival of a fraction of the cargo that a trading vessel carried, in return for a fee paid by the owner of the goods. Should the cargo suffer damage or loss at sea, the underwriters would reimburse the owner. Should the cargo arrive without mishap, the insurance fee contributed to the profits of the insurers. Within a few weeks or months, all the parties concerned would know the outcome of the voyage and would be able to total their profits or losses on the venture, clearing the books and freeing their money to be used for other purposes, perhaps to finance another voyage.

The scope and the scale of long-distance trade changed greatly in the wake of European voyages of exploration. As regular trade to Asia and America developed in the sixteenth century, the lines of credit and exchange had to be lengthened to accommodate the greater distances and times involved. A merchant who borrowed money for a shipment of goods to the Spanish colonies might not know the outcome of the voyage for several years. In the sixteenth century, typical fleets for the Indies sailed in spring or summer, stayed the winter to trade and acquire goods for the return voyage, and returned the following year. Delays or danger from foreign pirates might mean that a return trip took far longer than planned. Moreover, the risk of loss increased with distance from one's markets, because merchants had to predict changes in prices and demand that occurred thousands of miles away and took months or years to develop. The difficulties of the Asian trade were, if anything, even greater, although the potential profits were sometimes greater as well. As first the Portuguese and then other European merchants risked their livelihoods on long-distance trade to Asia, they were forced to develop some flexible methods of doing business and better ways of borrowing money and establishing credit over the long term. Maritime insurance, banks, sophisticated partnership contracts, and varied methods of ownership all evolved to spread the increased risks of global trade.[36]

All of these changes – in government, society, plants, animals, money, and trade – evolved in the aftermath of the voyages of Christopher Columbus. Yet we should take care not to attribute the changes solely to those voyages or to assume that they would not have occurred without him. Enormous changes in human history can rarely be attributed to one person or one set of events. Instead, we should try to view the voyages of Columbus as the culmination of one scene in a much broader drama. If Columbus had not sailed westward in search of Asia, someone else would soon have done so. The time was right for such a bold undertaking, and the European economy was poised to take advantage of the expanded trade that a direct ocean route to Asia would afford.

Yet Columbus was clearly well positioned for the role that history assigned him. Experienced with trade and with the sea, widely read in the cosmography of the day, and fortuitously given the opportunity to benefit from the best contemporary geographical knowledge, he was the right man in the right place at the right time. That, and his strength of character and perseverance, justly earned him the fame that he still enjoys, five hundred years after his first historic voyage. Columbus believed that great changes would transform the world as a result of his voyages: the conversion of all peoples to Christianity, the creation of a single world empire, and the Second Coming of Christ that would end world history altogether in the Last Judgment of humanity. The changes that actually occurred seem rather tame in comparison with the Apocalypse, yet they were profound enough to shape the modern world.

Notes

CHAPTER I

1 Francesco Guicciardini, *Storia d'Italia* (Florence, 1561), book 6, chapter 9. In the five-volume edition by Costantino Panigada (Bari, 1929), the quotation appears at 2:131. Guicciardini was a Venetian diplomat who served as ambassador to the Spanish court in 1511–12.

2 Juan Luis Vives, *De disciplinis* (Antwerp, 1531), preface. Translated by Foster Watson as *Vives: On Education* (Cambridge, 1913), p. 3.

3 Cited in Elisabeth Feist Hirsch, *Damião de Gois: The Life and Thought of a Portuguese Humanist, 1502–1574* (The Hague, 1967), p. 103.

4 Girolamo Cardano, *The Book of My Life*, trans. Jean Stoner (London, 1931), p. 189.

5 Gonzalo Fernández de Oviedo, *Historia general y natural de las Indias*, in Biblioteca de Autores Españoles, nos. 117–21 (Madrid, 1959), no. 117, p. 167 (book 6, chapter 9).

6 Washington Irving, *The Life and Voyages of Christopher Columbus*. First published in a 3-volume edition in New York and a 4-volume edition in London, both in 1828. The definitive scholarly version was edited by John Harmon McElroy (Boston, 1981). Irving's biography of Columbus was sensationally popular not only in the United States but around the world. It was reprinted thirty-nine times in English, and fifty-one editions in other languages appeared before the author's death in 1859. In all, one hundred seventy-five full editions and abridgments appeared between 1828 and 1900. Irving relied heavily on the document collection of Martín Fernández de Navarrete, *Colección de los viajes y descubrimientos que hicieron por mar los españoles desde fines del siglo XV*, 3 vols. (Madrid, 1825–37). The first volume contains most of the documents dealing with Columbus, many of them first published by Navarrete, as he is commonly known.

7 Undoubtedly the most important was the massive collection published by the Italian government, *Raccolta di documenti e studi pubblicati dalla Reale Commissione Colombina*, ed. C. de Lollis et al., 15 vols. (Rome, 1892–6).

8 Henry Harrisse, *Christophe Colomb, son origine, sa vie* (Paris, 1884); John Boyd Thacher, *Christopher Columbus: His Life, His Work, His Remains* (New York, vols. 1–2, 1903; vol. 3, 1904); Justin Winsor, *Christopher Columbus and How He Received and Imparted the Spirit of Discovery* (Boston, 1892).

9 We examined about two hundred fifty history textbooks used in schools in the United States during the nineteenth and twentieth centuries, focusing on their descriptions of Columbus. Our findings were presented to the Seventeenth International Congress of Historical Sciences, held in Madrid in August 1990.

10 Alfred W. Crosby contrasts the "bardic" interpretation – the traditional heroic view – with the "analytic" interpretation – placing Columbus in wider contexts. *The Columbian Voyages, the Columbian Exchange, and Their Historians* (Washing-

ton, D.C., 1987). As far as popular perception goes, the bardic interpretation has prevailed.

11 *Historie del S. D. Fernando Colombo; nelle quali s'ha particolare, & vera relatione della vita, & de' fatti dell'Ammiraglio D. Cristoforo Colombo, suo padre . . .* (Venice, 1571). Translated by Benjamin Keen as *The Life of the Admiral Christopher Columbus by his Son Ferdinand* (New Brunswick, N.J., 1959).

12 Antonio Rumeu de Armas, *Hernando Colón, historiador del descubrimiento de América* (Madrid, 1973).

13 Bartolomé de las Casas, *Historia de las Indias,* ed. Agustín Millares Carlo, 3 vols. (Mexico City, 1951).

14 Cristóbal Colón, *Textos y documentos completos,* ed. Consuelo Varela (Madrid, 1982); Consuelo Varela, *Colón y los florentinos* (Madrid, 1988); Juan Gil and Consuelo Varela, *Temas colombinos* (Seville, 1986).

15 *Pleitos colombinos,* ed. Antonio Muro Orejón et al., 5 vols. to date (Seville, 1964, 1967, 1983, 1984, 1989).

CHAPTER 2

1 Several older works remain valuable for surveys of medieval geographical knowledge. See G. H. T. Kimble, *Geography in the Middle Ages* (London, 1938; reprinted New York, 1968), and the sections on geography in Boies Penrose, *Travel and Discovery in the Renaissance, 1420–1620* (Cambridge, Mass., 1955). For more recent, well-informed syntheses, see J. H. Parry, *The Discovery of the Sea* (Berkeley and Los Angeles, 1981), especially chapter 3; and J. R. S. Phillips, *The Medieval Expansion of Europe* (Oxford, 1988).

2 Phillips, *Medieval Expansion of Europe,* pp. 188–9.

3 For a discussion of the controversy concerned with dating the first human migrations into the Americas, see Warwick Bray, "How Old Are the Americans," *Américas* 40 (May–June, 1988): 50–5.

4 For pre-Columbian American civilizations, see Robert Wauchope, ed., *The Indian Background of Latin American History: The Maya, Aztec, Inca, and Their Predecessors* (New York, 1970); Michael S. Coe, *The Maya,* 3d ed. (London, 1984); Norman Hammond, *Ancient Maya Civilization* (Cambridge, 1982); John S. Henderson, *The World of the Ancient Maya* (Ithaca, N.Y., 1981); Linda Schele, *Blood of Kings: Dynasty and Ritual in Maya Art* (Fort Worth, 1986); Linda Shele and David Freidel, *A Forest of Kings* (New York, 1990); Friedrich Katz, *The Ancient American Civilizations* (New York, 1972); George A. Collier, Renato I. Rosaldo, and John D. Wirth, eds., *The Inca and Aztec States, 1400–1800: Anthropology and History* (New York, 1982); Frances F. Berdan, *The Aztecs of Central Mexico: An Imperial Society* (New York, 1982).

5 Robert Eric Mortimer Wheeler, *Rome beyond the Imperial Frontiers* (London, 1954).

6 Frederick H. Russell, *The Just War in the Middle Ages* (Cambridge, 1975); T. P. Murphy, ed., *The Holy War* (Columbus, 1976).

7 For the Crusades, see Hans Eberhard Mayer, *The Crusades,* trans. J. Gillingham (Oxford, 1972; 2d ed., 1988); Jonathan Riley-Smith, *The Crusades* (London, 1987); K. M. Setton, ed., *A History of the Crusades,* 5 vols. (Philadelphia, 1955–85); A. Maalouf, *The Crusades through Arab Eyes* (London, 1984); F. Gabrieli, *Arab*

Historians of the Crusades (London, 1984); Joshua Prawer, The Latin Kingdom of Jerusalem: European Colonialism in the Middle Ages (London, 1972); Jean Richard, The Latin Kingdom of Jerusalem, trans. Janet Shirley, 2 vols. (Amsterdam, 1979); R. W. Southern, Western Views of Islam in the Middle Ages (Cambridge, Mass., 1961).

8 Noël Deerr, The History of Sugar, 2 vols. (London, 1949–50), 1:76–7; Jean Richard, The Latin Kingdom of Jerusalem, 2:351; Joshua Prawer, "Etude de quelques problèmes agraires et sociaux d'une seigneurie croisée au XIIIe siècle," Byzantion 22 (1952):5–61; Edmund O. von Lippman, Geschichte des Zuckers, seiner Darstellung und Verwendung (Leipzig, 1890), p. 181; Charles Verlinden, The Beginnings of Modern Colonization, trans. Yvonne Freccero (Ithaca, N.Y., 1972), pp. 78–80.

9 Robert S. Lopez, The Commercial Revolution of the Middle Ages, 950–1350 (Cambridge, 1976); Robert S. Lopez and Irving Raymond, eds., Medieval Trade in the Mediterranean World (New York, 1955); Harry A. Miskimin, The Economy of Early Renaissance Europe, 1300–1460 (New York, 1975).

10 William D. Phillips, Jr., "Sugar Production and Trade in the Mediterranean at the Time of the Crusades," in The Meeting of Two Worlds: Cultural Exchange between East and West during the Period of the Crusades, ed. Vladimir P. Goss and Christine V. Bornstein (Kalamazoo, Mich., 1986), pp. 393–403; J. H. Galloway, "The Mediterranean Sugar Industry," Geographical Review 67 (1977):177–94.

11 Wilhelm von Heyd, Histoire du commerce du Levant au Moyen-Age, trans. Furey Reynaud, 2 vols. (Leipzig, 1885–6; reprinted Amsterdam, 1967), 2:686.

12 Matthew Paris's English History from the Year 1235 to 1273, trans. J. A. Giles, 3 vols. (London, 1852; reprinted New York, 1968), 1:312–13.

13 For the Mongols, see J. J. Saunders, A History of the Mongol Conquests (London, 1971); D. Morgan, The Mongols (Oxford, 1986); René Grousset, The Empire of the Steppes: A History of Central Asia, trans. Naomi Walford (New Brunswick, N.J., 1970).

14 For a selection of works on the Black Death and its aftermath, see Philip Ziegler, The Black Death (London, 1969); Peter Laslett, The World We have Lost (New York, 1965); J. Hatcher, Plague, Population and the English Economy, 1348–1530 (London, 1977); J. F. D. Shrewsbury, A History of Bubonic Plague in the British Isles (Cambridge, 1970).

15 Lopez, Commercial Revolution; M. M. Poston, Medieval Trade and Finance (Cambridge, 1973); Frank J. Swetz, Capitalism and Arithmetic: The New Math of the Fifteenth Century (La Salle, Ill., 1987); A. P. Usher, The Early History of Deposit Banking in Mediterranean Europe (Cambridge, Mass., 1943); Jean-Albert Goris, Etude sur les colonies marchandes méridionales (Portugais, Espagnols, Italiens) à Anvers, 1477–1566 (Louvain, 1925); Ruth Pike, Enterprise and Adventure: The Genoese in Seville and the Opening of the New World (Ithaca, N.Y., 1966); Philippe Dollinger, The German Hansa (London, 1970); Raymond De Roover, The Rise and Decline of the Medici Bank, 1397–1494 (New York, 1966); Robert L. Reynolds, Europe Emerges: Transition toward an Industrial World-Wide Society, 600–1750 (Madison, 1961).

16 Fernand Braudel, The Structures of Everyday Life (New York, 1981); J. R. Hale, Renaissance Europe: Individual and Society, 1480–1520 (Berkeley and Los Angeles, 1978).

17 For the political situation in Europe, see Denys Hay, Europe in the Fourteenth and

Fifteenth Centuries (New York, 1966); Wallace K. Ferguson, *Europe in Transition, 1300–1520* (Boston, 1963); George Holmes, *Europe, Hierarchy and Revolt, 1320– 1450* (New York, 1976).

18 The classic by E. S. Creasy, *History of the Ottoman Turks,* 2 vols. (London, 1854– 6; reprinted Karachi, 1980), is still useful for an overview. See also Herbert A. Gibbons, *The Foundation of the Ottoman Empire* (Totowa, N.J., 1968); Halil Inalcik, *The Ottoman Empire: The Classical Age, 1300–1600* (London, 1973).

19 The best survey of Europe's intellectual and religious life is Margaret Aston, *The Fifteenth Century: The Prospect of Europe* (New York, 1979).

20 De Lamar Jensen, *Renaissance Europe: Age of Recovery and Reconciliation* (Lexington, Mass., 1981); Paul Oskar Kristeller, *Renaissance Thought: The Classic, Scholastic, and Humanist Strains* (New York, 1961); Walter Ullman, *Medieval Foundations of Renaissance Humanism* (Ithaca, N.Y., 1977).

21 Elizabeth L. Eisenstein, *The Printing Press as an Agent of Change* (Cambridge, 1979); Lucien Febvre and Henri-Jean Martin, *The Coming of the Book: The Impact of Printing, 1450–1800,* trans. David Gerard (New York, 1976).

22 Two recent books examine the relations between western Europe and the rest of Eurasia on the eve of European expansion. See Janet L. Abu-Lughod, *Before European Hegemony: The World System, A.D. 1250–1350* (Oxford, 1988); Archibald R. Lewis, *Nomads and Crusaders, A.D. 1000–1368* (Bloomington, 1988).

CHAPTER 3

1 For introductions to the European religious life of the period, see Francis Oakley, *The Western Church in the Later Middle Ages* (Ithaca, N.Y., 1979); Steven Ozment, *The Age of Reform, 1250–1550* (New Haven, 1980).

2 Quoted in Benjamin Z. Kedar, *Crusade and Mission: European Approaches toward the Muslims* (Princeton, 1984), p. 119.

3 See John Moorman, *A History of the Franciscan Order from Its Origins to the Year 1517* (Oxford, 1968), for a good overview of the interplay between Joachism and the early Franciscans.

4 For late medieval missionary activities and their connection with the crusading idea, see Kedar, *Crusade and Mission;* Robert I. Burns, "Christian–Islamic Confrontation in the West: The Thirteenth-Century Dream of Conversion," *American Historical Review* 76 (1971): 1386–1434; E. Randolph Daniel, *The Franciscan Concept of Mission in the High Middle Ages* (Lexington, 1975); John Leddy Phelan, *The Millennial Kingdom of the Franciscans in the New World* (Berkeley and Los Angeles, 1956). For how Columbus fit into this context, see Alain Milhou, *Colón y su mentalidad mesiánica en el ambiente fransciscanista español* (Valladolid, 1983); P. M. Watts, "Prophecy and Discovery: On the Spiritual Origins of Christopher Columbus's 'Enterprise of the Indies,' " *American Historical Review* 90 (1985): 73–102; Leonard Sweet, "Christopher Columbus and the Millennial Vision of the New World," *Catholic Historical Review* 72 (1986): 372–81.

5 J. R. S. Phillips, *The Medieval Expansion of Europe* (Oxford, 1988), pp. 60–73.

6 For Prester John, see V. Slessarev, *Prester John, the Letter and the Legend* (Minneapolis, 1959); C. F. Beckenham, *Between Islam and Christianity: Travellers, Facts, Legends in the Middle Ages and the Renaissance* (London, 1983).

7 K. N. Chaudhuri, *Trade and Civilisation in the Indian Ocean: An Economic History from the Rise of Islam to 1750* (Cambridge, 1985).

8 Jacques Heers, *Marco Polo* (Paris, 1983); Leo Olschki, *Marco Polo's Asia* (Berkeley and Los Angeles, 1970); *The Travels of Marco Polo*, trans. R. E. Latham (Harmondsworth, 1958; reprinted 1982).

9 Francesco Balducci Pegolotti, *La practica della mercatura*, ed. A. Evans (Cambridge, Mass., 1936; reprinted 1970).

10 Ibid.

11 For an overview of the commercial history of the eastern Mediterranean, see Eliyahu Ashtor, *Levant Trade in the Later Middle Ages* (Princeton, 1983); Frederic C. Lane, *Venice, A Maritime Republic* (Baltimore, 1973); Jacques Heers, *Gênes au XVe siècle: Activité économique et problèmes sociaux* (Paris, 1961).

12 Jacques Heers, "Le commerce du sel en Méditerranée occidentale au Moyen Age," in *Le rôle du sel dans l'histoire*, ed. Michel Mollat (Paris, 1968); Jean-Claude Hocquet, *Le sel et la fortune de Venise*, 2 vols. (Lille, 1978–9); Jean Delumeau, *L'alun de Rome (XVe–XIXe siècle)* (Paris, 1962).

13 Jesús Lalinde Abadía, *La Corona de Aragón en el Mediterráneo medieval (1229–1479)* (Zaragoza, 1979); Mario del Treppo, *I mercanti catalani e l'espansione della Corona d'Aragona nel sècolo XV* (Naples, 1972); Charles Emmanuel Dufourcq, *L'Espagne catalane et le Maghrib aux XIIIe et XIVe siècles* (Paris, 1966).

14 Phillips, *Medieval Expansion*, pp. 156–8; Florentino Pérez Embid, *Los descubrimientos en el Atlántico y la rivalidad castellano–portuguesa hasta el Tratado de Tordesillas* (Seville, 1948), pp. 51–8. There is a controversy about whether the Vivaldis were attempting a westward Atlantic voyage two hundred years before Columbus or whether they were trying to sail around Africa to the Indian Ocean. All the evidence and the legends mention the African coast, however, therefore supporting the idea of African circumnavigation.

15 On the African gold trade, see Fernand Braudel, *The Mediterranean and the Mediterranean World in the Age of Philip II*, trans. Siân Reynolds, 2 vols. (New York, 1976): 1:462–75; E. W. Bovill, *The Golden Trade of the Moors*, 2d ed. (Oxford, 1968); Philip D. Curtin, "The Lure of Bambuk Gold," *Journal of African History* 14 (1973): 623–31; Pierre Vilar, *Oro y moneda en la historia, 1450–1920* (Barcelona, 1969).

16 For studies of Portugal at home and overseas in this period, see Bailey W. Diffie and George D. Winius, *Foundations of the Portuguese Empire, 1415–1580* (Minneapolis, 1977); Antonio H. de Oliveira Marques, *History of Portugal*, 2 vols. (New York, 1972); Vitorino de Magalhães Godinho, *A economia dos descobrimentos henriquinos* (Lisbon, 1962); Vitorino Magalhães Godinho, *Os descobrimentos e a economia mundial*, 4 vols. (Lisbon, 1983–4), 1:65–174.

17 On the Portuguese enclave at Mina, see John Vogt, *Portuguese Rule on the Gold Coast, 1469–1482* (Athens, Ga., 1979). On the early Portuguese slave trade, see A. C. de C. M. Saunders, *A Social History of Black Slaves and Freedmen in Portugal, 1441–1555* (Cambridge, 1982). For the story of one important trade commodity, see Eugenia W. Herbert, *Red Gold of Africa: Copper in Precolonial History and Culture* (Madison, 1983).

18 For Spanish trade with Africa, see Antonio Rumeu de Armas, *España en el Africa atlántica*, 2 vols. (Madrid, 1956).

19 For the history of European exploration and conquest of the Canaries, see Felipe

Fernández-Armesto, *Before Columbus: Exploration and Colonization from the Mediterranean to the Atlantic, 1229–1492* (Philadelphia, 1987); Pérez Embid, *Los descubrimientos en el Atlántico;* Rumeu de Armas, *España en el Africa atlántica;* John Mercer, *The Canary Islanders: Their Prehistory, Conquest and Survival* (London, 1980); Miguel Angel Ladero Quesada, *Los primeros europeos en Canarias (Siglos XIV y XV)* (Las Palmas, 1979).

20 For slavery in the Canaries, see Manuela Marrero Rodríguez, *La esclavitud en Tenerife a raiz de la conquista* (La Laguna, 1966); Manuel Lobo Cabrera, *La esclavitud en las Canarias orientales en el siglo XVI: Negros, Moros, y Moriscos* (Gran Canaria, 1982).

21 For colonial society in the Canaries, see Ladero Quesada, *Los primeros europeos en Canarias;* Eduardo Aznar Vallejo, *La integración de las Islas Canarias en la Corona de Castilla (1478–1526): Aspectos administrativos, sociales, y económicos* (Seville and La Laguna, 1983); Felipe Fernández-Armesto, *The Canary Islands after the Conquest: The Making of a Colonial Society in the Early Sixteenth Century* (Oxford, 1982); Mercer, *Canary Islanders.* For a recent interpretive account of this period of Canarian history, see Alfred W. Crosby, *Ecological Imperialism: The Biological Expansion of Europe, 900–1900* (Cambridge, 1986). On the Canarian sugarcane industry, see Guillermo Camacho y Pérez-Galdós, "El cultivo de la caña de azúcar y la industria azucarera en Gran Canaria (1510–1535)," *Anuario de Estudios Atlánticos* 7 (1961): 1–60.

22 For accounts of Portuguese island colonization, see the relevant sections of Diffie and Winius, *Foundations of the Portuguese Empire;* T. Bentley Duncan, *Atlantic Islands: Madeira, the Azores, and the Cape Verdes in Seventeenth Century Commerce and Navigation* (Chicago, 1972). For sugar, see Philip D. Curtin, *The Rise and Fall of the Plantation Complex: Essay in Atlantic History* (Cambridge, 1990); Sidney M. Greenfield, "Madeira and the Beginnings of New World Sugar Cultivation and Plantation Slavery: A Study in Institution Building," in *Comparative Perspectives on Slavery and New World Plantation Societies,* ed. Vera D. Rubin and Arthur Tuden, Annals of the New York Academy of Sciences, no. 292 (New York, 1977), pp. 536–52; Sidney M. Greenfield, "Plantations, Sugar Cane and Slavery," *Historical Reflections / Réflexions Historiques* 6 (1979): 85–119.

CHAPTER 4

1 For an introduction to medieval European ship design and maritime practice, see J. H. Parry, *The Discovery of the Sea* (Berkeley and Los Angeles, 1981), pp. 3–23. For specialized studies, see Archibald R. Lewis and Timothy J. Runyan, *European Naval and Maritime History, 300–1500* (Bloomington, 1985); Richard W. Unger, *The Ship in the Medieval Economy, 600–1600* (Montreal, 1980); John H. Pryor, *Geography, Technology, and War: Studies in the Maritime History of the Mediterranean, 649–1571* (Cambridge, 1988); Archibald R. Lewis, "Northern European Sea Power and the Straits of Gibraltar, 1031–1350," in *Order and Innovation in the Middle Ages: Essays in Honor of Joseph R. Strayer,* ed. William C. Jordan, Bruce McNab, and Teófilo Ruiz (Princeton, 1976), pp. 139–64.

2 A number of books provide information on the history of ship design. Many points remain controversial, but the preceding discussion seems to us the most

logical scenario. For further reading in English, see Martin Malcolm Elbl, "The Portuguese Caravel and European Shipbuilding: Phases of Development and Diversity" (Lisbon, 1985); John F. Guilmartin, *Gunpowder and Galleys: Changing Technology and Mediterranean Warfare at Sea in the Sixteenth Century* (Cambridge, 1974); Joseph Jobé, ed., *The Great Age of Sail,* trans. Michael Kelly (Lausanne, 1967); Frederic Chapin Lane, *Venetian Ships and Shipbuilders of the Renaissance* (Baltimore, 1934); *The Lore of Ships,* rev. ed. (New York, 1975); Carla Rahn Phillips, *Six Galleons for the King of Spain: Imperial Defense in the Early Seventeenth Century* (Baltimore, 1986); Unger, *Ship in Medieval Economy.*

3 For studies of navigation, see Luís de Albuquerque, *Astronomical Navigation* (Lisbon, 1988); Parry, *Discovery of the Sea,* pp. 24–41; E. G. R. Crone, *The Havenfinding Art: A History of Navigation* (New York, 1957).

4 For the history of cartography, see G. R. Crone, *Maps and Their Makers* (London, 1953); J. B. Harley and David Woodward, *The History of Cartography,* vol. 1: *Cartography in Prehistoric, Ancient, and Medieval Europe and the Mediterranean* (Chicago, 1987); J. B. Harley, *Maps and the Columbian Encounter* (Milwaukee, 1990); Kenneth Nebenzahl, *Atlas of Columbus and "The Great Discoveries"* (Chicago, 1990). For the portolans specifically, see M. de la Roncière and M. Mollat du Jourdin, eds., *Les portulans: Cartes marines du XIIIe au XVIIe siècle* (Fribourg, 1984).

5 Many technical manuals describe the methods of celestial navigation. For our purposes, one of the clearest descriptions is Albuquerque, *Astronomical Navigation.* A handsome facsimile edition of one of the earliest manuals of navigation is included with Ursula Lamb's translation, *A Navigator's Universe: The "Libro de Cosmographía" of 1538 by Pedro de Medina* (Chicago, 1972).

6 Carlo M. Cipolla, *Guns, Sails and Empire: Technological Innovation and the Early Phases of European Expansion, 1400–1700* (New York, 1965); Robert B. Cunninghame Graham, *Horses of the Conquest* (London, 1930; reprinted Norman, Okla., 1949); John Grier Varner and Jeannette Johnson Varner, *Dogs of the Conquest* (Norman, Okla., 1983).

7 An excellent re-creation of the medieval world view is C. S. Lewis, *The Discarded Image* (Cambridge, 1964).

8 On the geography of the fifteenth century, see J. R. S. Phillips, *The Medieval Expansion of Europe* (Oxford, 1988); Parry, *Discovery of the Sea;* Kimble, *Geography in the Middle Ages;* N. Broc, *La géographie de la Renaissance* (Paris, 1980).

9 Nehemia Levtzion and J. F. P. Hopkins, eds., *Corpus of Arabic Sources Relating to West Africa* (Cambridge, 1981), pp. 272–3.

10 For the wind patterns, see Alfred W. Crosby, Jr., *Ecological Imperialism: The Biological Expansion of Europe, 900–1900* (Cambridge, 1986), chapter 4, "Winds," pp. 104–31; Pierre Chaunu, *European Expansion in the Later Middle Ages,* trans. Katharine Bertram (Amsterdam, 1979), pp. 111–16; Bailey W. Diffie and George D. Winius, *Foundations of the Portuguese Empire, 1415–1580* (Minneapolis, 1977), pp. 60–1; Philip D. Curtin, *Disease and Imperialism before the Nineteenth Century* (Minneapolis, 1990).

11 The Portuguese scholar Luís Adão da Fonseca gave a stimulating paper on this theme at a conference sponsored by the Camões Center at Columbia University in June of 1990.

CHAPTER 5

1 For Columbus's years in Genoa and Portugal, we have principally followed three major biographies: Paolo Emilio Taviani, *Christopher Columbus: The Grand Design,* trans. William Weaver (London, 1985); Jacques Heers, *Christophe Colomb* (Paris, 1981); Antonio Ballesteros Beretta, *Cristóbal Colón y el descubrimiento de América,* 2 vols. (vols. 4–5 of *Historia de América y de los pueblos americanos,* ed. Antonio Ballesteros Beretta) (Barcelona, 1945). Taviani's work, the best book available in English on the early life of Columbus, thoroughly examines every controversy surrounding his early life and provides detailed documentation for what we know and do not know. Heers, who has spent his professional life in the study of the economy and society of late medieval and Renaissance Genoa and its foreign trade, adds a broader context to the story of Columbus. His biography, presently available only in French, is especially informative on Genoese history and Genoese connections to Iberia. Ballesteros provides the most detailed account to date of Columbus's years in Portugal. Morison's biography also has useful material on Columbus's early life, although its strength lies in its treatment of his voyages from 1492 on. Samuel Eliot Morison, *Admiral of the Ocean Sea: A Life of Christopher Columbus,* 2 vols. (Boston, 1942). For Genoa, see Jacques Heers, *Gênes au XVe siècle: Activité économique et problèmes sociaux* (Paris, 1961), and Gaetano Ferro, *La Liguria e Genova al tempo di Colombo* (Rome, 1988).

2 C. Malloy, *De jure maritimo et navali* (London, 1682).

3 For discussion of the material up to 1985 and a listing of some of the more preposterous claims about Columbus's origins, see Taviani, *Christopher Columbus,* pp. 223–32. See Ballesteros, *Cristóbal Colón,* in *Historia de América,* 4:112–27, for refutation of the claims that Columbus was Spanish. Merely listing the titles of published works up to 1945 that assert a non-Genoese origin for Columbus requires three pages of small type in Ballesteros's book.

4 *Libretto de tutta la navigatione de re de Spagna de la isole et terreni novamente trovati* (Venice, 1504). Facsimile ed. (Paris, 1929), p. 3. Unless otherwise noted, we have supplied the English translations.

5 *Historia general y natural de las Indias,* in Biblioteca de Autores Españoles (B.A.E.), nos. 117–121 (Madrid, 1959), no. 117, p. 16.

6 *Historie . . . dell'Ammiraglio D. Cristoforo Colombo* (Venice, 1571), p. 7.

7 Bartolomé de las Casas, *Historia de las Indias,* ed. Agustín Millares Carlo, 3 vols. (Mexico City, 1951), book 1, chapter 2, 1:29. The Spanish word *garzos* is now usually translated as "light blue," but it seems to have connoted light grey-green or hazel eyes to Columbus's contemporaries. The word *rubio* can mean "blonde," "fair," or "ruddy."

8 Bernard Berenson, *Lorenzo Lotto* (London, 1956). Berenson did not include the painting in earlier editions of his book because he had seen only an engraving of it rather than the original. Provided with a photograph of the painting by its owners before his 1956 edition, he authenticated the painting as a Lotto. Unfortunately, the gallery that owned the Lotto portrait in 1956 has no record of its current whereabouts.

9 Sorolla's preliminary studies for this portrait, including ten large oil sketches and

several-dozen pencil sketches, are in the collection of the Hispanic Society of America in New York.

10 Ferdinand Columbus, *The Life of the Admiral Christopher Columbus by His Son Ferdinand*, trans. Benjamin Keen (New Brunswick, N.J., 1959). This is a translation of the Italian edition published in Venice in 1571. No earlier printed or manuscript version exists, although Hernando would surely have written in Castilian Spanish. Many scholars doubt that the biography is entirely Hernando's work, and some think it was written by someone else altogether. See Antonio Rumeu de Armas, *Hernando Colón, Historiador del descrubrimiento de América* (Madrid, 1973).

11 See the persuasive argument that Columbus was not of Jewish origin in Heers, *Christophe Colomb*, pp. 26–8.

12 Ibid., pp. 68–9.

13 Cristóbal Colón, *Textos y documentos completos*, ed. Consuelo Varela (Madrid, 1982), p. 252.

14 Oliver Dunn and James E. Kelley, Jr., eds. and trans., *The "Diario" of Christopher Columbus's First Voyage to America, 1492–1493, Abstracted by Fray Bartolomé de las Casas* (Norman, Okla., 1989), pp. 252–3.

15 Ferdinand Columbus, *Life of the Admiral*, p. 11. A "galleass" was a ship equipped with both sails and oars. A "carrack" was a sailing ship of the type that the Spanish often called a *nao*. (See Chapter 4 of the present volume.)

16 Columbus's letter was written during his second voyage, while he still enjoyed the monarchs' full favor. The manner in which he mentioned René of Anjou suggests that it was not the first time he had told the king of his service to René. Morison has an apt comment on scholarly speculation about the veracity of Columbus. "One finicky objection raised to the whole story is that it 'gave Columbus away' to King Ferdinand as a former enemy. Ferdinand would certainly not have cared, for everyone changed sides in the fifteenth century." Morison, *Admiral of the Ocean Sea*, 1:36, n. 6. A less finicky objection might be raised on the grounds of Columbus's age. René of Anjou died in 1470. According to the usual date for Columbus's birth, 1451, he would have been at most nineteen when he served the king, a remarkably early age at which to command a vessel.

17 The letter is available in Colón, *Textos y documentos*, pp. 280–3. In the course of his remarks, Columbus referred to a letter (no longer extant) that he had previously written to Fernando and Isabel, advising them on seasonal sailing conditions for the voyage of Margarita of Austria, the Habsburg princess coming to Spain to marry their son Prince Juan.

18 Ferdinand Columbus, *Life of the Admiral*, pp. 13–14.

19 Colón, *Textos y documentos*, p. 160.

20 Ibid., p. 252; Ferdinand Columbus, *Life of the Admiral*, p. 12; Dunn and Kelley, eds., *Diario*, pp. 252–3, entry for December 21, 1492.

21 Ramón Menéndez Pidal, *La lengua de Cristóbal Colón* (Madrid, 1942); Antonio Rumeu de Armas, *El "portugués" Cristóbal Colón en Castilla* (Madrid, 1982). It should be noted that Rumeu de Armas thinks Columbus was Genoese but so influenced by his years in Portugal that he could have been mistaken for a Portuguese by Spaniards.

22 The document of donation is printed in Bailey W. Diffie and George D. Winius, *Foundations of the Portuguese Empire, 1415–1580* (Minneapolis, 1977), pp. 303–4.

23 In addition to the standard biographies already cited, other works shed varying degrees of light on Columbus's years in Portugal and the position of his wife's family. See Nicolau Florentino (a pseudonym of Antonio Maria de Freitas), *A mulher de Colombo* (Lisbon, 1892); Gaetano Ferro, *Le navigationi lusitane nell' Atlantico e Cristoforo Colombo in Portogallo* (Milan, 1984). Although its thesis is unconvincing, the book by Augusto Mascarenhas Barreto does contain interesting details: *O português Cristóvão Colombo: Agente secreto do Rei Dom João II*, 2d ed. (Lisbon, 1988). We are grateful to Timothy Coates for locating and purchasing Portuguese materials for us.

24 Ferdinand Columbus, *Life of the Admiral*, p. 15.

25 Ibid., p. 23.

26 Unless otherwise noted, the following account of the rumors Columbus gathered comes from Ferdinand Columbus, *Life of the Admiral*, pp. 23–8.

27 Dunn and Kelley, eds., *Diario*, pp. 25–7, entry for August 9, 1492.

28 The Atlantic was assumed to be filled with islands. For the legendary islands, see Vincent H. Cassidy, *The Sea around Them: The Atlantic Ocean, A.D. 1250* (Baton Rouge, 1968). Initially, some Europeans even thought that the islands Columbus reached in the Caribbean were part of the Canary Island group. Felipe Fernández Armesto, *Before Columbus: Exploration and Colonization from the Mediterranean to the Atlantic, 1229–1492* (Philadelphia, 1987), p. 221, citing M. Giménez Fernández, "América, 'Ysla de Canaria por ganar,' " *Anuario de Estudios Atlánticos* 1 (1955):309–36. The title of the first Italian version of the 1492 voyage referred to the Caribbean Islands as "nuove insule de Channaria indiane": Giuliano Dati, *The History of the Discovery of the New Indian Islands of the Canaries*, ed. and trans. Theodore J. Chachey, Jr. (Chicago, 1989).

29 The date of Diogo de Teive's voyage is hard to ascertain. He made one important voyage to the Azores in 1452; Pedro de Velasco could easily have accompanied him and lived to tell Columbus about it some forty years later. But the pilot was said to be from Palos de Moguer, in Spain, a name for the town that became Palos de la Frontera in the last decade of the fourteenth century, far too early for its pilot to have lived to tell Columbus about it. Official names are not always reflected in popular usage, however. The 1452 date for the voyage seems likely.

30 The two prominent modern historians who support the pre-Columbian contact theory are Juan Manzano Manzano, *Colón y su secreto* (Madrid, 1976), and Juan Pérez de Tudela y Bueso, *Mirabilis in altis: Estudio crítico sobre el origen y significado del proyecto descubridor de Cristóbal Colón* (Madrid, 1983). See the analysis of these books by John Larner, "The Certainty of Columbus: Some Recent Studies," *History* 73 (February 1988):3–23.

31 Las Casas, *Historia de las Indias*, book 1, chapter 14, 1:70–1.

32 Fernández de Oviedo, *Historia general y natural de Indias* in B.A.E., no. 117, p. 16. Hernando Colón was annoyed by Fernández de Oviedo's story, either not realizing or refusing to acknowledge that it was presented as a rumor, not a fact. *Life of the Admiral*, p. 27.

33 See Dunn and Kelley, eds., *Diario*, pp. 21, 41, 51, 175.

34 Colón, *Textos y documentos*, pp. 281–2.

35 Ibid., p. 9.

36 Ibid., p. 167. Varela took this version from a manuscript by Las Casas now in the Biblioteca Nacional in Madrid. The letter, with slight variations, also appears

in Hernando Colón's biography. As translated by Benjamin Keen from the 1571 Italian edition, it says, "In the month of February, 1477, I sailed one hundred leagues beyond the island of Tile, whose northern [sic] part is in latitude 73 degrees N, and not 63 degrees as some affirm; nor does it lie upon the meridian where Ptolemy says the West begins, but much farther west. And to this island, which is as big as England, the English come with their wares, especially from Bristol. When I was there, the sea was not frozen, but the tides were so great that in some places they rose twenty-six fathoms, and fell as much in depth." *Life of the Admiral*, p. 11. Hernando's biography adds, "The Thule of which Ptolemy speaks does in fact lie where the Admiral says it does; nowadays it is called Frisland." *Life of the Admiral*, p. 11. Scholars have often identified Ptolemy's Thule with the Shetland Islands, off the northern coast of Scotland.

37 Taviani, *Grand Design*, pp. 81–6, 318–31.
38 Colón, *Textos y documentos*, p. 167.
39 Ibid., p. 45 (Oct. 28, 1492), and p. 67 (Nov. 27, 1492).
40 Ibid., pp. xxxii–xl.
41 Taviani, *Grand Design*, pp. 209–12.
42 See the discussion of wind patterns in the preceding chapter.
43 See the sources cited in Taviani, *Grand Design*, pp. 84–9, 174, 396–8, 450–5.
44 Colón, *Textos y documentos*, pp. 10–11.
45 See George E. Nunn, *The Geographical Conceptions of Columbus: A Critical Consideration of Four Problems* (New York, 1924; reprinted 1977), pp. 1–30. See also Taviani, *Grand Design*, pp. 413–16.
46 The distance came from Marco Polo's *Travels*. In a modern edition the statement reads: "Japan is an island far out to sea to the eastward, some 1,500 miles from the mainland [of Asia]." *The Travels of Marco Polo*, trans. Ronald Latham (Harmondsworth, 1958; reprinted 1982), p. 243.
47 W. G. L. Randles, "The Evaluation of Columbus' 'India' Project by Portuguese and Spanish Cosmographers in the Light of the Geographical Science of the Period," *Imago Mundi* 42 (1990):50–64, speculates that the cosmographers rejected Columbus's ideas because of medieval prejudices about the size of the known world, rather than rational calculations, as we argue.
48 There is no documentary account of what Columbus sought from the Portuguese king. Las Casas said that Columbus presented a list similar to what he received in Spain, but that statement may be no more than Las Casas's extrapolation.
49 Columbus's arrogance in dealings with King João was noted by the chronicler-historian João de Barros, writing in the mid-sixteenth century. Morison, *Admiral of the Ocean Sea*, 1:93–4.
50 Charles Verlinden, *The Beginnings of Modern Colonization: Eleven Essays with an Introduction*, trans. Yvonne Freccero (Ithaca, N.Y., 1970), chapter 9: "A Precursor of Columbus: The Fleming Ferdinand van Olmen," pp. 181–95.

CHAPTER 6

1 The useful work by Juan Manzano Manzano, *Cristóbal Colón: Siete años decisivos de su vida, 1485–1492,* (Madrid, 1964; 2d ed., 1989), clarifies much about those

crucial seven years, but his assertions must always be checked against other sources. See also Bartolomé de las Casas, *Historia de las Indias,* ed. Agustín Millares Carlo, 3 vols. (Mexico City, 1951); Paolo Emilio Taviani, *Christopher Columbus: The Grand Design,* trans. William Weaver (London, 1985); Jacques Heers, *Christophe Colomb* (Paris, 1981); Antonio Ballesteros Beretta, *Cristóbal Colón y el descubrimiento de América,* 2 vols. (vols. 4–5 of *Historia de América y de los pueblos americanos,* ed. Antonio Ballesteros Beretta) (Barcelona, 1945); Samuel Eliot Morison, *Admiral of the Ocean Sea: A Life of Christopher Columbus,* 2 vols. (Boston, 1942).

2 The Spanish wording of the phrase is "de las yslas de Canaria para yuso contra Guinea." John H. Parry and Robert G. Keith include a translation of the treaty in *The New Iberian World: A Documentary History of the Discovery and Settlement of Latin America to the Early Seventeenth Century,* vol. 1: *The Conquerors and the Conquered* (New York, 1984), pp. 266–71. This phrasing would be crucial in a dispute over whether Columbus's first discoveries fell within the area reserved for Portugal or that reserved for Castile. For a study of the dispute, see Luis Suárez Fernández, *Política internacional de Isabel la Católica: Estudio y documentos,* 3 vols. (Valladolid, 1965–9), 1:195–223. The Spanish text of the agreement, signed in Alcáçovas on September 4, 1479, and confirmed by Isabel on September 27, 1479, in Trujillo, is contained in Antonio de la Torre and Luis Suárez Fernández, eds., *Documentos referentes a las relaciones con Portugal durante el reinado de los Reyes Católicos,* 3 vols. (Valladolid, 1958–63), 1:277. For the Atlantic rivalry, see Florentino Pérez Embid, *Los descubrimientos en el Atlántico y la rivalidad castellano-portuguesa hasta el Tratado de Tordesillas* (Seville, 1945).

3 Ruth Pike, *Enterprise and Adventure: The Genoese in Seville and the Opening of the New World* (Ithaca, N.Y., 1966); Miguel Angel Ladero Quesada, *La ciudad medieval (1248–1492) (Historia de Sevilla,* vol. 2) (Seville, 1976).

4 Antonio Rumeu de Armas, *La Rábida y el descubrimiento de América* (Madrid, 1968), pp. 33–5.

5 For Franciscan missions in the Canaries, see Felipe Fernández-Armesto, *Before Columbus: Exploration and Colonization from the Mediterranean to the Atlantic, 1229–1492* (Philadelphia, 1987), pp. 234–40. For comments on the missionary work of friars from La Rábida, see Rumeu de Armas, *La Rábida,* pp. 90–1).

6 Ferdinand Columbus, *Life of the Admiral Christopher Columbus by his Son Ferdinand,* ed. and trans. Benjamin Keen (New Brunswick, N.J., 1959), p. 37.

7 Our construction of Columbus's connections with the Portuguese political elite is based on the following works. For the political events surrounding the reign of João II, see Elaine Sanceau, *The Perfect Prince: A Biography of the King Dom João II* (Porto, n.d.). Sanceau does not mention the Perestrelo or Moniz families. For the overtures of the Bragança faction to Fernando and Isabel and for the Bragança and Viseu exiles in Castile, see Suárez Fernández, *Política internacional de Isabel la Católica,* 2:61–2, 66, 68. Ballesteros Berreta, *Cristóbal Colón,* in *Historia de América,* 4:397–8, mentioned but did not believe a possible political reason for Columbus's departure from Portugal. He cites an author who asserted such a connection, however: Augusto Carlos Teixeira de Aragão, *Breve noticia sobre o descobrimento da America* (Lisbon, 1892). Taviani reported that the Moniz family was included in the expulsion order following the death of the duke of Bragança. *Grand Design,* p. 430.

8 Consuelo Varela, *Colón y los florentinos* (Madrid, 1988), pp. 46–7.

9 Most historians assume that Marchena was already *guardián* at La Rábida and that Columbus met him there, but they have no proof.

10 Las Casas, *Historia de las Indias,* book 1, chapter 32, 1:171.

11 Las Casas did not say who introduced Columbus to the court but said his most important early contact was Pedro González de Mendoza. *Historia de las Indias,* book 1, chapter 29, 1:156. Rumeu de Armas suggested that the duke of Medinaceli introduced him. *La Rábida,* p. 149.

12 The day-to-day movements of Fernando and Isabel can be followed in Antonio Rumeu de Armas, *Itinerario de los Reyes Católicos, 1474–1516* (Madrid, 1974).

13 See, for example, Henry Kamen, *Spain, 1469–1714: A Society of Conflict* (London, 1983), who asserts that Spain was unprepared in many ways for the empire that was thrust upon it. A similar interpretation is found in A. W. Lovett, *Early Habsburg Spain, 1517–1598* (Oxford, 1986).

14 There are several good books in English on medieval Spain, including J. N. Hillgarth, *The Spanish Kingdoms, 1250–1516,* 2 vols. (Oxford, 1976–8); J. F. O'Callaghan, *A History of Medieval Spain* (Ithaca, N.Y., 1975); Angus MacKay, *Spain in the Middle Ages: From Reconquest to Empire, 1000–1500* (London, 1977); T. N. Bisson, *The Medieval Crown of Aragon: A Short History* (Oxford, 1986). The best Spanish-language introduction is Miguel Angel Ladero Quesada, *España en 1492* (Madrid, 1978), of which a new Spanish edition will appear soon. See also Ladero Quesada, "El entorno hispánico de Cristóbal Colón," the inaugural lecture of the 17th International Congress of Historical Sciences, held in Madrid, August 26 to Sept. 2, 1990, (Madrid, 1990), 32 pp.

15 Manzano, *Siete años decisivos,* 2d ed., pp. 66–8. Columbus's trip to Alcalá is documented in Francisco Henríquez de Jorquera, *Crónica de la conquista de Granada,* ed. Antonio Marín Ocete, 2 vols. (Granada, 1934), 1:377. Columbus mentioned the date of his first royal audience in the diary of his first voyage. The entry for January 14, 1493, addressed the monarchs, noting the date when "I came to serve you, which now is seven years ago on January 20." *The "Diario" of Christopher Columbus's First Voyage to America, 1492–1493, Abstracted by Fray Bartolomé de las Casas,* ed. and trans. Oliver Dunn and James E. Kelley, Jr. (Norman, Okla., 1989), entry for January 14, 1493.

16 Peggy Liss helpfully pointed out the connection between Bartolomeu Perestrelo and Queen Isabel's grandfather to us. The information on Isabel's childhood comes from an early draft of Peggy Liss's forthcoming biography of Queen Isabel, which she very generously allowed us to see.

17 The circumstances of Isabel's childhood will be fully developed in Peggy Liss's forthcoming biography.

18 Andrés Bernáldez, *Memorias del reinado de los Reyes Católicos,* ed. Manuel Gómez-Morena and Juan de M. Carriazo (Madrid, 1962), p. 270. Juan Manzano (*Siete años decisivos,* pp. 74–80) argues that Columbus also asked the monarchs to listen to a Franciscan friar – probably Antonio de Marchena – during the audience, who spoke in favor of Columbus's ideas. They allowed time for the friar to reach court, which had left Alcalá and was seated in Madrid in late February of 1486. Manzano's assertions are based on the testimony of Andrés del Corral, who in a 1512 deposition claimed to have been at the court in Madrid with Columbus when the monarchs first considered his case. Corral stated that many members of the court were inclined to disbelieve Columbus but that a Franciscan called at

Columbus's request had corroborated his ideas. Corral's testimony is suspect, however. In 1512 he was a witness in a lawsuit for Diego Colón, Columbus's son, and identified himself as a citizen of Puerto Real, around thirty-two or thirty-three years of age, and a servant of Christopher and Diego, having served the latter for fourteen or fifteen years. If he really was present at the beginning of Columbus's negotiations with the crown, he was only five or six years old at the time. Antonio Muro Orejón et al., *Pleitos colombinos*, vol. 3: *Probanzas del Almirante de Indias (1512–1515)* (Seville, 1984), pp. 37–40.

19 Dunn and Kelly, eds., *Diario*, pp. 17–19.

20 Ibid., p. 291, entry for December 26, 1492.

21 Bernáldez, *Memorias del reinado de los Reyes Católicos*, pp. 184–6.

22 On the speculation about Beatriz de Bobadilla, see Ballesteros Berreta, *Cristóbal Colón*, in *Historia de América*, 4:461–2; Morison, *Admiral*, 1:144, 218. The marchioness of Moya, Beatriz Fernández de Bobadilla, was a cousin of the Beatriz de Bobadilla who governed the island of Gomera and who gave Columbus a rousing send-off on his second voyage. The two are sometimes confused. Ironically, the marchioness was also the sister of Francisco de Bobadilla, the royal official who arrested the Columbus brothers and sent them home in chains at the end of the third voyage.

23 José de la Torre y del Cerro, *Beatriz Enríquez de Harana y Cristóbal Colón* (Madrid, 1933).

24 Archivo General de Simancas, "Quitaciones de la Casa Real," printed in Martín Fernández de Navarrete, *Colección de los viajes y descubrimientos que hicieron por mar los españoles desde fines del siglo XV*, 3 vols. (Madrid, 1825–37), in Biblioteca de Autores Españoles, nos. 75–77 (Madrid, 1954), no. 75, p. 311.

25 Ferdinand Columbus, *Life of the Admiral*, p. 146.

26 Manzano, *Siete años decisivos*, 2d ed., pp. 170–5.

27 Las Casas, *Historia de las Indias*, book 1, chapter 30, 1:162.

28 Bernáldez, *Memorias del reinado de los Reyes Católicos*, p. 269.

29 Varela, *Colón y los florentinos*, pp. 18, 29. For a summary of printing and the book trade in fifteenth-century Spain, see Clive Griffin, *The Crombergers of Seville: The History of a Printing and Merchant Dynasty* (Oxford, 1988), pp. 1–19.

30 Charles Verlinden, *The Beginnings of Modern Colonization*, trans. Yvonne Freccero (Ithaca, N.Y., 1970), chapter 9, "A Precursor of Columbus: The Fleming Ferdinand van Olmen (1487)," pp. 181–95.

31 The text of the letter is available in Juan Gil and Consuelo Varela, eds., *Cartas de particulares a Colón y relaciones coetáneas* (Madrid, 1984), p. 142–3.

32 Christóbal Colón, *Textos y documentos completos*, ed. Consuelo Varela (Madrid, 1982), pp. 11–12. Italics added. It should be noted that Las Casas claimed that this marginal note had been written by Columbus's brother Bartolomeo, and not by Columbus himself. Las Casas, *Historia de las Indias*, book 1, chapter 29, 1:155.

33 Las Casas, *Historia de las Indias*, book 1, chapter 30, 1:161–4.

34 Columbus seems to have made valuable contacts in the duke's domain. The flagship that Columbus chartered for his 1492 voyage was the *Santa María*, whose Cantabrian owner Juan de la Cosa had registered it in Puerto de Santa María. The town was also one of Columbus's early stops after his return from the first

voyage, probably to settle affairs arising from the loss of the flagship off Española.

35 Immediately after Columbus's successful completion of the first voyage, Medinaceli wrote to Pedro González de Mendoza to remind him of his service to the crown in the Columbus affair and to ask for compensation in the form of trading licenses in the lands Columbus had discovered. The text of the letter is in Gil and Varela, eds., *Cartas . . . relaciones,* pp. 144–6.

36 Pérez had been a royal financial official, probably an accountant, but not the confessor he is so often said to have been.

37 Manzano, *Siete años decisivos,* 2d ed., p. 358.

38 Ibid., p. 366.

39 Ibid., pp. 367–81.

40 Ferdinand Columbus, *Life of the Admiral,* p. 44.

41 Tarsicio de Azcona, *Isabel la Católica: Estudio crítico de su vida y reinado* (Madrid, 1964). In a personal communication, Peggy Liss provided additional information on this transaction.

42 For the capitulations, see Navarrete, *Colección,* in B.A.E., no. 75, pp. 302–3. For the letter patent of April 30, ibid., pp. 304–5. The definitive English translation and editions of both versions will appear in Helen Nader's edition of Columbus's *Book of Privileges,* to be published by the University of California Press. Scholars have long wrestled with seemingly confusing provisions in those documents. Many of the problems have been solved by Antonio Rumeu de Armas, *Nueva luz sobre las Capitulaciones de Santa Fe de 1492* (Madrid, 1985). The line of argument that the details surrounding the first voyage represent an amalgam of Castilian and Aragonese traditions has been ably summarized by Stuart B. Schwartz, *The Iberian Mediterranean and Atlantic Traditions in the Formation of Columbus as a Colonizer* (Minneapolis, 1986). For notes on the Castilian precedents of the office of viceroy, see Manzano, *Siete años decisivos,* 2d ed., pp. 419–27.

43 Most prominent among them, H. Vignaud, in his *Histoire critique de la grande entreprise de Christophe Colomb,* 2 vols. (Paris, 1911), and in his *Etudes critiques sur la vie de Colomb avant ses découvertes* (Paris, 1905).

44 Manzano, *Siete años decisivos,* 2d ed., pp. 443–64. Manzano's speculations about Berardi's role, first put forth in 1964, have recently been corroborated by Varela, *Colón y los florentinos,* pp. 49–52.

CHAPTER 7

1 For preparations for the voyage, see Juan Manzano Manzano, *Cristóbal Colón. Sieto años decisivos de su vida, 1485–1492,* 2d ed. (Madrid, 1989). Several primary and secondary sources are useful for studying the voyage itself. First and foremost is Las Casas's redaction of Columbus's log book and diary, *The "Diario" of Christopher Columbus's First Voyage to America, 1492–1493, Abstracted by Fray Bartolomé de las Casas,* ed. and trans. Oliver Dunn and James E. Kelley, Jr. (Norman, Okla., 1989). We have cited the dates of diary entries in the text rather than citing page numbers in the notes, to facilitate finding the proper entry in editions other than Dunn and Kelley's. See also Ferdinand Columbus, *The Life of the Admiral Christopher Columbus by His Son Ferdinand,* ed. and trans. Benjamin

Keen (New Brunswick, N.J., 1959); and Bartolomé de las Casas, *Historia de las Indias,* ed. Agustín Millares Carlo, 3 vols. (Mexico City, 1951). We have cited Las Casas by book and chapter number, so that any edition can be used. There is a partial English translation of Las Casas: *History of the Indies,* ed. and trans. Andrée M. Collard (New York, 1971). Modern biographies of Columbus include Samuel Eliot Morison, *Admiral of the Ocean Sea: A Life of Christopher Columbus,* 2 vols. (Boston, 1942). This is the complete version; Morison also published an abridged one-volume edition without notes in the same year. He published a further abridged, unfootnoted version in 1955: *Christopher Columbus, Mariner,* which has remained in print ever since. Morison kept close watch on developing Columbian scholarship after 1942. For his comments and incorporation of it, see the notes to the relevant sections of his *European Discovery of America: The Southern Voyages, A.D. 1492–1616* (New York, 1974). His *Great Explorers: The European Discovery of America* (New York, 1978) is a condensation of the two volumes of *The European Discovery of America* and has few notes. Morison stressed the maritime aspects of the Columbian venture, and his approach and conclusions have become standard in English-language scholarship. The best Spanish-language biography is Antonio Ballesteros Beretta, *Cristóbal Colón y el descubrimiento de América,* 2 vols. (vols. 4–5 of *Historia de América y de los pueblos americanos,* ed. Antonio Ballesteros Beretta (Barcelona, 1945). See also Jacques Heers, *Christophe Colomb* (Paris, 1981). Paolo Emilio Taviani produced a handsomely illustrated study of Columbus's voyages: *I viaggi di Colombo: La grande scoperta,* 2 vols. (Novara, 1984). A Spanish edition has been published, but no English edition has appeared so far. For the story of the first voyage from the perspective of the Spanish captains who played a crucial role, see the first volume of Juan Manzano Manzano and Ana María Manzano Fernández-Heredia, *Los Pinzones y el descubrimiento de América,* 3 vols. (Madrid, 1988).

2 Miguel Angel Ladero Quesada, *España en 1492* (Madrid, 1978), pp. 79–80.

3 Manzano, *Siete años decisivos,* 2d ed., pp. 482–93; Miguel Angel Ladero Quesada, *Andalucía en el siglo XV: Estudios de historia política* (Madrid, 1973), pp. 2–10, 12–17, 19–25; Miguel Angel Ladero Quesada, "Palos en vísperas del descubrimiento," *Revista de Indias* 38 (1978):471–506.

4 For Juan de la Cosa's biography, see Antonio Ballesteros Beretta, *La marina cántabra,* 3 vols., vol. 1: *De sus orígenes al siglo XVI* (Santander, 1968), pp. 79–149.

5 Antonio Muro Orejón, Florentino Pérez-Embid, and Francisco Morales Padrón, eds., *Pleitos colombinos,* 5 vols. to date, not consecutively numbered, vol. 8: *Rollo del proceso sobre la apelación de la sentencia de Dueñas (1534–1536)* (Seville, 1964), pp. 334. For similar comments, see ibid., pp. 308, 312, 323, 339.

6 Ibid., pp. 300, 305, 312; Gonzalo Fernández de Oviedo, *Historia general y natural de las Indias* (1535), in Biblioteca de Autores Españoles, nos. 117–121 (Madrid, 1959), no. 118, p. 390.

7 Manzano and Manzano, *Los Pinzones,* pp. 16–20.

8 In March of 1484, a load of wheat sent by don Pedro Enríquez, *adelantado mayor* of Andalusia, was intercepted and stolen as it traveled to Genoa in a *nao* commanded by a Vicente Yáñez, described as a *vecino* (citizen) of Moguer. The alleged pirate was Martín de la Borda, a *vecino* of Fuenterrabía on the French border, who was therefore far away from his home base. Even though Vicente Yáñez Pinzón was said at various times to have been a *vecino* of both Palos and

Huelva, there was also in 1494 another man named Vicente Yáñez Enríquez of Moguer. See Manzano and Manzano, *Los Pinzones*, 1:16–20, 25–6.

9 In another variation of the prediscovery myth, some of the witnesses in the court cases twenty years later claimed that during his 1492 voyage to Rome, Martín Alonso Pinzón had secured a map of new islands in the western ocean sea from the Vatican librarian, a friend of his. Such an assertion was designed to magnify Pinzón's role and to diminish that of Columbus. See Manzano and Manzano, *Los Pinzones*, pp. 32–4.

10 *Pleitos colombinos*, 2:257, 278, 398.

11 The Latin version of the Toscanelli letter, in the Biblioteca Colombina in Seville, states: "auro solido cooperiunt templa et domos regias. . . ." (they cover the temples and royal houses with solid gold. . . .). Quoted in Antonio Rumeu de Armas, *Hernando Colón, historiador del descubrimiento de América* (Madrid, 1973), p. 438. Toscanelli likely got his ideas from Marco Polo, whose *Travels* claimed that the ruler of Japan had a "very large palace entirely roofed with fine gold. . . . Moreover, all the chambers, of which there are many, are likewise paved with fine gold to a depth of more than two fingers' breadth. And the halls and windows and every other part of the palace are likewise adorned with gold." *The Travels of Marco Polo*, trans. Ronald Latham (Harmondsworth, 1958, reprinted 1982), p. 244.

12 Bailey W. Diffie and George D. Winius, *Foundations of the Portuguese Empire, 1415–1580* (Minneapolis, 1977), pp. 444–5; Manzano and Manzano, *Los Pinzones*, 1:42; Ferdinand Columbus, in *Life of the Admiral*, p. 27, called him Pedro de Velasco.

13 *Pleitos colombinos*, 8:341–2.

14 Manzano, *Siete años decisivos*, 2d ed., p. 525.

15 Ibid., p. 501.

16 *Pleitos colombinos*, 8:314.

17 She shared her findings in a series of articles published between 1924 and 1944. Recently the articles were collected, indexed, and published by the Royal Academy of History in Madrid. See Alicia B. Gould, *Nueva lista documentada de los tripulantes de Colón en 1492* (Madrid, 1984).

18 *Raccolta di documenti e studi pubblicati dalla Reale Commissione Colombiana*, ed. C. de Lollis et al., 15 vols. (Rome, 1892–6), vol. 3, part 2, p. 103. The Spanish *tonelada* was a measure of both volume and weight, and its precise meaning has been subject to controversy. We consider its volume to have been 1.42 cubic meters in Columbus's time, the same as the old French "sea ton," or *tonneau de mer*. Cuneo wrote in Italian and used the word *tonnellate*, rather than the Spanish *tonelada*; nonetheless, we consider the terms to have been equivalent in the context of his letter.

19 See Eugene Lyon, "Fifteenth-Century Manuscript Yields First Look at *Niña*," *National Geographic* (November 1986), pp. 601–5.

20 Juan Escalante de Mendoza, *Itinerario de navegación de los mares y tierras occidentales* (Madrid, 1575), printed in Cesáreo Fernández Duro, *Disquisiciones náuticas*, 6 vols. (Madrid, 1876–81), 5:445.

21 Scholars' estimates of the *Santa María*'s dimensions differ widely, but the ones generally accepted are much larger than this. The distinguished Spanish naval historian José María Martínez-Hidalgo Terán used his own method to estimate

the size of Columbus's ships, rather than the official Spanish formula for calculating tonnage from a ship's dimensions. *Columbus's Ships,* ed. Howard I. Chapelle (Barre, Mass., 1966), pp. 40–2, 96–100. However, applying the official tonnage formula to Martínez-Hidalgo's figures gives an estimated size of 250.4 *toneladas* for the *Santa María,* which we consider unacceptable. For the official tonnage formula, see *Recopilación de leyes de Indias,* libro 9, título 28, ley 25, 3, pp. 363–9. See also Carla Rahn Phillips, "Sizes and Configurations of Spanish Ships in the Age of Discovery," *Proceedings of the First San Salvador Conference, Columbus and His World, Held October 30–November 3, 1986* (Fort Lauderdale, Fla., 1987), pp. 69–98.

22 Manzano, *Siete años decisivos,* 2d ed., pp. 558–64.

23 The precise length of the league (Spanish *legua*) used by Columbus is open to debate. Most likely it was no more than 4 miles, and no less than 3.75 miles. We will use the word "league" to retain the flavor of the original language, providing approximate equivalents in miles when that seems necessary.

24 Ferdinand Columbus, *Life of the Admiral,* chapters 21–22. For a discussion of Columbus's instructions, see Manzano and Manzano, *Los Pinzones,* 1:52–3.

25 For example, the journal *Terra Incognitae* devoted an entire issue to the recently revived controversy about the identity of Columbus's first landfall in the Caribbean (vol. 15, 1983), later published as *In the Wake of Columbus,* eds. John Parker and Louis DeVorsey (Detroit, 1985). *National Geographic* magazine entered the fray in November 1986, to revive an old claim that Columbus first landed on Samaná Cay, rather than San Salvador/Watling Island.

26 Dunn and Kelley, eds., *Diario.*

27 Dunn and Kelley, ibid., p. 29, also suggest this eminently logical possibility. See the discussion by James E. Kelley, Jr., "In the Wake of Columbus on a Portolan Chart," *Terra Incognitae* 15 (1983):77–111, particularly pp. 91–2 and appendixes B and C.

28 See Carla Rahn Phillips, *Six Galleons for the King of Spain: Imperial Defense in the Early Seventeenth Century* (Baltimore, 1986), pp. 152–80.

29 Ferdinand Columbus, *Life of the Admiral,* chapter 21.

30 *Pleitos colombinos,* 8:397.

31 This statement was included in the questionnaire to which witnesses were asked to respond in the legal cases arising in 1513. See, for example, *Pleitos colombinos,* 4:219.

32 Ibid., 4:270.

33 Ibid., 8:341–2.

34 For discussion of this testimony, see Manzano and Manzano, *Los Pinzones,* 1:77–82; and Juan Manzano Manzano, "Los motines en el primer viaje colombino," *Revista de Indias* 30 (1970):431–71.

35 Manzano and Manzano, *Los Pinzones,* 1:86–94; Pietro Martire d'Anghiera, *De orbe novo: The Eight Decades of Peter Martyr D'Anghera,* trans. Francis Augustus MacNutt, 2 vols. (New York, 1912; reprinted 1970), *First Decade,* book 1; Fernández de Oviedo, *Historia general y natural de las Indias,* in B.A.E., nos. 117–21 (Madrid, 1959), no. 117, pp. 23–6 (book 2, chapter 5); Andrés Bernáldez, *Memorias del reinado de los Reyes Católicos,* ed. Manuel Gómez-Morena and Juan de M. Carriazo (Madrid, 1962), p. 308.

CHAPTER 8

1 The Dunn and Kelley *Diario* is the best source for the remainder of the first voyage: *The "Diario" of Christopher Columbus's First Voyage to America, 1492–1493, Abstracted by Fray Bartolomé de las Casas,* ed. and trans. Oliver Dunn and James E. Kelley, Jr. (Norman, Okla., 1989). As we did in Chapter 7, for the most part in this chapter we will mention the dates of diary entries in the text rather than the notes. Other sources for this section are listed in Chapter 7, note 1. See also Carl Ortwin Sauer, *The Early Spanish Main* (Berkeley and Los Angeles, 1969); Troy S. Floyd, *The Columbus Dynasty in the Caribbean, 1492–1526* (Albuquerque, 1973); Samuel M. Wilson, *Hispaniola: Caribbean Chiefdoms in the Age of Columbus* (Tuscaloosa, 1990); Irving Rouse, *Migrations in Prehistory* (New Haven, 1986). For the landfall controversy, see the sources in Chapter 7, note 25.

2 Dunn and Kelley, eds., *Diario,* entry for October 13. His latitudes were incorrect. Hierro lies at about 28 degrees north, whereas the central Bahamas lie at about 25 degrees north.

3 Ibid., entry for October 14.

4 Samuel Eliot Morison, *Admiral of the Ocean Sea: A Life of Christopher Columbus,* 2 vols. (Boston, 1942), 1:326, suspected that the plant was actually agave.

5 Dunn and Kelley, eds., *Diario,* entries for October 19 and 23.

6 Ibid., entry for October 30.

7 Juan Manzano Manzano and Ana María Manzano Fernández-Heredia, *Los Pinzones y el descubrimiento de América,* 3 vols. (Madrid, 1988), 1:114–15.

8 Ferdinand Columbus, *Life of the Admiral Christopher Columbus by His Son Ferdinand,* ed. and trans. Benjamin Keen (New Brunswick, N.J., 1959), p. 75.

9 The latter is usually referred to as "the pilot Roldán." Alicia B. Gould supplied his first name through careful research. *Nueva lista documentada de los tripulantes de Colón en 1492* (Madrid, 1984), pp. 79–84.

10 Manzano and Manzano, *Los Pinzones,* 1:113–14.

11 There is some controversy about whether this was the same Bartolomeu Dias who discovered the Cape of Good Hope, but the general consensus is that it was not.

12 Bartolomé de las Casas, *Historia de las Indias,* ed. Agustín Millares Carlo, 3 vols. (Mexico City, 1951), book 1, chapter 74, 1:324–5.

CHAPTER 9

1 The letter to Santángel can be found in *Select Documents Illustrating the Four Voyages of Columbus,* ed. and trans. Cecil Jane, 2 vols. (London, 1930, 1933), 1:2–19. With few exceptions we have quoted from Jane's English translation. There are various Spanish editions. One is in Cristóbal Colón, *Textos y documentos completos,* ed. Consuelo Varela (Madrid, 1982), pp. 139–46. Another, with facsimiles of the letter, appears in Demetrio Ramos, *La primera noticia de América* (Valladolid, 1986), and the same author's *Carta de Colón sobre el descubrimiento* (Valla-

dolid, 1983). For interpretations of the letter, see Cecil Jane's introduction to *Four Voyages,* pp. cxxxv–cxliii, and the studies of Ramos just cited.

2 Colón, *Textos y documentos,* p. 139. A facsimile and English translation of Cosco's Latin version appears in Cristoforo Colombo, *Epistola de insulis nuper inventis,* trans. Frank E. Robbins ([Ann Arbor], 1965). Theodore J. Cachey, Jr., translated Dati's version into English as *The History of the Discovery of the New Indian Islands of the Canaries* (Chicago, 1989).

3 For a discussion of these passages and an effective case for the tamperings, see Ramos, *Primera noticia,* and Ramos, *Carta de Colón.*

4 J. H. Parry frequently wrote on these papal bulls and treaties. See, for example, *The Spanish Seaborne Empire* (New York, 1967), pp. 46–7, 153–4, and *The Age of Reconnaissance: Discovery, Exploration and Settlement, 1540–1650* (New York, 1963, and numerous subsequent editions), pp. 134–5, 151–2. English translations of the texts of the Treaty of Alcáçovas, the bulls *Inter caetera* and *Dudum siquidem,* and the Treaty of Tordesillas can be found in John H. Parry and Robert G. Keith, eds., *The New Iberian World: A Documentary History of the Discovery and Settlement of Latin America to the Early Seventeenth Century,* 5 vols., vol. 1: *The Conquerors and the Conquered* (New York, 1984), pp. 264–80. The agreements reached at Tordesillas also settled outstanding disputes between the two countries over their respective spheres of influence in Africa.

5 Juan Manzano Manzano, *Cristóbal Colón: Siete años decisivos de su vida, 1485–1492,* 2d ed. (Madrid, 1989), pp. 543–4.

6 Bartolomé de las Casas, *Historia de las Indias,* ed. Agustín Millares Carlo, 3 vols. (Mexico City, 1951), book 1, chapter 78, 1:332.

7 Consuelo Varela, *Colón y los florentinos* (Madrid, 1988), pp. 101–3, 131.

8 Las Casas, *Historia de las Indias,* book 1, chapter 78, 1:332–3.

9 Martín Fernández de Navarrete, *Colección de los viajes y descubrimientos que hicieron por mar los españoles desde fines del siglo XV,* 3 vols. (Madrid, 1825–37), in Biblioteca de Autores Españoles, nos. 75–77 (Madrid, 1954), no. 75, p. 311.

10 For the reception in Barcelona, see Las Casas, *Historia de las Indias,* book 1, chapters 78–80, 1:333–43. See also Antonio Rumeu de Armas, *Colón en Barcelona* (Seville, 1944).

11 Girolamo Benzoni, *Historia del mondo nuovo* (Venice, 1572), book 1, fols. 12–12v.

12 For the scene of the baptism of the islanders, see Gonzalo Fernández de Oviedo, *Historia general y natural de las Indias,* in B.A.E., nos. 117–21 (Madrid, 1959), no. 117, p. 31.

13 Las Casas, *Historia de las Indias,* book 1, chapter 81, pp. 343–5. The instructions appear in Navarrete, *Colección,* in B.A.E., no. 75, pp. 338–42. Bernardo Buil's name has been rendered in a variety of ways: first name: Bernal; last name Buil, Boyl, Boil, Boïl.

14 Samuel Eliot Morison, *Admiral of the Ocean Sea: A Life of Christopher Columbus,* 2 vols. (Boston, 1942), 2:53–4.

15 Las Casas, *Historia de las Indias,* book 1, chapter 78, 1:333.

16 Ibid., book 1, chapter 82, 1:346–9.

17 Ibid., book 1, chapter 83, 1:351.

18 Michele de Cuneo "Relación," in Juan Gil and Consuelo Varela, eds., *Cartas de particulares a Colón y relaciones coetáneas* (Madrid, 1984), pp. 239–40.

19 See, for example, Gianni Granzotto, *Christopher Columbus,* trans. Stephen Sartarelli (Norman, Okla., 1987), pp. 119–21. Beatriz de Bobadilla, governor of the island of Gomera, was a cousin of Beatriz Fernández de Bobadilla, the marchioness of Moya. See Chapter 6 in the present volume.

20 For Dr. Chanca's letter, see the Spanish edition (with an English translation on facing pages) in Jane, ed., *Four Voyages,* 1:20–73. On Chanca himself, see Aurelio Tió, *Dr. Diego Alvarez Chanca: Estudio biográfico* (N.p., 1966). For Michele de Cuneo, the most convenient complete edition is the Spanish translation in Gil and Varela, eds., *Cartas . . . relaciones,* pp. 235–60.

21 Chanca, in Jane, ed., *Four Voyages,* 1:32.

22 Cannibalism was also described by two other participants on the second voyage. From Simón Verde, a Florentine merchant resident in Spain, fragments of a letter remain. Gil and Varela, eds., *Cartas . . . relaciones,* pp. 208–11. See also the description of Guillermo Coma, in ibid., pp. 188–91. The existence of cannibalism in pre-1492 America is accepted by many historians and social scientists. Some anthropologists and literary critics suggest that it existed only in the minds of the Europeans. See, for example, Anthony Pagden, *The Fall of Natural Man: The American Indian and the Origins of Comparative Ethnology* (Cambridge, 1982). To deny that cannibalism existed, one needs to assume that a wide range of European commentators simply made up the stories, an interpretation that defies reason, logic, and the available evidence.

23 Michele de Cuneo is the main source for this incident. In Gil and Varela, eds., *Cartas . . . relaciones,* pp. 241–2.

24 Ibid., p. 242.

25 Dr. Chanca's account is the source for this and what follows.

26 Cuneo, in Gil and Varela, *Cartas . . . relaciones,* p. 243. La Isabela eventually failed as a settlement, despite hard work and extensive hydraulic engineering to provide water for drinking and for powering mills.

27 Gerald Weissmann, "They All Laughed at Christopher Columbus," *Hospital Practice* 21 (Jan. 15, 1986):30–7, 41. Weissmann argues that this syndrome can explain many of Columbus's physical afflictions in later life. We thank Helen Nader for calling the Weissmann article to our attention.

28 For Hojeda, see Las Casas, *Historia de las Indias,* book 1, chapters 84, 89, 1:354, 365–6.

29 Original text and English translation in Jane, ed., *Four Voyages,* 1:74–113. On p. 112, Jane mistakenly gives the date of Columbus's instructions as 1495. Fernando and Isabel wrote a letter acknowledging receipt of Columbus's reports and requests on April 13, 1494. Navarrete, *Colección,* in B.A.E., no. 75, p. 368.

30 Jane, ed., *Four Voyages,* 1:84.

31 It is possible, though unlikely, that the original supplies for the second voyage had not included livestock, except for the troopers' horses. Domestic animals are not mentioned in the royal instructions, dated May 29, 1493. Navarrete, *Colección,* in B.A.E., no. 75, pp. 338–42. Las Casas, on the other hand, does mention domestic animals among the items carried on the second voyage. Las Casas, *Historia de las Indias,* book 1, chapter 82, 1:346–49.

32 Jane, ed., *Four Voyages,* 1:92.

33 Ibid., 1:88.

34 Ibid., 1:102.

35 Gill and Varela, eds., *Cartas . . . relaciones*, pp. 244–5.
36 Ferdinand Columbus, *The Life of the Admiral Christopher Columbus by His Son Ferdinand*, trans. Benjamin Keen (New Brunswick, N.J., 1959), chapter 56, p. 135.
37 Andrés Bernáldez, *History of the Catholic Sovereigns*, in Jane, ed., *Four Voyages*, 1:118–21.
38 For the text, Gil and Varela, eds., *Cartas . . . relaciones*, pp. 217–23.
39 Antonio Ballesteros Beretta, *Cristóbal Colón y el descubrimiento de América*, 2 vols. (vols. 4–5 of *Historia de América y de los pueblos americanos*, ed. Antonio Ballesteros Beretta) (Barcelona, 1945), 5:251.
40 Navarrete, *Colección*, in B.A.E., no. 75, pp. 393–4.
41 Cuneo, in Gil and Varela, eds., *Cartas . . . relaciones*, p. 257.
42 Las Casas, *Historia de las Indias*, book 1, chapter 107, 1:421–2.
43 Cuneo, in Gil and Varela, eds., *Cartas . . . relaciones*, p. 251.
44 The royal instructions to Fonseca appear in Navarrete, *Colección*, in B.A.E., no. 75, pp. 398–9. Concerning the dogs, the monarchs specified "alanos e mastines" (two kinds of mastiff), a breed used in Spain and elsewhere in Europe for guarding livestock against predators. See John Grier Varner and Jeannette Johnson Varner, *Dogs of the Conquest* (Norman, Okla., 1983).
45 For the letter giving Aguado authority to investigate the colony, see Las Casas, *Historia de las Indias*, book 1, chapter 107, 1:422. For his instructions from the crown, see John H. Parry and Robert G. Keith, eds., *New Iberian World: A Documentary History of Discovery and Settlement of Latin America to the Early Seventeenth Century*, 5 vols. (New York, 1984), 2:206–8. For a discussion of the commission of experts, see Antonio Rumeu de Armas, *Política indigenista de Isabel la Católica* (Valladolid, 1969), pp. 127–47.
46 Samuel Eliot Morison, *The European Discovery of America: The Southern Voyages, A.D. 1492–1616* (New York, 1974), p. 138, surmised that they were suffering from hepatitis, citing Saul Jarcho, "Jaundice during the Second Voyage of Columbus," *Revista de la Asociación de Salud Pública de Puerto Rico* 2 (1958):24–7.

CHAPTER 10

1 Columbus was informed of Cabot's successful 1497 voyage by a letter from the English merchant John Day. Juan Gil and Consuelo Varela, eds., *Cartas de particulares a Colón y relaciones coetáneas* (Madrid, 1984), pp. 267–9.
2 The main sources for this chapter are the ones cited in Chapter 7, note 1, of the present volume.
3 Martin Fernández de Navarrete, *Colección de los viajes y descubrimientos que hicieron por mar los españoles desde fines del siglo XV*, 3 vols. (Madrid, 1825–37), in Biblioteca de Autores Españoles, nos. 75–77 (Madrid, 1954), no. 75, p. 408.
4 Andrés Bernáldez, *Memorias del reinado de los Reyes Católicos*, ed. Manuel Gómez-Moreno and Juan de M. Carriazo (Madrid, 1962), p. 333. Some scholars have assumed this means that Columbus was wearing the habit of a "tertiary Franciscan," i.e., that he had become a member of the Franciscans' Third Order, an association of laymen. That assumes rather more than Bernáldez's remark sup-

ports. In addition, some scholars have assumed that Columbus lived in Bernáldez's house while he was in Seville. The only evidence for this is a remark by Bernáldez, "I had as guests in my house the bishop don Juan de Fonseca and the admiral and the said don Diego" [tuve por huéspedes en mi casa al obispo don Juan de Fonseca e al almirante e al dicho don Diego], *Memorias,* p. 334. The passage more likely refers to a dinner party than to a lengthy stay. Besides, Columbus had his sister-in-law's house and the houses of other relatives in Seville to stay in.

5 Ferdinand Columbus, *The Life of the Admiral Christopher Columbus by His Son Ferdinand,* trans. Benjamin Keen (New Brunswick, N.J., 1959), chapter 65, pp. 173–5.

6 Bernáldez, *Memorias,* p. 334.

7 Pietro Martire d'Anghiera, *De orbe novo: The Eight Decades of Peter Martyr D'Anghera,* trans. Francis Augustus MacNutt, 2 vols. (New York, 1912, reprinted 1970), *First Decade,* book 4, p. 109.

8 Bartolomé de las Casas, *Historia de las Indias,* ed. Agustín Millares Carlo, 3 vols. (Mexico City, 1951), book 1, chapter 123, 1:468–9.

9 Ibid., book 1, chapter 105, 1:417.

10 For events on Española during Columbus's absence, see ibid., book 1, chapter 111–22, 1:431–68.

11 Ibid., book 1, chapter 126, 1:480.

12 Ibid., book 1, chapter 125, 1:478. The document is also in Navarrete, *Colección,* in B.A.E., no. 75, pp. 431–2.

13 Navarrete, *Colección,* in B.A.E., no. 75, p. 409.

14 John H. Parry and Robert G. Keith, eds., *The New Iberian World: A Documentary History of the Discovery and Settlement of Latin America to the Early Seventeenth Century,* 5 vols. (New York, 1984), 2:218. The royal instructions are at pp. 217–20. Spanish originals appear in Navarrete, *Colección,* in B.A.E., no. 75, pp. 409–12, 423–5. In the earlier set of instructions, dated April 23, 1497, the monarchs had given Columbus permission to increase the number of salaried employees to five hundred (Navarrete, *Colección,* in B.A.E., no. 75, p. 411), but on June 15, 1497, they were more explicit: he could change the number, so long as the original three hundred thirty was not exceeded. Ibid., p. 423.

15 Parry and Keith, eds., *New Iberian World,* 2:220.

16 Their appointment documents are dated February 18 and 19, 1498, and can be seen in Navarrete, *Colección,* in B.A.E., no 75, p. 433.

17 The ships and their officers were: *Santa Cruz* (pilot, Francisco Niño; master, Juan Bermúdez); *Santa Clara* or *Niña* (pilot, Juan de Umbria; master, Pero Francés); *La Castilla,* 70 *toneles* (master, Andrés García Galdín; owner, Alfon Gutiérrez); *La Gorda,* 60 *toneles* (master, Alfon Benítez; owner, Andrés Martín de la Gorda); *La Rábida* (master, Alfon García Cansino; owner, Bartolomé de Leza); *Santa María de Guía,* 101 *toneles* (master and owner, Cristóbal Quintero); *La Garza,* 70 *toneles* (master and owner, Francisco García de Palos); *La Vaqueña* (master and owner unknown). For the ships of the third voyage, see Consuelo Varela, ed., *Cristóbal Colón: Los cuatro viajes, Testamento* (Madrid, 1986), pp. 23–4. For the crews, see Juan Gil, "El rol del tercer viaje colombino," *Historiografía y Bibliografía Americanista* 29 (1985):83–110. Gil's article also appears in Juan Gil and Consuelo Varela, *Temas colombinas* (Seville, 1986).

18 Gil, "El rol del tercer viaje."

19 Las Casas, *Historia de las Indias,* book 1, chapter 126, 1:481–2. Las Casas considered the incident a portent of Columbus's later fall from royal favor.

20 Alain Milhou, *Colón y su mentalidad mesiánica en el ambiente franciscanista español* (Valladolid, 1983), pp. 125–8.

21 Gil and Varela, *Cartas . . . relaciones,* p. 234.

22 *Select Documents Illustrating the Four Voyages of Columbus,* ed. and trans., Cecil Jane, 2 vols. (London, 1930, 1933), 2:38.

23 Jane, ed., *Four Voyages,* 2:28–30. His extended discussion of geography is on pp. 26–42.

24 Ibid., 2:36.

25 Cristóbal Colón, *Textos y documentos completos,* ed. Consuelo Varela (Madrid, 1982), p. 224.

26 Ibid., p. 238. Las Casas also quotes the letter: *Historia de las Indias,* book 1, chapter 162, 2:109–13.

27 Colón, *Textos y documentos,* p. 240.

28 Ibid.

29 Louis-André Vigneras, *The Discovery of South America and the Andalusian Voyages* (Chicago, 1976).

30 Jane, ed., *Four Voyages,* 2:48.

31 Ibid., 2:66.

32 Revelation 21:1 (King James version).

33 Jane, ed., *Four Voyages,* 2:28–30.

34 Ibid., 2:30; Colón, *Textos y documentos,* p. 286.

35 Las Casas, *Historia de las Indias,* book 2, chapter 4, 2:219.

36 Helen Nader is translating and editing the *Book of Privileges,* due to be published shortly by the University of California Press as part of the *Repertorium Columbianum.*

37 Delno C. West and August Kling, eds., *The "Libro de las profecías" of Christopher Columbus* (Gainesville, Fla., 1991).

38 Ursula Lamb, *Frey Nicolás de Ovando: Gobernador de Indias, 1501–1509* (Madrid, 1956).

39 For many of the primary sources, see Navarrete, *Colección,* in B.A.E., no. 75, pp. 447–69.

40 Antonio Ballesteros Berreta, *Cristóbal Colón y el descubrimiento de América,* 2 vols. (vols. 4–5 of *Historia de América y de los pueblos americanos,* ed. Antonio Ballesteros Berreta) (Barcelona, 1945), 5:542; Samuel Eliot Morison, *Admiral of the Ocean Sea: A Life of Christopher Columbus,* 2 vols. (Boston, 1942), 2:321–2. For the crews of Spanish war fleets in 1601 and 1613, see Carla Rahn Phillips, *Six Galleons for the King of Spain: Imperial Defense in the Early Seventeenth Century* (Baltimore, 1986), p. 237.

41 Ferdinand Columbus, *Life of the Admiral,* chapter 89, pp. 231–3.

42 Ibid., chapter 103, pp. 272–3.

43 Jane, ed., *Four voyages,* 2:112–43, contains Méndez's tale.

44 Ibid., 2:90–2.

45 See Milhou, *Colón y su mentalidad mesiánica,* pp. 88–90; P. M. Watts, "Prophecy and Discovery: On the Spiritual Origins of Christopher Columbus's 'Enterprise of the Indies,'" *American Historical Review* 90 (1985):73–102; Leonard Sweet,

"Christopher Columbus and the Millennial Vision of the New World," *Catholic Historical Review* 72 (1986):372–81.
46 Jane, ed., *Four Voyages*, 2:104.
47 Gerald Weissmann, "They All Laughed at Christopher Columbus," *Hospital Practice* 21 (Jan. 15, 1986):30–7, 41.
48 For a description of the reordering of Spain, see J. H. Elliott, *Imperial Spain, 1469–1716*, a classic work first published in 1963 and reprinted many times. For more extended accounts, see Tarsicio de Azcona, *Isabel la Católica: Estudio crítico de su vida y obra* (Madrid, 1964), and the forthcoming biography by Peggy Liss.

CHAPTER 11

1 For the first circumnavigation, see Samuel Eliot Morison, *The European Discovery of America: The Southern Voyages, A.D. 1492–1616* (New York, 1974), pp. 313–73. The eyewitness account is Antonio Pigafetta, *A Narrative Account of the First Circumnavigation*, ed. R. A. Skelton, 2 vols. (New Haven, 1969).
2 Kenneth R. Andrews, *Trade, Plunder and Settlement: Maritime Enterprise and the Genesis of the British Empire, 1480–1630* (Cambridge, 1984), pp. 46–7. On supposed pre-Columbian voyages and Cabral's discovery of Brazil, see Samuel Eliot Morison, *Portuguese Voyages to America in the Fifteenth Century* (Cambridge, Mass., 1940), and the relevant sections of Morison's *European Discovery of America: The Northern Voyages, A.D. 500–1600* (New York, 1971), and his *Southern Voyages*.
3 For the range of opinion regarding the impact of early European expansion into the Americas, see Marvin Lunenfeld, ed., *1492: Discovery, Invasion, Encounter: Sources and Interpretations* (Lexington, Mass., 1991). Numerous authors have written on the conquests of Mexico and Peru. A thorough bibliographical essay can be found in *The Cambridge History of Latin America*, 2 vols. on *Colonial Latin America*, ed. Leslie Bethell (Cambridge, 1984). See also R. C. Padden, *The Hummingbird and the Hawk: Conquest and Sovereignty in the Valley of Mexico, 1503–1541* (Columbus, 1967); John Hemming, *The Conquest of the Incas* (London, 1970); Miguel León-Portilla, ed., *The Broken Spears: The Aztec Account of the Conquest of Mexico*, trans. Lysander Kemp (Boston, 1961); Nathan Wachtel, *The Vision of the Vanquished: The Spanish Conquest of Peru through Indian Eyes, 1530–1570* (New York, 1977). James Lockhart provided a collective biography of the conquerors of Peru in *The Men of Cajamarca* (Austin, Tex., 1972). For an excellent account of the socioeconomic changes that followed the Spanish conquest of the Aztec empire, see Ross Hassig, *Trade, Tribute, and Transportation: The Sixteenth-Century Political Economy of the Valley of Mexico* (Norman, Okla., 1985).
4 For the demographic history of the conquests, see Esther W. Stearn and Allen E. Stearn, *The Effect of Smallpox on the Destiny of the American Indian* (Boston, 1945); Alfred W. Crosby, Jr., *The Columbian Exchange: Biological and Cultural Consequences of 1492* (Westport, Conn., 1972).; William H. McNeill, *Plagues and Peoples* (Garden City, N.Y., 1976), pp. 176–207; Percy M. Ashburn, *The Ranks of Death: A Medical History of the Conquest of America* (New York, 1947).
5 For the history of smallpox, see Donald R. Hopkins, *Princes and Peasants: Smallpox in History* (Chicago, 1983); Cyril W. Dixon, *Smallpox* (London, 1962); Peter Razzell, *The Conquest of Smallpox* (Firle, 1977); Ann G. Carmichael and Arthur

M. Silverstein, "Smallpox in Europe before the Seventeenth Century: Virulent Killer or Benign Disease?", *Journal of the History of Medicine and Allied Sciences* 42 (1987):147–68.

6 Nicolás Sánchez-Albornoz, *The Population of Latin America: A History* (Berkeley and Los Angeles, 1974); Nicolás Sánchez-Albornoz, "The Population of Colonial Spanish America," in Bethel, ed., *Colonial Latin America*, 2:3–35; William M. Denevan, ed., *The Native Population of the Americas in 1492* (Madison, 1976).

7 Colin McEvedy and Richard Jones, *Atlas of World Population History* (Harmondsworth, 1978). Modern work consistently challenges the pioneering work of S. F. Cook and W. Borah in the 1960s and 1970s, which estimated the preconquest population of Latin America at upward of 100 million. See their books *The Aboriginal Population of Central Mexico on the Eve of the Spanish Conquest* (Berkeley and Los Angeles, 1963), and *Essays in Population History: Mexico and the Caribbean*, 2 vols. (Berkeley and Los Angeles, 1971–4).

8 See Russell Thornton, *American Indian Holocaust and Survival: A Population History since 1492* (Norman, Okla., 1987), pp. 15–56, for a thorough discussion of the range of speculation.

9 Leslie Bethell, "A Note on the Native American Population on the Eve of the European Invasions," in Bethell, ed., *Colonial Latin America*, 1:145–6, provides a brief bibliographical survey of recent work.

10 Noble David Cook, *Demographic Collapse: Indian Peru, 1520–1620* (Cambridge, 1981), p. 94.

11 Amherst's correspondence is quoted at length in Francis Parkman, *The Conspiracy of Pontiac and the Indian War after the Conquest of Canada*, 9th ed. rev. (Boston, 1883), pp. 38–42.

12 For discussions of labor organization and supply, see James Lockhart and Stuart B. Schwartz, *Early Latin America: A History of Colonial Spanish America and Brazil* (Cambridge, 1983); Mark A. Burkholder and Lyman L. Johnson, *Colonial Latin America* (New York, 1990); Herbert S. Klein, *African Slavery in Latin America and the Caribbean* (Oxford, 1986); William D. Phillips, Jr., *Slavery from Roman Times to the Early Transatlantic Trade* (Minneapolis, 1985), pp. 171–217.

13 For an introduction to Las Casas, see Juan Friede and Benjamin Keen, eds., *Bartolomé de las Casas in History: Toward an Understanding of the Man and His Work* (DeKalb, Ill., 1971). See also the numerous works of Lewis Hanke, including *The Spanish Struggle for Justice in the Conquest of America* (Boston, 1949, reprinted 1965).

14 Eric Wolf, *Sons of the Shaking Earth* (Chicago, 1959), pp. 195–6.

15 Crosby, *Columbian Exchange*, pp. 122–64; McNeill, *Plagues and Peoples*, pp. 193–5. Scholars of disease still argue over the origin of syphilis.

16 Francisco López de Gómara, *Primera parte de la historia general de las Indias*, Biblioteca de Autores Españoles, no. 22 (Madrid, 1852), p. 156.

17 Diego de Ribero, "Carta Universal," Vatican Library.

18 Armillary sphere of Caspar Vopell Medebach, 1543, now in the National Museum, Copenhagen.

19 Two excellent overviews of European analyses of America are John H. Elliott, *The Old World and the New, 1492–1650* (Cambridge, 1970), and Fredi Chiappelli et al., eds., *First Images of America: The Impact of the New World on the Old*, 2 vols. (Berkeley and Los Angeles, 1976).

20 For an overview of the development of global trade, with extensive citations, see Carla Rahn Phillips, "The Growth and Composition of Trade in the Iberian Empires, 1450–1750," in *The Rise of Merchant Empires: Long-distance Trade in the Early Modern World, 1350–1750,* ed. James D. Tracy (Cambridge, 1990), pp. 34–101.

21 See the classic work by William Lytle Schurz, *The Manila Galleon* (New York, 1939, reprinted 1959). See also the article by Eugene Lyon, "Track of the Manila Galleons," *National Geographic* (September 1990): 5–37.

22 For interpretive overviews of food crops, domestic animals, and diet worldwide, see Fernand Braudel, *The Structures of Everyday Life: The Limits of the Possible,* vol. 1 of *Civilization and Capitalism, 15th–18th Century,* trans. Siân Reynolds (New York, 1981); Alfred W. Crosby, *The Columbian Exchange: The Biological Consequences of 1492* (Westport, Conn., 1972); Alfred W. Crosby, *Ecological Imperialism: The Biological Expansion of Europe, 900–1900* (Cambridge, 1986); Henry Hobhouse: *Seeds of Change: Five Plants That Transformed Mankind* (New York, 1986).

23 Bartolomé de las Casas, *Historia de las Indias,* ed. Agustín Millares Carlo, 3 vols. (Mexico City, 1951), book 1, chapter 83, 1:351.

24 In the entry for January 25, 1493, a little over a week after the return voyage began, the following comment appears: "The sailors killed a porpoise and a tremendous shark, and . . . they had quite some need of it because they were carrying nothing to eat except bread and wine and yams from the Indies." *The "Diario" of Christopher Columbus's First Voyage to America, 1492–1493, Abstracted by Fray Bartolomé de las Casas,* ed. and trans. Oliver Dunn and James E. Kelley, Jr. (Norman, Okla., 1989), p. 353. The word translated as "porpoise" (*tonina*) has several meanings in modern Spanish, including "tuna." The word *ajes,* translated as "yams," really means "sweet potatoes." See Carl Ortwin Sauer, *The Early Spanish Main* (Berkeley and Los Angeles, 1966), p. 53.

25 Carla Rahn Phillips, *Six Galleons for the King of Spain: Imperial Defense in the Early Seventeenth Century* (Baltimore, 1986), p. 164.

26 Redcliffe Salaman, *The History and Social Influence of the Potato,* rev. and ed. J. G. Hawkes (Cambridge, 1985).

27 Columbus, letter to the monarchs, in *Select Documents Illustrating the Four Voyages of Columbus,* ed. and trans. Cecil Jane, 2 vols. (London, 1930, 1933), 2:22.

28 For a good overview of this process, see Ralph Davis, *The Rise of the Atlantic Economies* (Ithaca, N.Y., 1973).

29 Sidney W. Mintz, *Sweetness and Power: The Place of Sugar in Modern History* (New York, 1985); Stuart B. Schwartz, *Sugar Plantations in the Formation of Brazilian Society: Bahia, 1550–1835* (Cambridge, 1985); Richard S. Dunn, *Sugar and Slaves: The Rise of the Planter Class in the English West Indies, 1624–1713* (Chapel Hill, 1972).

30 Immanuel Wallerstein, *Mercantilism and the Consolidation of the European World-Economy, 1600–1750,* vol. 2 of *The Modern World System* (New York, 1980), especially pp. 129–75, provides a useful discussion of plantation agriculture and the profits it generated for European merchants. See also Philip D. Curtin, *The Rise and Fall of the Plantation Complex: Essays in Atlantic History* (Cambridge, 1990).

31 Wallerstein, *Mercantilism and the Consolidation of the European World-Economy;* Kristof

Glamann, "The Changing Patterns of Trade," in *Cambridge Economic History of Europe,* vol. 5, ed. E. E. Rich and C. H. Wilson (Cambridge, 1977), pp. 185–289.

32 Earl J. Hamilton, *American Treasure and the Price Revolution in Spain* (Cambridge, 1934), pp. 32–42. See also the discussion and notes in Carla Rahn Phillips, "The Growth and Composition of Trade in the Iberian Empires," pp. 82–96.

33 The classic proponent of this conclusion was Hamilton, *American Treasure and the Price Revolution in Spain,* especially pp. 283–306.

34 Fernand Braudel and Frank C. Spooner, "Prices in Europe, 1450–1750," in *Cambridge Economic History of Europe,* vol. 4, ed. E. E. Rich and C. H. Wilson, (Cambridge, 1967), pp. 378–486. A short overview is in Elliott, *The Old World and the New,* pp. 54–68.

35 Ward Barrett, "World Bullion Flows, 1450–1800," in *The Rise of Merchant Empires: Long-distance Trade in the Early Modern World, 1350–1750,* ed. James D. Tracy (Cambridge, 1990), pp. 224–54, provides a summary and critique of both classic and current research. See also Artur Attman, *American Bullion in the European World Trade, 1600–1800* (Goteborg, 1986).

36 Fernand Braudel, *The Wheels of Commerce,* vol. 2 of *Civilization and Capitalism, 15th–18th Century* (New York, 1982), provides a wide-ranging summary of business methods in early modern Europe and its colonies.

Bibliography

PRIMARY SOURCES

Benzoni, Girolamo. *Historia del mondo nuovo*. Venice, 1572.

Bernáldez, Andrés. *Memorias del reinado de los Reyes Católicos*. Ed. Manuel Gómez-Morena and Juan de M. Carriazo. Madrid, 1962.

Cardano, Girolamo. *The Book of My Life*. Trans. Jean Stoner. London, 1931.

Colombo, Cristoforo. *Epistola de insulis nuper inventis*. Facsimile of Leander del Cosco's Latin version, with English translation by Frank E. Robbins. [Ann Arbor], 1965.

Colón, Cristóbal. *Textos y documentos completos*, ed. Consuelo Varela. Madrid, 1982.

Columbus, Ferdinand. *Historie del S. D. Fernando Colombo; nelle quali s'ha particolare, & vera relatione della vita, & de' fatti dell'Ammiraglio D. Cristoforo Colombo, suo padre* . . . Venice, 1571.

The Life of the Admiral Christopher Columbus by His Son Ferdinand. Trans. Benjamin Keen. New Brunswick, N.J., 1959.

Dati, Giuliano. *The History of the Discovery of the New Indian Islands of the Canaries*. Ed. and trans. Theodore J. Chachey, Jr. Chicago, 1989.

Dunn, Oliver, and James E. Kelley, Jr., eds. and trans. *The "Diario" of Christopher Columbus's First Voyage to America, 1492–1493, Abstracted by Fray Bartolomé de las Casas*. Norman, Okla., 1989.

Escalante de Mendoza, Juan. *Itinerario de navegación de los mares y tierras occidentales*. Madrid, 1575. Reprinted in Cesáreo Fernández Duro, *Disquisiciones náuticas*, 6 vols. Madrid, 1876–81, 5:413–515.

Fernández de Navarrete, Martín. *Colección de los viajes y descubrimientos que hicieron por mar los españoles desde fines del siglo XV*. 3 vols. Madrid, 1825–37. Modern edition: Carlos Seco Serrano, ed., Biblioteca de Autores Españoles, nos. 75–7. Madrid, 1954.

Fernández de Oviedo, Gonzalo. *Historia general y natural de las Indias*. Seville, 1535. Modern edition: Juan Pérez de Tudela Bueso, ed., in Biblioteca de Autores Españoles, nos. 117–21. Madrid, 1959.

Gil, Juan, and Consuelo Varela, eds. *Cartas de particulares a Colón y relaciones coetáneas*. Madrid, 1984.

Guicciardini, Francesco. *Storia d'Italia*. Florence, 1561. 5 vols. Modern edition: Costantino Panigada, ed. Bari, 1929.

Henríquez de Jorquera, Francisco. *Crónica de la conquista de Granada*. Ed. Antonio Marín Ocete. Granada, 1934.

Jane, Cecil, ed. and trans. *Select Documents Illustrating the Four Voyages of Columbus*. 2 vols. London, 1930, 1933.

Levtzion, Nehemia, and J. F. P. Hopkins, eds. *Corpus of Arabic Sources Relating to West Africa*. Cambridge, 1981.

Las Casas, Bartolomé de. *Diario del primer y tercer viaje de Cristóbal Colón*. Ed. Consuelo Varela. In *Obras completas,* vol. 14. Madrid, 1989.
  Historia de las Indias, ed. Agustín Millares Carlo. 3 vols. Mexico City, 1951.
  History of the Indies. Abridged edition: ed. and trans. Andrée M. Collard. New York, 1971.
López de Gómara, Francisco. *Primera parte de la Historia general de las Indias*. Ed. Enrique de Vedía. Biblioteca de Autores Españoles, no. 22. Madrid, 1852.
Martire d'Anghiera, Pietro. *De orbe novo: The Eight Decades of Peter Martyr D'Anghera*. Trans. Francis Augustus MacNutt. 2 vols. New York, 1912; reprinted 1970.
Medina, Pedro de. *A Navigator's Universe: The "Libro de cosmographía" of 1538 by Pedro de Medina*. Ed. and trans. Ursula Lamb. Chicago, 1972.
Navarrete. See Fernández de Navarrete.
Oviedo. See Fernández de Oviedo.
Paris, Matthew. *Matthew Paris's English History from the Year 1235 to 1273*. Trans. J. A. Giles. London, 1852; reprinted New York, 1968.
Parry, John H., and Robert G. Keith, eds. *New Iberian World: A Documentary History of the Discovery and Settlement of Latin America to the Early Seventeenth Century*. 5 vols. New York, 1984.
Pegolotti, Francesco Balducci. *La practica della mercatura*. Ed. Allan Evans. Cambridge, Mass., 1936; reprinted 1970.
Pigafetta, Antonio. *A Narrative Account of the First Circumnavigation*. Ed. R. A. Skelton. 2 vols. New Haven, 1969.
Pleitos colombinos. Ed. Antonio Muro Orejón et al. 5 vols. to date. Seville, 1964, 1967, 1983, 1984, 1989.
Polo, Marco. *The Travels of Marco Polo*. Trans. R. E. Latham. Harmondsworth, 1958; reprinted 1982.
Raccolta di documenti e studi pubblicati dalla Reale Commissione Colombina, ed. C. de Lollis et al. 15 vols. Rome, 1892–6.
Recopilación de leyes de los reinos de las Indias. 3 vols. Madrid, 1791.
Torre, Antonio de la, and Luis Suárez Fernández, eds. *Documentos referentes a las relaciones con Portugal durante el reinado de los Reyes Católicos*. 3 vols. Valladolid, 1958–63.
[Trivigiano, Angelo.] *Libretto de tutta la navigatione de re de Spagna de la isole et terreni novamente trovati*. Venice, 1504. Facsimile ed.: Paris, 1929.
Varela, Consuelo, ed. *Cristóbal Colón: Los cuatro viajes, testamento*. Madrid, 1986.
Vives, Juan Luis. *De disciplinis* (Antwerp, 1531). Modern edition: *Vives: On Education,* trans. Foster Watson. Cambridge, 1913.
West, Delno C., and August Kling, eds. and trans. *The "Libro de las profecías" of Christopher Columbus*. Gainesville, Fla., 1991.

SECONDARY SOURCES

Abu-Lughod, Janet L. *Before European Hegemony: The World System, A.D. 1250–1350*. Oxford, 1989.
Albuquerque, Luís de. *Astronomical Navigation*. Lisbon, 1988.
Andrews, Kenneth R. *Trade, Plunder and Settlement: Maritime Enterprise and the Genesis of the British Empire, 1480–1630*. Cambridge, 1984.

Ashburn, Percy M. *The Ranks of Death: A Medical History of the Conquest of America.* New York, 1947.

Ashtor, Eliyahu. *Levant Trade in the Later Middle Ages.* Princeton, 1983.

Aston, Margaret. *The Fifteenth Century: The Prospect of Europe.* New York, 1979.

Attman, Artur. *American Bullion in the European World Trade, 1600–1800.* Goteborg, 1986.

Azcona, Tarsicio de. *Isabel la Católica: Estudio crítico de su vida y reinado.* Madrid, 1964.

Aznar Vallejo, Eduardo. *La integración de las Islas Canarias en la Corona de Castilla (1478–1526): Aspectos administrativos, sociales, y económicos.* Seville, 1983.

Ballesteros Beretta, Antonio. *Cristóbal Colón y el descubrimiento de América.* 2 vols. Vols. 4–5 of *Historia de América y de los pueblos americanos,* ed. Ballesteros Beretta. Barcelona, 1945.

La marina cántabra. 3 vols. Vol. 1: *De sus orígines al siglo XVI.* Santander, 1968.

Barreto, Augusto Mascarenhas. *O português Cristóvão Colombo: Agente secreto do Rei Dom João II.* 2d ed. Lisbon, 1988.

Barrett, Ward. "World Bullion Flows, 1450–1800." In *The Rise of Merchant Empires: Long-distance Trade in the Early Modern World, 1350–1750,* ed. James D. Tracy. Cambridge, 1990, pp. 224–54.

Beckenham, C. F. *Between Islam and Christianity: Travellers, Facts, Legends in the Middle Ages and the Renaissance.* London, 1983.

Berdan, Frances F. *The Aztecs of Central Mexico: An Imperial Society.* New York, 1982.

Berenson, Bernard. *Lorenzo Lotto.* London, 1956.

Bethell, Leslie, ed. *The Cambridge History of Latin America.* Vols. 1–2: *Colonial Latin America.* Cambridge, 1984.

"A Note on the Native American Population on the Eve of the European Invasions." In Bethell, *Colonial Latin America,* 1:145–6.

Bisson, T. N. *The Medieval Crown of Aragon: A Short History.* Oxford, 1986.

Bovill, E. W. *The Golden Trade of the Moors.* 2d ed. Oxford, 1968.

Boxer, C. R. *The Portuguese Seaborne Empire, 1415–1825.* New York, 1969.

Braudel, Fernand. *The Mediterranean and the Mediterranean World in the Age of Philip II.* Trans. Siân Reynolds. 2 vols. New York, 1976.

The Structures of Everyday Life: The Limits of the Possible. Vol. 1 of *Civilization and Capitalism, 15th–18th Century.* Trans. Siân Reynolds. New York, 1981.

The Wheels of Commerce. Vol. 2 of *Civilization and Capitalism, 15th–18th Century.* New York, 1982.

Bray, Warwick. "How Old Are the Americans?" *Américas* 40 (May–June 1988): 50–5.

Broc, N. *La géographie de la Renaissance.* Paris, 1980.

Burkholder, Mark A., and Lyman L. Johnson. *Colonial Latin America.* New York, 1990.

Burns, Robert I. "Christian–Islamic Confrontation in the West: The Thirteenth-Century Dream of Conversion." *American Historical Review* 76 (1971): 1386–1434.

Camacho y Pérez-Galdós, Guillermo. "El cultivo de la caña de azúcar y la industria azucarera en Gran Canaria (1510–1535)." *Anuario de Estudios Atlánticos* 7 (1961):1–60.

Carmichael, Ann G., and Arthur M. Silverstein. "Smallpox in Europe before the Seventeenth Century: Virulent Killer or Benign Disease?" *Journal of the History of Medicine and Allied Sciences* 42 (1987): 147–68.

Cassidy, Vincent H. *The Sea around Them: The Atlantic Ocean, A.D. 1250.* Baton Rouge, 1968.

Chaudhuri, K. N. *Trade and Civilisation in the Indian Ocean: An Economic History from the Rise of Islam to 1750.* Cambridge, 1985.

Chaunu, Pierre. *L'Amérique et les Amériques.* Paris, 1964.

Conquête et exploitation des nouveaux mondes (XVIe siècle). Paris, 1969.

L'expansion européenne du XIIIe au XVe siècle. Paris, 1969. Translated as *European Expansion in the Later Middle Ages* by Katharine Bertram. Amsterdam, 1979.

Chaunu, Pierre, and Huguette Chaunu. *Séville et l'Atlantique (1504–1650).* 12 vols. Paris, 1956–60.

Chiappelli, Fredi, ed. *First Images of America: The Impact of the New World on the Old.* 2 vols. Berkeley and Los Angeles, 1976.

Cipolla, Carlo M. *Guns, Sails, and Empires: Technological Innovation and the Early Phases of European Expansion, 1400–1700.* New York, 1965.

Coe, Michael D. *The Maya.* 3d ed. London, 1984.

Collier, George A., Renato I. Rosaldo, and John D. Wirth, eds. *The Inca and Aztec States, 1400–1800: Anthropology and History.* New York, 1982.

Cook, Noble David. *Demographic Collapse: Indian Peru, 1520–1620.* Cambridge, 1981.

Cook, Sherburne F., and Woodrow Borah. *The Aboriginal Population of Central Mexico on the Eve of the Spanish Conquest.* Berkeley and Los Angeles, 1963.

Essays in Population History: Mexico and the Caribbean. 2 vols. Berkeley and Los Angeles, 1971–4.

Creasy, E. S. *History of the Ottoman Turks.* 2 vols. London, 1854–6; reprinted Karachi, 1980.

Crone, G. R. *The Haven-finding Art: A History of Navigation.* New York, 1957.

Maps and Their Makers. London, 1953; reprinted 1968.

Crosby, Alfred W., Jr. *The Columbian Exchange: Biological and Cultural Consequences of 1492.* Westport, Conn., 1972.

The Columbian Voyages, the Columbian Exchange, and Their Historians. Washington, D.C., 1987.

Ecological Imperialism: The Biological Expansion of Europe, 900–1900. Cambridge, 1986.

Cunninghame Graham, Robert B. *Horses of the Conquest.* London, 1930; reprinted Norman, Okla., 1949.

Curtin, Philip D. *Cross-cultural Trade in World History.* Cambridge, 1984.

Disease and Imperialism before the Nineteenth Century. Minneapolis, 1990.

"The Lure of Bambuk Gold." *Journal of African History* 14 (1973): 623–31.

The Rise and Fall of the Plantation Complex: Essays in Atlantic History. Cambridge, 1990.

Daniel, E. Randolph. *The Franciscan Concept of Mission in the High Middle Ages.* Lexington, 1975.

Davis, Ralph. *The Rise of the Atlantic Economies.* Ithaca, N.Y., 1973.

Deagan, Kathleen. "Spanish–Indian Interactions in Sixteenth-Century Florida and the Caribbean." In *Culture in Contact,* ed. W. Fitzhugh. Washington, D.C., 1985.

Deerr, Noël. *The History of Sugar.* 2 vols. London, 1949–50.

Delumeau, Jean. *L'alun de Rome (XVe–XIXe siècle).* Paris, 1962.

Denevan, William M., ed. *The Native Population of the Americas in 1492.* Madison, 1976.

Diffie, Bailey W. *Prelude to Empire: Portugal Overseas before Henry the Navigator.* Lincoln, Nebr., 1960.

Diffie, Bailey W., and George Winius. *Foundations of the Portuguese Empire, 1450–1580.* Minneapolis, 1977.

Dixon, Cyril W. *Smallpox.* London, 1962.

Dollinger, Philippe. *The German Hansa.* London, 1970.

Dufourcq, Charles Emmanuel. *L'Espagne catalane et le Maghrib aux XIIIe et XIVe siècles.* Paris, 1966.

Duncan, T. Bentley. *Atlantic Islands: Madeira, the Azores, and the Cape Verdes in Seventeenth-Century Commerce and Navigation.* Chicago, 1972.

Dunn, Richard S. *Sugar and Slaves: The Rise of the Planter Class in the English West Indies, 1624–1713.* Chapel Hill, 1972.

Eisenstein, Elizabeth L. *The Printing Press as an Agent of Change.* Cambridge, 1979.

Elbl, Martin Malcolm. "The Portuguese Caravel and European Shipbuilding: Phases of Development and Diversity." Lisbon, 1985.

Elliott, John Huxtable. *Imperial Spain, 1469–1713.* New York, 1963.

The Old World and the New, 1492–1650. Cambridge, 1970.

Febvre, Lucien, and Henri-Jean Martin. *The Coming of the Book: The Impact of Printing, 1450–1800.* Trans. David Gerard. New York, 1976.

Ferguson, Wallace K. *Europe in Transition, 1300–1520.* Boston, 1963.

Fernández-Armesto, Felipe. *Before Columbus: Exploration and Colonization from the Mediterranean to the Atlantic, 1229–1492.* Philadelphia, 1987.

The Canary Islands after the Conquest: The Making of a Colonial Society in the Early Sixteenth Century. Oxford, 1982.

Ferro, Gaetano. *La Liguria e Genova al tempo di Colombo.* Rome, 1988.

Le navigazioni lusitane nell'Atlantico e Cristoforo Colombo in Portogallo. Milan, 1984.

Florentino, Nicolau [Antonio Maria de Freitas]. *A mulher de Colombo.* Lisbon, 1892.

Floyd, Troy S. *The Columbus Dynasty in the Caribbean, 1492–1526.* Albuquerque, 1973.

Friede, Juan, and Benjamin Keen, eds. *Bartolomé de las Casas in History: Toward an Understanding of the Man and His Work.* DeKalb, Ill., 1971.

Gabrieli, Francesco. *Arab Historians of the Crusades.* London, 1984.

Galloway, J. H. "The Mediterranean Sugar Industry." *Geographical Review* 67 (1977): 177–94.

Gibbons, Herbert A. *The Foundation of the Ottoman Empire.* Totowa, N.J., 1968.

Gil, Juan. "El rol del tercer viaje colombino." *Historiografía y Bibliografía Americanista* 29 (1985): 83–110.

Gil, Juan, and Consuelo Varela. *Temas colombinos.* Seville, 1986.

Giménez Fernández, M. "América, 'Ysla de Canaria por ganar.' " *Anuario de Estudios Atlánticos* 1 (1955): 309–36.

Glamann, Kristof. "The Changing Patterns of Trade." In *Cambridge Economic History of Europe,* vol. 5, E. E. Rich and C. H. Wilson, eds. Cambridge, 1977, pp. 185–289.

Godinho, Vitorino de Magalhães. *Os descobrimentos e a economia mundial.* 2d ed. 4 vols. Lisbon, 1983–4.

A economia dos descobrimentos henriquinos. Lisbon, 1962.

L'économie de l'empire portugais au XVe et XVIe siècles. Paris, 1969.

Goris, Jean-Albert. *Etude sur les colonies marchandes méridionales (Portugais, Espagnols, Italiens) à Anvers, 1477–1566.* Louvain, 1925.

Gould, Alicia B. *Nueva lista documentada de los tripulantes de Colón en 1492.* Madrid, 1984.

Granzotto, Gianni. *Christopher Columbus.* Trans. Stephen Sartarelli. Norman, Okla., 1987.

Greenfield, Sidney M. "Madeira and the Beginnings of New World Sugar Cultivation and Plantation Slavery: A Study in Institution Building." In *Comparative Perspectives on Slavery and New World Plantation Societies,* ed. Vera D. Rubin and Arthur Tuden. Annals of the New York Academy of Sciences, no. 292. New York, 1977, pp. 536–52.

"Plantations, Sugar Cane and Slavery." *Historical Reflections/Réflexions Historiques* 6 (1979): 85–119.

Griffin, Clive. *The Crombergers of Seville: The History of a Printing and Merchant Dynasty.* Oxford, 1988.

Grousset, René. *The Empire of the Steppes: A History of Central Asia.* Trans. Naomi Walford. New Brunswick, N.J., 1970.

Guilmartin, John F. *Gunpowder and Galleys: Changing Technology and Mediterranean Warfare at Sea in the Sixteenth Century.* Cambridge, 1974.

Hale, J. R. *Renaissance Europe: Individual and Society, 1480–1520.* Berkeley and Los Angeles, 1978.

Hamilton, Earl J. *American Treasure and the Price Revolution in Spain.* Cambridge, Mass., 1934.

Hammond, Norman. *Ancient Maya Civilization.* Cambridge, 1982.

Hanke, Lewis. *The Spanish Struggle for Justice in the Conquest of America.* Boston, 1949; reprinted 1965.

Harley, J. B. *Maps and the Columbian Encounter.* Milwaukee, 1990.

Harley, J. B., and David Woodward. *The History of Cartography.* 1 vol. to date: *Cartography in Prehistoric, Ancient and Medieval Europe and the Mediterranean.* Chicago, 1987.

Harrisse, Henry. *Christophe Colomb, son origine, sa vie.* Paris, 1884.

Hassig, Ross. *Trade, Tribute, and Transportation: The Sixteenth-Century Political Economy of the Valley of Mexico.* Norman, Okla., 1985.

Hatcher, J. *Plague, Population and the English Economy, 1348–1530.* London, 1977.

Hay, Denys. *Europe in the Fourteenth and Fifteenth Centuries.* New York, 1966.

Heers, Jacques. *Christophe Colomb.* Paris, 1981.

"Le commerce du sel en Méditerranée occidentale au Moyen Age." In *Le rôle du sel dans l'histoire,* ed. Michel Mollat. Paris, 1968,

Gênes au XVe siècle. Activité économique et problèmes sociaux. Paris, 1961.

Marco Polo. Paris, 1983.

Hemming, John. *The Conquest of the Incas.* London, 1970.

Henderson, John S. *The World of the Ancient Maya.* Ithaca, N.Y., 1981.

Herbert, Eugenia W. *Red Gold of Africa: Copper in Precolonial History and Culture.* Madison, 1983.

Heyd, Wilhelm von. *Histoire du commerce du Levant au Moyen-Age.* Trans. Furey Reynaud. 2 vols. Leipzig, 1885–6; reprinted Amsterdam, 1967.

Hillgarth, J. N. *The Spanish Kingdoms, 1250–1516.* 2 vols. Oxford, 1976–8.

Hirsch, Elisabeth Feist. *Damião de Gois: The Life and Thought of a Portuguese Humanist, 1502–1574.* The Hague, 1967.

Hobhouse, Henry. *Seeds of Change: Five Plants That Transformed Mankind.* New York, 1986.

Hocquet, Jean-Claude. *Le sel et la fortune de Venise.* 2 vols. Lille, 1978–9.

Holmes, George. *Europe, Hierarchy and Revolt, 1320–1450.* New York, 1976.

Hopkins, Donald R. *Princes and Peasants: Smallpox in History.* Chicago, 1983.

Hulme, Peter. "Tales of Distinction: European Ethnography and the Caribbean." Paper presented to the Implicit Ethnographies conference, Minneapolis, October 1990.

Inalcik, Halil. *The Ottoman Empire: The Classical Age, 1300–1600.* London, 1973.

Irving, Washington. *The Life and Voyages of Christopher Columbus.* 3 vols., New York, 1828; 4 vols., London, 1828. Modern ed.: John Harmon McElroy, ed. Boston, 1981.

Jarcho, Saul. "Jaundice during the Second Voyage of Columbus." *Revista de la Asociación de Salud Pública de Puerto Rico* 2 (1958): 24–7.

Jensen, De Lamar. *Renaissance Europe: Age of Recovery and Reconciliation.* Lexington, Mass., 1981.

Jobé, Joseph, ed. *The Great Age of Sail.* Trans. Michael Kelly. Lausanne, 1967.

Kamen, Henry. *Spain, 1469–1714: A Society of Conflict.* London, 1983.

Katz, Friedrich. *The Ancient American Civilizations.* New York, 1972.

Kedar, Benjamin Z. *Crusade and Mission: European Approaches toward the Muslims.* Princeton, 1984.

Kelley, James E., Jr. "In the Wake of Columbus on a Portolan Chart." *Terra Incognitae* 15 (1983): 77–111.

Kimble, G. H. T. *Geography in the Middle Ages.* London, 1938; reprinted New York, 1968.

Klein, Herbert S. *African Slavery in Latin America and the Caribbean.* Oxford, 1986.

Kristeller, Paul Oskar. *Renaissance Thought: The Classic, Scholastic, and Humanist Strains.* New York, 1961.

Ladero Quesada, Miguel Angel. *Andalucía en el siglo XV: Estudios de historia política.* Madrid, 1973.

   La Ciudad medieval (1248–1492). Vol. 2, *Historia de Sevilla.* Seville, 1976.

   "El entorno hispánico de Cristóbal Colón." Inaugural lecture of the Seventeenth Congress of Historical Sciences. Madrid, 1990.

   España en 1492. Madrid, 1978.

   "Palos en vísperas del descubrimiento." *Revista de Indias* 38 (1978): 471–506.

   Los primeros europeos en Canarias (Siglos XIV y XV). Las Palmas, 1979.

Lalinde Abadía, Jesús. *La Corona de Aragón en el Mediterráneo medieval (1229–1479).* Zaragoza, 1979.

Lamb, Ursula. *Frey Nicolás de Ovando: Gobernador de Indias, 1501–1509.* Madrid, 1956.

Lane, Frederic C. *Venetian Ships and Shipbuilders of the Renaissance.* Baltimore, 1934.

   Venice, A Maritime Republic. Baltimore, 1973.

Larner, John. "The Certainty of Columbus: Some Recent Studies." *History* 73 (1988): 3–23.

Laslett, Peter. *The World We Have Lost.* New York, 1965.

León-Portilla, Miguel, ed. *The Broken Spears: The Aztec Account of the Conquest of Mexico.* Trans. Lysander Kemp. Boston, 1961.

Lewis, Archibald R. *Nomads and Crusaders, A.D. 1000–1368.* Bloomington, 1988.

——— "Northern European Sea Power and the Straits of Gibraltar, 1031–1350." In *Order and Innovation in the Middle Ages: Essays in Honor of Joseph R. Strayer,* ed. William C. Jordan, Bruce McNab, and Teófilo Ruiz. Princeton, 1976, pp. 139–64.

Lewis, Archibald R, and Timothy J. Runyan. *European Naval and Maritime History, 300–1500.* Bloomington, 1985.

Lewis, C. S. *The Discarded Image.* Cambridge, 1964.

Lippman, Edmund O. von. *Geschichte des Zuckers, seiner Darstellung und Verwendung.* Leipzig, 1890.

Lobo Cabrera, Manuel. *La esclavitud en las Canarias orientales en el siglo XVI: Negros, Moros, y Moriscos.* Gran Canaria, 1982.

Lockhart, James. *The Men of Cajamarca.* Austin, Tex., 1972.

Lockhart, James, and Stuart B. Schwartz. *Early Latin America: A History of Colonial Spanish America and Brazil.* New York, 1983.

Lopez, Robert S. *The Commercial Revolution of the Middle Ages, 950–1350.* Cambridge, 1976.

Lopez, Robert S., and Irving Raymond, eds. *Medieval Trade in the Mediterranean World.* New York, 1955.

The Lore of Ships. Rev. ed. New York, 1975.

Lovett, A. W. *Early Habsburg Spain, 1517–1598.* Oxford, 1986.

Lunenfeld, Marvin, ed. *1492: Discovery, Invasion, Encounter.* Lexington, Mass., 1991.

Lyon, Eugene. "Fifteenth-Century Manuscript Yields First Look At Niña." *National Geographic* (November 1986): 601–5.

——— "Track of the Manila Galleons." *National Geographic* (September 1990): 5–37.

Maalouf, A. *The Crusades through Arab Eyes.* London, 1984.

McAlister, Lyle N. *Spain and Portugal in the New World, 1492–1700.* Minneapolis, 1984.

McEvedy, Colin, and Richard Jones. *Atlas of World Population History.* Harmondsworth, 1978.

MacKay, Angus. *Spain in the Middle Ages: From Reconquest to Empire, 1000–1500.* London, 1977.

McNeill, William H. *Plagues and Peoples.* Garden City, N.Y., 1976.

Manzano Manzano, Juan. *Colón y su secreto.* Madrid, 1976.

——— *Cristóbal Colón: Siete años decisivos de su vida, 1485–1492.* 2d ed. Madrid, 1989.

——— "Los motines en el primer viaje colombino." *Revista de Indias* 30 (1970):431–71.

Manzano Manzano, Juan, and Ana María Manzano Fernández-Heredia. *Los Pinzones y el descubrimiento de América.* 3 vols. Madrid, 1988.

Marques, Antonio H. de Oliveira. *History of Portugal.* 2 vols. New York, 1972.

Marrero Rodríguez, Manuela. *La esclavitud en Tenerife a raíz de la conquista.* La Laguna, 1966.

Martínez-Hidalgo Terán, José María. *Columbus's Ships.* Ed. Howard I. Chapelle. Barre, Mass, 1966.

Mayer, Hans Eberhard. *The Crusades.* Trans J. Gillingham. 2d ed. Oxford, 1988.

Menéndez Pidal, Ramón. *La lengua de Cristóbal Colón*. Madrid, 1942.

Mercer, John. *The Canary Islanders: Their Prehistory, Conquest and Survival*. London, 1980.

Milhou, Alain. *Colón y su mentalidad mesiánica en el ambiente franciscanista español*. Valladolid, 1983.

Mintz, Sidney W. *Sweetness and Power: The Place of Sugar in Modern History*. New York, 1985.

Miskimin, Harry A. *The Economy of Early Renaissance Europe, 1300–1460*. New York, 1975.

Moorman, John. *A History of the Franciscan Order from Its Origins to the Year 1517*. Oxford, 1968.

Morales Padrón, F. *Historia del descubrimiento y conquista de América*. Madrid, 1963.

Morgan, David. *The Mongols*. Oxford, 1986.

Morison, Samuel Eliot. *Admiral of the Ocean Sea: A Life of Christopher Columbus*. 2 vols. Boston, 1942.

Christopher Columbus, Mariner. Boston, 1955.

The European Discovery of America: The Northern Voyages, A.D. 500–1600. New York, 1971.

The European Discovery of America: The Southern Voyages, A.D. 1492–1616. New York, 1974.

The Great Explorers: The European Discovery of America. New York, 1978.

Portuguese Voyages to America in the Fifteenth Century. Cambridge, Mass., 1940.

Murphy, T. P., ed. *The Holy War*. Columbus, 1976.

Nebenzahl, Kenneth. *Atlas of Columbus and "The Great Discoveries."* Chicago, 1990.

Nunn, George E. *The Geographical Conceptions of Columbus: A Critical Consideration of Four Problems*. New York, 1924; reprinted New York, 1977.

Oakley, Francis. *The Western Church in the Later Middle Ages*. Ithaca, N.Y., 1979.

O'Callaghan, Joseph F. *A History of Medieval Spain*. Ithaca, N.Y., 1975.

Olschki, Leo. *Marco Polo's Asia*. Berkeley and Los Angeles, 1970.

Ozment, Steven. *The Age of Reform, 1250–1550*. New Haven, 1980.

Padden, R. C. *The Hummingbird and the Hawk: Conquest and Sovereignty in the Valley of Mexico, 1503–1541*. New York, 1970.

Pagden, Anthony. *The Fall of Natural Man: The American Indian and the Origins of Comparative Ethnology*. Cambridge, 1982.

Parker, John, and Louis DeVorsey, eds. *In the Wake of Columbus*. Detroit, 1985.

Parkman, Francis. *The Conspiracy of Pontiac and the Indian War after the Conquest of Canada*. 9th ed., rev. Boston, 1883.

Parry, John H. *The Age of Reconnaissance*. New York, 1963.

The Discovery of the Sea. Berkeley and Los Angeles, 1974.

The Spanish Seaborne Empire. New York, 1966.

Pearson, M. N. *Merchants and Rulers in Gujarat: The Response to the Portuguese in the Sixteenth Century*. Berkeley and Los Angeles, 1976.

Penrose, Boies. *Travel and Discovery in the Renaissance, 1420–1620*. Cambridge, Mass., 1955.

Pérez Embid, Florentino. *Los descubrimientos en el Atlántico y la rivalidad castellano-portuguesa hasta el Tratado de Tordesillas*. Seville, 1948.

Pérez de Tudela y Bueso, Juan. *Mirabilis in Altis: Estudio crítico sobre el origen y significado del proyecto descubridor de Cristóbal Colón*. Madrid, 1983.

Phelan, John Leddy. *The Millennial Kingdom of the Franciscans in the New World.* Berkeley and Los Angeles, 1956.

Phillips, Carla Rahn. "The Growth and Composition of Trade in the Iberian Empires, 1450–1750." In *The Rise of Merchant Empires: Long-distance Trade in the Early Modern World, 1350–1750,* ed. James D. Tracy. Cambridge, 1990, pp. 34–101.

——— *Six Galleons for the King of Spain: Imperial Defense in the Early Seventeenth Century.* Baltimore, 1986.

——— "Sizes and Configurations of Spanish Ships in the Age of Discovery." *Proceedings of the First San Salvador Conference.* Fort Lauderdale, Fla., 1987, pp. 69–98.

Phillips, J. R. S. *The Medieval Expansion of Europe.* Oxford, 1988.

Phillips, William D., Jr. *Slavery from Roman Times to the Early Transatlantic Trade.* Minneapolis, 1985.

——— "Sugar Production and Trade in the Mediterranean at the Time of the Crusades." In *The Meeting of Two Worlds: Cultural Exchange between East and West during the Period of the Crusades,* ed. Vladimir P. Goss and Christine V. Bornstein. Kalamazoo, Mich., 1986, pp. 393–406.

Pike, Ruth. *Enterprise and Adventure: The Genoese in Seville and the Opening of the New World.* Ithaca, N.Y., 1966.

Postan, M. M. *Medieval Trade and Finance.* Cambridge, 1973.

Prawer, Joshua. "Etude de quelques problèmes agraires et sociaux d'une seigneurie croisée au XIIIe siècle." *Byzantion* 22 (1952): 5–61.

——— *The Latin Kingdom of Jerusalem: European Colonialism in the Middle Ages.* London, 1972.

Pryor, John H. *Geography, Technology, and War: Studies in the Maritime History of the Mediterranean, 649–1571.* Cambridge, 1988.

Ramos, Demetrio. *La carta de Colón sobre el descubrimiento.* Valladolid, 1983.

——— *La primera noticia de América.* Valladolid, 1986.

Randles, W. G. L. "The Evaluation of Columbus' 'India' Project by Portuguese and Spanish Cosmographers in the Light of the Geographical Science of the Period." *Imago Mundi* 42 (1990): 50–64.

Razzell, Peter. *The Conquest of Smallpox.* Firle, 1977.

Reynolds, Robert L. *Europe Emerges: Transition toward an Industrial World-wide Society, 600–1750.* Madison, 1961.

Richard, Jean. *The Latin Kingdom of Jerusalem.* Trans. Janet Shirley. 2 vols. Amsterdam, 1979.

Riley-Smith, Jonathan. *The Crusades.* London, 1987.

Roncière, M. de la, and M. Mollat du Jourdin, eds. *Les portulans: Cartes marines du XIIIe au XVIIe siècle.* Fribourg, 1984.

Roover, Raymond De. *The Rise and Decline of the Medici Bank, 1397–1494.* New York, 1966.

Rouse, Irving. *Migrations in Prehistory.* New Haven, 1986.

Rumeu de Armas, Antonio. *Colón en Barcelona.* Seville, 1944.

——— *España en el África atlántica.* 2 vols. Madrid, 1956.

——— *Hernando Colón, historiador del descubrimiento de América.* Madrid, 1973.

——— *Itinerario de los Reyes Católicos, 1474–1516.* Madrid, 1974.

——— *Nueva luz sobre las Capitulaciones de Santa Fe de 1492.* Madrid, 1985.

——— *Política indigenista de Isabel la Católica.* Valladolid, 1969.

El "portugués" Cristóbal Colón en Castilla. Madrid, 1982.

La Rábida y el descubrimiento de América. Madrid, 1968.

Russell, Frederick H. *The Just War in the Middle Ages.* Cambridge, 1975.

Salaman, Redcliffe. *The History and Social Influence of the Potato.* Rev. ed. Ed. J. G. Hawkes. Cambridge, 1985.

Sanceau, Elaine. *The Perfect Prince: A Biography of the King Dom João II.* Porto, n.d.

Sánchez-Albornoz, Nicolás. "The Population of Colonial Spanish America." In Leslie Bethell, ed., *Colonial Latin America,* vols. 1–2 of *The Cambridge History of Latin America,* ed. Bethell. Cambridge, 1984.

The Population of Latin America. Trans. W. A. R. Richardson. Berkeley and Los Angeles, 1974.

Sauer, Carl Ortwin. *The Early Spanish Main.* Berkeley and Los Angeles, 1966.

Saunders, A. C. de C. M. *A Social History of Black Slaves and Freedmen in Portugal, 1441–1555.* Cambridge, 1982.

Saunders, J. J. *A History of the Mongol Conquests.* London, 1971.

Scammell, G. V. *The World Encompassed: The First European Maritime Empires, c. 800–1650.* Berkeley and Los Angeles, 1981.

Schele, Linda. *Blood of Kings: Dynasty and Ritual in Maya Art.* Fort Worth, 1986.

Schele, Linda, and David Freidel. *A Forest of Kings.* New York, 1990.

Schurz, William Lytle. *The Manila Galleon.* New York, 1939; reprinted 1959.

Schwartz, Stuart B. *The Iberian Mediterranean and Atlantic Traditions in the Formation of Columbus as a Colonizer.* Minneapolis, 1986.

Sugar Plantations in the Formation of Brazilian Society: Bahia, 1550–1835. Cambridge, 1985.

Setton, K. M., et al., eds. *A History of the Crusades.* 5 vols. Philadelphia and Madison, 1955–85.

Shrewsbury, J. F. D. *A History of Bubonic Plague in the British Isles.* Cambridge, 1970.

Slessarev, V. *Prester John, the Letter and the Legend.* Minneapolis, 1959.

Southern, R. W. *Western Views of Islam in the Middle Ages.* Cambridge, Mass., 1961.

Stearn, Esther W., and Allen E. Stearn. *The Effect of Smallpox on the Destiny of the American Indian.* Boston, 1945.

Suárez Fernandez, Luis. *Política internacional de Isabel la Católica: Estudio y documentos.* 3 vols. Valladolid, 1965–9.

Sweet, Leonard. "Christopher Columbus and the Millennial Vision of the New World." *Catholic Historical Review* 72 (1986): 372–81.

Swetz, Frank J. *Capitalism and Arithmetic: The New Math of the Fifteenth Century.* La Salle, Ill., 1987.

Taviani, Paolo Emilio. *Christopher Columbus: The Grand Design.* Trans. William Weaver. London, 1985.

I viaggi di Colombo: La grande scoperta. 2d ed. 2 vols. Novara, 1986.

Taviani, Paolo Emilio, et al. *Christoforo Colombo nella Genova del suo tempo.* Turin, 1985.

Thacher, John Boyd. *Christopher Columbus: His Life, His Work, His Remains.* 3 vols. New York, 1903–4.

Thornton, Russell. *American Indian Holocaust and Survival: A Population History since 1492.* Norman, Okla., 1987.

Tió, Aurelio. *Dr. Diego Alvarez Chanca: Estudio biográfico*. San Germán, Puerto Rico, 1966.

Todorov, Tzvetan. *The Conquest of America: The Question of the Other*. Trans. Richard Howard. New York, 1984.

Torre y del Cerro, José de la. *Beatriz Enríquez de Harana y Cristóbal Colón*. Madrid, 1933.

Treppo, Mario del. *I mercanti catalani e l'espansione della Corona d'Aragona nel sècolo XV*. Naples, 1972.

Ullman, Walter. *Medieval Foundations of Renaissance Humanism*. Ithaca, N.Y., 1977.

Unger, Richard W. *The Ship in the Medieval Economy, 600–1600*. Montreal, 1980.

Usher, A. P. *The Early History of Deposit Banking in Mediterranean Europe*. Cambridge, Mass., 1943.

Varela, Consuelo. *Colón y los florentinos*. Madrid, 1988.

Varner, John Grier, and Jeannette Johnson Varner. *Dogs of the Conquest*. Norman, Okla., 1983.

Verlinden, Charles. *The Beginnings of Modern Colonization*. Trans. Yvonne Freccero. Ithaca, N.Y., 1970.

Vignaud, H. *Etudes critiques sur la vie de Colomb avant ses découvertes*. Paris, 1905.
Histoire critique de la grande entreprise de Christophe Colomb. 2 vols. Paris, 1911.

Vigneras, Louis-André. *The Discovery of South America and the Andalusian Voyages*. Chicago, 1976.

Vilar, Pierre. *Oro y moneda en la historia, 1450–1920*. Barcelona, 1969.

Vogt, John L. *Portuguese Rule on the Gold Coast, 1469–1682*. Athens, Ga., 1979.

Wachtel, Nathan. *The Vision of the Vanquished: The Spanish Conquest of Peru through Indian Eyes, 1530–1570*. New York, 1977.

Wallerstein, Immanuel. *The Modern World-System: Mercantilism and the Consolidation of the European World-Economy, 1600–1750*. New York, 1980.
The Modern World-System: Capitalist Agriculture and the Origins of the European World-Economy in the Sixteenth Century. New York: 1974.

Watts, P. M. "Prophecy and Discovery: On the Spiritual Origins of Christopher Columbus's 'Enterprise of the Indies,' " *American Historical Review* 90 (1985): 73–102.

Wauchope, Robert, ed. *The Indian Background of Latin American History: The Maya, Aztec, Inca, and Their Predecessors*. New York, 1970.

Weissmann, Gerald. "They All Laughed at Christopher Columbus." *Hospital Practice* 21 (Jan. 15, 1986): 30–7, 41.

Wheeler, Robert Eric Mortimer. *Rome beyond the Imperial Frontiers*. London, 1954.

Wilson, Samuel M. *Hispaniola: Caribbean Chiefdoms in the Age of Columbus*. Tuscaloosa, 1990.

Winsor, Justin. *Christopher Columbus and How He Received and Imparted the Spirit of Discovery*. Boston, 1892.

Wolf, Eric R. *Europe and the People without History*. Berkeley and Los Angeles, 1982.
Sons of the Shaking Earth. Chicago, 1959.

Ziegler, Philip. *The Black Death*. London, 1969.

Index